W9-BAF-609

BRAIN POWER

LEARN TO IMPROVE YOUR THINKING SKILLS

Discard

Karl Albrecht

is a management consultant, lecturer, and instructor at the University of California extension, San Diego. He works with business executives to increase organizational effectiveness through management teamwork, effective problem solving, and innovation.

A FIRESIDE BOOK
Published by Simon & Schuster
New York London Toronto Sydney Tokyo Singapore

F

FIRESIDE

Rockefeller Center
1230 Avenue of the Americas
New York, New York 10020
Copyright © 1980 by Prentice Hall Press

All rights reserved, including the right of reproduction
in whole or in part in any form.

Published in 1987 by Prentice Hall Press
Originally published by Prentice-Hall, Inc.

First Fireside Edition 1992
FIRESIDE and colophon are registered trademarks of
Simon & Schuster Inc.

Manufactured in the United States of America

29   30   28

Library of Congress Cataloging-in-Publication Data

Albrecht, Karl G.
Brain power.
Bibliography; p.
Includes index.
1. Thought and thinking.   2. Success.   I. Title.
BF455.A43   153.4'2   80-309

ISBN 0-671-76198-6

contents

preface

Let us admit the case of the conservative: if we once start thinking, no one can guarantee where we shall come out; except that many ends, objects and institutions are doomed. Every thinker puts some portion of an apparently stable world in peril, and no one can wholly predict what will emerge in its place.

JOHN DEWEY

George Bernard Shaw once remarked, "Few people think more than two or three times a year. I've made an international reputation for myself by thinking once or twice a week." Perhaps Shaw overstated the case a bit, but it certainly does seem that thinking as an individual human skill has received remarkably little attention in our society in general, and especially in our educational process.

That situation has now begun to change. New findings about the brain and its functions, newly developed practical techniques for teaching the skills of clear thinking, and an increasing interest in thinking among educators have brought us to the threshold of a potential revolution in our mental abilities. We can now make thinking *a subject in itself* — one we can analyze, organize, develop, learn, and teach. To my knowledge, this book represents the first real attempt to do that, by organizing a great deal of what we know about thinking into a comprehensive handbook of practical techniques.

By learning and applying the various concepts and techniques assembled here, you can

1. Understand how your brain works and learn to use it more effectively.
2. Think more clearly and logically; get to the heart of a confused situation and make sense of it.
3. Solve problems and make decisions more effectively, using an organized approach based on a six-step thinking model; overcome "decidophobia."
4. Tune in more perceptively to what is going on around you; "think on your feet" in difficult or challenging situations; use your hunches more effectively.
5. Free yourself from dogmatic thinking and mental rigidity; become more mentally flexible, open-minded, and adaptive; learn to understand various points of view; find the truly important factors in a situation; overcome "opinionitis" and change your mind when necessary.

v

6. Think critically when necessary; recognize hogwash no matter how cleverly or misleadingly it comes packaged; think for yourself instead of having your responses manipulated by others.
7. Maintain a healthy curiosity about your world and about ideas themselves; increase your interest and involvement with the world around you.
8. Mobilize your skills for thinking creatively; come up with new, novel, and useful ideas by connecting available ideas together.
9. Maintain a fully positive frame of mind and remain immune to the negativism that pervades so much of society; think positively and thereby maintain a high happiness level.
10. Improve brain skills such as concentration, memory, visualization, and intuition.

This book makes a major contribution, I modestly believe, by establishing an extensive *vocabulary* of useful terms that help to define the subject of thinking. Virtually every subject of human study—history, music, finance, art, carpentry, politics—has its basic defining vocabulary—terms that to a great extent shape the subject itself. Thinking has so far not had such a body of well-recognized terms, and so we haven't really recognized it as a subject in its own right. These terms, italicized as they appear throughout the book, help to capture many of the concepts and techniques of thinking and to express them in easily understandable form.

I hope you will find the concepts and techniques presented in the following pages interesting, fun to learn, and above all useful. If any one of them serves you well in some specific situation, the book will have achieved its purpose. The more of them you can acquire and put to use, the more effective you will become as a thinker—the more you will promote the triumph of reason over reflex.

special note to teachers

We are beginning to see a renaissance of interest in thinking, signaled by an unprecedented increase in sales of thinking games, books, and puzzles, use of microprocessors in teaching machines and electronic games, and in experimental classes in thinking offered in high schools, colleges, and university extensions. I believe this may become a large revolution—a virtual epidemic of interest in using the mind in all of its dimensions.

Teachers at all levels of the educational process can play a central part in helping it happen. I urge you as a teacher, whatever your "subject," to learn the techniques presented in this book and to build as many of them as possible into your classroom activities. If you've a mind to do some pioneering, you can create a complete course in thinking within your institution. I've arranged this book so it can serve as a practical textbook as well as a general interest book, in the hope that many teachers will do just that.

I also urge parents and students to contact the administrators of their schools about establishing thinking courses for students. Thinking *as a subject* for serious, practical study may turn out to be the greatest — and most overdue—educational innovation of this century.

acknowledgments

At various points throughout this book, I've interspersed quotations to emphasize or amplify important points. These brief observations, opinions, remarks, witticisms, and "one-liners" give us a rich and stimulating insight into the thought processes of other people, many of them well known.

In using quotes this way, a writer always faces the difficult and ambiguous problem of attribution—did so-and-so actually say such-and-such? Did he or she really say it first? And did he or she actually say it quite that way? When someone expresses an important idea in a well-turned phrase, others naturally pick it up, make use of it, and pass it on. As they circulate, these quotes unfortunately quite often get separated from the names of their originators. As they go from person to person, the wording often shifts as well, under the influence of selective memory and an occasional attempt to improve upon them. In some cases, there may be substantial question about whether the supposed originator ever said a certain thing at all. He or she may have picked it up from some lesser-known person and adopted it for personal use. In some cases, two or more individuals may have coined roughly the same expression independently of one another. All of this makes attribution of clever and profound sayings to their originators a conjectural matter at best.

Nevertheless, a responsible author must make every attempt to sort them out, associating each particular quote with its most likely originator. I have done that in this book to the best of my ability.

In those cases of doubtful origin or possible multiple sources, I simply made the most reasonable attribution possible, based on available information. In some cases, attribution of a particular quote to a particular person rests on a rather slim factual basis. Where the phrasing of the quote varies from one reference to another, I have used the wording that seems most popular, or at any rate most descriptive of the supposed originator's viewpoint.

In every case, my intention was the same: to make reasonably certain that the originator of the quote receives proper recognition of his or her contribution to the ideas of our time.

Specific acknowledgments of known published sources are as follows: Page 6: attributed to Allen Ginsberg in Buckminster Fuller's book *I Seem to Be a Verb*, page 165A. Fuller cites the original source as "a two-part profile by Jane Kramer, *The New Yorker*."

Page 30: Rudolf Flesch, in *The Art of Clear Thinking.*

Page 45: Comment by Hermann Goering, quoted in G. M. Gilbert's book *Nuremberg Diary.*

Pages 66, 119, 187, 232: Specified excerpts from #41, #56, #63, and #68 in *The Way of Life According to Lao Tzu*, translated by Witter Bynner (John Day). Copyright 1944 by Witter Bynner; renewed 1972 by Dorothy Chauvenet and Paul Horgan. Reprinted by permission of Harper & Row, Publishers, Inc.

Page 102: Wendell Johnson, in *People in Quandaries.*

Page 126: Helen Keller in *Three Days to See.* Quoted in Reader's Digest Association Booklet, *Great Words From Great Lives*, 1970.

Page 153: From "The Elephant's Child" in *Just So Stories* by Rudyard Kipling, Copyright © 1900. Reprinted by permission of Doubleday and Company and the estate of Mrs. George Bambridge.

Page 173: Attributed to H. L. Mencken by Alistair Cooke in his book *The Vintage Mencken*, page 73.

Page 190: Laurence Peter, in his delightful book *Peter's Quotations: Ideas for Our Times.*

Page 235: Robert M. Lindner, in *Must You Conform?*

Page 264: From *Happy Marriage and Other Poems* by Archibald MacLeish. Copyright 1924 and renewed 1952 by Archibald MacLeish. Reprinted by permission of Houghton Mifflin Company.

K. G. A.

why many people don't think clearly

The spirit of the age is filled with disdain for thinking.

ALBERT SCHWEITZER

how thinking almost went out of style

Not many years ago, to call someone "an intellectual" was usually considered a high compliment. Today, many people use the term freely as a general put-down. Perhaps thinking as a basic human skill has never really enjoyed a fashionable status, but the period following World War II has seen a remarkable decline in the general significance that Americans have attached to it. We see today in the United States certain styles of talking and patterns of living that virtually discount the use of our brains except for the mundane, mechanical aspects of functioning. For many people, especially the young, this has become the official Age of Emotion. The head is out—the gut is in.

We've seen an enormous number of changes in the American culture since World War II, many of which should have helped Americans become much more effective in using their brains. Yet, despite the changes, the importance of using one's gray matter in enlightened, sophisticated, and creative ways seems to have taken quite a beating.

At a time when we know a great deal about thinking processes and how to develop them, we find a curious scarcity of courses on thinking in high schools, colleges, universities, university extensions, and in business organizations. And we find a notable shortage of practical, how-to books on thinking offered by the publishing industry. In view of the fact that thinking skills are among the most basic and the most important life skills we can ever learn, such a general lack of attention to the topic seems truly remarkable.

the "instant" society

 Ours is the age that is proud of machines that think and suspicious of men who try to.

H. MUMFORD JONES

One of the curious side effects of America's tremendous industrial capacity for producing and distributing consumer goods and for providing creature comforts is the tendency of people to become oriented to *passive experience* much more than active experience. With the ability to trade their money for solutions to the various logistical problems of living, Americans may be losing their ability to solve problems, to innovate, to improvise, and to repair. For a toothache, one goes to a dentist. For a muscle pain, one goes to the doctor. For a leaky pipe, one calls a plumber. For a cranky television set, one calls a repair shop. For a malfunctioning car, one goes to a service station. For a torn shirt, one buys a new shirt. Probably very few people, especially under the age of twenty, know how to darn a sock or have ever even thought of doing anything other than throwing it away. Americans have instant breakfast cereal, instant news, instant sex, and instant vacations. The fast food restaurant more or less epitomizes the American obsession with making things easier and faster. Television and movies have made many Americans into habitual consumers of synthetic experience—audiovisual fantasies that simply pass the time.

The American technological attitude occasionally borders on downright arrogance. One lady remarked on seeing the Grand Canyon for the first time, "You can't tell me *that* was done without human help!"

In America during the last quarter of the twentieth century, most people face *fewer mental challenges* than ever before—fewer demands to deal actively and logically with their environments. Even the fruits of technology have been simplified enormously for use by people who can't or don't want to think. Microwave ovens, cameras, color television sets, automobiles, calculators—all have been designed to be readily operable by persons with average to dull-normal mental faculties. Although Americans command enormous amounts of energy, and have at their disposal extremely sophisticated items of equipment, they face even fewer challenges to use their thinking abilities than ever before.

the american education system:
obedience training

 The object of the education of children lies not in communicating the values of the past, but in creating new values of the future.

JOHN DEWEY

2

Many criticisms have been aimed at the American public school system over the past few years—most of them fully justified. As a mass delivery system for dead information, American schools have functioned fairly well. As a mechanism for helping growing children to acquire and use the skills of thinking—especially critical thinking—the schools have been a spectacular flop. In retrospect, this is understandable, and not necessarily "wrong."

Wave after wave of new educational theories, technological advances, social movements among teachers, infusions of enormous amounts of tax revenues, and the inevitable government programs have deluged the American educational system. Yet, never has it showed the slightest signs of veering from the primary task assigned to it by our society, namely the useful function of incarcerating children between the ages of about six and eighteen to free their parents from the tiresome task of raising them. A casual glance around a typical grade school, a junior high, or a high school will show any observer who chooses to take a neutral look that the facility is optimized for obedience and conformity.

The subject matter of the school system itself generally reflects conformity to conveniently measured norms. Subjects such as English grammar, spelling, arithmetic, geometry, history, and science are all easily measured, easily packaged, easily spooned out, and easily tested. Musical skills, artistic skills, creative craftwork, journalism, and drama receive only the smallest attention, if they are included at all. Individualized skills like these are inconvenient and difficult for the school to "deliver."

Many teachers, especially new ones, who bring fresh ideas and imaginative techniques to their jobs find themselves pressed into the mold of ritual and conformity by the structure of the school system itself. And many of them, exasperated by the lack of freedom, oversized classes, and narrowminded school board policies, find themselves at midcareer with a "what the hell" attitude. The teachers get the same message that the students get: conform or get out. Very few teachers or administrators manage to retain a real enthusiasm for their careers and for the learning experiences of the students in the "factory" setting that characterizes so much of the educational system.

I'm not contending that children don't learn anything at all of value in this setting, nor that the setting is particularly harmful to them. But I am emphasizing the fact that the overall school system, as a social apparatus, has always operated according to unspoken but clearly communicated values about how growing children should be handled. And I think we make a mistake if we assume that the development of creative, logical, or critical thought *in and of itself* has been the principal value governing the "teaching" process.

Many parents apparently don't want teachers to show their children how to think critically, to question, to challenge the values and purposes of the adult world, or to explore alternatives that might be uncomfortable for the parents. They do, of course, approve of such objectives in principle, but when the teaching process begins to have an impact on their parental authority over a child's value systems and behavioral standards, they conveniently and firmly draw the line.

One school administrator confided an incident that brought home this point emphatically. He had pioneered the development of a course in problem solving and decision making for a group of junior high school students. He found himself under attack by the irate parents of one teenager who took it upon himself to apply the decision model he had learned to the question of whether he should smoke marijuana. The youngster had weighed the various elements of the question and decided to go ahead and try it. Far from admiring the teenager's flair for independent thought, the parents were outraged that he had elected such a course of action on his own, against their desires.

By the time they finish high school, most Americans have become so accustomed to the pursuit of irrelevance that they take it quite nicely in stride. It seems perfectly reasonable, or at least acceptable, to sit for hours each day going through the motions prescribed by the teacher. Unfortunately, most of them automatically carry their obedience training well into their adult lives, and usually with them to the grave.

A charming story told by a grade-school teacher in Seattle illustrates the typical classroom situation as well as any I've heard. In response to a quiz covering the lesson unit on the human body, one youngster wrote: "The human body is composed of three parts—the Brainium, the Borax, and the Abominable Cavity. The Brainium contains the brain. The Borax contains the lungs, the liver, and the living things. The Abominable Cavity contains the bowels, of which there are five: A, E, I, O, and U."[1]

My experiences in teaching university extension classes for business people have convinced me that the typical adult "learner" brings the very same habits and expectations to the classroom in grown-up life that he or she learned so well in obedience school. Many business people who have enrolled in a course for the first time since leaving high school (or college—a more sophisticated form of obedience school) will sit passively in a classroom and grant the teacher absolute authority to decide what they should learn, how, when, and why. The notion that they are customers, and that the teacher is there to perform a service for them, seems to escape most of them altogether.

Years of obedience training seems to make the trainees highly skilled at conforming—at finding how things are "supposed to be done" and at doing them the "right" way. And it makes them into excellent consumers—uncritical respondents to a constant barrage of television news and adver-

---

[1]Walt Evans in *Seattle Times*, reprinted in *Reader's Digest* (April 1978), p. 132.

tising. If we're looking for ways to foster creative, imaginative, and critical thinking skills among American citizens, the public educational system as we presently have it arranged is probably not the best place to find them.

television:
chewing gum for the mind

The experience of watching television continuously for several hours relates to active thinking in about the same way that chewing a wad of gum relates to talking. Part of the same apparatus is involved, but there is no output. Extensive television watching apparently inhibits the development and use of active mental skills, due to its essentially *passive* nature. It is no accident that intellectual pablum dominates the programming of most television networks. Situation comedies, soap operas, melodramas, sports events, and movies outnumber documentaries and educational programs by a wide margin, but not because television watchers are unintelligent or incapable of concentration and logical reasoning. It is because the television watcher drifts along in an *altered state of consciousness*—a trancelike stupor in which active thinking becomes an unwanted distraction from a narrowly fixated sensory state.

A number of investigations have shown that, after spending about 30 minutes or more staring into a television screen at typical programming material, a viewer's brain is in a condition qualitatively similar to hypnosis. The body becomes more or less inert, with markedly diminished kinetic processes. Respiration and heart rate may decline somewhat. Attention narrows to include only the images on the screen and the sounds coming from the speaker. Shifting attention to other events or processes in the room requires an unwanted mental effort. The popularity of automatic channel-selecting devices, operable from the easy chair, probably stems from this condition of quasi-hypnosis more than from any supposed characteristic of "laziness" on the part of the viewer. From the point of view of brain activity, passivity is self-reinforcing. The longer one remains fixated on a sensory process that requires little or no active thought, the more fixated one is likely to become, until it takes a moderate effort to break out of the semitrance condition.

If you'd like to experiment with this passivity phenomenon, try watching a thirty minute TV program while standing up. Resist the urge to kneel, crouch, or sit on the edge of some item of furniture. I'll bet you find yourself much more alert and much more aware of what you're doing. And you might find yourself taking a much more observant, critical attitude toward the commercials. This illustrates fairly dramatically the interactions between your bodily processes and your mental processes.

For many people, watching TV merely offers a way to kill time. Because they've watched television so much in the past, they have trouble thinking of other ways to structure their evening hours, so they repeatedly opt for sitting in front of the set, absorbing synthetic experiences, as a ready-made way to pass the time. Some researchers estimate that Americans average as much as five to six hours per day in front of television sets. This average includes the effects of people who don't even own TV sets and those who only watch occasionally. Over ninety-six percent of American homes have television sets, and over fifty percent have two sets or more. Publishers estimate that only five to ten percent of Americans read books on a regular basis.

> We're in science fiction now. Whoever controls the media—the images—controls the culture.
>
> ALLEN GINSBERG

Because television stations operate for twelve to eighteen hours each day, seven days a week, fifty-two weeks a year, they need a heavy supply of broadcast material. TV is an enormously hungry medium. Scriptwriters, programmers, and producers must work steadily at the task of turning out programming material and pouring it into the hopper of their greedy broadcast machines.

Television had gained a central place in American life by about 1960. By about 1970, TV scriptwriters had run out of material. Of course, that didn't slow them down. They merely continued to redo the same basic material—human interest situations with simplified plots—in different forms. They substituted one cadre of stock characters for the previous set, changed the story lines a bit, readjusted the ratio of sex to violence, and brought out the next season's series.

> Nobody ever lost money underestimating the taste of the American public.
>
> H.L. MENCKEN

The mass production of more than 50,000 hours of program material over about ten years inevitably lead to the level of intellectual mediocrity that characterized nearly ninety percent of the programs offered by the three major broadcasting networks by about 1970. With the notable exception of a few media events of great cultural significance, such as the live telecast of the Apollo 11 moon landing in 1969, television programming had become a vast intellectual and cultural wasteland. Of course, the movie industry had traveled much the same road, although it emphasized a smaller number of more spectacular productions in contrast to the television networks' virtually continuous use of the airwaves.

Television, together with radio and the record industry, converted a number of obscure performers into instant celebrities. Mass-produced

Television Suckling Its Young. From LAN-
GUAGE IN THOUGHT AND ACTION,
Third Edition by S.I. Hayakawa, copyright © 1972 by Harcourt Brace Jovanovich, Inc. Reproduced by permission of the
publisher and George Allen & Unwin (Publishers) Ltd.

music, mass-produced comedy, and mass-produced personalities had become the primary fare of the television viewing public by the 1970s.

> *We used to have actresses trying to become stars. Now we have stars trying to become actresses.*
>
> **SIR LAURENCE OLIVIER**

One of the most talented TV show hosts, Steve Allen, not long ago expressed his disappointment with the decline in American intellectual and cultural standards within television as a medium. As an actor, songwriter, composer, comedian, author, and respected intellectual, Steve Allen has probably had more to say about the effects of TV's mass-production processes on American taste than any other show business personality. Allen says

Most music on the "Top 40" today is junk. There are at least 57 reasons for this, but one is the popularity of the guitar in the last 20 years. Another reason is Elvis Presley, who became a sensation after one appearance on my show in 1956. Of all the singers who have ever been popular in our culture, he was the most popular. But his songs were the worst, averaged out, that any established singer has ever recorded. The fact that someone with so little ability became the most popular singer in history says something significant about our cultural standards.

Allen comments further on the possible effects of television in displacing other experiences that had previously enabled young people to develop the skills of verbal and logical thought. He observes

I have the impression that we are becoming dumber. It may well be that the brightest people now are brighter than ever because they have available to them resources of information that none of the geniuses of the past ever had.

But it is measurable that college examination scores are dropping. Like all people

in television, I get mail, and I have observed a deterioration of handwriting and the ability to compose a simple English sentence. The ability even to speak an English sentence is becoming rarer. A lot of speech now consists of broken phrases not very reasonably strung together. The common problem of simply completing one sentence and then starting another relates to our difficulty in thinking, reasoning.

Most people watch far too much television. Much of television is what I call junk food for the mind. Like junk food for the stomach, it's not terribly harmful in itself. It's just that it's empty, escapist—just something to pass the time. [2]

At the time when television was emerging as an enormously significant cultural phenomenon, American schools were apparently going through a period of changing educational philosophies, marked by a decline in emphasis on basic skills, achievement standards, study requirements, and grading. Recent studies of educational processes and scholastic achievement levels during the period 1960–1975 have shown a marked decline in verbal and logical skills among high school graduates of that period. This decline in the effectiveness of the secondary school system, coupled with the tremendous incursion of television watching into the available time of young people during that period, probably accounts for most of the decline in these skills.

Average scores on the Scholastic Aptitude Test, widely accepted as a measure of college readiness, declined steadily between 1963 and 1975, showing no signs of leveling off until 1976 and 1977. Scores on the verbal part of the examination dropped by about ten percent over that period, while scores on the mathematical part dropped by about six percent. Over a million students took the tests each year, giving a very large statistical base for evaluating results from year to year.

This inarticulateness shows up very clearly in the speech of many young people between the ages of fifteen and twenty-five. Over and above the transient forms of slang that enrich the conversation of young people, one can detect an awkward groping for words—a fumbling attempt to put together a string of imprecise clichés, slogans, and metaphors into a fashionable-sounding but inexpressive jumble. The term "Y' know" seems to tumble out like every fifth bead on a string. Many of the sentences of people who talk this way are merely a patchwork of stock phrases.

While pausing at the top of a ski slope in Utah recently, I overheard a teenage girl replying to her companion's request for some suggestions about how to make it down a rather steep section of the hill. The answer went something like "Well, you just . . . y'know . . . like, just go for it." Her companion looked at her for a second, mumbled something, and proceeded down the slope.

In a hotel lobby, I overheard a clerk who was apparently discussing a

---

[2]"Steve Allen: TV Is 'Junk Food for the Mind.' " Reprinted from *U.S. News & World Report*, 13 March 1978. Copyright 1978 U.S. News & World Report, Inc.

guest's laundry order with him. The clerk said, "Well, did you have any . . . like . . . shirts, or anything?" The extraneous word "like" caught my attention. It seems to serve some useful function as a space filler in the conversation of some marginally articulate people, especially in the age range of the TV generation.

Another youngster explained to a companion over lunch, "She's a nice person y'know . . . but, like . . . I dunno, y'know . . . I mean . . . she's always, y'know . . . she loses her temper easy, y'know?"

Apparently television has been a mixed blessing for the American society, at least from the point of view of the development of the basic linear skills of verbal description and logical thought.

the encounter fad: the cult of "feelings"

 | *America is the only nation in history that has gone directly from barbarism to decadence without the usual interval of civilization.*

GEORGES CLEMENCEAU

The social phenomenon of the early 1960s and the 1970s known as the encounter group has drawn a great deal of attention from magazine writers and others in the media field. Partially because of this attention, perhaps, the philosophical values and the terminology of the encounter setting have influenced many Americans in various ways. The encounter phenomenon appears to have been a decidedly mixed blessing, bringing with it new possibilities for understanding one's emotional processes, and at the same time leading some people to adopt an intense preoccupation with emotion for its own sake, often at the expense of useful forms of rational thinking.

The original form of the encounter group—also known as the sensitivity group and sometimes as the T-group (short for "training group" as used in business)—began with therapist Carl Rogers,[3] who formulated the approach of getting people together in loosely structured group situations for the purposes of exploring personal problems and helping one another. Behavioral theorist Kurt Lewin is generally credited with bringing encounter techniques into business organizations.

Rogers believed that individuals could learn to understand themselves and their problems better if they had opportunities to interact with others in a group setting, while learning to observe the group's processes and their own individual roles in those processes. By interacting with others rather intensively under the guidance of a trained psychologist, Rogers believed, a person could learn to relinquish counterproductive interpersonal strategies and begin to adopt productive new ones.

[3]Carl Rogers, *Carl Rogers on Encounter Groups* (New York: Harper & Row Pub., 1970).

Probably neither Rogers nor Lewin foresaw the intense fascination the encounter situation would hold for some people, nor did they foresee the enormous interest in popularized forms of psychology. While sensitivity training had run its course in the business environment and fizzled out by about 1970, the encounter group had become somewhat of a fad among laypeople and was in full swing among a noticeable segment of the population.

There arose from these various movements a veritable industry of "growth," with its schools, centers, popular writers, popular therapists, gurus, movement leaders, and packaged programs. The small resort area of Esalen, in the picturesque Big Sur region of the California coast, became the mecca for encounter enthusiasts as well as a training center for encounter group leaders (most of whom preferred to label themselves "facilitators"). This True Self industry, as educator Neil Postman terms it, found quite a number of willing and eager customers, especially among young and relatively affluent people, many of whom brought various emotional adjustment problems with them. It also spawned a significant number of frauds, quack therapists, and downright irresponsible opportunists, who set themselves up in the business of helping other people "grow," without the slightest qualifications or competence.

Imaginative techniques such as nude encounters, body awareness training sessions, dance therapy, "rolfing" (a form of vigorous massage), "rebirthing" (a re-enactment of one's own birth scene), primal screaming, gestalt therapy (developed by the colorful Fritz Perls), psychodrama (in which other participants help the seeker act out his or her life's difficulties), and a variety of techniques lifted from Asian philosophical systems and religious movements offered the prospective buyer a wide range of choices. In most cases, the central element of the approach was emotion— emotion as a thing unto itself, something to be evoked, intensified, reveled in, savored, and exalted as an end in its own right.

America saw, beginning with the encounter group and continuing with the diversification of the personal growth market, the development of the "cult of the hypothalamus." Rational thought was ridiculed as the prison of the unenlightened. Emotional incontinence and personal transparency to others became the new values for growth cultists. "Let it all hang out," "Do your own thing," and "Go with the feeling" became the new slogans. The ability to cry in public and the ability to skip merrily through a park, smelling flowers and hugging trees became for some people the proof that they had "grown." Popular singer Neil Diamond recorded a rock song titled "Don't Think—Feel!" A line from another popular song assured the singer's beloved that its message was ". . . comin' from my heart and not my head."

Like virtually all topics that gain widespread interest, the encounter fad produced a distinctive vocabulary—a metaphorical lexicon of emotion.

Favored terms and expressions included "getting my head together," "a heavy experience," "going with my feelings," "staying in the here and now," "he knows where his head's at," "going through heavy changes," "where I'm coming from," "I was in a bad place at that time in my life," "the space I'm in," "be a whole person," and the extremely hackneyed password "getting in touch with your feelings." (The latter term brings to my mind an image of a person dialing a telephone and putting through a call to someone named My Feelings.)

Probably the ultimate put-down in encounter lingo is to be accused of "intellectualizing," or more bluntly, being "on a head trip." A newcomer to an encounter group who begins a statement with "I think . . ." is likely to hear the scornful response, "I don't give a damn what you *think*. Tell me what you *feel!*" Any attempt at a logical train of thought is usually equated as an attempt to escape from the emotional immediacy of the situation, and condemned as a "head trip." Various metaphorical references to "your head" seem to convey an impression of the head as some kind of useless gourd—a troublesome appendage that contains that disreputable organ, the brain.

This kind of metaphorical language seems to have caught on strongly with young people of high school and college age, possibly as a kind of elitist slang that can differentiate them from older members of the population. Writer R.D. Rosen uses the term *psychobabble* to describe this hip, metaphorical, and sometimes banal slang of the pop-psych arena. Rosen believes it may signal a suppression of normal descriptive language in favor of empty metaphors, which are phonetically pleasing but uninformative. The objective of psychobabble, according to Rosen, may be to prevent significant communication about one's self and one's inner experience, under the safe guise of pretended frankness.[4]

In any case, it does seem that the encounter movement has had a substantial impact on the thinking processes of many Americans, particularly young ones. A growing preoccupation with emotion, or at least with talking about emotion, seems to have displaced some useful modes of logical thinking and logical talking. The kind of verbal, descriptive thought that helps one to deal with situations and problems in his or her life seems to have taken a back seat for the time being.

However, I'm willing to bet we'll see an increasing sense of disappointment with the pop-psych fad and an increasing sense of boredom with the banality of much of it. We may see a much better grasp of everyday operational psychology on the part of many people, and a greater willingness on the part of people to think about themselves, their lives, and the ways in which they deal with their world. The encounter phase undoubt-

[4]See R. D. Rosen, "The Baffling World of Psychobabble," *Reader's Digest* (April 1978), p. 239. For a fuller treatment, see Richard D. Rosen, *Psychobabble* (New York: Atheneum, 1975, 1976, 1977).

edly has had a number of useful effects, especially the enormous interest it has generated in self-understanding and personal growth. However, the fad itself is just about bankrupt. I believe many people are ready to get back to using their brains for their own benefit, to thinking logically about themselves and their problems, and to renewing their respect for their own intellectual processes. I hope this book will make a useful contribution to this renaissance of the mind.

2

learning to think more effectively

The world is a tragedy to those who feel, and a comedy to those who think.

SHAKESPEARE

thinking about thinking

By taking a conscious interest in your brain and how it works, and by consciously trying some of the techniques that follow, you can acquire a variety of useful mental skills. It isn't really very difficult, but it won't happen by accident. The prevalence of negative thinking, fuzzy and illogical thinking, and rigid thinking in our society attests to the fact that these higher level thinking skills do not come naturally. The cross section of our society represents the "average" level of thinking skill—the level one might expect of a large number of people who have never thought very much about thinking. To move beyond the level of average thinking, you must *think about thinking*. You must pay attention to how your brain works, and you must experiment with new techniques. Once you do that, you will clearly see the value of it.

Studying any subject becomes much easier if we can break it down into its component parts, learn them one by one, and put them together into a whole package. Thus, we can subdivide the composite skill of thinking into its primary components, so we can work on them individually. Most psychologists recognize certain specific brain skills, or *cognitive functions*, which constitute a person's basic mental repertoire. We will work with these specific brain skills throughout this book. Different writers or researchers may use different labels or may subdivide these processes in a different way, but for this book, we'll use ten categories, as follows:

1. Concentration.
2. Observation.
3. Memory.
4. Logical reasoning.
5. Making inferences.

6. Forming hypotheses.
7. Generating options.
8. Making associations between ideas.
9. Recognizing patterns.
10. Spatial and kinesthetic perception.

Actually, it is more important to study the *applications* of these skills to real life situations rather than try to study them as isolated brain processes. Therefore, most of this book deals with combinations of the ten cognitive skills in ways that promote practical and useful results. For example, almost all of the basic skills come into play during the processes of problem solving and decision making. Creative thinking involves most of them. The function of effective judgment involves several of them. Our task is more a matter of *releasing* these basic brain skills, which are available in ample measure in every normal human brain. No one can really teach you to reason logically—that function already exists in your cerebral cortex. What you *can* learn to do better is to focus your logical reasoning abilities more effectively on the problems and situations that face you in your life. In this respect we want to develop certain *functional thinking skills*—skills of applied thinking.

I choose to group most of our useful thinking skills into six functional categories, in terms of their value in dealing with various life situations. By developing and applying these skills, we will be properly mobilizing the ten primary brain skills previously listed. I've given them simple descriptive labels which might not please the average psychologist, but which do capture the essence of their usefulness. My six functional skill categories are

1. Fact finding.
2. Crap detecting.
3. Thinking on your feet.
4. Idea production.
5. Problem solving and decision making.
6. Happying.

You may find my choice of terms somewhat provocative. I'll explain each of these skills in depth as we go along, and show how it works, why it is useful, and how to develop it to a high level. For the time being, a brief definition of these terms will show how each includes one or more of the "natural" brain skills that we all have as part of our neurological makeup.

Fact finding is the broad skill of finding out things of value and importance about the world around you. It is the ability to open up your perceptual field of view, to search, to observe, to inquire, to investigate; to take in facts, figures, ideas, opinions, clues, hints, signals, pictures, sights, sounds, impressions, and sensations that might help you to know more about what's going on around you. And knowing what's going on around you, in your near neighborhood and in the extended world, plays an essential part in thinking effectively. The effective fact finder is one who is deliberately curious.

Crap detecting is the skill of critical observation. I've chosen this term precisely because of its charming bluntness. In their thought-provoking book, *Teaching as a Subversive Activity*, Neil Postman and Charles Weingartner credit Ernest Hemingway with coining the term.[1] According to the anecdote, someone asked Hemingway what personal or intellectual traits he thought a good writer should have. After some reflection, Hemingway is said to have replied, "A built-in, shock-proof crap detector." Postman and Weingartner contend that a major objective of education should be to teach children the essential skill of crap detecting to enable them to understand and cope with the myriad absurdities of a culture in upheaval such as the American culture.

Thinking on your feet is the skill of situational thinking. It involves presence of mind, judgment, alertness for the unusual, strategic observation, goal orientation, and, above all, the skill of adapting one's actions effectively to the requirements of a situation.

Idea production is a simple, learnable thinking skill, which many people make unnecessarily complicated by confusing themselves with terms like "creativity." As a later section shows, a workable definition of the skill of thinking creatively is simply the skill of *producing new and novel ideas.* You can learn to put two or more ideas together to make another idea, and you can make this process such a regular mental habit that you become virtually an "idea machine." Idea production is an acquired skill, not an in-born gift. The more you practice idea production in a given area, the more "creative" you become in that area, by the conventional definition.

Problem solving and decision making is the combined skill of consciously going after problems with an active mental approach and working out solutions with the help of a logical model or framework. Decision making, according to my definition, is the final stage of the overall problem-solving process. It involves choosing a course of action from a group of known alternatives, according to a consciously stated objective that you want to achieve. Problem solving, according to this definition, includes all the thought processes you go through to arrive at the choice point, as well as the actual process of making the decision.

Happying may seem like a curious companion to the other functional thinking skills, but in my opinion it is just as much a thinking skill as the first five. Being happy is a decision, together with a strategy for carrying through on the decision, and a state of mind that tells you that you're living

[1] Neil Postman and Charles Weingartner, *Teaching as a Subversive Activity* (New York: Dell Pub. Co., Inc., 1969), p. 3.

effectively according to your decision. Although many people seem to consider happiness as the result of good luck, accidental circumstances, or the actions of other people, the fact is that people decide for themselves how happy they are going to be. Unfortunately, many unhappy people don't realize that they've made the decision. Once you understand that your state of mind—happy, unhappy, or in between—is your own responsibility, you can decide to be happy and begin to do the things that will enable you to become happy. Actually, we should use a verb rather than an adjective to describe this skill. We need a word like "happying," to imply that one *does* happiness rather than *has* it.

Throughout this book, we will use these ten cognitive processes, and especially the six functional thinking skills, as convenient categories to organize our study and practice of useful thinking techniques. We will also see how to use various *utility thinking skills* such as drawing pencil-and-paper *thinking models*, verbalizing thoughts, thinking out loud, categorizing facts, visualizing situations, sequential thinking, and asking questions skillfully, to help us organize our thoughts more effectively and put the six functional thinking skills into practice.

a vocabulary for thinking

Mind, n. A mysterious form of matter secreted by the brain.

AMBROSE-BIERCE

Through a number of years of studying the human computer, I've noticed that certain useful terms have been helpful in clarifying basic aspects of its function. Various self-explanatory terms and metaphors, like option thinking, thinking on your feet, mechanical thinking, crap detecting, and mental arthritis, make it easier to isolate a specific thinking skill or thinking malfunction, and to study it in a fairly organized way. I've found myself collecting many of these simple descriptive terms and using them to think about thinking. In conducting seminars on thinking and problem solving for business people, I've often used these terms as a way of organizing the subject so we could study it methodically.

When I wondered for the one-thousand-and-first time why we have so very few courses on thinking in our colleges, universities, and high schools, and why writers have covered it so sparsely in their books, it occurred to me that we have never had a basic *defining vocabulary* of terms that would enable us to describe it, and consequently we haven't recognized it as a *subject* that could be analyzed, studied, taught, and learned. *Every other subject I know about has such a defining vocabulary.* Indeed, for many subjects, the vocabulary forms almost the complete content. That is, if you know the language of a subject, you understand most of what practitioners of that specialty do, say, and think.

Having realized this and having recognized the need to make a subject of thinking, I proceeded to collect, organize, and refine such a basic inventory of terms. You've already seen some of them as you've read this far. These terms appear throughout the book in italics, with definitions, when they first appear. I've tried to keep the terms as simple as possible, and the definitions simple as well. Many times, the simplicity of a term, its self-evident connotations, and the context in which I've used it are quite sufficient to define it.

The Index (starting on page 307) contains all of the thinking terms that appear throughout the book, identifying them by italics. You may want to browse through the list ahead of time, to get some advance notice of the kinds of thinking processes and techniques we will be studying.

I suggest you become familiar with this Thinker's Vocabulary, and make as many of the terms a part of your own vocabulary as you can. Use them in your everyday conversation and you'll find yourself becoming much more aware of your own thinking processes and the thinking processes of others.

how your brain works

. . . . an enchanted loom where millions of flashing shuttles weave a dissolving pattern, always a meaningful pattern though never an abiding one.

SIR CHARLES SHERRINGTON

Situated inside your skull is the most complex biological structure known to exist anywhere on earth. A rubbery blob of tissue about the size of a grapefruit and weighing about three pounds, it nestles inside the bony fortress of your cranium. It is perhaps the best-protected organ in your entire body, and it enjoys the highest priority when blood, oxygen, and nutrients are distributed. Your brain is sheathed in several layers of a tough membrane tissue, and it is suspended in a circulating fluid medium. It actually floats inside a shock-proof vault.

The design of your entire body reflects the pre-eminent role of your brain in coordinating and controlling virtually all of its functions. The brainstem, emerging from the lower part of its structure, merges with the spinal cord to form the central control and communication axis of your body.

There is a great deal we do not know about the brain and its functions, but what we do know is awesome. The twelve billion or so neurons, or nerve cells, of your brain interlock in such a way as to make it potentially a phenomenal information processor. Each neuron has hundreds or even thousands of branching threadlike extensions that connect it to other neurons, and each connection plays a part in the transmission of signals throughout your brain and body. Your thought processes arise from an incredibly complex pattern of electrical-chemical signals flitting rapidly about through this blob of tissue, a biological computer of awesome capability.

> *Brain, n. An apparatus with which we think that we think.*
>
> AMBROSE BIERCE

Scientists have not so far found any particular correlation between brain size or shape and mental capabilities. Although systematic studies on this point are rather scarce, the brains of a few eminent and highly intelligent people have been examined after death. The brains of Napoleon, Lenin, and Einstein, for instance, seem very similar to those of more ordinary people, from the point of view of general physical characteristics.

For all the complexity and microscopic detail of the brain, its overall functional structure is so highly organized, so elegantly designed, and so efficient as to raise the eyebrows of even the most sophisticated electronic engineer or computer scientist. The following brief description of how your brain carries out its thinking processes will be useful in learning about new thinking methods and techniques. It should also help you to understand and internalize the fact that thinking is *a skill* which you can improve if you want to.

First, your brain does not merely hibernate in isolation within your skull. It communicates with all other parts of your body through the nerve pathways that go down your spinal cord to your muscles and all your internal organs. Activities going on in your brain can conceivably affect every single cell in your body, directly or indirectly, because of the extensive nerve network lacing throughout all of your body tissues. Even your blood vessels dilate and constrict in response to the steady stream of pulse signals originating in the lower centers of your brain. And, of course, your brain receives an enormous number of pulses every second from the many sensor nerves that originate in the tissue of your muscles and organs. This is how your brain makes sense of what's happening all over your body and responds with the necessary regulatory signals. This interactive relationship between your brain and the other parts of your body also forms the basis for psychosomatic disease and psychosomatic wellness.

Second, your abstract thinking processes represent only one of three levels of operation involving your brain and spinal cord. The three levels are the spinal cord, the basal region, and the cerebral cortex. At the lowest level, the *spinal cord* itself, some primitive processes go on in the form of reflex activities. These include the patellar knee jerk, which the physician tests with a little hammer, and automatic withdrawal reactions to sharp pain or to touching something uncomfortably hot or cold.

At the *basal region* of your brain, your spinal cord enlarges just before it merges with the cerebral cortex. At this midbrain level, your *autonomic*, or *involuntary*, functions are controlled by various specialized structures. Originating here are the signals that control your heart rate, breathing, hunger, thirst, sexual drives, sleep and wakefulness, functions of liver, kidneys, and other organs, blood pressure, dilation and constriction of pupils of your eyes, and the general level of activity of your entire nervous system. This area also produces a number of *hormones*, or chemical message substances. These include such hormones as *growth hormone*, others that activate your adrenal glands to cause them to secrete the excitation hormone familiarly known as *adrenalin*, and others that stimulate the thyroid gland to supply *thyroxin*, which controls the overall pace of your body's cellular combustion processes, that is, your *metabolism*. While you go blithely along, assuming that your brain is merely the organ with which you form abstract thoughts, this midbrain region is working away faithfully below the level of your awareness, keeping your body's intricate organic processes running smoothly.

This same basal region has a special structure that is easily noticeable in any photograph or anatomical drawing of the brain. Tucked just below your cortex, or upper part of your brain, is a plum-sized blob of special nerve tissue called the *cerebellum*. Your cerebellum takes care of all of your habitual motor functions, such as balance and coordination, walking, routine hand and arm movements, control of your vocal apparatus, eye movements, and other well-learned motor processes such as a tennis serve, operating a typewriter, or driving a car. Some of these processes require the cerebellum to operate in conjunction with higher level thinking centers, while others are handled by the cerebellum almost exclusively. To become more aware of this automatic motor control function—your body's *autopilot*—try to take over conscious control of the process of walking across the room, or of writing your name, or of clapping your hands together. Note how the process seems to proceed almost of its own accord, making it very difficult—and strange—to control it by conscious thought. Your brain has a built-in neural tendency to structure its operations in the form of stored "programs" like these, at all levels up to and including abstract reasoning.

The third level, or *cerebral cortex*, carries out the more complex and consciously experienced processes. As we have seen, it does not operate in isolation from the two lower regions, but rather in close conjunction with them. A good example of the close interplay among these regions is the *stress reaction*, or "fight or flight" mobilization of your entire body, which can happen in response to an abstract thought such as being late for an airplane flight or a rude or insulting remark made to you by someone else.

The cerebral cortex, highest of the three levels, carries out three basic functions. It receives and organizes incoming messages from the five senses; it manipulates that information along with similar data previously stored in the form of memories; and it sends out motor commands to the various voluntary muscles of the body. Even at the level of the cortex, there is a close interplay between abstract thoughts and basic body functions.

For example, you may be explaining a complex idea to another person by forming it in your mind, finding the words to express it, operating your speech apparatus, making facial expressions and illustrative hand gestures, observing the other person's reactions for cues you can analyze to decide how well you're getting the idea across, and experiencing the emotional "tone" of the whole situation. Thinking is really a whole-brain function, and indeed even a whole-body function. Very few of the body's processes, especially thinking, go on in isolation from the other processes. Figure 2.1 illustrates the basic architecture of the brain.

The various functions of your cortex are not scattered randomly about within it, but are arranged in a rather well-defined pattern. And your brain organizes all incoming sensory signals into distinct patterns as well. For instance, all the signals coming from your eyeballs go to an area at the rear of your brain, at the base of your skull. Signals from the other sense channels go to their own characteristic regions. Certain special association areas apparently merge the data from all five senses and pass it on to a small region known as the *common integrating area*, which for about ninety percent of people is located slightly above and behind the left ear. This one area, about the size of a dime, appears to be the seat of conscious, purposive intellectual processes, those that give shape and meaning to all that your cortex does.

Physical damage to any particular region of the brain will affect the stored patterns and functions normally carried out by that region. For example, a stroke—blockage of a blood vessel supplying some region of the brain's tissue—will deny oxygen to that particular portion of tissue, causing it to die. It can then no longer carry out its function. Destruction of the common integrating area, for example, will render a person functionally an idiot, unable to form a complete thought or to develop a sufficient basis for purposive action. Destruction of the motor area for speech, usually located just behind the left temple, will leave the person capable of forming thoughts properly, but utterly unable to speak. Conversely, destruction of the verbal processing center, located for most people just in front of the left ear, will leave the person able to speak normally, but the speech will be a semantic jumble, properly articulated, yet devoid of meaning. Damage to the frontal region just behind the forehead, which can be caused by advanced alcoholism or heavy drug use, diminishes the capacity for abstract thought, such as developing a concept of a future action, forming an

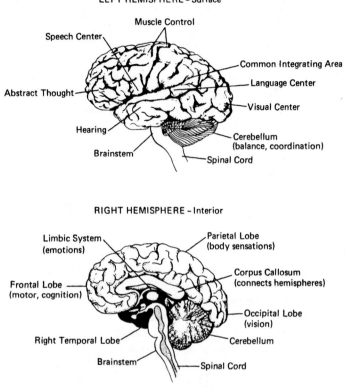

LEFT HEMISPHERE - Surface

Muscle Control

Speech Center

Common Integrating Area

Language Center

Abstract Thought

Visual Center

Hearing

Cerebellum
(balance, coordination)

Brainstem

Spinal Cord

RIGHT HEMISPHERE - Interior

Limbic System
(emotions)

Parietal Lobe
(body sensations)

Corpus Callosum
(connects hemispheres)

Frontal Lobe
(motor, cognition)

Occipital Lobe
(vision)

Right Temporal Lobe

Cerebellum

Brainstem

Spinal Cord

Figure 2.1 Architecture of the Brain

intention, carrying out a logical sequence of thoughts, or making judgments about the propriety of one's behavior. Physicians can often diagnose the nature and extent of brain damage due to a stroke or physical injury by testing the patient's various cognitive and motor functions. Any impaired function implies a corresponding damage to the associated region of the brain that controls it. Your brain, incidentally, cannot perceive the effects of trauma to its own tissue. It has no sensor nerves of its own.

Although we have been able to localize a number of functions within the cortex, we do not by any means understand all of its operation. In fact, there is probably much more about the cortex that is a mystery than that which is known. For example, we still have no clear idea of exactly how the brain stores its memories. It appears that an individual memory, such as an early experience, an image of a place or a scene, or a particular physical sensation, is not stored in one tiny location as would be the case for storage of numerical data inside an electronic computer. Most neuroscientists now believe that such memories are somehow "distributed" across relatively large regions of the cortex. Experiments with brain-damaged patients have shown that various memories become dimmer and less distinct, but they usually do not vanish abruptly with the loss of small regions of brain tissue. One prevailing theory holds that brain tissue records sensory data very much like a hologram—the three-dimensional photographs produced by laser light.

The most striking physical feature of the deeply wrinkled and convoluted cortex is its division into two distinct halves, or right and left hemispheres. These hemispheres physically are mirror images of each other, but they process information quite differently. In terms of motor functions, we know that the right hemisphere controls the left side of the body and the left hemisphere controls the right side. Signals from your sense organs cross over before they enter your brain, going to the opposite hemispheres. For example, images from the right visual field of each eye go to the left hemisphere of your brain, and the left field images go to the right hemisphere.

Recent research on brain function seems to indicate that most people have one dominant hemisphere, that is, one side that seems more "in charge" than the other. For perhaps ninety percent of people, this is the left hemisphere. Brain wave studies seem to indicate that the dominant hemisphere is somewhat more electrically active than the recessive one, and that the individual somehow relies on that particular hemisphere more than on the other. The evidence does not suggest a clear-cut left-right dominance in all cases, however. For example, not all left-handers are right brain dominant. About half of them have dominant left hemispheres just as most right-handers do. Left-handers account for about ten percent of the population, and they seem to vary in brain dominance more than do right-handers.

Some research seems to indicate that women are not as extensively "lateralized" as men in brain function. There also seem to be individuals of both sexes who are more or less "ambidextrous" in brain function. For these people, language and speech functions may be shared or duplicated between hemispheres rather than confined to the left side. They may be manually ambidextrous as well, or they may perform some tasks well with their left hands and other tasks well with their right hands.

When it comes to the more abstract forms of thought, the right and left hemispheres of the brain operate in remarkably contrasting ways. Brain researchers have concluded that the "left brain" deals primarily with information which can be represented in sequential or linear form. Such inputs include sequences of sounds, words, and sentences, the repetitive features of visual patterns, written language, numbers, and logical "if-then" relationships. In terms of data processing, the left brain seems to prefer verbal thought, linear sequences, numbers, mathematical relationships, logical chains of reasoning, and time relationships. For example, the task of determining which of two signals, a flash of light and an audible tone, occurred first would probably be handled primarily by the left brain. Decoding a spoken message would be mostly a left brain activity. The ability to organize a concept in words and explain it logically seems to be primarily a left brain skill.

The right hemisphere, or "right brain," seems to deal with whole forms, especially visual and spatial structures, rather than elements in a sequence. Your right hemisphere contains your subjective body image—the sense of your physical boundaries, your visual image of your appearance in a mirror, and the relative positioning of your arms, legs, and other body parts at any instant. Your right brain also seems to prefer visual and spatial data much more than your left brain does. Your right brain would probably take the lead in the task of determining how another object is positioned in space with respect to your body, or with respect to other objects. Spatial perception and spatial problem solving are primarily right brain functions. Your right brain would also probably be dominant for the task of comparing two musical tones or for recalling the pitch contours of a particular melody. Of course, the two hemispheres would always cooperate, such as for singing a song. The right brain would probably supply the subjective sense of rhythm and melody, with the left brain supplying the words and operating your vocal apparatus.

Brain wave studies have shown, through measurements of the relative amounts of electrical activity in various parts of the brain, that the two hemispheres work together, but that one or the other tends to become more active for its particular kinds of tasks. During normal waking activities, the left brain seems to be generally more active, with the right brain being somewhat recessive. During sleep, however, especially during dream activity, the right hemisphere seems to become much more active, while the left hemisphere recedes into a supporting role. This seems to align with our subjective experience, in that we seem to think verbally during waking hours and we seem to dream much more in visual images than in words. Some psychologists believe that certain people characteristically rely on right brain functions much more than others, and that they tend to think with visual and structural patterns in situations where "left brain" thinkers would rely more heavily on verbal patterns. Many artists and musicians might fall into this category.

Information flows freely back and forth between the two hemispheres by means of signals passing across a connecting bridgelike band of nerve fibers called the *corpus callosum* (Latin for "callous body"). If you didn't have a corpus callosum, your two hemispheres would have to operate in isolation. For example, you couldn't sing a familiar tune because the melody and pitch levels would reside primarily in your right brain, and that information couldn't flow across to the left brain, which contains the motor center for operating your vocal cords. Conversely, you would probably have great difficulty forming a mental picture of a scene that you heard someone describe, because your right brain couldn't decode the spoken message by itself (that's primarily a left brain task) in order to activate its stored visual memories. Figure 2.2 illustrates these functions.

Scientists have found out many things about the interactions between

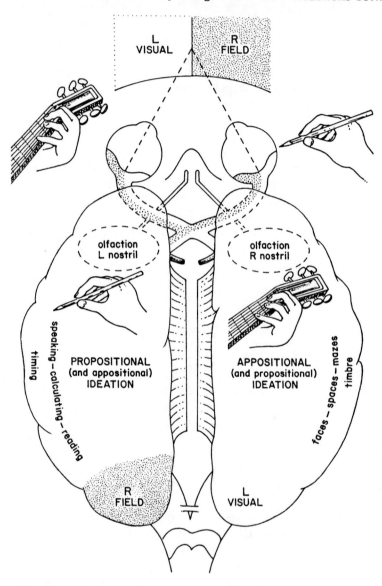

Figure 2.2   Each of the brain's hemispheres processes information in its own distinctive way. This diagram represents the lateralization of brain functions, as seen from above. (From M.C. Wittrock, et al., *The Human Brain*. Englewood Cliffs, N.J.: Prentice-Hall, 1977. Used with permission of the publisher and J.E. Bogen.)

right and left hemispheres by studying human beings who have had their corpus callosa surgically divided, usually as a last-resort treatment for otherwise untreatable epilepsy. Surprisingly, such a grossly intrusive surgical procedure does not cause total chaos in the brain's operation, as one might expect. The changes in brain function manifest themselves in rather subtle form, usually in terms of increased difficulty in performing certain mechanical tasks and in verbalizing experiences.

Now let's see how these physical and neural features of your brain play a part in your thought processes. To do so, we will study the brain's operation as an *organ of information*.

the three "languages" of conscious thought

Have you ever tried to "tune in" on your thoughts? Have you sometimes wondered how you think—what your thoughts seem to be made of? Perhaps you've tried to figure out whether you think mostly in words, in pictures, or in some other form. This seems to be a difficult question for a person to answer, because thoughts are fleeting things. They flash across your internal "screen" of consciousness one after another, so rapidly that it is extremely difficult to study them as they go by.

Actually, most of your thinking goes on automatically, rapidly, and more or less below the level of your conscious inspection. What psychologists call *conscious thought* is actually a slower, more limited form of thought than that which proceeds rapidly and invisibly at a steady pace all through your waking hours and possibly even while you are asleep.

Think for a moment about the many things you say and do automatically, even while you are consciously doing something else. You can take the proper freeway exit while driving your car and talking to your friend at the same time. If you must put on the brakes quickly to avoid another driver, you need not go through an elaborate process of verbalizing what you are doing—you simply do it. You recognize a friend or acquaintance on the street, decide to wave and say hello, and you do it, with all of your decisions and motor commands having been organized below the level of your immediate attention.

We can distinguish two separate levels of thought as the *conscious* level and the *preconscious* level. The *preconscious* level is the level of rapidly flowing, automatic thought processes that account for most of your brain's activity. The *conscious* level is the level of carefully encoded thought forms to which you can pay close attention. In labeling these two levels, I choose to avoid using terms like "the unconscious" or "unconscious mind," only because they have acquired so many mysterious and awesome connotations over the years. Sigmund Freud originally used the term "unconscious mind" to try to describe thought processes that went on beyond the immediate reach of one's instantaneous field of attention. Popularization of Freudian theory during the early part of the twentieth century made the term into a cliché, often used in ways quite different from Freud's intended meaning. (Incidentally, Freud did not use the term "subconscious" in explaining his theory. That was later connected with psychoanalysis by popular writers rather than psychotherapists.)

> *Our normal waking consciousness . . . is but one special type of consciousness, whilst all about it, parted from it by the flimsiest of screens, there lie potential forms of consciousness entirely different. We may go through life without suspecting their existence; but apply the requisite stimulus, and at a touch they are there in all their completeness.*
>
> **WILLIAM JAMES**

Figure 2.3 shows schematically the relationship between this "underground," or preconscious, mental activity and the "aboveground," or conscious, mental activity. Further, we can refer to the immediate focus of your attention, such as the words you're reading at this moment, as the "foreground," or your conscious thought. And we can refer to your stored memories, such as previously read words and ideas, as the "background" to your instantaneous focus of attention. These terms can help to clarify the forms of thought your brain uses to carry out its many functions.

This visual analogy of a cylinder (Figure 2.3) reinforces the notion that most of our continuous thinking activity goes on underground, beyond the level of convenient expression in symbolic form. The foreground area can be compared to a projection screen, on which we may choose to display projected versions of the various inexpressible thought forms going on at the underground level. For example, as you are reading this book, you might reach the bottom of the page and decide quite automatically to turn to the next page. You might say that you turned the page "without even

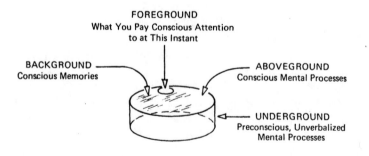

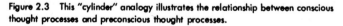

Figure 2.3 This "cylinder" analogy illustrates the relationship between conscious thought processes and preconscious thought processes.

thinking about it." But, in fact, you did think about it, at least at the preconscious underground level. You didn't have to express the thought at the conscious foreground level in order to carry it out. If you had chosen to try to verbalize that underground thought, for example, by saying "now it's time to turn the page, because I've finished reading this one and I have to turn it over to see what's on the next one," you would no longer have been thinking the original thought. You would have constructed a new thought, at the foreground level. Your underground thoughts would continue right along, moving on to take care of other matters even while you were talking. In a sense, conscious thoughts are like the shadows of preconscious thoughts.

You can consider your conscious thought processes—those which you can tune in to and observe as they happen—as being expressed in any or all of three thinking "languages," which are

1. Verbal thought.
2. Visual thought.
3. Kinesthetic thought.

Verbal thought is "hearing" your mental "voice" just as if you were expressing your mental processes aloud in words, phrases, and sentences.

Visual thought is "seeing" mental pictures, which are often fuzzy and fragmentary and which are usually recalled from your memory as composite images; pictures, fragments of pictures, and scenes you have observed or can imagine; spatial structures and relationships.

Kinesthetic thought is experiencing overall sensations, including various emotional reactions (which are merely whole-body reactions), subjective tension level, and general creature reactions to immediate experience.

You can represent just about any conscious thought in visual form by responding to it at the level of your generalized creature reactions. For example, you can think about your mate, lover, relative, or friend by saying that person's name in your mind, by forming a mental picture of the person, and by tuning in to your overall feeling response to the total concept of the person. For most of your conscious thought, all three of these thinking languages come into play simultaneously, with one or another playing the dominant role depending on the topic and your own mental habits.

These three thinking languages—visual, verbal, kinesthetic—are the means by which you project snapshots of your rapidly moving preconscious thoughts onto the "screen" of your immediate attention, that is, the foreground of your conscious thought. You can capture some of these fleeting thoughts and translate them into conscious form, but the vast majority of them flow on invisibly and reliably without your conscious attention.

According to this description of brain function, your preconscious level of thought is perfectly capable of reasoning logically, of making decisions, and of directing a large share of your moment-to-moment actions. This point of view may also explain the basis for hunches, or intuitive thought processes, which seem to tell you what to do, but offer no well worked-out verbal reasoning processes to substantiate the proposed course of action. What we customarily refer to as *intuition* is, in my opinion, a preconscious process of logical reasoning, which has not (yet) manifested its effects in conscious, systematic form. A hunch can be every bit as logical as a consciously verbalized reasoning process.

Albert Einstein, generally considered one of the foremost scientific thinkers in human history, commented especially on the function of intuition. "The really valuable thing is intuition," he said. "A thought comes and I may try to express it in words afterwards." Trusting your hunches, then, comes down to "listening" for the subtle cues which play about the edges of the foreground of your conscious thought, and which cast the shadows of a preconscious reasoning process that may have resulted in a valuable conclusion.

Skill in using your hunches and other kinds of preconscious thought requires the skill of translating these fleeting forms into one or more of the three thinking languages. By expressing your ideas effectively in words, in pictures, and in kinesthetic form, you can tap into your mental underground of thought. An effective interplay between the preconscious and conscious levels is the basis of the so-called creative thinking process, as well as intuition, playing hunches, and generally thinking on your feet.

Using visual thinking—mental pictures—is also a very effective way to improve your memory. If you can "file" a memory in visual and kinesthetic form as well as in words, for example, by making an amusing mental picture of it, you bring larger regions of your brain into play and improve your chances of recalling it later.

abstract thought

The ability to deal with abstract ideas plays a very important part in a person's overall mental capability. People vary widely in the extent to which they feel comfortable with abstract thinking and in the extent to which they can move freely along the conceptual "scale" from the very concrete to the very abstract.

In one sense, virtually all of your thinking operates at some relative level of abstraction because your thoughts are mostly the echoes of your past perceptions. When you primarily verbalize your thoughts in the form of familiar perceptual structures such as objects, people, and processes, you operate toward the concrete end of the conceptual scale. When you verbalize largely in the form of "unreal" structures such as intangible concepts and processes, you operate toward the abstract end of the scale.

Early education experiences seem to play an important part in a person's orientation toward abstract thought. A child who becomes confused and discouraged in classroom activities, especially in mathematics, will very likely grow up apprehensive and will possibly avoid math and other forms of abstract thought. The adult who says, "I'm terrible at math," probably felt confused and defeated in early experiences and had no one to turn to for help or encouragement. Such an adult might shy away from exposure to technical subjects, mechanical devices, and philosophical topics of conversation. The confirmed concrete thinker might even feel uncomfortable with a chart, a graph, or another abstract representation of factual information.

You can estimate a person's general level of fluency with abstract thought from several key features of his or her behavior. For example, the confirmed concrete thinker tends to use a relatively concrete vocabulary almost exclusively in talking and writing. This person will probably seldom read books or magazine articles for enjoyment, except for fiction or very light subject matter, and will prefer movies and TV programs that emphasize escape and entertainment rather than complex "social messages." A distinct aversion to mathematics, technical subjects of all kinds, and philosophical discussions also betrays an imprisoning inclination toward concrete thought. Conversely, a person who reads extensively, speaks and writes freely with relatively abstract terms, and works comfortably with mathematics and other complex concepts probably has a high level of fluency with abstract thought and also probably enjoys it.

If you would like to increase your own fluency with abstract thinking, just do more of the kinds of things mentioned above. Make it a practice to read about new subjects from the abundant literature of non-fiction. Browse around bookstores and buy books that will challenge your ideas. Watch thought-provoking films and TV programs and go to lectures that deal with interesting topics. Discuss these topics with your friends and spend more time with people who have intellectual interests. Also make it a point to add various abstract terms to your vocabulary and use them more freely. If you have an aversion to mathematics, try taking a refresher course to build up your confidence in logical thinking and to gain some useful thinking techniques. Many adults who re-study mathematics find it much easier to master, and consequently more enjoyable, the second time around

In addition to the practical value of fluency in abstract thinking, those who have developed it find that it makes their lives more interesting and enjoyable. The adaptive, fluent thinker enjoys a rich mental life and finds many interesting things to do. Those who enjoy thinking seldom allow themselves to become bored.

mental patterns

Don't forget that everybody, including yourself, has only his own experience to think with.

RUDOLF FLESCH

One of the most important facts about the human brain is that it does most of its conscious thinking not with tiny bits of information, but with whole thought units. From the moment of birth, and perhaps even before, your brain begins organizing the signals brought to it by your senses into *mental patterns*, and it uses these patterns as the building blocks of conscious thought.

A mental pattern is simply a memory trace in your brain tissue, which records something you have perceived a number of times. As you see, hear, feel, smell, or taste the same thing or approximately the same thing many times, your brain will build a recognition pattern of that perceptual event, using certain defining cues that identify it. When you perceive it again, or you perceive something like it, the memory trace is activated. An important fact of human perception (which we will explore in more depth in Chapter 7) is that if the memory trace is strongly enough embedded, the brain will tend to substitute the memory trace for the incoming sensory signals and deal with the trace instead of the fresh sensory data in its information-processing activities.

For example, if you have seen photographs of Leonardo da Vinci's Mona Lisa many times, or if you have seen the actual painting in the Louvre, you can probably recognize the work at a moment's glance. What defining cues does your brain use to recognize the famous portrait as the Mona Lisa and not as some other young woman? At a glance, your perception could probably be fooled by a cleverly contrived substitute painting, which included those basic cues but differed substantially in detail from the original. Upon closer inspection, your brain would depend less on its stored pattern and more on direct observation, so you could tell the difference. Mental patterns help you to recognize familiar objects and experiences efficiently and to think about them, but they can also sometimes imprison your thinking processes if you depend on them inappropriately.

Think for a moment about the enormous number of mental patterns you use in dealing with your day-to-day experiences. Each of your five senses brings in data to the brain, which it tends to organize into patterns. Visual patterns are probably easiest to identify. For example, the characters of the alphabet, numbers, street and highway signs, traffic signals, and advertising messages are symbolic patterns; they carry consciously encoded messages. Other easily recognized patterns that are quite famous include the Eiffel Tower in Paris, the Statue of Liberty in New York, and the

Washington Monument in Washington, D.C. Your brain tends to organize as many as possible of its repeated experiences into convenient mental patterns. You tend to see commonplace objects—trees, houses, streets, clouds, tables, chairs, and many others—in terms of *recognition* cues, not in terms of their detailed structures. You might glance out the window and say, "There goes a man on a bicycle," based on a very brief and fragmentary perception of the process you are describing. Mostly, these recognition patterns serve extremely well in organizing the brain's information into higher level building blocks.

But occasionally the brain reacts inappropriately to some specific recognition cue, and fails to take in other significant information about what's going on. For example, I recently got out of my car and headed for the small print shop where I have for several years had photocopying work done. Thinking about other things, I merely headed for the familiar brightly colored awning in the middle of the block. As I walked inside, I was startled and confused to find myself surrounded by racks of clothing! The print shop had been moved across the street during the few weeks I had been out of town. The proprietor of the new shop chuckled at my bewilderment. "I can usually recognize someone who's looking for the print shop," he said. "They all have the same surprised look on their faces." Looking at the shop from the street, I realized that my only recognition cue for finding it had been the brightly colored awning, which had not changed.

The brain also constructs and stores other sensory patterns. A musical melody is an example of an auditory pattern. No single note carries any information about the song itself. It is only a certain "arrangement" of notes in a fairly precise time sequence that your brain recognizes as familiar. Slogans, proverbs, and famous sayings fall into this category of auditory or verbal patterns.

Similarly, tactile patterns tell you when you are touching something familiar. Blind people who read by the Braille system rely on raised patterns of dots to recognize verbal information. You can pick up a familiar object without looking at it, and you know what it is. Only when objects are quite similar do you sometimes mistake one for another. Then you must direct your attention below the level of pattern recognition and inspect the object more closely. Similarly, tastes and odors seem familiar or unfamiliar, according to your own distinctive mental patterns that organize your olfactory and gustatory memories. Perhaps you've had the experience of smelling some vaguely familiar odor and getting a "flashback" memory of a childhood experience, complete with the accompanying feelings.

Pattern thinking is basic to your brain's operation, and it serves to make your perceptual processes extremely efficient. Unfortunately, pattern thinking can sometimes imprison your thinking if you fail to notice important differences between what's in front of you and what you've perceived in the past. The tendency of your brain to use its stored mental patterns whenever possible is so strong that it sometimes interferes with accurate observation. The brain seems to try to assign "meaning" to everything it takes in, to categorize it, and relate it to what you already know. This means that the brain *interprets* sensory data as it takes it in.

To explore this pattern-making feature of your mental computer, look at Figure 2.4. What is the "meaning" of the figure in the center of the group? Does it seem to shift back and forth as you look at it? Can you divorce it from pre-established patterns and explore it as an independent object of perception? What else could you allow it to "be"?

Figure 2.5 shows a well-known visual illusion, which also illustrates your brain's pattern-making and pattern-recognition processes. Can you see two faces in profile, nose-to-nose, as well as see a cuplike object formed by the black area of the figure? You will probably find it quite difficult to dismiss these patterns from your perceptual field and see the arrangement of black and white areas without assigning meanings to it. In such a case, the mental patterns stored in your memory are competing with your immediate sensory information for dominance as your brain tries to decide what it's looking at.

Figure 2.6 shows another familiar pattern, buried within an unusual arrangement of information. *Before reading any further, glance at the figure right now.* What did you see? If you can't recognize a familiar pattern, look again, with the idea of finding a familiar English word presented in an unusual way. Does knowing what to look for help to spot the pattern? Try placing a straightedge along the top or bottom edge of the figure. Once you recognize the pattern, can you then get rid of it and call it back as you choose?

Figure 2.4   What "is" the figure in the center of the group?

Figure 2.5 What do you see here?

Becoming more aware of pattern thinking and the effects it can have in organizing your mental picture of a situation can help you to think more freely and in a much more versatile manner. Begin looking for mental patterns in your thinking processes and in situations where you find yourself having difficulty. These patterns can range from simple perceptual patterns all the way to the abstract, such as relationships between people, accepted approaches to problems, and accepted ways of doing things. Look at the patterns that define your relationships with people who are close to you. Study your patterns for living, for dealing with others, for talking, for arguing, for compromising, for socializing. How do you do your daily work? What patterns define your relationships with your coworkers or fellow students or casual acquaintances?

mental routines

In addition to using mental patterns as building blocks of thought, your brain also uses a vast number of *mental routines,* or programmed thought sequences, to carry out its work of information processing. These mental routines bear a close resemblance to the routines and subroutines used by an electronic computer to process data.

A mental routine is simply a sequence of mental steps, usually taking

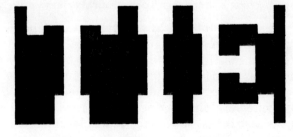

Figure 2.6 Can you find a familiar pattern here?

place so fast you can't consciously observe them, and serving to organize and manipulate memories for some given purpose. Your brain has committed a vast number of these standard sequences to memory and can call them up when it needs them.

The more times you think a certain thought, the more likely you are to think that thought again. Apparently the memory traces that come into play for a particular thought take on a kind of electrical "readiness," which makes it easier for them to respond again. With repeated activation, the thought patterns probably become grooved into that particular channel, especially if that thought is comparatively important or useful and if it involves relatively large regions of your cortex. A close analogy to this process is the effect of erosion on a bare hillside. Each additional downpour of rain tends to carve deeper into the crevices and channels that already exist, reinforcing them. New channels tend to develop only occasionally, if at all.

It is no accident that many people become less inquisitive, less creative, and less willing to try unfamiliar experiences as they "mature." It is a biological tendency of their cortical structures. After a certain point in life, they stop acquiring new mental routines and they learn to get along with the ones they have. Anthropologist Ashley Montagu calls this condition *psychosclerosis*. Another term for it is "hardening of the categories." You can overcome or avoid this mentally-fossilized condition, but only by conscious attention to developing mental flexibility.

Old age puts more wrinkles in the mind than in the face.

MONTAIGNE

To explore some of these mental routines, try carrying out the following thought processes:

1. $2 + 7 =$ _____.
2. Mary had a little _____.
3. The largest city in China is _____.
4. I eat when I am _____.
5. If Mary is older than John and John is older than Mike, then Mary is _____ than Mike.

You solve these simple problems by deploying your standard programs, or stored mental routines. A great deal of your verbal memory is organized in this way. You can recall the words to a song most easily by singing it through. The words seem to fall into place as if from nowhere; actually, you are recalling them as integrated parts of a complete pattern. Similarly, you can probably recite the alphabet forward more reliably than you can recite it backward, because that's the way you probably memorized it as a child.

Of course, one can become so dependent on fixed mental programs as to become rigid, dull, and mechanical in his or her thinking processes. One character in a slapstick movie illustrated such an extreme dependence on mental routines when someone asked him his name. He thought for a moment, screwed up his face, frowned, scratched his head, and finally began waving his hands back and forth rhythmically as if leading an orchestra. Then he brightly announced, "Norman. That's my name—Norman." The other person asked, somewhat cautiously, "Would you mind telling me why you went through all of that, just to remember your name?" He replied, "Sure." Then he repeated the sequence, singing "Happy birthday to you, happy birthday to you, happy birthday dear—Norman!"

Mental routines usually employ standard mental patterns, giving the brain an extremely efficient way to process information quickly and simply. By putting together a number of such building blocks, your brain can solve a typical problem and arrive at a conclusion without having to examine every tiny element of information.

Sometimes, however, these automatic processes can short-circuit your thinking when you choose an inappropriate mental routine or a mental pattern that doesn't fit the situation. Here's another simple mental task to help you explore the ways in which your brain uses patterns and routines. Look at the figure below and note the number of squares. *Do this now, before reading any further.*

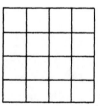

If you responded like most people who try this experiment, you looked at the drawing and concluded that there were sixteen squares. But look again. What constitutes the definition of a "square?" How about two-by-two squares? How about three-by-three squares? Actually, you can find thirty squares of various sizes in the diagram. If your answer was sixteen, you were probably victimized by your brain's pattern-making tendency and by a faulty mental routine.

You may have responded to the request to "note the number of squares" in something like the following way. You glanced at the diagram, your attention was drawn immediately to the neat four-by-four arrangement, and you defined a square for this particular situation as a one-by-one element of the overall diagram. And you probably didn't count them either. You probably noted that there were four elements in each direction, so you multiplied four by four (another mental routine) and came up with sixteen.

If you left out the other possibilities, it was because the automatic mental routines you brought into play did not allow for them.

When the only tool you have is a hammer, you tend to treat everything as if it were a nail.

ABRAHAM MASLOW

Take a moment to reflect on the ways in which mental routines like these might play a part in your thinking processes. How about listening to another person explain an idea you believe you already understand? How about making a decision when you don't have as many facts as you would like? How about hearing an opinion with which you strongly disagree? Well-selected mental routines in these situations can help you to deal with them effectively. If poorly selected, because of a lack of awareness of thinking traps like the one just demonstrated, they can misdirect your thinking processes and thwart your intentions in the situation.

The difference between the dogmatic, rigid, categorical thinker and the adaptive, creative, and strategic thinker is basically in the ability to escape the imprisoning effects of fixed thinking routines, and to bring to the situation whatever point of view or pattern or mental program is needed to get effective results. In a sense, this entire book is about how to gain mastery over your thinking routines and thought patterns, rather than to allow them to master you.

the mental "set"

One evening on "The Tonight Show," bandleader Doc Severinson became the butt of a practical joke, prearranged between host Johnny Carson and the members of the band. As Severinson prepared to start the music that traditionally signaled the opening of the show, the television camera was trained on him. He rasied his baton to bring the band to readiness. All the musicians briskly raised their instruments in preparation. Then, as Severinson gave the vigorous downstroke to signal the start of the music, *nothing happened!* The musicians sat like statues, with no one playing a note. They simply stared at Severinson while he flailed his arms in desperation, trying to understand what was going on.

For those few seconds, Severinson was the prisoner of a *mental set,* an expectation so strong that it organized his entire thinking process. He was so completely prepared for the expected event, and quite naturally so, that he was thrown into a kind of mental tailspin when it didn't happen. It took him several seconds to shake off the mental set and make a quick "reality test" to find out what was really going on and to deal with it effectively. Once he recognized the joke, he joined in the laughter with the others.

When Carson asked him how the experience felt, Severinson said, "It felt like somebody hit me behind the neck."

A mental set is a strongly held expectation—an attitude or a belief about a situation or about an upcoming experience. It has the useful effect of preparing you to recognize and categorize certain incoming perceptions and to respond quickly and effectively. Unfortunately, it can also sometimes lead you to deal with the situation in a narrow, highly programmed manner, which may not be the best approach. *Mental sets are normal, natural, and routine aspects of your brain's patterned way of organizing information.* To develop a high degree of mental freedom requires developing the ability to recognize your mental sets under certain circumstances, and in some cases to change them, rearrange them, or abandon them.

A few other examples might help to show how commonplace mental sets are and how basic to human thought processes. One Sunday morning, the chairman of a certain church committee stood before the congregation to present a minor matter of church business for a vote. After the vote, his next agenda item was to lead the congregation in singing several hymns. He confidently presented his project for a vote, fully expecting routine acceptance by the congregation. But to his surprise, the matter failed. The vote was no. He was so completely rattled by this surprising turn of events that the fragments of his shattered mental set confounded his thought processes as he introduced the next hymn. Instead of inviting the group to join him in singing "I Stand All Amazed," he introduced it as "I Stand All Opposed."

Some mental sets have much more subtle effects on our thinking than others. The essence of the magician's art is to invite you to adopt a certain mental set, and then to surprise you with a turn of events you didn't expect. The magician may lead you to conclude very confidently that the card you previously selected is not in the group of ten cards he has just shown you one at a time, possibly by deftly skipping over the card he knows to be yours. A few seconds later, when he turns up your card, you are so completely unprepared to see it that you are momentarily stunned. The fun of being fooled by a magician comes from the sudden demolition of the mental set he has helped you to adopt.

Similarly, the surprise effect of a joke comes from the sudden destruction of a mental set. The punch line (an interesting term from this point of view) is so far removed from what you could possibly have expected to hear, that you experience a mild mental "thunderstorm." Your laughter expresses your involuntary response to the sudden discovery that your mental set has led you astray. This *monorail thinking*, as Edward deBono calls it, is the basis of narrow and rigid forms of thought as well as the basis of jokes.

For example, try to anticipate the punch line as you read the following story:

A new bridegroom looked at the results of his bride's first attempt at cooking breakfast and said glumly, "It isn't like Mom used to make."

Disappointed, she tried all the harder the next morning, producing a nicely cooked, attractive breakfast. He looked at it and muttered, "It just isn't like Mom used to make."

This went on for a number of mornings in succession. She would go to great lengths, sure she had created a tasty, well-prepared breakfast, only to be greeted with "It isn't like Mom used to make."

Finally she became so exasperated with his cruel comments that she decided to rebel. She deliberately fried the eggs until they were like hard rubber, virtually cremated the bacon, burned the toast black, and overcooked the coffee until it was almost unfit to drink.

Her husband sat down at the table, looked at the food, and beamed. "Hey! Just like Mom used to make!"

the mechanical thinker
and the adaptive thinker

 He who will not reason is a bigot; he who cannot is a fool; he who dares not is a slave.

WILLIAM DRUMMOND

Those people who have developed their thinking abilities to a high level all have one thing in common, which the vast majority of mediocre thinkers lack. They have freed themselves to a great extent from the confinement of fixed mental routines, and they have learned to adapt their mental processes to the needs of situations as they arise. But, unfortunately, adaptive thinkers form a relatively small population. The great majority of people do most of their thinking mechanically, habitually, reactively, and unimaginatively—not because they can't think adaptively, but because they don't realize they can.

Each of us has certain *adaptive thinking* skills that increase our freedom, and each of us has certain *mechanical thinking* habits that imprison us without our knowing it. We will draw two sharply contrasting profiles for comparison, one of the extremely mechanical thinker and one of the adaptive thinker. Very few people fit either of these two profiles completely, but the profiles will help us to understand the mental processes we must explore if we are to develop our thinking skills and increase the benefits we derive from using our brains.

First, let's look at the extreme version of the mechanical thinker. This person is typically an adult, since children tend to think very freely and imaginatively until they are processed by the school system. The mechanical thinker is just as likely to be a woman as a man, although the following description uses the nonspecific pronoun "he" in describing the stereotype.

First, the mechanical thinker takes considerable pride in his opinions, which he believes to be "right." It is proper and necessary, he believes, for a person to "take a stand" on things—on just about everything, in fact. Although he doesn't realize it, each time he voices a sweeping generalization or a dogmatic opinion on some topic, he commits himself to adopt a rigid stand on similar topics. He must, above all, be "consistent."

If you study the mechanical thinker closely, you will probably notice a singular lack of apparent curiosity. He seldom asks questions (except loaded ones during debates with others, which he likes to call "discussions"), and he seldom seeks new information about his world. He would seldom concede to having learned something from another person. He rarely reads books and certainly not nonfiction material. If a man, he may read the sports pages, which is acceptable behavior for a male in his society—or if a woman she may read the women's section of the paper. The mechanical thinker may reveal a noticeable uneasiness in unfamiliar situations and may be embarrassed when confronted with a fact that forces him to revise a strongly held opinion.

The mechanical thinker hates more than anything else to change his mind. New ideas and new points of view bring ambiguity, and the mechanical thinker is allergic to ambiguity. He likes to have things settled, with all issues decided, all questions answered as simply as possibly, and all philosophical problems put to rest. And because he unconsciously invests his ego in his opinions, he unconsciously views changing his mind as a form of weakness.

He might be deeply religious, and if so he is likely to be highly dogmatic about his religion as being the only "true" one. He believes his country is the "best" in the world, and he views all other citizens of the world as inferior second-stringers who have had the genetic misfortune to be born un-American. Religious leaders love him, political demagogues love him, and advertising copywriters love him, because he is controllable. Ironically, although he takes fierce pride in "thinking for himself," the mechanical thinker is much more easily manipulated than is the adaptive thinker, because he responds automatically to messages designed to trigger his limited repertoire of thought processes.

The mechanical thinker likes slogans, stock phrases, pat answers, and categorical statements that help him to simplify his conception of his world. His favorite phrase is "I always say . . ." He likes simple terms such as right and wrong, good and bad, win and lose. He does not like shades of gray because they tend to leave situations and issues unresolved. He becomes impatient (and uneasy) with people who won't commit themselves as dogmatically as he has, who won't "take a stand." He likes bumper stickers with slogans like, "America—Love It Or Leave It!"

The mechanical thinker loves to pass judgment on people, ideas, and things, since it feels good to play the role of Chief Justice of the World. He has evaluated the President, any other national figures he knows about, his state governor, the mayor, his boss, his neighbor, his own spouse, his children, and his children's friends. Then he proceeds to take care of various categories, such as Blacks, Orientals, Mexicans, Jews, politicians, lawyers, union members, gays, movie stars, the younger generation, the older generation, and on and on—except, of course, any group to which he himself belongs.

He may have very simple conceptions about what men are supposed to be like and what women are supposed to be like. If a male, he may ridicule viciously what he calls "Women's Lib." (A female would be likely to ridicule it as well, although with perhaps different jibes than a mechanical-thinking male would use.) As a result of these simple role definitions, both males and females with the mechanical-thinking orientation are likely to lead very truncated role-locked lives, unwilling to explore roles and behaviors even slightly outside the boundaries of their conventional definitions of maleness and femaleness.

The mechanical thinker has firm opinions on movies, art, and music. His stock phrase is "I don't know much about art, but I know what I like." If he would then go on to say things such as "I like this," "I like that a lot," and "I don't particularly like that," he would be thinking at least somewhat adaptively. Instead, he is more likely to say "That's ugly" or "That's stupid" or "That's the most ridiculous thing I ever saw." He probably has never thought about value judgments as individualized mental processes. He would probably consider the distinctions between the two kinds of statements given above to be splitting hairs. So far as he is concerned, something that's stupid is stupid, and that's that. He doesn't like to "mess around with semantics." He may be a very literal thinker, simply bypassing or skipping over ideas that are expressed in slightly abstract or metaphorical terms.

Indeed, you can spot the mechanical thinker most easily by listening to the way he uses words. You will probably hear a large proportion of declarative statements, many phrased in dogmatic terms, and a relatively small portion of open-ended questions. If you listen carefully, you will probably hear certain words which semanticists refer to as *allness terms*— all, every, everybody, always, never, nobody, and none. These terms tend to channel his thinking processes into rigid forms, preventing him from expressing—and in fact, perceiving—shades of gray, degrees of things, and comparative aspects. He may convey an *either-or orientation* by the words he chooses, with verbal structures like win or lose, for and against, good and bad, success and failure, right and wrong. These prevent him from recognizing and dealing with the matter of relativity in talking about people and ideas, and especially in discussing matters that involve human values.

> *What passes for common sense is often stupidity hardened into habit.*
>
> **HERMAN WOUK**

The mechanical thinker may also have an underdeveloped sense of humor. Even if he doesn't see the world as basically a grim place, he probably gets most of his laughs at the expense of others. He likes jokes that illustrate how stupid other people are, but he usually has great difficulty laughing at himself or at the institutions of which he considers himself a part. Because humor involves ambiguity and newness, and because the mechanical thinker avoids ambiguity, he misses a great deal of the charming absurdity in the world about him.

But probably the single most self-limiting feature of the mechanical thinker's habit pattern, which prevents him from developing his thinking skills any further, is that *he simply doesn't use his brain very much unless it's necessary.* The mechanical thinker goes through the day with his higher mental powers simply gathering dust because he failed to learn (or was taught otherwise in obedience school) that using his brain in non-routine ways can be stimulating and pleasurable. He mostly responds to the demands of the moment, with whatever mental patterns and routines he has acquired by hit or miss during his life. If he needs to figure out his car's gas mileage or to double a recipe, he does it. If he needs to discuss a business problem with someone, he does it. If he has to talk to his son or daughter about school, he does it. He is a creature of habit—mental habits, physical habits, and social habits. Nonroutine thinking is foreign to his habit patterns. To explore his world for the sake of *possibly* learning something new and exciting just doesn't appeal to him. The mechanical thinker is *mentally sedentary.*

> *When I works, I works hard;*
> *When I sits, I sits loose;*
> *When I thinks, I falls asleep.*
>
> **ANONYMOUS**

From time to time, even the most confirmed mechanical thinker experiences brief episodes of adaptive thinking. He may, on occasion, get a very exciting idea or put two ideas together in a new and novel way, and he may experience that joyous burst of energy which the adaptive thinker knows so well. And at those moments, the mechanical thinker has become an adaptive thinker, using his brain more in the direction of its potential. Unfortunately, he doesn't realize that what he did can be developed into a skill that he can call on time and again. He has been trained by the labeling and categorizing process of his society (and probably his schooling) to consider himself dull and "uncreative," so he regards a creative new thought as something accidental—a bolt from the blue or a cosmic ray that struck his brain. The mechanical thinker is fully capable of becoming an adaptive thinker, but his mechanical thinking habits usually keep him from realizing it.

Now let's examine the contrasting style of the adaptive thinker. The adaptive thinker's primary characteristic is a kind of mental and psychological "neutrality" toward the situation he finds himself in at any one moment. This neutral orientation is relatively free of fixed mental sets and enables the adaptive thinker to maintain an investigative approach. He simply finds out what's going on in front of him and around him, and he uses his brain to adapt his responses most effectively to it. He can scan the situation, think on his feet, and deal with it in whatever way he determines is best for his own needs and purposes. (Whereas the adaptive thinker knows he is doing this, the mechanical thinker doesn't realize that such an orientation is possible.) The adaptive thinker's "let's see" orientation is the key to his entire repertoire of mental skills.

The adaptive thinker continually explores his world, even (and especially) when exploration is not necessarily demanded by the immediate situation. He inquires into the goings-on around him, looking for new, novel, or interesting aspects of the situation, which may later become useful. He asks questions, questions, and more questions. He speculates about other goings-on and tries to check out his speculations. "I wonder if (or how, or what, or when, or who, or where). . .," "Could it be that. . .?" and "What would happen if. . .?" are his favorite terms. He gathers in bits and pieces of information about his world as a matter of mental habit, with the unconscious faith that much of it will sooner or later turn out to be useful. The fact that he doesn't know which of the bits and pieces will eventually become useful and which will not doesn't bother him in the least. He has a basic conviction about the value of knowing. The skill of what-if thinking comes easily to him.

The adaptive thinker likes new ideas, whereas the mechanical thinker retreats to the familiar ground of tried and true (or at least the tried). The adaptive thinker comes up with new ideas by combining known ideas. He puts together new options, new points of view, and new approaches, in many cases for the sheer pleasure of playing with ideas. He usually finds that a surprising number of these new possibilities work better than tried and true approaches. Thomas Edison once commented about his exhausting search for the best material to use as the filament in his new incandescent lamp. "I'll try anything. I'll even try Limburger cheese." This kind of indomitable faith in the value of mental effort is the hallmark of adaptive thinking.

The adaptive thinker creates opinions rather sparingly. He realizes that an opinion is simply a temporary point of view, a mental set adopted for the purpose of organizing further incoming information. While the mechanical thinker considers his opinions to be the end point of a thought process, to be defended against all comers, the adaptive thinker considers an opinion a temporary way station in a thinking process, and a rather dangerous one at that. He has little difficulty abandoning opinions or revising them when new information tells him that the opinions are no longer workable. He is less likely to distort or filter his perceptions to match his preconceived opinions, because he has generally fewer opinions to begin with and because he holds on to them less tenaciously.

The adaptive thinker freely questions the status quo. Whereas the mechanical thinker retreats to the status quo because it is familiar, the adaptive thinker tends to suspect the status quo just because it is familiar. He looks for the dominant factors in a given situation and asks (at least to himself) whether they could or should be changed, and what might be the result if they were changed. He spots the hidden assumptions and controlling values in a situation, and he thinks about the effects they might be having on the thinking processes of the mechanical thinkers who are subject to them but haven't recognized them. This is one area in which adaptive thinkers and mechanical thinkers often have trouble relating to one another. Indeed, the antagonism between adaptive thinking and *status quo-ism* has characterized the entire developmental history of the human race.

The adaptive thinker can say "I don't know" simply and unapologetically. He feels confident in his ability to deal with new situations once he learns whatever it is that he needs to know, and even to deal more effectively with familiar situations when he fills in some gap in his knowledge. He does not imprison himself in the pretense of knowing about everything that is important, not even when he is "supposed to." He deals with some discovered gap in his knowledge very simply—he asks someone to help him fill it. He doesn't claim to be an expert and so he doesn't have to pretend to be one. This ability to say "I don't know" without having to defend his ego grants the adaptive thinker an enormous range of freedom, which the cautious, ego-protecting mechanical thinker does not have. It makes the adaptive thinker much more comfortable in problem-solving situations involving other people. He keeps his emotional reactions within reasonable, healthy bounds by detecting the many potential trigger signals coming from other people and choosing not to get hooked by them. He does not snap-react to key words, phrases, or specific actions of others, because he has learned to detect them and to deal with them for what they are—objective features of the unfolding situations in which he finds himself. He has acquired the psychomotor skill of maintaining a positive frame of mind, and he seldom gets particularly frustrated when events do not meet with his hopes or expectations. He adapts rapidly to reality as it unfolds before him.

And much more than the mechanical thinker, the adaptive thinker is highly aware of situations as situations. He can move into some particular setting or situation, especially one involving dealings with other people, and check it out. He can scan the situation to see who is there, what they are doing, how they are dealing with one another, how they are offering to deal with him, what they seem to be trying to do, what overall "meaning" or structure they seem to have given to the situation, what factors tend to organize and dominate their overall relationships to one another, and what options he himself has for playing a part in what is going on. He is highly aware of environmental messages, verbal and nonverbal, which have the purpose of manipulating him or of eliciting action without critical thought. He responds from an awareness of each situation and his personal objectives for being there. He can "think on his feet."

So here we have two contrasting profiles, two very different styles of thinking. The first, the mechanical thinker, may not exist in the pure form as described, but he certainly shows up in each of us from time to time. The second, the adaptive thinker, serves as a goal image of what each of us can become if we choose to.

3

crap detecting

> The only motive that guided me was my ardent love of my people.
>
> HERMANN GOERING

a key mental skill

If you're a fairly typical citizen of twentieth-century America, you belong to the most mentally manipulated, brainwashed society on earth. You are bombarded with up to 50,000 advertising messages a year. Your buying patterns are well programmed and possibly your voting habits as well. You probably watch the television "news" broadcasts faithfully and you tune in your car radio a little better when the radio "news" comes on, confident that the announcer is telling you all about the significant events going on in your world.

You purchase most of the products presented to you on the TV screen, and you pay the prices that include the cost of selling them to you in your living room. You and your fellow consumers (that word has now acquired a wholly positive connotation) buy the products of American industry in a bewildering variety of forms. You live in a style that could readily be classified as vulgar by world standards, yet you're convinced you're falling behind. A central aim in your life is to acquire and own consumer "things" for yourself and your loved ones.

> Many of the luxuries, and many of the so-called comforts of life, are not only not indispensable, but positive hindrances to the elevation of mankind.
>
> HENRY DAVID THOREAU

More than twenty years after we discovered that smoking cigarettes is extremely damaging to the human body, more than thirty percent of Americans still smoke. Tobacco sales total well over $15 billion a year. Along with over half of your fellow citizens, many of whom are below the age of twenty, you are probably at least partially addicted to the caffein-sugar combination of heavily promoted Coca Cola and similar soft drinks.

45

You probably believe that things go better with Coke, that Walter Cronkite knows what's going on in the world, that Dristan drains all eight sinus cavities, and that ring around the collar is the greatest personal disgrace a human being can suffer. And remarkably, you probably believe you're immune to the effects of advertising! The greatest testimonial to advertising as a form of brainwashing is that most people seem utterly convinced that only their neighbors are influenced by it.

If you're a typical middle-class American, you're thoroughly brainwashed and you don't even know it. What you wear, what your drive, where you live, how you spend your disposable income, what you believe, your values, wants, and aspirations—most of these have been shaped to a great extent by the media environment within which you live and breathe day after day. You are solely a creature of that environment, unless you are aware of it and the various forces it brings to bear on you, predisposing you to behave in certain preprogrammed ways.

On the other hand, if you are a very untypical American, you may have developed the mental skills necessary to sift through the welter of directive messages coming to you in various forms and to evaluate them in terms of their real meaning to you personally. This is the skill of *crap detecting*. It is a key mental skill—virtually a survival skill—and it can be developed to a very high level fairly easily.

A story concerning Lyndon Johnson illustrates the point very well. During a regulatory dispute, Johnson was discussing a basic issue with several representatives of one of the contending factions. One of the attorneys opened the topic with "Well, Mr. President, I'm just an ole country boy m'self, and . . ." Johnson stopped him with "Hold it right there! Where I come from, when a fellow starts with that kind of talk, we immediately put our hands over our wallets." In essence, Johnson served notice that he didn't intend to respond to the ulterior message with which the speaker had intended to convey the image of naivete and sincerity.

Another delightful example, taken from Neil Postman's thought-provoking book, *Crazy Talk, Stupid Talk*, deals with the ways in which we use our language to contribute to our own maladjustment. Postman quotes a letter sent by a school teacher to a group of ninth-grade students just before the start of their Christmas holidays. It read

Dear Student:

May I take this opportunity to wish each and every one a very holy and merry holiday season. Kindly extend this greeting to the members of your household and those who will help you celebrate this festive time of year.

Writers remind us constantly that with the arrival of a new year, we must become cognizant of the fact that it is time to proclaim our New Year's resolutions. As a class, let us accept for the theme of the New Year the ever-powerful meaning of the need and desire for "Enthusiasm." Remember, my dear students, that "En-

thusiasm" can and will achieve the unheard of and the miraculous. *Place within your minds and the deep recesses of your hearts the need for enthusiasm. An unknown writer once said: "Carry enthusiasm in your attitude and manner; it spreads like a contagion; it begets and inspires effects you did not dream of."*

To aid and guide you on your pathway to learning, the following assignments will help you to activate vehemently your newly acquired aim, "Enthusiasm."

1. *A vocabularly test will be given the day that you return to school.*
   Period One: "Nouns and Verbs" and "Workaday Words."
   Period Four: The words which were given to you on Monday, December 10.

2. *Oral book reports will be given the first week of school.*

We must remember the reality of the fact that we are beginning a program of study that will mold our future. This presents to us responsibilities. I did not prepare this epistle to harass you, but I sincerely wish to prepare you for the demands of high school and college, with which some of you will be confronted in the near future.

I once again extend to you and your family my season's greetings.

Aside from exemplifying a third-rate essay, which would probably earn no better than a "C" in another English teacher's class, this letter is a fine example of crap. In Postman's analysis

What this letter is about, of course, is a couple of tests and assignments which the teacher is hard put to justify. I would almost go so far as to say that what this teacher's classroom is about is tests and assignments, the purposes of which have long since been forgotten, if they were ever known.[1]

In the words of the philosopher Stendahl, "The shepherd always tries to persuade the sheep that their interests and his own are the same."

Crap detecting is a simple skill that develops rapidly once one takes a conscious approach to it. I was pleasantly surprised to see how much more alert I became to the ulterior messages and institutionalized absurdity in the world around me, after I stumbled across this useful term in Postman and Weingartner's *Teaching as a Subversive Activity.* I think you'll also find that, with a little practice, you'll quickly develop your own personal version of Hemingway's "built-in, shock-proof crap detector."

varieties of crap

The great masses of the people will more easily fall victims to a great lie than to a small lie.

ADOLPH HITLER

[1]Neil Postman, *Crazy Talk, Stupid Talk* (New York: Dell Pub. Co., Inc., 1976), pp. 182–83.

In developing the skill of crap detecting it is important to avoid a cynical, pious, or superior attitude characterized by the assumption that everybody is "on the con" or that nothing you see or hear deserves to be taken as it comes, on face value. And it is equally important to recognize the prevalance of humbug in an "advanced" society such as ours, which depends so heavily on mass communication and organized persuasion. Let's review some of the varieties of crap in order to identify the areas in which increased alertness to the message itself will be useful.

Commercial crap is so widespread in the media-dominated culture of late twentieth-century America that it merits special treatment later in this chapter, in the section called Advertising in Particular.

Institutionalized crap tends to escape detection the longest and to resist the stoutest attempts to eliminate or replace it. Every culture has a variety of customs, beliefs, values, traditions, and accepted explanations for "the way things are." These fixed modes of living, behaving, and thinking create a useful "flywheel" effect, which helps to stabilize the social order of things. But as the times change, some of these accepted beliefs and practices cease to serve useful purposes. Some outmoded processes pass into oblivion as people find new ways to meet their needs, while some others seem to remain long after their time has passed. When a custom, belief, value, or practice is defended and worshipped for its own sake instead of for the definite benefits it offers, it has become Crap—with a capital "C." If it survives by means of formalized procedures such as laws, government policies, or formal schooling, it becomes institutionalized crap.

For example, almost every major country in the world has well worked-out rationalizations to justify the conduct of its wars. The United States is no different in that respect than any other nation. We fought a War to Make the World Safe for Democracy, the War to End All Wars, conducted a "police action" in Korea, and rendered "military assistance" to Vietnam. We justify the expenditure of well over $100 billion in taxes every year as the "defense" budget. (After the close of World War II, the leaders of the War Department changed the name of the organization to the Defense Department.)

During an interview in his cell in Nuremberg, Hermann Goering, one of Adolph Hitler's inner circle of Nazi leaders, remarked

"Why, of course the people don't want war. Why should someone want to risk his life in a war when the best he can get out of it is to come back in one piece? Naturally, the common people don't want war; neither in Russia nor in England nor in America, nor for that matter, in Germany. That is understood. But after all, it is the leaders of the country who determine the policy and it is always a simple matter to drag the people along, whether it is a democracy or a fascist dictatorship or a parliament or a Communist dictatorship. Voice or no voice, the people can always be brought to the bidding of the leaders. That is easy. All you have to do is tell them

they are being attacked and denounce the pacifists for lack of patriotism and exposing the country to danger. It works the same in any country."[2]

The Americans who actively protested the Viet Nam war from the beginning, and who resisted Lyndon Johnson's efforts to escalate the level of military operations there, could be called traitors, or pacifists, or crap detectors, according to your point of view. Unfortunately, there is nothing self-evident about crap. What is crap to one person is a cherished tradition or a fundamental social value to another. There can never be a simple test for an institutionalized value to which all would agree. Crap, unfortunately, is a matter of opinion.

> In modern war there is nothing sweet nor fitting in your dying. You will die like a dog and for no good reason.
>
> *ERNEST HEMINGWAY*

Every society needs a small supply of crap detectors—people who question and challenge prevailing social values and institutions, and who invite others to question them. We need the essential flywheel effect of tradition, and we must also occasionally recognize when the changing times have converted some particular asset into a liability. Various people at various points in history, some well known and some less well known, have challenged the status quo. Some of them have paid high prices for their opposition to institutionalized values, often at the hands of the people who embraced those values.

The members of the Continental Congress, who drafted and passed the Declaration of Independence from England, were urging that the colonists set aside their accepted view of their relationship with the king. Indeed, there was a great deal of initial opposition to this insane idea—setting up an independent country of their own.

Some civil rights leaders lost their lives trying to challenge prevailing values concerning relationships between black and white people in America. The murders of Medgar Evers and Martin Luther King are grim testimony to the hostility with which some people will respond when they perceive threats to their value systems.

Comedian Lenny Bruce is another example of a person who blatantly challenged prevailing social standards, in his case the standards of obscenity. In his view, Bruce's nightclub act was not "dirty." He believed his matter-of-fact use of that peculiar private vocabulary of sexual terms, which everyone knew but pretended did not exist, could startle people into

[2]Kenneth S. Keyes, Jr., *How to Develop Your Thinking Ability* (New York: McGraw-Hill Book Company, Inc., 1950), p. 226.

reexamining their views about themselves, their relationships with one another, and their hypocrisy.

Ralph Nader, who caused a furor over automobile safety with his book, *Unsafe at Any Speed,* challenged rather successfully the widespread assumption that the Big Three auto manufacturers always did everything humanly possible to make sure that the cars they sold were as safe as could be. His later efforts at questioning the ethics of various corporate entities and their dealings with consumers won him praise from many and hostility from some.

Howard Jarvis, the 74-year-old crusader who masterminded California's famous Proposition 13 tax initiative in 1978, drew mixed reactions of anger, resentment, hatred, approval, admiration, and applause for his accomplishment.

There is no attempt here to offer opinions in favor of or against any of the reformers mentioned. But it is important to point out that they all had one thing in common. They decided to *challenge prevailing norms* and to try to change what they considered institutionalized crap.

Political crap probably deserves relatively less attention than the other forms, only because so much of it is so inept and so easily detectable. Americans today see their politicians through the window of a very skeptical and critical television and print-media reporting system. A great deal of ordinary crap gets detected simply by close scrutiny. Political crap of the simpler kinds becomes dangerous only when a large number of people believe it, and especially when they need to believe it.

Political crap detecting—and crap generating for that matter—probably reached its highest form during the Watergate investigations. The essence of the attempts of Richard Nixon and others to evade careful scrutiny of their motives in the Watergate operation centered on their *use of language.* Nixon, Haldeman, and Ehrlichman persisted in using terms that suggested noble motives—patriotism, concern for national security, and courage in the face of danger. Richard Nixon's memorable skill with labels enabled him to assert that the members of his campaign team were guilty of nothing more than "an excess of zeal." Senator Sam Ervin, who chaired the hearings, as well as other senators, insisted on using terms such as burglary, bribery, and perjury. The creative choice of words made the hearings into a debate about whether Nixon and his colleagues were "patriots" or "crooks." A similar classic choice of words during the same painful period had Ron Ziegler, Nixon's press secretary, refer to a previous press release as "inoperative," meaning that the new one he was offering was the truth and that the previous one wasn't.

Some men are discovered; others are found out.

ANONYMOUS

"packaging" techniques

Skill at crap detecting amounts to the ability to recognize "packaging" techniques—techniques people often use to promote concepts, values, actions, or institutions of questionable value. It calls for something like Superman's x-ray vision, enabling you to see through a pretty package or a clever presentation and recognize the content for what it is. You might or might not, after examining the real evidence, agree with the conclusion. But the packaging does not help you to decide the matter logically.

 There are two ways to slide easily through life: to believe everything and to doubt everything. Both ways save thinking.

ALFRED KORZYBSKI

We can divide packaging techniques into three general categories, as follows:

1. Empty arguments
2. Pandering
3. Hidden persuaders

An *empty argument* offers to convince you of something with "facts" and conclusions that do not really hang together logically. This technique falls into the category of logical fallacies. Some logical fallacies are very easy to spot, while others do their work in a much more subtle manner.

For example, many people seem to buy more of those consumer products advertised by Hollywood celebrities. The underlying argument of such a commercial says, "Mister X, a famous person, uses such-and-such a headache remedy. Therefore, you should too." But, in reality, the fact that Mister X uses it (if indeed he really does) does not prove that it will meet your needs. This is the fallacy of *appeal to authority*. It becomes a transparently empty argument when you take a close look at it, but if you don't have your crap detector tuned in you might very well respond unconsciously to the subtly directive message of the commercial.

Pandering is the technique of appealing to human weakness, bias, prejudice, or any other of a whole gamut of emotions in order to promote a course of action or a point of view. Ego appeals, for example, invite a person to feel more important or significant by taking whatever action they urge. Advertisements for status-oriented products capitalize on the desire of the buyer to feel socially superior to other people. In his book, *Test Pattern for Living*, Nicholas Johnson quotes the following television commerical:

Announcer: Listen to Mr. and Mrs. Ken Davis tell why their 1970 Buick LeSabre is something to believe in . . .

51

Mrs. Davis: We're a young family and we're driving a Buick, and people think, well, gee maybe, maybe you're really coming up in the world.

Mr. Davis: This car, I think it's going to be the best I have owned.

Announcer: The 1970 Buick is something to believe in. Wouldn't you really rather have a Buick?[3]

Hidden persuaders are relatively new techniques used in consumer advertising, particularly mass advertising. Based on the psychology of human perception, these packaging techniques have come largely from the marketing research of the 1950s, which has come to be known as motivational research. The marketing specialist's definition of motivational research calls it an investigative approach to determining the real reasons why people buy various products. An alternative definition is the search for techniques to induce people in large numbers to buy things they ordinarily would not want. The next section deals extensively with modern advertising (commercial crap) as a body of packaging techniques for the one basic message that underlies the entire structure of the contemporary consumer economy—"Buy—anything and everything; just buy."

 | *Every crowd has a silver lining.*

PHINEAS T. BARNUM

advertising in particular

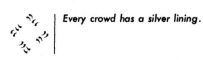

You can fool some of the people all the time, and that's enough to make a profit.

ANONYMOUS

Sometime between the turn of the century and the early 1950s, advertising in America as a form of communication underwent a profound philosophical change. It changed from a primarily informative mode to a largely manipulative, persuasive, directive mode. Here is a sample of a charmingly frank advertising message posted in a general store many years ago:

To my customers: I respectfully suggest that you try ABC Tooth Powder, for the practical benefits it may offer in cleaning your teeth and keeping them white. It is not much better nor much worse than other brands, but I have tried it and find it to be effective. My son has invented it, and has established himself in business to market it. He hopes to be married soon on the strength of it.

[3]Nicholas Johnson, *Test Pattern for Living* (New York: Bantam, 1972), p. 40.

Contrast that to the smooth, slickly packaged, subtly directive style of a more recent magazine advertisement for Camel cigarettes. A photograph shows a young, muscular man with a swarthy complexion and "macho" stance, leaning against a pole on the porch of a rustic cabin. Beside him, an attractive woman clings to his arm and gazes at him intensely as he looks into the camera. He has a cigarette dangling from his lips. The text extols the rugged individuality of the man and the cigarette. After challenging the reader to affirm his manhood by smoking this particular brand, the message concludes with the legally required statement: *"Warning: The Surgeon General Has Determined That Cigarette Smoking Is Dangerous to Your Health."* (In the foreground is a photograph of a package of cigarettes.) How ironic that the advertising copywriter chose to put the message directly above the warning about the health effects of cigarettes! Confidence, no doubt.

Advertising messages seem so commonplace, so familiar, and so innocuous that many people apparently assume that they have little or no effect. But the simple fact is that advertising messages, especially those presented over television, have an enormous directing effect on the people who watch them, and the sales of the products advertised usually correlate closely with the use of the advertisements.

Product names, for instance, often convey certain kinds of impressions by virtue of their connotations. Even though the hearer may realize that they have that effect, nevertheless he or she automatically responds to them in certain ways because of the deeply ingrained meanings he or she has learned. Indeed, the marketing department selects the product name for that very reason. A few years ago, we had automobiles with aggressive-sounding names like Mustang, Mach II, Cutlass, Cougar, and Marauder. More recently, car names have been tending toward status-loaded connotations—Monte Carlo, Caprice, LTD, Sedan de Ville, and Continental. To grasp the significance of the effect that names have on your thinking, imagine for a moment that manufacturers gave names to their cars like Rattletrap, Klunker, Lemon, Guzzler, and Rip-off. Would you prefer to drive a Lemon over a Monte Carlo? A Guzzler over an LTD?

What's in a name? Almost everything, in terms of the hearer's automatic responses. Instead of football teams with names like the Rams, the Colts, the Bears, the Cowboys, and the Chargers, try to imagine teams with names like the Flamingoes, the Rosebuds, the Rabbits, the Mice, and the Teddy Bears. How many times would you have to repeat the name of a team called the Mice in order to conjure up an image of ferocity, courage, and aggressiveness?

Instead of cigarettes with brand names like Kool, Marlboro, Parliament, Kent, and True, how about names like Cancer, Bronchitis, Hack, Wheeze, and Emphysema? How many cigarettes might people buy with names like those?

Honesty is the best policy in the long run, but for the short distance humbug has made pretty good time.

JOSH BILLINGS

I found an amusing advertising billboard along a freeway recently. It proclaimed in huge letters, "Uncle Bud's Used Cars." I reflected on the implications of such a name. "Now how," I asked myself, "could someone named 'Uncle Bud' be anything but friendly, helpful, and honest as the day is long? Could someone named 'Uncle Bud' ever cheat anybody?" And the answer came to my mind in about a thousandth of a second: "Certainly." By simply reading the sign, I can't tell whether Uncle Bud (if anybody by that name actually exists) is a crook or a philanthropist or somewhere in between.

Advertising in America lost virtually all semblance of innocent, straightforward communication during the middle 1950s with motivational research. The techniques of persuasion developed by psychologist Ernest Dichter and his colleagues proved so effective that they evolved into a well-understood technology of advertising. Vance Packard's famous book, *The Hidden Persuaders*,[4] explained these techniques in some depth. However, the widespread availability of this information hasn't seemed to have had any noticeable effect on consumer behavior. For the most part, advertisers continue to use the most carefully contrived strategies, and consumers continue to respond predictably to them.

The Hard Sell. From LANGUAGE IN THOUGHT AND ACTION, Third Edition by S.I. Hayakawa, copyright © 1972 by Harcourt Brace Jovanovich, Inc. Reproduced by permission of the publisher and George Allen & Unwin (Publishers) Ltd.

During the height of the controversy over so-called subliminal advertising techniques, such as single-frame messages flashed on TV screens, Johnny Carson quipped, "I don't believe there's anything to this business of subliminal advertising. But the other day I was watching TV and I got up and went out and bought a tractor."

Using famous people to sell consumer products also seems to work quite well, but an advertising campaign planned around a celebrity can fall apart

[4]Vance Packard, *The Hidden Persuaders* (New York: D. McKay, 1957).

without warning if the star falls from the heavens. The Ideal Toy Corporation saw the sales of its line of Evel Knievel toys drop disastrously after Knievel went to jail for slugging a writer who published a book about him. The firm had to discontinue the entire line of toys in the United States.

The basic mode of mass advertising is to arouse and direct a general "buying impulse" in the consumer. With larger and larger disposable incomes (money available after paying for necessities), middle-class Americans have an enormous buying power. The function of mass advertising is to mobilize this buying power by creating dissatisfaction—the feeling that one lacks something important in one's life. The design of virtually every mass advertising commerical centers on the attempt to persuade the potential buyer that something is currently missing. Your car is too old, or too small, or too large, or too low class. Your hair is too dry, or too oily, or too stringy, or lacking in body. Your breath might be ruining your love life. Your body might give off offensive odors, such as perspiration or normal breath. You need a better house, a better TV set, a mobile home. Above all, you need to "get ahead."

The Christmas season in America offers the greatest demonstration of the powerful influence of advertising in arousing the buying impulse within the consumer. Christmas advertising begins as early as October for some products. "Holiday" decorations begin to appear early in November. And like clockwork every year, the first day of December brings the inevitable Christmas carols over the ever-present background music systems in stores and shopping centers. These environmental cues have proven since the 1950s to arouse and maintain the buying impulse in most well-trained consumers. It is truly an awesome sight to see hundreds of people pouring out of department stores with shopping carts jammed with purchased gifts and to watch them load their cars with the produce of American factories. For many retail operations, such as record shops, clothing stores, toy stores, bookstores, and gift shops, the months of November and December account for as much as one-third of all sales for the year.

Mass advertising in America has also contributed to the establishment of a middle-class drug culture that far outweighs the traffic in marijuana and other "recreational" chemicals by young people. The massive promotion of aspirin and other pain-killing drugs, sleeping pills, stomach and cold remedies, and various other patent medicines has trained a majority of Americans to look for solutions to their problems in the medicine chest. The enormous popularity of tranquilizers like Valium and other nervous system depressants seems closely connected with the mass merchandising of pills in America.

The advertising environment in which we live presents a fundamental challenge to our crap-detecting skills. Although some commercials present their messages honestly and straightforwardly, most do not. The question becomes not *what* to buy, but *whether* to buy. A person who sits in front of a

TV set might consider him- or herself a spectator who wants only to be amused or informed. But from the point of view of the corporation whose comptroller writes the check to pay for the program, that person is a *student*, sitting in front of a *teaching machine*. Television stations do not sell products to consumers. Instead, *they sell consumers*. They sell them in predictable numbers to the advertisers who want to present their messages. A station charges prices for its commerical time according to the number of consumers of various ages, sexes, social levels, income levels, and educational levels whom the advertisers can expect to be sitting in front of their screens during a given time slot on a given day of the week.

 Advertising may be defined as the art of arresting human intelligence long enough to get money from it.

STEPHEN LEACOCK

tuning up your crap detector

Skill at crap detecting comes mostly from increased awareness. You can tune up your crap detector by adopting a balanced attitude; a combination of open-minded willingness to see and hear and a healthy skepticism for messages that come packaged in tricky ways. Without trying to find dishonesty in everything you see and hear, but simply staying alert for the nature of the message itself, you can develop your crap-detecting ability so well that it becomes nearly impossible to manipulate you.

My son and I sometimes call each other's attention to messages with a high crap content that we hear on the radio while driving. Should one of us find a commercial or a political message especially slanted, he will hold up the first two fingers of one hand and wiggle them like an antenna, saying, "beep. . .beep. . .beep. . . ." This signals that his crap detector has found something worthy of note. Occasionally I use this nonverbal "comment" during business meetings with colleagues and clients whom I know well. When someone cites a questionable "fact," I may say casually, "beep. . .beep. . .beep. . . ." When the other person asks, "What does that mean?" I say offhandedly, "Oh, that's just my crap detector beeping." It usually gets the point across with a light touch.

Teach yourself to listen for key terms, phrases, slogans, and explanations that might tell you more about the sender's motivations than the sender might consciously intend to share. Be alert for what is not said as well as what is said. Pay attention to the significance of who speaks as well as the significance of the person spoken to. Ask youself a few key questions about the message? Does it seem "straight," without a great deal of emphasis on persuasion? Does it rely mostly on facts and readily verifiable conjectures? Does the message offer you sufficient decision-making autonomy, or does it seem to attempt to forcibly narrow your decision options? Make a quick assessment of the *crap-to-fact ratio.*

Try a few practice exercises to tune up your crap detector. Page through a typical magazine, analyzing the advertisements as you go. Find any hidden persuaders and manipulative appeals. Browse through several of the articles and note the proportion of straightforward information or persuasion, as contrasted to highly manipulative or interpretive techniques. Read a typical editorial column and see how well the writer helps you to understand the issue, or the extent to which he or she beclouds it in order to sell an opinion.

Listen especially for the logical fallacies that people sometimes use to try to convince one another of various points of view or courses of action. Chapter 8 explains many of these informal fallacies, so common to our experience that many people overlook them altogether. Learn their names and use them as a mental checklist to analyze some of the obviously manipulative messages in your environment.

While you listen more carefully to what others say, make it a point to listen to yourself as well. To what extent do you yourself generate and purvey crap? To what extent do you find yourself trying to manipulate others, or to manipulate them without presenting the facts fairly? S.I. Hayakawa, semanticist and senator, recommends that you ask yourself from time to time, "What am I talking about, if anything?" Rely on straight talk and honest persuasion in dealing with others.

4

thinking
on your feet

Don't trust any thought you have sitting down.

FRIEDERICH NIETZSCHE

A story about a vigorous, hard-campaigning politician of the old school illustrates the fundamental skill of *thinking on your feet*. As he was smiling, waving, shaking hands, patting children, and kissing babies, one eager young mother thrust her infant into his arms. He was startled for a moment because the baby was the ugliest infant he had ever seen. How could he say something nice and believable at the same time? But after the briefest of pauses, he held the child up for all to see and beamed, "Now *there's* a baby!"

Thinking on your feet is a metaphor for an important functional skill that incorporates the skills of observing, generating options, and making quick decisions. Perhaps each of us has at some time regretted having responded narrowly or ineptly in some situation, only to think of several more clever or effective options afterward. "On-time" reacting is a skill you can develop by conscious attention to the factors that make it possible. Thinking on your feet is the triumph of reason over reflex.

developing presence of mind

Oh, goddammit! We forgot the silent prayer!

DWIGHT EISENHOWER (at a cabinet meeting)

We might equate the familiar term *presence of mind* with *situation awareness*, a skill that is difficult to define in simple terms, but is easy to spot in action and fairly easy to exemplify. It involves examining the situation in which you find yourself from several different points of view, looking for key factors that might affect you or your purposes, and assess-

58

ing how the various parts of the situation relate to one another. It calls for a special kind of alertness, which you can develop by conscious attention and a bit of practice.

As two hens were strolling through the barnyard, chatting about the affairs of the day, one hen paused, looked at the other thoughtfully and inquired, "Say, with all the eggs we've been laying, doesn't it strike you that there should be more of us around here?"

Psychologists sometimes use the terms *field dependence* and *field independence* in speaking of one's basic mental orientation. "Field" refers to the immediate surrounding environment, with its physical, social, and communicative processes bearing on the individual. A person who is highly field dependent tends to react more or less unconsciously and automatically to the situation as it unfolds, with relatively little awareness of alternative ways of reacting. A field-independent person, on the other hand, tends to look at the situation itself more frequently and to reassess his or her own role in it. We could consider any particular individual as operating somewhere along a continuum scale ranging from highly field dependent to highly field independent.

You can conceivably find yourself in a wide variety of situations, each with its own peculiar features, yet all of them having certain aspects in common. Within a fairly short span of time, you might be visiting your parents, buying a house, riding on a train, making love, having a job interview, attending a PTA meeting, teaching a class, getting married or getting divorced, breaking up a squabble between children, sitting in a business meeting, attending a cocktail party, shopping for clothes, or playing tennis. Each of these pursuits takes place within a *situational context*, and each context calls for a certain approach to dealing with it.

Full awareness of the situational context involves an awareness of activities, processes, events, roles, relationships between people, rules— either formal or implied—customs, traditions, norms, values, and expectations. It involves an awareness of the cues and signaling systems around you that tell you how you are "supposed" to act. This awareness can enable you to decide more or less consciously to what extent you choose to behave as others expect.

Situation awareness also plays an important part in the functional skill of crap detecting, as described in Chapter 3. Because the essence of certain forms of absurdity is in the situation itself, situational awareness can help you to detect and deal with it.

Situation awareness can involve simple *spatial* and *kinesthetic* perception as well as the more abstract perception of social structures and processes. Have you ever known someone who seemed to lack anything more than the most rudimentary sense of his or her own body and spatial relationships to others? Such a person might stand at the counter in a bank or post office, take care of her business, and remain there fumbling with money and papers while others wait for her to clear out. When she finishes, she might turn around and crash into the person standing behind her. Another person might back his car out of a parking space without thinking to look behind him for approaching cars. He might also board an airplane, find his seat, and then block the entire aisle while putting away his packages and overcoat, completely oblivious to the other people waiting behind him. Such a lack of sensitivity to the interests of others may pervade a person's entire life and relationships to other people.

Knowing how to proceed in a given situation depends on knowing what you want. Making choices from the perspective of your own values requires that you have a clear idea of what you value and what you're willing to pay to get it. Psychologist Abraham Maslow referred to the ability to resist *enculturation* as a basic skill of the self-actualizing person. By this he meant the willingness to make personal choices that might run counter to strongly communicated values and norms existing around one. It is the attitude of the self-directed individual.

> *We are discreet sheep; we wait to see how the drove is going, and then we go with the drove. We have two opinions: one private, which we are afraid to express; and another one—the one we use—which we force ourselves to wear to please Mrs. Grundy, until habit makes us comfortable in it, and the custom of defending it presently makes us love it, adore it, and forget how pitifully we came by it.*
>
> MARK TWAIN

Along with situation awareness and the skill of choice making goes the skill of fitting the response to the situation. What we so often admire as a "quick wit" amounts to the ability to come up with an idea or a point of view that others find novel and provocative within a particular situation. You can develop this skill like any other thinking skill, by paying conscious attention to it and by actually trying it.

A philosophy professor found himself challenged during a lecture one morning when a student interrupted icily, saying, "Doctor Gesundheit, can you prove I exist?" The professor paused for a moment, tilted his head as if listening, and said, "Did somebody say something?"

The art of the snappy comeback involves making a split-second assessment of the situation rather than reacting immediately and robotically. In the space of about a half-second, your brain can run through a wide range of possibilities for something to say. Teach yourself to pause for an instant before you say something in a challenging situation, and see how much more often you come up with a novel reply that fits the situation well.

He: You kiss with your eyes open.
She: How can you tell?

An amusing anecdote concerning George Bernard Shaw involved a very attractive but superficial actress who approached him at a social gathering and gushed, "Oh, Mr. Shaw! I've admired you so much! We should get together and make a baby. With my looks and your brains, the child would certainly become famous." "No thank you, my dear," Shaw is said to have replied. "There's at least an equal probability that it would have *my* looks and *your* brains."

seeing the big picture

The skill of *strategic thinking,* more prosaically known as "seeing the big picture," seems rather rare among people in typical social situations, and especially rare in business organizations. Big picture thinking can give you a substantial advantage in these situations. From your personal point of view, that is, deciding how to deal with some situation, the big picture amounts to the answers to questions like "What's going on here?" or "What do I want out of this situation?" or "What are the possibilities for achieving my objective?"

During a hectic field campaign in Europe, General Dwight Eisenhower is said to have asked one of his intelligence officers for a brief assessment of the enemy situation. The young officer quickly replied, "Sir, picture a donut. We're the hole!"

You can build the skill of seeing the big picture by teaching yourself to ask "What's going on—right here and right now?" Learn to scan the situation, making a quick inventory of the physical setting, the number of people, their apparent roles and relationships, what they're doing or about to do, and how they're offering to deal with you. Check to see who seems to be "in charge," either formally or practically. How do the other people respond to that person? What are the implied "rules" for behaving?

You can scan a situation most effectively if you have some idea of what to look for. Out of the virtually uncountable number of features you could pay attention to, you will usually find a few of primary importance to you. You can identify these key factors by first deciding what your personal interests are in the situation. Then, by "keeping your eye on the ball," that is, keeping your personal objective firmly in mind, you can more easily assess what happens and identify the options available to you for responding. Those two questions—"What's going on?" and "What's my objective in this situation?"—will equip you to fit your actions to the situation and to make intelligent choices.

Often you may find that one or two key factors really dominate the overall situation and have the effect of structuring the entire process. If you can scan the situation and "lock on" to the key factor, you will often know immediately how to proceed. For example, I was once engaged as a consultant by a group of investors who wanted advice on what to do about the financially troubled company they were backing. They wanted to decide whether or not to advance an additional sum of money—a sizeable sum—to the president of the company, in view of the fact that he seemed to have lost control of the operation.

As we convened our conference, I noted that the backers of the company all grouped themselves on one side of the room, facing the company president as a monolithic body. His posture and nonverbal processes suggested that he felt quite uncomfortable with the situation. Since the success of the operation would depend very strongly on teamwork among this entire group, this factor caught my attention. The key factor in this situation was not necessarily that sales were down, but that *this group of people didn't get along well enough to make a success of the operation.* After a brief review of the situation, I brought the group's attention to this obvious fact. The members chose not to deal with it directly. The company eventually went into bankruptcy, with an exchange of lawsuits, accusations of dishonesty, and generally hard feelings all around.

The obscure we see eventually. The completely apparent takes longer.

E.R. MURROW

The big picture concept also aligns with the skill of situation awareness, and particularly with the functional skill of crap detecting. Sometimes the situation itself has a structure which a well tuned-in crap detector will tell you represents questionable values from your point of view. For example, the physical arrangement of a supermarket, department store, or small shop might be contrived to induce you to buy certain items on impulse. The next time you go into a quick-stop market, look around at the layout. Do you find a variety of impulse items near the door and the checkout counter—candy, snacks, cigarettes, magazines, chewing gum, mints, or fad toys?

You may not be aware of it, but retail merchandising rests primarily on the concept of traffic flow, with the notion that the layout of the various items should maximize the number of products exposed to the customer's attention as he or she walks from the entrance to the shelf that has the desired product, and then returns to the checkout counter. Self-service markets have become popular in America largely because of this "maximal exposure" advantage. Typically, the merchant will place staple items such as milk, bread, and canned goods at the back of the store so that you will pass by as many impulse products as possible. Ask yourself how many times you bought some snack or impulse item without giving it much thought, merely because it appeared within easy reach. Merchandisers and marketing theorists refer to this technique as "arousing the buying impulse" in the customer. Once you get into a buying mood, you will unconsciously react to these cues. To the extent that you pay attention to such situations around you, you can decide how to respond. To the extent that you lack this awareness of the big picture, you tend to respond relatively automatically, as other people want you to.

Start looking around at the nonverbal messages communicated to you by the arrangements of homes, offices, and business establishments. Have you ever looked carefully at a typical junior high school? At a glance, the casual observer might mistake many a public school for a prison or some other correctional facility. The structure communicates obedience, conformity, and control. Have you noticed that many large department stores have women's clothing displayed just inside the main entrance, so that the shopper can browse while she feels fresh and has enough time?

Scan the situation in a typical doctor's office. Do you ever consider the doctor-patient interaction as one between a service person and a customer? Can you see yourself as a customer as you sit in the waiting room? Probably not, if you respond unconsciously to the situational cues that lend structure to the relationship. A typical doctor resides in an inner sanctum, with crisp nurses and a formal front office separating him or her from the patient. The nurses schedule patients in and out at the doctor's convenience. Each patient only gets so much time with the doctor, who, after all, is a busy and important person. Because medical care is currently a seller's market, ploys like this work effectively to inspire awe in the customer. A person who wouldn't think twice about debating a suspiciously high bill with a plumber or a gas station mechanic may feel acutely guilty about even mentioning the crass subject of money in the doctor's office. To some extent, lawyers operate in the same way.

Try walking into an expensive jewelry store and looking at the layout. In what ways might the situation itself send signals to the customer that say "Prepare yourself to part company with a big sum of money"?

Think about each of the following settings and identify the primary features you think might convey various unspoken rules for behaving:

1. Airport waiting lounge
2. Bank
3. Fancy, expensive restaurant
4. Government service organization, such as a motor vehicle department, unemployment bureau, or welfare office
5. Movie theater
6. Las Vegas gambling casino
7. Cocktail lounge or disco
8. Public rest room
9. Office of a very high ranking executive
10. Courtroom
11. Church

12. Funeral
13. Wedding
14. Crowded elevator
15. Cocktail party

From time to time you may find it helpful to ask yourself, "What unconscious rules might I be following because of the structure of the situation, which would enable others to manipulate me?"

option thinking

Wisdom is merely knowing what to do next.

ANONYMOUS

As a doctor was making the rounds in a ward of terminally ill patients, he asked each of them whether he or she had any final requests. To one old lady, he said, "Is there anything you especially want before you pass on?" She replied stoically, "Yes, I'd like to see my immediate family one more time." "Of course," said the doctor. "We'll arrange it." He asked a second patient for his wishes. "I'm a Catholic," murmured the old man. "I'd like to see a priest for confession and the last rites." "Certainly," replied the doctor. Then he approached the third patient, an elderly Jewish man. "Have you any last wish, sir?" he inquired. "Yes," gasped the old man. "My last wish is to see another doctor."

That's *option thinking*. To the extent that you can clearly identify useful options for proceeding in a challenging situation, you can maximize your chances for meeting your own needs and goals. The old man in the example did something that represents a very high level of mental functioning—he added an option to the situation.

In many situations, especially where there is manipulation going on, you may find yourself offered only one course of action. Perhaps the person urging you to take this course will find it to his or her advantage to have you do so, and may try to sell you on it. If you fail to think through the ramifications of acting as he or she urges you to act, you might not serve your own best interests. The ability to *optionize* a situation is a very high level mental skill, which you can develop with a little attention and practice.

Benjamin Franklin liked to tell a parable about a farmer and his animals to illustrate the relationship between the overtaxed colonies in the New World and the monarchy of England. In advocating a declaration of independence, he was calling for a new view of the relationship. According to his story, the farmer called a group of his animals together and said, "Well, my little ones, I've decided to have a big feast. I've called you together to discuss the matter of how I might cook you, and particularly which sauces to use to make you most delicious to eat." One chicken piped up, "But sir! We don't want to be eaten at all!" "My dears," chided the farmer, "you wander from the point!"

What is "the point" for one person in a given situation may not be the point for another. Someone skilled in manipulating may want you to accept one factor as "the point," when you might really have a different kind of an interest in the situation. An alertness for varying *points of view* in the same situation can enable you to evaluate what's going on much more effectively. (Chapter 6 deals more extensively with the concept of points of view and offers some skill-building exercises to help you become more effective at identifying the different points of view operating in a given situation.)

The skill of optionizing the situation can enable you to deal with other people more assertively and to prevent them from manipulating you. If you have a clear idea of your objective in a situation, if you keep your eye on the ball—that is, keep your objective firmly in mind—and if you scan the situation to see what's going on, you can often identify the options that offer real value to you personally. In some cases, people may cooperate and help you to clarify your options. In other cases, they may try to confuse you or intimidate you, hoping to prevent you from forming a clear idea of the avenues open to you.

As I passed through the checkout line in a supermarket in Los Angeles, I gave the clerk a ten dollar bill to pay for several items costing about three dollars. She put the bill into the drawer, counted out some money, and gave me change for five dollars. "Excuse me," I said. "I gave you a ten. You've only given me change for a five." "You gave me a five," she said curtly. "Gee, I could be wrong, but there's very little doubt in my mind that I gave you a ten. I only had a single ten dollar bill in my wallet when I came in." As the other customers in line began to fidget, we came to a standoff on the issue. "Well," she said, "just write down your name and address and leave it. If we turn out to be five dollars over at the end of the day, we'll send it to you." I said, "I've got a better idea. Let's call the store manager over and have him total up the money in your register. That way, we can settle it right now." She angrily called the store manager, who simply took the entire tray from her register and substituted a new one with a standard quantity of cash. He then counted the money, compared it to the register receipt, and gave me back my five dollars.

Perhaps she would have sent the money to me. Perhaps not. The "point" for me in this case was immediate action. Too many people let themselves be intimidated in retail situations, simply because they haven't firmly made up their minds what they want. If you know what you want in a situation such as this and you know that what you are asking is reasonable, it becomes fairly simple to stick to your guns and get it. Assertive com-

munication requires a high level of situation awareness, a clear idea of
your objective, and the skill of optionizing situations.

It is also very important in thinking on your feet to avoid getting sidetracked or distracted by factors that do not bear directly on what you want
to accomplish. Sometimes a secondary factor may so captivate your attention that you lose sight of your primary objective. This mistake is analogous
to the combat phenomenon of *target fixation*, which victimized some
military pilots in World War II. Sometimes a pilot would make a low level
bombing run, release his bombs, and then fly over the target again to strafe
it with machine guns. Many pilots would attack in a diving maneuver,
pulling out at the last possible second in order to shoot most accurately.
Occasionally a pilot became so fixated on the target itself that he forgot to
pull up altogether, and flew his plane into the ground. A number of deaths
were attributed to this psychological phenomenon, and more than one
pilot came back from a bombing mission with mud on his airplane. Target
fixation usually does not have such serious effects in most social situations,
but the concept is the same.

For example, I participated in a technical conference some years ago
involving several people from an aerospace company and a high-ranking
scientist in an influential position in a government agency. The purpose of
the conference, from the point of view of the company, was to establish a
friendly rapport with this individual, which could be the basis for a continuing exchange of ideas leading to a substantial contract with the agency.
One of the company representatives, a bright, creative senior engineer,
prided himself on his technical competence and judgment. After a few
minutes of polite chatter, the discussion drifted into a key technical area.
The government scientist voiced a strong and somewhat dogmatic opinion
in favor of a certain technical approach, which the company engineer
considered unworkable. The two proceeded to debate the issue, with an
ever-increasing level of intensity and hardening of positions. The marketing representative of the company managed to shift the topic of discussion,
but not before the engineer had succeeded in thoroughly alienating the
scientist.

It appeared to me that the engineer had mixed up his own ego in the
situation and had taken his eye off the ball. Instead of softening the discussion and perhaps changing the scientist's mind at some later date, he
became target-fixated on the technical question and what seemed to him a
"stupid" point of view. To the best of my knowledge, the scientist never
invited them back for any more discussions.

The best captain does not plunge headlong
Nor is the best soldier a fellow hot to fight.
The greatest victor wins without a battle . . .

LAO TZU

When your ego or your emotions get inappropriately involved in a situation, you run the risk of becoming target-fixated and losing sight of your objective. Emotion is a valid and important aspect of your functioning, but it is a very poor basis for making decisions. Especially when you become angry, your logical faculties become much less effective. Occasionally we find it necessary to overcome our feelings in a situation and proceed as best we can. Knowing how to control your ego and how to manage your feelings to some extent can make for better feelings in the long run.

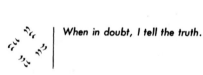

Anger is a wind that blows out the lamp of the mind.

ARAB PROVERB

trusting your hunches

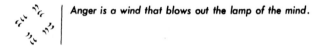

When in doubt, I tell the truth.

MARK TWAIN

The term *hunch* often brings to mind the term *intuition*. Some people describe themselves as basically "intuitive," often contrasting that orientation with a so-called "logical" orientation. According to psychologist Carl Jung, who built an entire theoretical system around that mysterious region of thought which he considered inexpressible in words, intuition is "a perception of realities which are not known to consciousness, and which goes via the unconscious." Jung tried to classify people according to the four psychological functions of thinking, feeling, sensing, and intuition, together with his well-known overall distinction of introversion and extroversion. Apparently Jung considered thinking and feeling to be more or less opposite modes of evaluating one's experiences, and he considered sensing and intuition as opposite modes of taking in information about the world. The fact that he could not offer a simple operational definition of the terms *feeling* and *intuition* did not slow him down in formulating a theory. Jungian theorists today would probably dismiss a request for a working definition of these terms as simply a manifestation of the requester's heavy orientation to thinking and sensing.

I question, however, the notion that people should be divided into simple categories like these. I further question the notion that one is *either* intuitive or logical. I believe we need a more definite framework for describing the brain's operation if we are to make the term "hunch" into a useful verbal tool. I'd like to offer here a model for brain function which may help to do that, and which I believe Jung could probably accept as valid if he were with us today. This model incorporates our current knowledge of brain structure and function as described in Chapter 2.

We can consider preconscious thought to be the primary form of the brain's activity, from the point of view of information processing. Countless preconscious thoughts go on routinely, with very few of them having enough significance to warrant projection on the special "viewing screen" of conscious thought, that is, of being expressed in words, mental pictures, and/or kinesthetic sensations associated with the words and pictures. The innumerable perceptions, associations, decisions, and logical processes involved in routine preconscious problem solving and motor activity do not generally warrant such conscious inspection. But when one of these preconscious thoughts is important enough, your brain maps out a *verbal version* of it in the cortex that it can deal with. The conscious thought thus formed is obviously not the same as the preconscious original thought. It is a "translation" of that inexpressible thought into a crude symbolic form, namely a linear sequence of words. By a process which scientists have fairly well traced within the brain, certain electrical thought patterns originating at lower levels—even as low as the cerebellum and portions of the brainstem—get transferred to appropriate regions of the cortex, which reorganizes them into verbal form. This is my proposed model of how preconscious thoughts lead to conscious thoughts. I believe it may also be the mechanism for those thought processes we refer to as "hunches" and "intuitive flashes."

A Hunch

Based on the foregoing model of the brain's operation and its construction of conscious thoughts from the raw material of preconscious thoughts, here is my working definition of a hunch: A hunch is a preconscious thought which is important enough to warrant expression in conscious form, but which is initially too complex to be easily verbalized.

How many times have you begun a sentence with the phrase "Something tells me. . . ."? That "something" is really your own thought process, and it signals the presence of a preconscious thought which is probably worthy of an attempt at conscious translation. Some researchers who support the concept of extrasensory perception, or ESP, believe that the brain can receive information via various channels as yet undiscovered, and that such information becomes available in preconscious form. This might partially explain why psychics sometimes give reports in vague terms and sometimes in very specific terms. Perhaps some of their preconscious thought forms lend themselves easily to verbalization, while others may not.

A colleague, Dr. Judythe Kelley, believes that many children have highly developed intuitive processes, but that the growing-up process somehow "rigidizes" their thought patterns into standard verbal forms, which make translation from the preconscious to the conscious levels progressively more difficult. "Ask a little child some question," she says, "and note carefully how the child responds. As likely as not, he'll pause for a second or so, as if 'listening' for the answer. Probably he's organizing the answer intuitively first. Then he puts it into words."

It has become commonplace to refer to artists and other "creative" people as having highly developed intuitive powers, even though the definition of "intuitive" has remained somewhat vague. I believe our new knowledge of brain function, as described in Chapter 2, supports this idea and makes it more definite. In fact, it points to a number of avenues for developing the skills of expression in anyone who wants to give sufficient energy to it. My working definition of artistic skill is: *the ability to formulate new ideas preconsciously, clarify them consciously, and express them in observable form.* Rather than conceive of new and novel ideas as arriving from somewhere in outer space (the "cosmic ray" theory of creativity), why not consider them the products—deliberate as well as accidental—of the brain's normal activity? I believe the person we label as "artistic" or "creative" has taken the trouble to develop and put to use the preconscious levels of his or her thought processes. Indeed, many artists, writers, and other idea producers seem to resent the common notion that they somehow have unusually "lucky" brains, that ideas just "come" to them without effort. Many productive people report taking an active mental approach to their worlds, exploring, questioning, experimenting, and above all taking in large quantities of experience. Probably this mentally active approach equips the idea producer's brain with much more raw material for putting together new ideas than does the activity of a mentally sedentary person. (Chapter 10 deals extensively with idea production as a functional thinking skill and with specific techniques for developing it.)

For the present discussion, we can think of hunches as playing a useful part in the skill of thinking on your feet. You can make it a general policy to stay alert for hunches; they may signal the availability of certain preconscious thoughts of potential value. You can also try to verbalize your hunches whenever possible, in order to form a better "bridge" between preconscious and conscious levels of thought.

You might find it interesting to try to assess your personal "track record" in following your hunches. Try to recognize those instances where you change your course in response to that "something" telling you what to do. Make a note of several of these occurrences and think them over later. How many of them seemed to give you a clear suggestion of a course of action, a "do" or a "don't"? How many of them did you listen to but override? How many did you follow? How did you feel about the results? To what extent did following a hunch or not following one seem to pay off?

thinking under pressure

While walking through the offices of an engineering firm in which the employees accept unrelenting pressure and a fast pace as a way of life, I noticed a hand-lettered placard on someone's wall which warned, "Old age and treachery will triumph over youth and skill." Although we probably don't want to take this message entirely seriously, it does imply a certain attitude of clever adaptation and mental resilience, which we can develop. Effective preparation goes a long way in enabling one to operate effectively under pressure.

When an airline pilot gets into the cockpit of a plane, he has many things to think about as he prepares the plane for takeoff. He can't simply start the thing up and fly away—the task is much too complex for that. He has to make over fifty different checks, adjustments, and decisions before he pulls back the throttle to go. And every professional pilot uses a *formal checklist* to help him organize his thoughts during this critical phase of the job. Despite our common view of the pilot as a calm, cool, and collected individual, he is under a certain amount of pressure every time he undertakes a flight.

An unfortunate fact of human physiology is that when a person becomes aroused, for instance, when under pressure, his or her higher level thinking processes, such as memory, logical reasoning, idea production, and decision making, tend to suffer. The nervous activation of the brain, combined with the increased flow of stress hormones, tends to cause whole portions of the brain to more or less shut down their activities. This biological fact means that complex mental tasks present much more difficulty to a person when he or she is experiencing the tension of a pressure situation than when fully relaxed. For this reason, the professional pilot relies on *preprogrammed thought process* in the form of a preflight checklist as well as a prelanding checklist. This helps the pilot to account for every important factor without having to remember them all.

We can learn a great deal from the professional pilot to help us deal with our own pressure situations. By having a simple mental checklist of things to do in any pressure situation, you can make it more likely that you will respond effectively, even under pressure and when you feel tense and excited.

Think through a few kinds of pressure situations you might find yourself in, and think about how you might handle them. Practice on the following examples:

1. You've overslept and cannot possibly get to the office on time to give your briefing at the important 8:00 A.M. staff meeting.
2. You've received a letter from the Internal Revenue Service saying they intend to audit your tax returns for the past three years.
3. You're about to give a speech before a large audience, and the master of ceremonies has just told the joke you had planned to lead off with.
4. You have fifteen minutes to catch a plane in an airport far from home, and you discover you've lost your wallet.
5. You like the new house the sales person has shown you, but you haven't really looked around at others. The salesperson is pressing you with an attractive price and warns that the next people to look at the house want to buy it.
6. You're traveling in a foreign country, and you discover your passport is missing.
7. You're being introduced to a famous person, and you find that the two of you will be alone for a few minutes until the person who introduced you returns.
8. You get a telephone call from the police informing you that your son or daughter is one of a group of young people arrested for creating a disturbance.
9. Your spouse or lover tells you that the relationship is over; he or she wants out.
10. You've just been summoned into the boss's office, and you think the boss plans to reprimand you or threaten to fire you for something you're not guilty of.

In all of these situations, the basic rule is the same: *stop and think.* Pause for a second or two and let your brain's higher level processes come into play, and prepare to think on your feet. Here are some useful rules and techniques for making the most of a given situation.

First, scan the situation. Find out who's involved, what's involved, and what's likely to happen.

Decide on your objective, that is, "the ball." Get a clear idea of what you want to accomplish in the situation and perhaps decide what, as a minimum, you will settle for.

Above everything else, keep your eye on the ball. Don't get sidetracked by secondary issues that won't help you achieve your objective. Don't let your emotions carry you away to the point that you become irrational or lose sight of your own interests. Avoid target fixation by scanning the situation again from time to time and checking to see that you're making progress toward your objective, or at least to a reasonable compromise.

> *Anger gets us into trouble. Pride keeps us there.*
>
> ANONYMOUS

Optionize the situation to your best advantage. Ask yourself whether you like the options that seem available. Do you need an alternative approach? What courses of action can you devise that might resolve the situation more effectively?

Have a few simple strategies in mind for handling at least those eventualities you can think of. Keep your goal simple, keep your plan simple, and keep your options simple. Don't try to solve too complex a problem while under pressure.

Prepare in advance of the situation if possible. If you can foresee certain things happening, you might be able to handle them effectively by finding out a few key facts ahead of time, by forming a key alliance with another key person, by preselling a certain course of action to one of the key players in the situation, or by thinking the problem over thoroughly before the pressure is on.

Rehearse the situation if possible. If you can picture the upcoming situation in your mind and mentally run through a scenario of possible outcomes, you can work out some effective options. You can also keep your stress level lower if you have mentally "been there before."

Keep your crap detector tuned in as the situation unfolds. Stay on the lookout for the kinds of manipulative strategies, logical dodges, and confusion factors other people sometimes use to try to keep you from thinking straight. By keeping your eye on the ball, you can compare what's happening with what you want to happen, and you can see through the smoke screens that others sometimes put up.

Don't fall victim to *snap reactions*. Stay alert for *trigger words* possibly intended to hook your automatic emotional responses. Don't allow another person to make you feel guilty, or ashamed, or unnecessarily fearful, or inferior, or jealous. Teach yourself to pause for about one second when someone else says something provocative or challenging, to give your brain time to analyze the message. By delaying your reactions in this way, you become much more difficult to manipulate or to antagonize.

Keep in mind the *principle of indirect action*. You may find it best to delay or avoid a direct confrontation, or delay a certain action, or accept a temporarily unpleasant option, in order to get an effective overall solution. Remember that the easiest route to your objective may not always be a straight line.

Check on your hunches from time to time. You might discover that you're solving some of the "equations" of the problem at the preconscious level even while wrestling with it consciously. Pause for a second or so if possible, and "listen" for ideas or options you might be able to come up with intuitively.

Pay special attention to expressing yourself clearly in pressure situations. Recognize that a few well-chosen words may do much more good than a few hundred poorly chosen ones. Concentrate on getting one or two important ideas across simply and clearly rather than trying to say too much. Start with the big picture, get the other person or people on your wavelength, and only then proceed to fill in those selected details that will serve your objective. Don't get bogged down in unnecessary details. If you tend to get tongue-tied under pressure, just *slow down and let your words come at a comfortable rate*. Take plenty of time to explain your views. Perhaps a convenient starting point, a simple and effective analogy, or a workable metaphor will help you to organize what you have to say. Explain your idea clearly and simply, editing out all unnecessary details and side issues. Stick to those facts, opinions, ideas, and points of view that are best suited to the particular individuals you are dealing with. Keep in mind that how you say it might turn out to be just as important as what you have to say.

> *When more and more people are thrown out of work, unemployment results.*
>
> CALVIN COOLIDGE

Buy time if necessary. You may not have to solve the problem or make a decision or take action at the instant the problem comes up. Although others may pressure you to commit yourself, you might find it more effective to take time to think over the situation. Even in a business conference, you might respond to a surprise issue by saying, "I haven't thought about that factor. Let me have a half-minute to think it over." You can do a great deal of thinking in thirty seconds, and you may find that others increase their respect for you as you act more assertively and with more confidence in your mental skills. Make the decision and take action *in your time* whenever possible. Give an interim reply and promise to follow up. Or set a deadline for making a decision. Call for a postponement of the process to give you time to prepare better. Set a time for a new meeting if possible. Do whatever you need to do to acquire thinking time.

Similarly, do not make hasty deals or get pushed into "sudden death" solutions. Realize that when someone else presses you to make a decision or to take action, you might have the option of not deciding. Beware of the salesperson who tells you the deal is off if you walk out the door. If you get a very attractive job offer, the personnel officer might press you for a quick decision. Don't be afraid to ask for a few days to think it over. Decide when you're ready to decide and on your own terms whenever possible. And don't be too timid to say "No."

And do your best to create and maintain positive relationships with the other people in the situation. Get them on your side as much as possible without surrendering your objective. It is much easier to handle pressure situations among friends than among adversaries. Even if you have only one friend in a trouble situation, you will probably fare much better than if you had none.

> *The proper office of a friend is to stick by you when you're in the wrong. Nearly anybody will stick by you when you're in the right.*
>
> MARK TWAIN

And just as the professional pilot does, keep a mental checklist handy for dealing with pressure situations. The following checklist, with only three key questions, should suffice:

1. What's going on here?
2. What's my objective?
3. What are my options?

how your words shape your thoughts

 Men imagine that their minds have the command of language, but it often happens that language bears rule over their minds.

FRANCIS BACON

The following paragraph, taken from *How To Develop Your Thinking Ability* by Kenneth Keyes, describes a famous person. As you read it, try to assess the kinds of words it uses and the ways in which they might influence your reactions to the person. Also, try to guess the name of the person described.

Mr. X. had an unhappy childhood and little formal education. His ambition to become an artist was bitterly opposed by his father. Although self-educated, he became the author of a book, the sales of which in his country ranked next to the Bible. Obstacles did not discourage him. People would say, "Why you can't do that!" but he hurdled one barrier after another. He placed a great deal of emphasis on improving the health of young people, and he was known throughout the world as a dynamic speaker. His closest associates said of him: "(He) accomplishes great deeds out of the greatness of his heart, the passion of his will, and the goodness of his soul."[1]

Can you recognize the person described? What terms might give you useful clues? Notice that the person offering the description seems to evaluate the famous individual in highly positive terms.

The paragraph describes Adolf Hitler. If you read the description again with that in mind, does your reaction to the various terms change? Or, if you had known the identity of the person before you read the paragraph, would you have reacted differently to the words used? This example demonstrates as clearly as any I know, the subtle and significant effects that words can have on human thinking processes.

[1]Kenneth S. Keyes, Jr., *How to Develop Your Thinking Ability* (New York: McGraw-Hill, 1950), p. 11. Used with permission.

verbal maps

Language, n. The music with which we charm the serpents guarding another's treasure.

AMBROSE BIERCE

Probably all of us, at some time or other, have had a vague sensation that the words we use seem to lack a certain something—a sense of definiteness, a finality, or a firmness that might give us confidence in them as tools to mentally "capture" and hold on to various aspects of our experience. Each of us has struggled at some time with the seemingly hopeless task of trying to express a complex idea, a feeling, or a profound realization in simple terms. Perhaps you've played the child's game of saying some common word over and over again, such as book, book, book, book, until it began to sound strange and unreal; until it seemed to lose its natural sense of meaning. Or perhaps you have stood on an ocean shore at sunrise or sunset and watched a glorious display of color and light, and realized how utterly inadequate words were to deal with the experience. At these times we realize, with greater or lesser clarity, that *there are experiences and then there are words*, and they are not the same.

Not only do we think *with* words, but we think *in* words. A word is not only a tool for thought; in one sense, a word or a string of words *is* a thought. The late Alfred Korzybski, who created the science of general semantics, offered a useful metaphor for thinking about words. He said, "If we reflect upon our languages, we find that at best they must be considered only as *maps*." He referred to any statement, of any kind, made in any language as a *verbal map*, to emphasize the fact that words can only represent selected features of the perceived world in fragmentary ways. Let's explore the implications of this metaphor in dealing with our verbal thought processes.[2]

Just as a map of some part of the world, some part of a country, or part of the local terrain is an abstract representation of the real territory, so is a verbal map an abstract representation. A map is useful precisely because it is reductive—it simplifies, it summarizes, and it selects certain key features of the territory for presentation. Just as a highway map leaves out many terrain features while emphasizing certain other features of special interest, so does a verbal description of a person, an event, or a process leave out a great deal of detail in favor of those features someone considered worth talking about.

And just as a highway map inevitably distorts what it represents, so does a verbal map inevitably distort the original happening by adding the unavoidable connotative bias of the speaker. Very few freeways are really

[2]Alfred Korzybski, *Science and Sanity* (Lakeville, Conn.: International Non-Aristotelian Library Pub. Co., 1933).

colored red, very few cities are star-shaped, and very few areas of the countryside have huge dotted lines stretching across them. These distortions make little or no difference; we realize that they help to make the map useful, and they usually do not interfere in our dealings with the original territory they represent. If we could say the same about verbal maps, this would be a very short chapter. Unfortunately, the verbal maps people make and use do inevitably color, distort, and shape their thought processes, often in unconscious ways. Here we begin to part company with the simple analogy between verbal maps and freeway maps, as we try to understand the inevitable transformations involved in verbalizing about our inner experiences.

A simple example: One person might see a group of people riding on motorcycles and refer to them as a "motorcycle club." Another observer might choose to label them a "motorcycle gang." What seems like a minor variation between these two verbal maps can create an enormous difference in reactions on the part of the speaker and the hearer. Consider the differences between words like politician and statesman, government official and bureaucrat, police officer and pig, child and brat, businessperson and rip-off artist, and so on. Even at the simplest verbal level of ordinary description, we can see that the mere choice of labels unavoidably carries a fundamental connotation, a point of view, and to some extent an evaluation.

learning to analyze verbal maps

Abraham Lincoln liked to ask a riddle to illustrate the kinds of confusion that political messages sometimes create with clever words. "If you call the dog's tail a leg," Lincoln would ask, "how many legs does he have?" Typically, a person would answer, "Five." "No," Lincoln would answer. "He has four legs. Calling a dog's tail a leg doesn't make it a leg."

You can make yourself nearly immune to the unconscious tyranny of verbal maps by developing the skill of recognizing them and classifying them in terms of their functions. The following categorical system provides a convenient way to analyze most of the verbal maps that come to you and to deal with them at a conscious level.

We can divide verbal maps into three primary categories in terms of their intended functions in communications. These categories are

1. Directive
2. Affiliative
3. Informative

Directive verbal maps simply urge the hearer, either directly or indirectly, to act in some way or to believe some idea. Although they may cause ill feelings sometimes, they are not so likely to confuse or mislead people in unconscious ways. Many directive verbal maps serve simple, everyday functions such as getting work done.

Affiliative verbal maps do not usually convey significant information. Rather they simply convey by their very use the speaker's relative sense of attraction or enmity toward the hearer. Simple terms like *Hello* convey high levels of affiliation. Others—for example, *Go to hell!*—often signal very low levels of affiliation.

Informative verbal maps will receive most of our attention because they have the greatest potential for manipulation and for creating unconscious misunderstandings. An informative verbal map purports to give or get information in an exchange between people, and its use presupposes that it can be related back to some aspect of the world of the thinker who uses it. What we are calling informative verbal maps can also include those which deliberately misinform. The emphasis here is on their operational functions, not on their "truthfulness."

Since informative-type verbal maps offer the greatest potential for misinforming us and for channeling our thinking in subtle ways, let's look closer at this category. First, let's subdivide informative verbal maps into *descriptive* messages and *evaluative* messages, or personal judgments. The distinction between the two may become a bit blurred for certain kinds of statements, but we will find it convenient to classify them as predominantly one or the other.

Further, messages purported to be informative can vary greatly in the *levels of abstraction* at which they operate. One senses immediately the qualitative difference between the statement "It's raining right now" and the statement "Democracy is better than socialism any day." One is much more definite and deals with features of the world which the hearer can readily perceive. The second statement seems to defy immediate perception or verification. The level of abstraction that a statement conveys is the level of difficulty the hearer would have in recognizing and agreeing to those features of the world which the speaker has tried to identify. Broad generalizations, broad categories or classifications, and broad judgments or opinions are fairly reliable "tip-offs" to high levels of abstraction.

To gain some practice in analyzing verbal maps, try arranging the following interrelated statements in order of increasing levels of abstraction:

1. Here is a form of human communication.
2. Here are 427 sheets of paper with words typed on them.
3. Here is an important contribution to human knowledge.
4. Here is a book manuscript.

The third dimension of our classification system for informative verbal maps is the level of "verifiability" built into the message itself. We can rank verbal maps on a four-stage scale of relative uncertainty: direct observations you make yourself, reports you get from someone else, inferences made by you or someone else based on available information, and assumptions made by you or someone else based on little or no information.

To clarify this notion of verifiability levels, arrange the following statements in the order of "provable" information, that is, the effort and exploration probably required for two people to reach agreement on each of them:

1. Thinking should be taught in every school and college.
2. The square root of 70 is between 8.5 and 8.9.
3. The president of the United States is the leader of the country.
4. The book you are reading has an attractively designed cover.
5. Most two-year-old children cannot perform simple addition.

By putting together these three aspects of informative verbal maps, we can create a classification framework that will enable us to spot and analyze them rather quickly. First, we have the distinction between descriptive and evaluative messages, and within each of those categories we have the four levels of observation, report, inference, and assumption, and for each of those eight possibilities we have various possible levels of abstraction. Figure 5.1 pictures these categories as units of an elongated "cube" formed by the three perpendicular categories.

Although this simple system necessarily leaves out many of the subtleties of language use, such as ritualistic use of words, riddles and paradoxes, tone of voice and pitch patterns, and meta-verbal figures of speech that convey status differences and other subjective messages, its

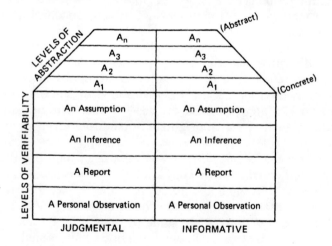

Figure 5.1 We can analyze verbal maps by classifying them according to informativeness, verifiability, and level of abstraction.

simplicity does nevertheless make it useful for dealing with a large proportion of the potentially troublesome kinds of verbal maps you find in your day-to-day environment.

Human understanding and misunderstanding seems to parallel fairly closely the range of variation in the verbal maps people use. When you reflect on the situations in which people argue and debate with one another, in which they confuse and manipulate one another, and in which they confuse themselves, you will probably agree that the verbal maps they use often play a central role in how they get along. It is very difficult to argue at great length about whether eight plus six equals fifteen or whether it equals fourteen. The protagonists can usually settle the matter readily. We don't seem to fight with one another very much over matters which we can easily settle. It is much easier to argue about whether "corporate profiteering is bleeding the American public," simply because *the terms in which the argument proceeds are too far removed from concrete reality for the matter to be easily settled.* We can justifiably say that most heated arguments sooner or later turn out to be arguments over the meanings of words, with automatic emotional reactions displacing logical thought.

As you begin to pay closer attention to the language habits of other people, you will probably notice that whenever two or more people get locked into a dispute, there is sure to be some relatively abstract or indefinite verbal map involved in their disagreement, and they are arguing because they don't realize they have failed to clarify their common verbal ground.

Referring again to the cube model in Figure 5-1, we can say that verbal maps originating perceptually "close" to the real world of direct sensory experience tend to cause much less debate and unconscious confusion than verbal maps originating further away. We could consider the level of descriptive observations at a low level of abstraction to offer the "safest" ground in human thought and communication. We could consider the other extreme, consisting of evaluative assumptions at high levels of abstraction, as offering the greatest likelihood of irresolvable disagreement. A later section of this chapter deals further with human language malfunctions, most of which originate in confused levels of verbal mapping.

Here are more selected verbal maps for use in building the skills of recognition and classification. They are taken from books and magazines. Classify them within the cubic model according to whether they are descriptive or evaluative, at high or low levels of uncertainty, and at high or low levels of abstraction. Since some of them may be mixtures of the various categories, try to break them down into subunits such as key terms or phrases and classify them on a piece-by-piece basis.

1. Washington, a rather primitive region on the Potomac River, is inhabited by two tribes. One tribe, called government, has money to give away in the form of grants,

contracts, revenue sharing, and subsidies; the other, called lobbyists, tries to get the money.

2. Gadgets, creams, lotions, and pills that are supposed to confound heredity, nature, and the calendar rake in an estimated $150,000,000 yearly from ever-trusting buyers.

3. At the National College Fairs, sponsored by the National Association of College Admissions Counselors, representatives of over 200 colleges will answer prospective students' questions on planning, admission, part-time job opportunities, and continuing education programs.

4. Power wielders respond to their subjects' needs and motivations only to the extent that they have to in order to fulfill their own power objectives, which remain their primary concern. True leaders, on the other hand, emerge from, and always return to, the wants and needs of their followers.

5. When the first U.S. space laboratory was placed into orbit in May 1973, its meteoroid and thermal shielding and one of its solar cell wings were torn away.

You can develop a high level of skill in analyzing verbal maps just by using this simple system of categories as a guide and by looking and listening carefully. A highly developed awareness of your verbal environment and the effects it can have on your thinking processes can enable you to think more flexibly, to keep your crap detector well tuned in, and to think on your feet as well.

the "cookie cutter" effect of language

The individual's whole experience is built upon the plan of his language.

HENRI DELACROIX

An anthropologist got a confusing impression when he asked a woman of an African tribe how many children she had. She answered, "Three." This answer confused the scientist because the woman's husband had earlier responded to the same question with "Four." The scientist discovered later that, in this particular tribe, a man counts only male offspring as children, while a woman includes only females. He became even more confused when he asked, "What is the total number of children you have of both sexes?" To his surprise, they both answered, "Nine." Only later did he find out that these people counted deceased children as well as living ones in numbering their total offspring.

It is one of the great curiosities—and one of the areas of potential confusion—that human languages create categories, and these categories become *perceptual subdivisions* as well as descriptive subdivisions. It is as if each word in a thinker's language system works like a cookie cutter, dividing up the substance of his or her perception into its own distinctive kind of shape or package.

Your words do not really describe the world outside your head so much as they describe the perceptual pattern existing in the neurons of your cerebral cortex. In a sense, your acquired descriptive system—your language—"dices up" your total perceptual field into small elements, and these elements become the bits and pieces your brain manipulates as you think in verbal form. Just as a beginning artist may use a grid pattern of lines overlaid on a picture he or she wants to sketch and then draws the forms isolated by each of the grid squares, so each of us superimposes a kind of verbal grid pattern over our preconscious perceptions, and we deal with the elements presented to us by the grid. The grid, in this case, is our language system. We don't verbalize about the world so much as we verbalize our perceptions of it.

Anthropologists use the term *language community* to denote a group of people who share a common set of verbal maps by virtue of their common membership in a cultural framework.[3] Americans form a language community that has many similar features to the British language community. Hopi Indians of the Southwest form a well-defined language community. To some extent, teenagers form a language community characterized by contemporary slang and "in" languages, and they also belong to the broader language community of their national citizenship. One person can simultaneously belong to several language communities. It may happen from time to time that the verbal behavior expected of a person in the context of one language community varies from the customary verbal behavior he or she learned as part of a different language community. In such a case, the person must adjust his or her verbal patterns to suit the situation, by calling on those language habits characteristic of one community.

Black children, especially from urban or ghetto areas, often face this situation when they attend white schools taught by white teachers. Certain language patterns are highly characteristic of the black community, and the black child learns them quite readily as he or she grows up there. At school, a black child might feel quite ill at ease if the teacher "corrects" his or her "improper" use of English. The child concludes that the teacher has more or less outlawed his or her basic language habits and may become very insecure and reluctant to speak at all. A black person, hearing another black person using the "correct" form of academic English, may refer to him—perhaps disdainfully—as "talkin' white."

Our brains use words so rapidly and so automatically that, after many years of verbal thinking and talking, we come to identify each word or term closely with the corresponding perceptual event. After a large number of repetitions, the word and the perceptual image tend to evoke one another interchangeably and automatically. Advertisers often exploit this well-

[3]For a very readable and intriguing description of the curiosities of language habits around the world, see Peter Farb, *Word Play* (New York: Knopf, 1973).

known feature of the brain by highly repetitive "product awareness" advertising, to the extent that an advertising slogan or jingle will produce a characteristic brain drool (to use the analogy to Pavlov's trained dogs) whenever the consumer hears it.

Sometimes the brain malfunctions slightly in verbalizing an idea, especially when its attention becomes divided between two thought processes. For example, after reading a radio news item that reported on HEW Secretary Califano's announcement that as many as 12 million Americans have serious drinking problems, the announcer said, ". . . and in local news, the city of Escondido won a bottle with—er, ah—make that a battle with the state of California over Proposition 13 relief funds."

It appears that the descriptive categories, or "cookie cutters," that a thinker learns to use have more than a minor effect on his or her brain's data-processing activities. The following examples might help to sketch out the range of variation in human thought created by language structures.

An English thinker goes to a ticket counter to make a purchase and says, "Two, please." But a Japanese thinker says, "Nimai, kudasai." He uses the counting vocabulary reserved for paper items like tickets, postage stamps, or writing paper. To purchase eggs or other round objects, he would use the counting words ikko, niko, sanko, yonko, and so on. If he wanted to count pens, pencils, or other cylindrical objects, he would use the forms ippon, nihon, sanbon, yonhon, and so on. But if he wanted to enumerate things in liquid form residing in containers, such as cups of coffee or jars of paint, he would use ippai, nihai, sanbai, yonhai, and so on. The Japanese have counting words for things in small bunches like carrots, words for counting tiny round items of food like grapes, peas, or beans, and words for counting books. The Japanese thinker might consider it a novel feature of English that it has only a single group of universal counting words. While the English thinker might consider his system easier and more convenient, the Japanese thinker might consider it simply crude and inelegant. Each thinker learns to cut his cookies in his own characteristic way and to consider that way "natural"—if indeed he thinks about it at all.

To the Hottentot of southern Africa, counting does not have the extreme importance as an everyday experience that it has for industrialized peoples. For the Hottentot, four numbers are sufficient. They translate into English roughly as one, two, three, and a lot. For the Hottentot thinker, any group of four or more friends, family members, items of food, wild animals, or consecutive days of rain is a whole bunch. He apparently deals with larger numbers than three as indefinite.

One of the most striking differences among languages, and consequently among cultures, is this variation in the degree to which each makes fine distinctions in applying labels to experiences. The English thinker has one basic word for a particular kind of precipitation—snow. To the Eskimo, it would seem extremely inconvenient to confuse falling snow with snow that has just fallen, or to confuse either of them with old snow that has become crusted and hard. A fixed snowdrift is obviously different to the Eskimo than snow that is drifting at the moment of perception and discussion. Because the Eskimo finds it helpful to make these perceptual distinctions within his world, the Eskimo has many terms for the substance. The English thinker uses only one.

Anthropologists sometimes find their greatest fascination in studying cultural differences when they examine the various terms used to denote kinship. English speakers have one of the simplest and least precise systems of any of the world's cultures for describing tribal and familial relationships. Many African thinkers would consider it absurd to use a single word like cousin to describe both male and female relatives, or not to distinguish whether the person described is related by blood to the speaker's father or to his mother. To be unable to distinguish a brother-in-law as the brother of one's wife or the husband of one's sister would seem hopelessly confusing within the fabric of personal relationships existing in many cultures. Similarly, how is it possible to make sense of a situation in which a single word—uncle—applies to the brother of one's father and to the brother of one's mother? The Hawaiian language uses the same term to refer to one's father and to the father's brother. People of Northern Burma, who think in the Jinghpaw language, have eighteen basic terms for describing their kin. Not one of them has a direct equivalent in English.

Curiously, industrialized cultures and others that depend heavily on symbols and written communication seem to make finer distinctions in describing colors than do cultures whose people live in less complex social patterns. Several tribes in New Guinea use only two basic terms to distinguish light colors from darker ones. The Shona of Rhodesia recognize only four colors across the visible band. English thinkers, and especially American thinkers, seem to use a much wider variety of terms to denote not only colors, but shades of colors and their relative saturations and intensities. Metaphors like peach, midnight blue, shell pink, and birch grey tend to emphasize fine distinctions.

Bible scholars still debate significant points of biblical history that turn on the interpretation of single words or brief phrases in Hebrew, which often do not have direct counterparts in English. The Hebrew language system enabled biblical writers to describe their ideas in certain forms, using their characteristic cookie cutters. Those who translated the Bible into English had no choice but to make certain assumptions about meanings. In some cases, they had to choose certain English idioms or figures of speech to approximate concepts that they understood in the Hebrew mapping system of their brains but could not express in the English mapping system. This process is analogous to translating from one kind of map, such as an aerial photograph, to another kind, such as a city street map. To the extent that the two mapping methods do not have common structures, the original territory gets represented in a distorted fashion.

English-speaking semanticists have discovered various interesting features of American Indian languages. Hopi in particular has intrigued a number of researchers, notably Benjamin Lee Whorf and Edward Sapir. They found that Hopi and English conceptualize the surrounding world in some remarkably different ways. And they concluded that, while English and its family of European languages tend to emphasize the organization of space and time, Hopi tends to emphasize processes and the description of events. Hopi thinkers have no way to measure or even to describe what English thinkers call *time*. Hopi has no words for minutes, hours, days, weeks, months, years, or any other spans of time. Instead of describing the span of time it would take to do something, a Hopi language user would describe the events involved in doing it and would explain how the string of events would produce the result.

The fragility of language as a means for encoding thoughts became frustratingly obvious to early researchers working on the problem of computerized translation from one language to another. According to one story, they presented the computer with the English figure of speech "out of sight, out of mind," had it translated into Russian, and then had the translated version reconverted to English. The machine came up with "invisible idiot."

how to hold an intelligent conversation

If dogs could talk, we'd probably have as much trouble getting along with them as we do with people.

KAREL CAPEK

Having studied the role of verbal maps in human thinking and having developed a simple system for analyzing them, we can now identify fairly easily the kinds of semantic malfunctions that can sometimes occur when people try to think and talk. A great deal of human misunderstanding, antagonism, confusion, misery, and even insanity stems directly or indirectly from the misuse of words.

Referring back to Figure 5-1, we can trace many semantic malfunctions to the fact that the speaker or the hearer, or both, are confusing themselves about which "compartment" of the semantic cube their verbal maps occupy. In general, we can say that those verbal maps operating closest to the bottom-right corner of the cube, that is, the level of concrete-descriptive-observation, tend to cause the least misunderstanding and tend to permit the quickest resolution and agreement when misunderstanding does arise. Verbal maps closest to the far upper-left corner of the cube—the level of abstract-judgmental-assumptions—tend to offer the weakest basis for human agreement and mutual action and tend to impede the process of achieving consensus and cooperation.

Much of what passes for social conversation, and even problem-solving discussions in business situations, actually amounts to preaching, dogmatic assertions, ego building, and scoring "status points," "success points," and "smart points" instead of the organized exchange of ideas. By studying the verbal maps people use, and by carefully choosing those you use, you can hold effective, worthwhile, and enjoyable conversations much more often than if you fall victim to various semantic malfunctions.

A story concerning actress Zsa Zsa Gabor exemplifies a fairly simple social conversation. The famous actress is said to have been chatting with a gentleman at a cocktail party when she realized she had talked about herself, her career, and her activities for the entire conversation. "But we've talked enough about me, dahlink," she said. "Let's talk about you. How do you like my new dress?"

By training yourself to monitor the ways in which you and others use verbal maps in conversation, you can develop the skills of self-expression to a high level. Note the ways in which some speakers use their verbal tools to get people on their wavelengths and sell their ideas, while others seem to flounder about with no apparent plan and no particular organization to their approach to the other person. Of all the factors that psychologists have tried to associate with success in the business world, perhaps the only consistent one is the command of the written and spoken word. Those who can use verbal maps effectively tend to get where they want to go much easier than those who cannot.

An acquaintance commented recently on the *evaluative labels* often applied to people, in this case by psychotherapists. "The shrink has you coming and going," he grumbled. "If you arrive late for your appointment, you're 'resisting therapy.' If you get there early, you're 'anxious.' And if you get there right on time, you're 'compulsive!' "

Much unnecessary labeling goes on in English by means of the simple word *is* and its linguistic family, the various forms of the verb to be. A person might say, "He is an idiot" or "She's cheap" or "That's a stupid idea" or "I'm just a failure." Languages that do not have these simple A equals B verb forms tend to force their users to describe their worlds more in action terms than in terms of abstract categories or traits.

How many derogatory labels can you spot in one day's casual listening? Do you hear words like communism, socialism, welfare-ism, big business, big government, politician, bureaucrat, profiteer, hippie, long-hair, redneck, crook, Jew, nigger, wop, spic, or teeny-bopper used as the basis for arguing certain points of view? Do you hear laudatory labels—taxpayer,

A Spade Calling a Spade a Spade. From LANGUAGE IN
THOUGHT AND ACTION, Third Edition by S.I. Hayakawa,
copyright © 1972 by Harcourt Brace Jovanovich, Inc. Reproduced by permission of the publisher and George Allen &
Unwin (Publishers) Ltd.

citizen, free enterprise, American youth, the American Way, the American
Dream, mom, the worker, a true friend—applied for the same purpose?

This comment, attributed to the director of the National Cowboy Hall of
Fame, concerns America's conversion to the metric system of measurement. "Metric is definitely Communist. One monetary system, one language, one weight and measurement system, one world—all Communist!
We are playing into Communist hands. Here in the West, we're closer to our
heritage—the land. We know that the West was won by the inch, foot, yard,
and mile."

> *When a thinker states that any thing is "only" some other thing, he is usually on the brink
> of a blunder.*
>
> *MARY EVEREST BOOLE*

Another semantic malfunction, *confusing levels of abstraction,* can take
more subtle forms. Have you ever heard people discussing questions like
"Does man have free will?" or "Is there life after death?" or "What is the
ideal form of government?" A fundamental feature of these types of questions, as verbal maps, is that they begin at such a high level of abstraction
that the speaker or hearer can proceed from them in almost any direction.
The extremely high level of abstraction tends to expand the mental playing
field, rather than to reduce it to a level at which a number of people could
possibly achieve some measure of agreement. When such a question helps
the discussion degenerate into a heated debate, the protagonists will most
likely end up arguing over the meanings of words, although they may not
realize it.

The next time you read a newspaper editorial or other viewpoint, count
the number of fairly concrete words in the text. Note the number of words
you consider highly abstract. See how the relative proportion of abstract

and concrete words plays a part in the presentation of the author's message, and note your reaction to them. To what extent does consciously identifying the abstract terms help you to evaluate the arguments and viewpoints presented?

An especially interesting form of high-level abstraction involves *personification*, describing an inanimate or even imaginary entity as if it were a living thing. Semanticists also call this phenomenon *reification*. News reporters refer to the stock exchange as having rallied, slumped, recovered, or tested its resistance level. How many news reports begin with "The White House said today that . . ."?

Metaphor constitutes another special case of abstract verbal mapping, in which the maker of the map offers to substitute a selected idea or process as a model for describing the process at hand. If you start listening for metaphors in conversation around you and begin detecting them in the things you read, you may be surprised at how much of our discourse depends on these figures of speech. Note especially how many of our common terms and expressions convey the idea of spatial structures and physical actions. For example, we speak of grasping an idea, facing a problem, and shooting down a project.

A news article began with the lead statement "The 1980s loom as a bloody battlefield for U.S. industry." It went on to speak of one of the major electronics manufacturing firms with the view that "TI's struggle to the top and its game plan for the hot trade competition of the 1980s with Japan, certainly America's chief adversary, stand as strong examples of what other U.S. companies must do if they, too, are to survive in the next decade." This writer uses the metaphors of warfare mixed with the metaphors of sport (note the term *game plan*) to create a certain impression.

Euphemisms form another interesting class of abstract verbal maps. A fundamentalist Southern preacher got up in front of the congregation one Sunday morning and said, "Brothers and sisters, today I wants to tell ya about the status quo." A member of the group interrupted him. "Excuse me, Reverend. What's the status quo?" "The status quo," replied the minister, "is a Latin term for the mess we is in."

Euphemisms amount to more than mere semantic curiosities, however. Usually, a person who chooses a euphemism in favor of some more commonly used term does so for a specific reason: to persuade in an indirect fashion—to induce the hearer to adopt a mental set that predisposes him to approve of the object of description. Hitler referred to the murder of millions of Jews as "extermination" for the objective of "purifying the race." When Lyndon Johnson persuaded Congress to increase the income tax temporarily, he referred to the extra amount as merely a "surtax." Well, now. If it's only a surtax, it isn't really a regular tax. Therefore, the government hasn't really increased our taxes.

Another distinctive semantic phenomenon, usually characteristic of rigid thinking, is the *allness orientation*, the tendency to speak in terms that suggest totality, finality, or unequivocal certainty. Do you know anyone who frequently uses such terms as everybody says, all the time, always, I never, or nobody, in expressing ideas? This habit of allness talking apparently mirrors a habit of allness thinking. Many semanticists believe that when a person makes a habit of allness talking, his entire mental orientation leans toward rigid all-or-nothing ways of perceiving the world. He apparently becomes more likely to conclude, for example, that everybody in a given situation favors a certain point of view simply because he heard several people speak in favor of it.

A related form of unconscious semantic rigidity, known as the *two-valued orientation* (also called the *either-or orientation*), operates in more subtle ways than the habits of indiscriminate labeling and allness talking. The two-valued orientation shows up in the tendency to state issues, problems, situations, points of view, opinions, and evaluations in terms that suggest a forced choice between only two directly opposed alternatives. Many people take pleasure in saying "Well, there are always two sides to every argument" with an air of assurance. But a more semantically flexible view recognizes that every problem has multiple "sides"—as many as a person can think of. Learning to speak in multivalued terms tends to help one think in multivalued terms.

Revising your language habits toward increased semantic flexibility can help you to organize your thoughts more effectively and can help you to influence others more effectively. In his autobiography, Benjamin Franklin commented on his discovery of this point, as follows:

> I made it a rule to forbear all direct contradiction to the sentiments of others, and all positive assertion of my own. I even forbid myself the use of every word or expression in the language that imported a fixed opinion, such as certainly, undoubtedly, etc., and I adopted instead of them I conceive, I apprehend, or I imagine a thing to be so or so, or it so appears to me at present.

> When another asserted something that I thought an error, I denied myself the pleasure of contradicting him abruptly and of showing immediately some absurdity in his proposition; and in answering, I began by observing that in certain cases or circumstances his opinion would be right, but in the present case there appeared or seemed to me some difference, etc. I soon found the advantage of this change in my manner; the conversations I engaged in went on more pleasantly. The modest way in which I proposed my opinions procured a readier reception and less contradiction; I had less mortification when I was found to be in the wrong, and I more easily prevailed with others to give up their mistakes and join with me when I happened to be in the right.[4]

Another useful skill in using verbal maps is simply to keep the majority of your statements as definitive as possible. Train yourself to avoid

[4]Keyes, *How to Develop Your Thinking Ability*, pp. 152–53.

generalizations when the situation calls for a specific report. Develop a level of verbal precision that will help you get to the point and eliminate confusion, without splitting hairs or making a pest of yourself with unnecessary distinctions.

For example, as several executives discussed their upcoming sales trip, one commented that he wanted to leave a day early in order to take a train. A second executive asked, "Why do you want to take the train?" "I don't like airplanes," he replied. "Are you afraid of flying?" asked the second. The first executive replied, "No—crashing."

 One should, each day, try to hear a little song, read a good poem, see a fine picture, and if it is possible, speak a few reasonable words.

GOETHE

positive thinking and positive talking

The greatest discovery of my generation is that human beings, by changing the inner attitudes of their minds, can change the outer aspects of their lives . . . It is too bad that more people will not accept this tremendous discovery and begin living it.

WILLIAM JAMES

Many people talk about positive thinking, but relatively few seem to make a consistent habit of it. The actual technique of positive thinking is so utterly simple that it appears to have eluded a large majority of our fellow thinkers. Positive thinking merely means fixing your attention on positive subjects and using positive language to form and express your thoughts. You can easily train yourself to think more positively just by training yourself to choose what you pay attention to and what to say about it, both silently and aloud.

In Chapter 2 we explored the three languages of conscious thought—words, pictures, and kinesthetic patterns. We noted that when a word comes to mind it will usually bring with it some kind of visual or spatial image, whether clearly or vaguely defined, and it will also bring to mind an overall sensation, a kinesthetic pattern your brain automatically associates with it. Our usual term for this kinesthetic pattern is a *feeling*. In my view, what we commonly call "feelings" are kinesthetic responses—whole-body reaction patterns—which coincide with our cortical activity. We might interrelate the three thinking languages in the form of three overlapping circles, with each representing one of the languages, as in Figure 5-2. A simple experiment will show how they work together.

First, say the words "poisonous snake" in your mind two or three times. Then allow whatever image seems natural to emerge and accompany the words. Keep the words and the image together as you visualize the snake

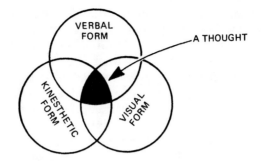

Figure 5.2 Your brain forms an idea simultaneously in
three "languages."

moving toward you. Unless you happen to have some kind of avocational
or professional affinity to poisonous snakes, you will probably begin to
experience the vague traces of an anxious feeling. This sensation is your
kinesthetic representation of the thought of the snake or, if you like, your
"feeling" about the snake. Your brain expresses the thought simultaneously in the three languages, verbal, visual, and kinesthetic. If you explore
these three thinking languages, you will probably find that you can start
with any one of the three and it will elicit the others.

Having demonstrated the effects of a verbal thought that has negative
connotations, let's demonstrate the effects of positive verbal thoughts. Say
"delicious meal" in your mind several times. Form a picture of having just
finished eating a delicious meal in pleasant surroundings, with pleasant
company. Imagine feeling very satisfied. Probably your *kinesthetic memory* will bring back to your conscious field of thought the familiar feelings
you've had in the past after a delicious meal. Of course, if you happen to be
very hungry while reading this paragraph, your kinesthetic memory might
trigger a hunger reaction and your mouth might water.

What we have demonstrated here is the basic neurological fact of positive thinking: Paying attention to positive experiences and using positive
words to express your thoughts will elicit positive images from your visual
memory and positive feelings from your kinesthetic memory. These form
the "substance" of positive thought.

This tells us that positive thinking simply amounts to choosing to use
positive attention and a *positive vocabulary* to maintain a three-dimensional positive frame of mind. In simple terms, if you pay attention to
enjoying delicious meals more often than you pay attention to poisonous
snakes, you will have positive feelings more often than you have negative
feelings. The same fact applies if you talk about success more often than
failure, love more often than hate, happiness more often than misery,
friendship more often than animosity, confidence more often than fear,
cooperation more often than combat, satisfaction more often than dissatisfaction, human kindness more often than cruelty, good news more often

than bad news, what's right more often than what's wrong, and how to solve a problem more often than how terrible a problem it is.

Have you taken a close look at the number of negative, morbid, critical, and unpleasant messages transmitted back and forth in our extremely media-oriented, urbanized culture every day? A thinker in America must develop a very high degree of environmental awareness and a rugged crap detector to block out the constant barrage of negativism that pervades his or her verbal environment. Television and radio newscasts present a steady stream of bad news. Commercials explain what's wrong with his or her teeth, hair, car, sex life, clothes, life's work, and political views. Newspaper headlines blare out the message every day: The world is going to hell.

I was amazed how much more positively I began to feel toward the world and toward my fellow creatures once I stopped watching television, quit reading the "anxiety columns" in the newspapers, and adopted the practice of changing radio stations during news broadcasts. I finally got tired of hearing about the hotel fire in Argentina that killed 100 people, the little girl in Michigan who froze to death after her parents abandoned her, the elderly man who was run down by a gang of teenagers in a van, the old lady who was raped and murdered in her home, the earthquake that destroyed a village in Peru, and the constant complaints about the cost of living. I concluded that television and radio "news" people are in the "Bad News Business," and that their primary strategy for selling products seems to be to appeal to the morbid sense of apprehension in all of us about our own well-being and safety. Ask yourself how many of these inputs enable you to live your life more effectively, and how many of them you can do without.

I've looked in on a few daytime soap operas, and the levels of negativism and morbidity have amazed me. The idea of several million housewives wallowing every day in what I can only describe as emotional garbage (an admittedly evaluative verbal map) is a bewildering prospect. Unwed mothers, suicides, incestuous relationships, divorces, runaway children, alcoholics, and dedicated losers form the nucleus of the soap opera population.

Some television commercials may actually have the effect of programming people for sickness. Have you ever heard a commercial for a headache remedy finish with the line, "The next time you have a headache . . ."?

Have you ever listened closely to the lyrics of popular songs? Can you recall some of the titles? If you would like to increase your awareness of positive and negative messages around you, take a pen and paper and make two lists, side by side. On one side list the titles of any songs you can think of that you consider to have basically positive, confident, happy, or uplifting messages. On the other side, list titles of songs that you consider to have sad, self-critical, complaining, mournful, or lamenting messages. You may have a very difficult time making the positive list as long as the negative list. This is not to suggest that we should all stop listening to popular music or that listening to or singing a sad song always constitutes a despicable act of negative thinking. But I do believe that the predominance of songs with negative themes mirrors a predominantly negative view of the world on the part of many, many of our fellow thinkers. And our songs do account for quite a few of the host of messages, both positive and negative, that soak into our senses every day.

Have you ever listened to a fundamentalist religious sermon on the radio? Many of these preachers invite listeners to condemn and criticize themselves and to wallow in self-accusation. Much of the institutionalized "Christian" doctrine portrays people as basically evil creatures, put on earth to suffer. Anybody who is having a good time with his life and who is not condemning himself must be somehow "cheating."

Have you noticed the kinds of placards and slogans some people hang on their walls in offices? How many of them convey messages of cheerfulness, a sense of accomplishment, or enjoyment of life? How many convey a sense of despair, frustration, gloom, and surrender, thinly disguised as humor? One placard has a forlorn little character saying, "I Used to be Lost in the Shuffle. Now I Just Shuffle Along with the Lost." How would you like to start your day with a boost like that? Another shows a character winding up to swing at a golf ball. The message is "I sometimes make a number of false starts before I make my final deadly mistake." Although it seems funny at first, the lingering impression is one of defeatism. After seeing a number of these kinds of messages on postcards and placards in gift shops, I finally found a card that I purchased immediately. It shows two cartoon people joining hands and dancing wildly up and down. The message is "Life is a very special occasion." I gave it an honored place on my bathroom mirror, where it gives me a little boost in the mornings.

As you look around you, try to identify the kinds of messages that bring you good news and the kinds that bring you bad news. To what extent can you choose to pay attention to some of these messages and reject others? To what extent can you deliberately arrange your immediate environment—your home, your work place, your car, or the place where you read or study—in such a way as to send your positive messages? To the extent that you pay attention to ideas and experiences that lead to positive feelings, you can make the most of your environment.

Negative verbalizations come in a variety of forms. For a brief discussion, we can divide them into four principal categories, as follows:

1. Self-critical statements.
2. Negative value judgments.
3. Negative expectations.
4. Verbal "dead-ending."

Statements we make about ourselves to others or to ourselves, some-times referred to as *self-talk*, form the topic of the next section. *Self-critical statements* represent an especially damaging form of self-talk, which one can fairly easily learn to revise.

Negative value judgments lead the thinker to find negative aspects in others and to dwell on them, often with additional undesirable side effects.

Statements of *negative expectations* lead the thinker to anticipate a negative experience, to worry about it, and even possibly to make it more likely to happen.

Verbal dead-ending includes those forms of wasted mental energy, such as blaming others and rejecting responsibility for one's own mistakes, worrying about the future, agonizing about the past, resenting the suc-cesses of others, and general types of complaining known as the "poor me" effect. These have the effect of taking your thought processes down a verbal dead end, leading you to waste mental energy and wallow in bad feelings, and especially preventing you from getting on with whatever type of problem-solving activity the situation calls for.

A straightforward strategy for learning to think more positively is to consciously exclude from your speaking and thinking vocabulary those words which have predominantly negative connotations, and to teach yourself to use mostly words with positive connotations. If you can't say it, you can't think it. Think of your entire stock of words as composed of three subvocabularies, as illustrated in Figure 5-3. Positive thinking amounts to setting aside the negative subvocabularly and finding ways to organize and express your ideas without it.

The following terms are proposed as typical candidates for exclusion from all of our verbal maps:

1. I'm afraid (that, of)
2. I hate (to, him, her, that)
3. I dread

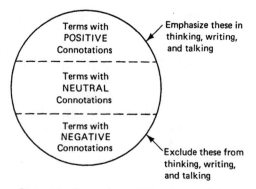

Figure 5.3   The words you think with can affect your feelings. Choose them carefully.

4. I'm sick of, I'm sick and tired of
5. That drives me crazy
6. That blows my mind
7. That blew me away
8. That kills me
9. I'm dead
10. I'm dying to (know, meet, try)
11. I'm wiped out
12. That turns me off
13. I can't
14. I was psyched out
15. I'm (any negative adjective)
16. I'm a (any negative noun)
17. I'll probably blow it
18. With my luck, I'll probably (negative forecast)
19. You're (he, she, that, it) stupid
20. That'll never work
21. It's all my fault
22. It's all your fault
23. If only (any statement that agonizes over the past)
24. See what you made me do?
25. If it weren't for you (him, her, the kids, my job), I could (complaining or "poor me" statement)
26. This is awful (terrible, stupid, and so on)
27. Why do these things always happen to me?
28. Nobody likes me
29. Everything I do turns out wrong
30. I never do anything right

Perhaps you can add others to the list. Some of the items may seem uncomfortably familiar. Many of the people in my thinking classes have reported with amazement the number of negative, cynical, defeatist, or self-critical terms they have found in their everyday habitual speech, once they started monitoring what they said. They have also reported surprise at the prevalence of routine negative statements in everyday conversation. I have known many people, students and colleagues alike, who have achieved a great deal of personal satisfaction and positive feelings by amending their use of language. You may find it becomes a bit of a challenge, once you have eliminated the more obvious negatives. But you will probably find that a consciousness of your language habits comes rather quickly, and you will probably find that positive thoughts and feelings come more readily and automatically.

We can diagram the possibilities for positive thinking, in terms of *positive attention* and *positive verbalization*, as shown in Figure 5-4. In the

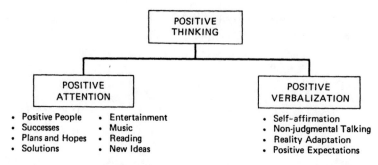

Figure 5.4   Positive thinking means deliberately organizing your thoughts in positive terms.

area of positive attention, we generally replace bad news with good news, unless, of course, some item of bad news is really significant and warrants close attention. We replace ideas of failure with ideas of success, worries about problems with thoughts about solutions, fears with hopes, worries with plans, unpleasant movies with pleasant ones, morbid literature with positive, uplifting literature, moronic television shows with nothing, morbid news programs with nothing, negative, unpleasant people with positive, supportive ones, and frustrations with the past with new ideas for the future.

In the area of positive verbalization, we focus on *positive expectations*. We realize that we can influence our own success, and we begin doing so by concentrating on success and by verbally forecasting success. We talk success, we talk achievement, and we talk confidence. We use phrases like "I can do it," "Let's give it a try," and "Why not?"

We replace self-condemnation and self-criticism with *self-affirmation*. We speak well of ourselves—not to brag or to put others down, but to give ourselves our due. We speak as kindly to ourselves as we would speak to our best friends. We focus only on our strengths and do not cancel them out with statements about "weaknesses." We acknowledge and affirm our worth as individuals, with the notion that each of us is exactly as worthwhile as any other in human terms.

We substitute *nonjudgmental acceptance* whenever possible for the kinds of negative value judgments we are sometimes tempted to make. We deal as much as possible with descriptions rather than evaluations and as much as possible with options and investigative thinking rather than dogmatic opinion.

We substitute *reality adaptation* for dead-end thinking, whereby we catch on to what's happening in a given situation and acknowledge the reality of the events in order to adapt to them most effectively. We waste little mental energy on frustration, self-pity, blaming others, or sour grapes thinking. We acknowledge reality and proceed rapidly to adapt to it.

You can maintain a conscious policy of bringing relatively positive thoughts into your mind and dismissing negative thoughts. You can use the mental technique of *thought stopping* to chase away a negative, morbid, or preoccupying thought. To do this, merely "hear" the shouted word STOP! in your mind and use it to bring your thoughts abruptly to a standstill. The worrisome thought will disappear, and you can immediately focus on a more positive thought. If you find yourself preoccupied with an especially morbid or troublesome thought, keep repeating the thought stopping technique every few minutes until you get rid of it. In conjunction with the technique, give yourself something mentally demanding and positive to do at the same time. You can make the thought stopping effect more emphatic by occasionally shouting the word *STOP!* aloud, such as when you're alone in a car. Let the sound fill the space around you and memorize the sensation of it ringing in your ears. Then you'll be able to use the technique silently with a stronger effect.

Another useful technique for deliberately maintaining a positive feeling is to visualize yourself kicking negative thoughts out of your mind. If you find yourself feeling somewhat sad, depressed, or discouraged, simply make a mental picture of the negative feeling as a hateful little gremlin. Arouse a strong feeling of aggressiveness toward this negative creature, and see yourself violently kicking it out of sight. At the same time, feel yourself becoming more positive and uplifted, and substitute a much more positive attitude for the one you kicked out.

self-talk

Self-talk includes anything you say to yourself about yourself, either in your mind or aloud. Just as you can consider your overall stock of words as composed of the three subvocabularies shown in Figure 5-3, that is, positive, neutral, and negative, so you can consider self-talk in the same categories. You may find it very revealing to make a small study of the things you say to yourself. Begin monitoring your silent conversations as well as those you mumble to yourself at various times, listening for terms such as those listed in the preceding section. Make a note also from time to time of the ways in which you describe yourself in conversation with other people.

For example, what comment, if any, do you make at the instant when you spill something, knock over someone's glass of water in a restaurant, or realize you've left something important at home instead of bringing it with you? Do you at these times hold a kind of criminal trial in your mind, find yourself guilty, and pass judgment? To what extent do you make derogatory joking comments about yourself ? Most of us do this, at least occasionally. With conscious attention, we can make the occasional self-critical comment extremely rare. And the more positively we speak of ourselves, the more positively our feelings will follow from our words.

Begin experimenting with two very important types of self-talk terms and eliminating them from your vocabulary. One is the derogatory adjective, which I like to call the "deradjective." A deradjective is any judgmental adjective you use in referring to yourself that has the effect of condemning you and criticizing you, whether or not you believe it to be "true."

Typical deradjectives are:

1. Dumb		9. Spastic
2. Stupid		10. Crazy
3. Fat		11. Disorganized
4. Lazy		12. Neurotic
5. Clumsy		13. Schizy
6. Ugly		14. Spacy
7. Klutzy		15. Inept
8. Old		

The other important type of self-talk term is the derogatory noun, which we could contract to "doun" or, in more contemporary terms, a "downer." A downer is any judgmental name you apply to yourself that has the effect of condemning you or making you seem less worthy than you have a right to be. Typical downers are

1. Idiot		9. Failure
2. Dummy		10. Coward
3. Klutz		11. Clod
4. Nitwit		12. Jerk
5. Dimwit		13. Slob
6. Dingdong		14. Old bag
7. Fool		15. Old dog
8. Loser		

A very reliable measure of maturity and personal adjustment is the length of time a person takes to recover from an emotional upset. For the positive thinker, an upset is a temporary block in progress. For the dead-end thinker, the upset or the problem causing it becomes an end in itself. He dwells on it as if it were the most important happening in the universe, and thereby invests it with much more negative influence over his thoughts than it deserves to have.

Emotional dead-ending shows up in self-talk by means of terms and expressions like the following:

1. This is terrible.
2. This is awful.

3. Why me?
4. I hate it when this happens.
5. It's your fault.
6. It's not my fault.
7. You made me mad.
8. I don't know what to do.
9. Screwed again.
10. You can't fight City Hall.
11. If only—.
12. I have no choice.
13. See what you made me do.
14. I need you, I can't live without you.
15. That dirty—.

Some people even use terms of negation when they try to express positive news. In answer to the question "How are you?" such a person might say, "Not bad." They might use the same term in giving a compliment to someone else, for example, "That's not a bad-looking dress" or "That's not a bad idea." It may well be that their brains decode this message rather crudely at the preconscious level, focusing on the words *not* and *bad*, producing a slightly negative connotation. Try a little psychosemantic experiment by alternately repeating the terms *not bad* and *good* a number of times out loud. See if you sense a subjective difference in your reaction to the two forms.

You might even consider giving your brain the challenge of minimizing the number of times you use the word *no* and *not*, and others related to them, in speaking. See what it would take to reconstruct some of your habitual expressions in affirmative terms. Instead of "I don't like eggplant," you might say, "There are lots of foods I like more than eggplant." Instead of "I don't want to pay too much money for a new pair of shoes," you could say, "I want to get a new pair of shoes for a good price." Perhaps this verbal distinction strikes you as splitting hairs. But consider that focusing on the positive form of expression tends to cause a subtle shift in the meaning of the sentence from the idea of avoidance or rejection to the idea of accomplishment or affirmation.

You can also put yourself in a positive mood whenever you feel low or fatigued just by saying words or phrases in your mind that have highly positive connotations and then letting your kinesthetic response follow the words. These *affirmations* can be sentences like "I am healthy, happy, positive, and full of the joy of life" or "I live, move, and act with perfect balance and harmony" or "I am free to live, free to be happy, and free to enjoy my life." I often let affirmations like these drift through my mind while I'm jogging, or I may just say a few positive words like "joy," "happy," "strong," "free," "powerful," "love," and "life." The response follows automatically.

Remember that whatever you fasten your attention on, you tend to bring into your life. And keep in mind also that you define yourself as a person in the way you talk about yourself—literally, *you are whatever you say you are.* By teaching yourself the two key skills of positive attention and positive self-talk, you can develop a winning attitude and maintain lifelong happiness.

Change your thoughts and you change your world.

NORMAN VINCENT PEALE

6

developing
mental flexibility

I am free of all prejudice. I hate everyone equally.

W.C. FIELDS

psychosclerosis, or jumping at the left-hand door

In his book, *Language in Thought and Action*, S.I. Hayakawa cites an experiment performed with laboratory rats, which demonstrates the characteristic inability of some animals to adapt to new circumstances and to make new choices.

Professor N.R.F. Maier of the University of Michigan performed a series of interesting experiments in which "neurosis" is induced in rats. The rats are first trained to jump off the edge of a platform at one of two doors. If the rat jumps to the right, the door holds fast, and it bumps its nose and falls into a net; if it jumps to the left, the door opens and the rat finds a dish of food. When the rats are well trained to this reaction, the situation is changed. The food is put behind the other door, so that in order to get their reward they now have to jump to the right instead of to the left. (Other changes, such as marking the two doors in different ways, may also be introduced by the experimenter.) If the rat fails to figure out the new system, so that each time it jumps it never knows whether it is going to get food or bump its nose, it finally gives up and refuses to jump at all. At this stage, Dr. Maier says, "Many rats prefer to starve rather than make a choice."[1]

Researchers have explored a similar tendency toward behavioral rigidity in a species of fish known as the pike. Ordinarily a pike will quickly devour any minnow it finds swimming in its neighborhood. When researchers lower a bottomless bell jar into the pike's aquarium and put minnows into it, the pike will lunge at them many times, bumping its face painfully on the glass barrier. After many tries, it gives up and ignores them. When the researchers remove the bell jar so the minnows can swim

[1]S.I. Hayakawa, *Language in Thought and Action*, 3rd ed. (New York: Harcourt Brace Jovanovich, Inc., 1972), p. 242. Reprinted by permission of the publisher and George Allen & Unwin (Publishers) Ltd.

around freely, the pike never tries to eat them. The minnows can swim all around the pike and right past its nose, but it will not attack. It has become fully fixated in its behavior, unable to adapt to a new reality. It may even eventually starve surrounded by an abundant food supply.

This kind of *fixated reaction*, sometimes called the pike *syndrome*, shows up in human beings just as in animals. For example, a child who receives a great deal of criticism, ridicule, and disapproval will probably become a permanently shy adult. Such a person will probably never reexamine the situation and realize that he or she has outgrown the oppressive adults and left them behind. The vast majority of extremely shy adults have simply carried the behavior patterns that helped them "survive" childhood into their grown-up years.

Each of us can occasionally fall into a pattern of dealing with a problem situation by means of a fixated reaction. You may get into an argument with a clerk, a garage mechanic, a family member, a boss, or an employee, with both of you hardening your positions so completely that compromise becomes virtually impossible. The unworkable actions—shouting, criticizing, interrupting, name calling, or rebutting—may temporarily become your only means for dealing with the situation. You become fixated in these particular reactions, even though in your more reasonable moments you would agree that they don't work. When that happens, you have temporarily lost your perspective on the situation and (to use Hayakawa's expression) you continue "jumping at the left-hand door."

Each of us may resort to fixated reactions from time to time, and often they lead to no lasting harm. However, if your overall style consists of a fixed and limited repertoire of reactions to all situations that confront you, then you have made a mental habit of jumping at the left-hand door. Anthropologist Ashley Montagu refers to this mental pattern as *psychosclerosis*, a form of mental "aging" process that inhibits the person and limits his options for living just as surely as if he had advanced hardening of the arteries. We might call psychosclerosis a "disease" of mental adaptation. One of my colleagues calls it *hardening of the categories*.

To a mouse, cheese is cheese. That's why mousetraps are effective.

WENDELL JOHNSON

eliminating snap reactions

A curious feature of the human brain makes each of us just a little crazy at times. Mostly we stay reasonably alert to what's going on around us, and we adjust our reactions fairly well to the requirements of the situation. Each of us has a kind of "executive" function operating to monitor our sense inputs and to organize our overall mental response. This mental program seems to operate more or less preconsciously and continously as we interact with the world around us.

But occasionally something will happen, or someone will say a certain thing or do something we find extremely provocative. In such a case the incoming sense data may override the executive monitoring circuits (which probably can be localized to a certain region of the cortex) and trigger a snap reaction. Have you ever become extremely angry at someone for having committed some social atrocity and later reflected on how suddenly you responded? You might say something like "I just saw red" or "I got so mad I couldn't see straight" or "I just freaked out." Probably you could sense the utterly automatic quality of your reaction, as if your brain had responded to a radio signal transmitted from afar, or as if you had received a jolt from an electrode.

This kind of "electrode response," also known as a signal reaction (or knee-jerk reaction, spinal reaction, or reflex response), is a biological response rather than an intellectual one. When the "signal" comes in the form of a verbal message such as an insult, your brain processes the message at a high level in order to understand it, but thereafter the reaction proceeds at lower levels of your brain's structure. The various processing centers of your cortex, particularly the common integrating area, in connection with brainstem structures such as the hypothalamus, pituitary gland, and the medulla organize your entire emotional response to the signal. This response constitutes the kinesthetic form of the total thought, as explained in Chapter 2.

Frustration in particular derives from just this kind of signal reaction. Frustration constitutes your whole-body kinesthetic response to the realization that your mental set has been dashed. When you make up your mind very firmly that something or other will happen—indeed, that it must happen—and you hang your hopes firmly on its occurrence, then you've programmed yourself to signal-react and become frustrated if it doesn't happen. You can avoid or minimize frustration in day-to-day activities if you can develop a high-speed reality detecting skill and teach yourself to revise your mental sets rapidly if circumstances go differently than you had hoped.

Frustration amounts to a condition in which your reality testing skills temporarily malfunction. For a few seconds—or a few hours or days if you make a career of getting frustrated—you find yourself unable to accept the reality of what has happened. Someone broke a promise; someone acted unfairly or dishonestly; something you purchased doesn't work or doesn't fit; your car has broken down in the worst of possible circumstances; you missed your plane. In such a situation, you may say, "I can't believe it! I just can't believe it!" What you actually mean is "I won't accept it!" For a moment, you have refused to accept reality as it is unfolding; you cling to your more pleasant alternative conception of things as they should have happened. As soon as you relinquish this temporary form of craziness and begin to try to figure out what to do next, your reality testing skills and your adaptive mode of thinking have returned.

Signal reactions afflict all of us occasionally, but for some people the electrode response has become a pronounced habit. The signal-reactive person may get angry at small provocations, take offense at small slights, get frustrated easily when things unexpectedly go wrong, and become alarmed at small and insignificant setbacks. Overreaction seems to be this person's characteristic neurological style.

Not all signal reactions are strong enough to produce extreme emotional arousal. Many people simply snap-react to ideas with fixed thinking patterns. Sometimes a person will hear a question or statement as he or she prefers to hear it and will react with a favorite slogan, recipe, or formula. For example, a parishioner asked his priest one day, "Father, what causes arthritis?" The priest fixed him with a critical glare and said, "Arthritis? What causes arthritis? Immoral living, that's what causes it. Smoking! Drinking! Running around!" With a bit of a smug look and an especially acid tone, he continued, "And why do you ask?" "Oh, no particular reason, Father," said the parishioner. "It just says here in the paper that the Pope has arthritis."

Probably more people have frustrated themselves by dealing with other people unrealistically in the area of romantic love than in all other areas put together. People throughout Western cultures, especially young people, seem to have the most unrealistic views on matters of "real love," "faithfulness," "loyalty," "commitment," and "obligation." Many people use the term "love" with an almost reverent tone, sometimes to dignify certain feelings and attitudes that are not nearly as noble as they would like to believe. Indeed, most of our notions of romantic love in English-speaking countries trace directly to a handful of poets of the Romantic period—a small group of neurotic, sentimental, passive-dependent men who wrote what little literature the available technology could print and distribute. Most modern books and movies perpetuate the passive-dependent view of romantic love in preference to more mature mutual-growth themes.

> *Love is an ideal thing; marriage is real. Confusing the real with the ideal never goes unpunished.*
>
> GOETHE

The principle of *multiple expectations* offers a great deal of help in avoiding signal reactions and staying on the sane track as things happen in defiance of your plans. If you can approach a situation with a number of possible outcomes in mind, you can work out an appropriate strategy for each of them. In this way you won't get frustrated so easily, because you have no strongly held mental set.

If you're going to panic, at least panic intelligently.

ANONYMOUS

If you feel you snap-react too often for your own good, try making a written inventory of your *grabbers*. A grabber amounts to any external happening that usually or often sets off your strong reaction. Focus especially on *trigger words* such as stupid, dumb, should, and any others that seem especially "loaded" for you. Do you overract to hearing others use profanity or "obscene" language? By studying the list, you can detect some of your more troublesome reaction patterns and spot the ways in which you allow others to get your goat. By thinking about these reactions during your more quiet moments, you can begin to prevent them from arising. You can make your "goat" unavailable.

outgrowing opinionitis

Absurdity, n. A statement or belief manifestly inconsistent with one's own opinion.

AMBROSE BIERCE

The mental "disease" of *opinionitis* probably afflicts more human beings than all known physical diseases put together. Strong opinions, uncritically arrived at and doggedly clung to, confuse more people and create more alienation and misunderstanding than perhaps any other causes. Apparently many people consider it virtually one of nature's laws that a person must have opinions about things. But the tendency to have and hold on to strong opinions in the face of facts that tend to refute them can cause a great deal of trouble for any thinker. The inability or unwillingness to surrender or amend an opinion, when faced with a clear disconfirmation of it, borders on the kind of loss of contact with reality that makes the crazy person crazy.

An extreme example of this inability to adapt to new information is the old tale of the man who went around telling his friends that he was dead. He kept referring to himself in the past tense and frequently reminded others that he had passed on. His friends finally persuaded him to see a psychiatrist. He did so, and after hearing the man's story the therapist asked him to undertake a certain experiment.

The therapist said, "I'd like you to practice, every day for a month, standing in front of a mirror and looking at yourself while you say 'Dead men do not bleed.' We'll make another appointment thirty days from now and have another look at the problem." The man did as he was asked, and at the end of the month he came in again.

The psychiatrist asked the man to stand in front of the mirror, clench his fists, and say "Dead men do not bleed." As the man clenched his fists, the veins in his arms distended. Just as he was about to recite the statement again, the psychiatrist jabbed a scalpel into his arm. As the blood flowed freely down his arm, the man looked at it in amazement and said, "Well, I'll be damned. Dead men do bleed!"

For our purposes here, we can define opinionitis as a general tendency to adopt and hold on to strong opinions with little consideration of the evidence for or against them. The extremely opinionated person has an opinion on just about any subject, question, or issue he happens to have heard about. And if an issue arises which he hasn't heard about, he can form an opinion in a split second, no matter how complex the issue may be. For the extremely opinionated thinker, not having an opinion is a sign of weakness—an indication of a person's lack of resolve, lack of *self*-confidence, and even lack of ability to think things through. Opinionitis amounts to inadvertently making the opinion itself more important than the thinking process that produces it.

You can generally spot the highly opinionated thinker by listening to the kinds of statements he makes or doesn't make. He usually has an answer, regardless of the question. He may seldom say "I don't know" or "I haven't thought about it." He may also seldom ask other people for their views in a simple, straightforward way, encouraging them to share their ideas. He frequently makes flat, unequivocal statements. He seems to regard the goal of each conversation as to make sure the other person agrees with him or, failing that, to vanquish the other person in open debate. He may express his opinions in a strong tone of voice, choosing words that suggest finality—the subject is closed once he has spoken. He may speak in dog-matic, all-ness terms—"everybody knows," "obviously," "no one in his right mind would believe," and "any idiot knows." He may make decisions on the spur of the moment, with little consideration of the evidence and little attempt to identity very many options. Many of the people around him might refer to him as opinionated, and they might approach conversa-tions with him very guardedly to avoid getting bombarded with his fixed opinions. The highly opinionated person may go to great lengths to avoid having to change his mind, at least publicly.

A certain amount of opinionitis and mental rigidity arises when a person suffers from a characteristically low *tolerance for ambiguity*. People vary considerably in this respect. Some people feel quite comfortable in situa-tions having minimal structure, where the rules for behaving are not well defined, where roles and relationships seem to shift, and where problems and issues go unresolved. A certain amount of tolerance for ambiguity enables a person to proceed effectively in a confusing situation, keeping the options open until the situation clears up. Conversely, a low tolerance for ambiguity may lead a person to jump to conclusions, to seize and hold on to fixed opinions, to adopt fixed points of view, and to make decisions prematurely, in order to acquire a comfortable structure for his thinking. The person with low tolerance may unconsciously value certainty, resolution of issues, and situational stability more than he or she values imaginations, creative approaches to problems, and even effective solutions. Ambiguity tolerance is a skill you can increase by consciously working at it.

An extremely low ambiguity tolerance makes a person a *rectangular thinker*—one with an almost compulsive desire for certainty, structure, and familiarity of ideas and solutions. The rectangular mind seeks to arrange and classify every idea, every problem, every issue, every point of view, and every approach into mental pigeonholes. Potential solutions to a problem are either good or bad for this person. People are either good or they are bad. Something either should be done or it should not be done.

> *Most of our so-called reason consists of finding reasons to go on believing as we already do.*
>
> J.H. ROBINSON

If you feel your opinion-making processes need loosening up a bit, you can do several things. You can cure and avoid opinionitis by

1. Verbalizing your opinions more flexibly, that is, beginning sentences with "It seems to me," "At this point, I think," or "Based on what I know about the situation." This will remind you as well as others of the constant possibility of learning something new.
2. Consciously and carefully selecting those issues on which you want to develop

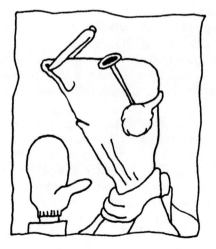

Intolerance Listening to Reason. From LAN-GUAGE IN THOUGHT AND ACTION, Third Edition by S.I. Hayakawa, copyright © 1972 by Harcourt Brace Jovanovich, Inc. Reproduced by permission of the publisher and George Allen & Unwin (Publishers) Ltd.

sound, reliable opinions, leaving others, especially more "distant" issues, open for further thought if you have no particular need to hold opinions about them.

3. Deliberately subjecting your opinions to the risk of revision; re-asking the original question that led you to form the opinion; reconsidering the factors involved; testing to see whether the situation or the issue has changed significantly.

These suggestions all add up to one basic policy: *Try to keep all of your opinions on probation, all the time.* To the extent that you can do so, you can continue to perceive adaptively, to think adaptively, and to form mental models of your world which will enable you to interact with that world adaptively.

understanding other points of view

Bigot n. One who is obstinately and zealously attached to an opinion that you do not entertain.

AMBROSE BIERCE

The ability to recognize and understand more than one *point of view* in a situation enables a thinker to avoid becoming imprisoned in a fixed pattern of reacting. Many people seem to adopt certain points of view, or "positions," in various situations automatically, often without recognizing that there could even be other points of view. A fixed point of view often becomes more apparent when we suddenly find ourselves forced to abandon it in favor of another one.

For example, a Montana rancher took two of his friends out one afternoon to hunt wildcats, in order to show off his new hunting dog. The dog was an enormous beast with huge teeth and a surly disposition. "You can bring your guns if you wanta," said the rancher. "But you won't need 'em. This animal's a born killer. He can finish off any wildcat in this territory."

They went out into the woods and soon spotted a wildcat. When the cat went up a tall tree, the rancher said to his friends, "Now watch. I'll do the rest." He climbed up the tree and began to shake the limb on which the wildcat was perched. With vigorous shaking, the wildcat lost its grip and fell down through the branches. No sooner had it hit the ground than the dog attacked it and killed it.

The rancher's companions were suitably awed. The group treed two more wildcats the same way. The rancher shook them loose, and the dog dispatched each of them in the same brutal fashion. As dusk came on, the rancher said, "Let's get one more wildcat, and then we'll head for supper." Soon they had another cat treed. The rancher climbed the tree, but he had a great deal of difficulty shaking this particular cat loose. It clung to the limb tenaciously. The rancher climbed part of the way out on the limb and began to shake it vigorously, but he lost his balance. As he was falling down through the branches of the tree, he shouted in panic to his friends on the ground, "Shoot the dog!"

Changed his point of view rather quickly, didn't he? This leads us to a simple and useful definition of a point of view, in terms of the ways in which it can affect a person's thinking. We can define a point of view as *a particular way of assigning priorities to the factors involved in a situation.* You may find it useful to train yourself to scan the situations you find yourself in and reflect on the various points of view the other participants might have adopted. This skill can be especially helpful in problem situations where people have trouble reaching agreement or cooperating. If they have adopted fixed points of view as defined by their initial approaches to one another, they may not be able to break out of the deadlock. If you can examine and appreciate more than one of the points of view involved, you can sometimes help them to clarify their problem and to seek compromise solutions. You can also prevent yourself from getting dragged into "win-lose" adversary situations.

Think about the following situations or happenings and see how well you can picture the points of view that each of the participants might adopt:

1. A person threatening to commit suicide
   a. the suicidal person
   b. the person's closest friend or relative
   c. the psychiatrist trying to dissuade the person
2. A research project sponsored with tax funds is ridiculed in the press by a senator; the project included a visit to an Agrentinian brothel to "study the environmental factors involved in prostitution"
   a. a taxpaper who reads the newspaper account
   b. the senator who discovered it
   c. the researcher conducting the grant project
3. A bank error on a customer's account
   a. the customer
   b. the clerk who made the error
   c. the clerk's supervisor
4. A highway construction project creates a traffic bottleneck
   a. a driver who is held up by the flagman
   b. the flagman
   c. the road workers whose safety depends on slowing down the passing cars
5. A father and mother forbid their teenaged daughter to smoke
   a. the daughter
   b. the father or mother
   c. the daughter's friends
6. A customer has waited a long time for service in a crowded restaurant
   a. the customer
   b. the waitress
   c. the restaurant owner

7. A person has terminal cancer, but his doctor and family haven't told him about it
   a. the person with the disease
   b. the doctor
   c. the closest family member
8. An airline flight has been canceled because of equipment difficulties
   a. a passenger in a hurry to get to another city
   b. the ticket agent who delivers the news to 150 passengers
   c. a bystander in the airport
9. An employee gets fired
   a. the employee
   b. the supervisor
   c. a coworker
10. A married woman flirting heavily at a party
    a. the woman
    b. her husband
    c. the flirting companion

Recognize that in any situation, anywhere, any time, *each person has a point of view*, and that point of view determines the priorities that he assigns to the various factors involved. It is impossible not to have a point of view on a situation, even if your point of view is boredom and complete disinterest. Keep in mind that people often disagree, argue, and fail to cooperate because of unrecognized differences in their respective points of view. And recognize also that your own point of view may color the way in which you try to describe another person's point of view.

For example, an elderly lady was attending a fundamentalist church service in the little Arkansas town where she had lived for sixty years. When the preacher spoke out on the evils of drinking, she nodded her head emphatically. When he got to smoking, she agreed wholeheartedly. Point for point, she felt the preacher to be dead right, and she said so to her neighbor sitting beside her. Then the preacher started talking about the evils of dipping snuff. The old lady sat bolt upright, with her jaw set in a look of stern disapproval. "Now he's done quit preachin'," she said, "and took to meddlin'!"

taming your ego

Bore, n. A person who talks when you wish him to listen.

AMBROSE BIERCE

An unruly ego can do more to block adaptive thinking than any other single factor. As a general rule, when an individual allows his sense of personal importance to get tangled up with his logical or perceptual processes, logic and perception will tend to suffer. Ego building often over-shadows adaptive thinking.

For example, much of what passes for casual conversation amounts to two or more participants firing barrages of words at one another, trying to score "one-up points." A person may talk loudly, or rapidly, or emphatically so as to dominate the conversation. In doing so, he boosts his sense of personal importance, but often at the expense of the good will of the others. Later the person may wonder vaguely why people don't seem to seek him out as a luncheon companion or conversation partner.

Or a person may bully others with dogmatic statements, fixed opinions, or ready answers, blocking off their chances to participate effectively in the conversation. Such a person may brag, in obvious or subtle ways, to show how important he is and to score "success points." He may criticize or ridicule other people in the conversation to show how superior he is. He may ridicule people who are not present, ranging all the way from various categorical groups of people to the president or the pope or a movie star or a sports figure, to show how smart he is and how dumb they are. He may drop names of well-known or highly regarded people to score "status points."

Conversation, n. A fair for the display of minor mental commodities, each exhibitor being too intent upon the arrangement of his own wares to observe those of his neighbor.

AMBROSE BIERCE

The chronic ego builder enjoys blasting the ideas and opinions of others, to prove to them—and himself, which is where the real doubt lies—that he is a better thinker. This person reacts to an opposing idea or viewpoint as if it were a poisonous snake to be attacked and eradicated. He falls easily into opinionated mental sets, from which he cannot afford to emerge without feeling that his personal importance will diminish. As we have seen, a fixed opinion can often distort one's perceptions to the point where one's picture of reality becomes dangerously inaccurate. *Ego thinking* and opinionitis often go hand in hand.

Positive, adj. Mistaken at the top of one's voice.

AMBROSE BIERCE

When people settle for the smug feelings of personal power and signifi-cance they get from overriding others with dogmatic statements, flat decla-rations, sweeping generalizations, judgmental labels and categories, they jeopardize their ability to take in fresh information and to change their minds. Statements like "That's just more socialism," "Those guys have a lot of fancy theories, but they've never lived in the real world," "We should take all these soft-headed liberals (Communists, Socialists, hippies, punks, radicals, and so on) and send them over to Russia," or "You kids today don't know how good you've got it" force them into rigid positions on various issues from which they find it very difficult to retreat. Because the chronic ego builder fears more than anything else the loss of a sense of personal importance—that's why he keeps trying to build up his sagging ego—he relegates accurate perception and adaptive thinking to second-class status whenever they conflict with his unconscious mission of grabbing more ego points.

Many people become progressively more rigid and unchanging as they grow older. Although advancing age does not automatically mean increasing ego rigidity, for the majority of human beings this seems to be the case. Typically, a person who passes through the age range of about forty to fifty begins to set personal attitudes firmly in concrete. The person finds fewer and fewer things to be interested in, and there seem to be fewer and fewer topics of any "real" importance about which he doesn't know. He tends to see himself as becoming more "mature," which may really amount to becoming more fossilized. At a certain stage he begins to talk about the old days, to criticize the present times, and to talk about the "younger generation" in scornful terms. His case of mental arthritis is fully advanced.

> Denunciation of the young is a necessary part of the hygiene of older people, and greatly assists in the circulation of their blood.
>
> LOGAN P. SMITH

Picture the chronic ego builder as analogous to a man driving an ancient flivver with soft, leaky tires. He drives along all right for a while, but soon the tires—analogous to his feeling of personal importance—begin to deflate. When this happens, he must stop going where he's going and pump them up. He does a little ego building until he feels better, and then he can jump back in and get on his way, but only until the tires start to deflate again. Each time he has to stop and pump up his leaky "ego-tires," he gets sidetracked from more positive mental objectives. A person with extremely leaky ego-tires spends so much time pumping them up, especially at the expense of other people, that he never gets very far. A person with high-quality ego-tires, a feature psychologists refer to as a healthy level of ego strength, doesn't need to spend much time in this sidetracked mode.

The chronic ego builder may detest more than anything else having to admit being wrong or letting other people know they have caused him to change his mind. The ego builder may have unconsciously associated the idea of changing his mind with weakness, lack of confidence, and lack of thinking ability. The unconscious notion is that one should be able to make up one's mind firmly about any issue, once and for all. Changing one's mind shows that it was never made up properly in the first place. For this reason, the chronic ego builder may resort to some highly combative conversational ploys, logical dodges, rationalizations, and semantic tricks to avoid having to give up an opinion or belief that doesn't hold water.

> *A man should never be ashamed to own that he has been in the wrong, which is but saying in other words that he is wiser today than he was yesterday.*
>
> ALEXANDER POPE

In addition to ego building, some people invest a fair amount of mental energy in ego-defense processes. Many very shy people, for example, will go to great lengths to avoid exposing their thinking processes to others, for fear that people will laugh at them or disapprove of them. The extremely shy person lives in constant fear of ridicule and disapproval from others, and his ego-defense strategies show it. What may seem like "illogical" behavior to another person seems very logical to the shy person, in terms of his internal priority system, which has as its primary rule: Protect your ego from the slings and arrows of the outside world first and then accomplish whatever else you can within that constraint.

You can begin to tame your ego by adopting several simple strategies. First, teach yourself to say three things freely, openly, confidently, and without apology. They are

1. I don't know.
2. I made a mistake.
3. I changed my mind.

If you can say these things, you can think them. For example, in a conversation another person might ask you a factual question. Even though you feel you "should" know, if the objective fact is that you do not know, you must carefully avoid the trap of trying to pretend that you do. You can sidestep the trap simply by saying "I don't know." The same applies in business situations. You may be surprised to find that no one else in the room knows either, and they feel relieved to hear you say so. Then everyone becomes free to find out.

> *I am not ashamed to confess I am ignorant of what I do not know.*
>
> CICERO

Practice spotting the ego-building strategies in various interpersonal situations, both as others use them and as you use them. Study the ways they influence the thinking of the people involved. Review your language habits and make sure that you don't unnecessarily box yourself into fixed opinions, points of view, or adversary positions from which you cannot retreat without feeling a loss of your sense of personal importance. Teach yourself to lay claim to your right not to know various things, your right to get confused occasionally, to change your mind from time to time, and above all to explore your world for new and significant information. If you can keep your ego firmly under control in most situations, you can think flexibly and adaptively. And curiously, you may find that this style of thinking and talking brings you much closer to other people and makes for much more enjoyable social interactions, which in turn provide much more reinforcement for your ego than the clumsy techniques of ego building could ever have brought.

learning to change your mind

Faced with the choice between changing one's mind and proving there is no need to do so, almost everyone gets busy on the proof.

JOHN KENNETH GALBRAITH

A young man was hitchhiking through Kentucky when a farmer driving an extremely dilapidated old truck stopped to give him a lift. As they rode along, they talked of many things. One topic of conversation concerned the local moonshine whiskey. The farmer extolled the merits of moonshine, although the young man allowed as how he didn't drink very much and would probably find the stuff too strong for his tastes. "Nonsense!" said the farmer. "You gotta try some. Matter of fact, I got a little taste here behind the seat." He fished around behind him and finally produced a small liquor jug with some oily-looking fluid in it. "Here," he said, handing the jar to the lad. "Take a pull!" "Oh, no thanks," said the young man. "I really don't think I care for any." "No, I insist," pressed the farmer. "Have some." "No, thanks—really." The farmer became more and more insistent, to the point of angrily stopping the truck, reaching into the back seat, and fetching a sawed-off shotgun. He pointed the gun at the lad and roared, "I said, take a pull!" "Okay! Okay! I've changed my mind! I guess I will have some after all." The young man took a few enthusiastic swallows before he realized how powerful the stuff really was. His throat muscles went into spasm, his eyes watered, and he gagged intensely. "Whataya think of it?" said the farmer. "Good, ain't it?" "Yeah. . .good. . .good," gasped the lad. Then the farmer handed him the shotgun and grinned. "Here! Now you hold the gun on me and make me take a pull!"

Some people seem to change their minds only at gunpoint. Opinionitis, ego thinking, and semantic rigidity often form a deadly combination. A person who can't change his mind easily and flexibly when new facts or points of view emerge has imprisoned himself in one of the most self-limiting of all mental orientations.

It ain't what a man don't know that makes him a fool, but what he knows that ain't so.

JOSH BILLINGS

You can consider changing your mind to be a mental skill, just as adding a column of figures, recalling the words to a song, or making a decision are mental skills. When the circumstances call for it, you need to be able to relinquish the mental set associated with your opinion or point of view, and take a fresh look at the facts.

You can improve your skill at changing your mind by keeping all of your opinions on permanent probation, by staying alert to new facts and points of view, by practicing semantic flexibility, and by repeated practice in consciously changing your mind. For a few days, pay close attention to the occasions on which you do change your mind and consciously review them. Verbalize the process of dropping one point of view and replacing it with a more effective one. Take the opportunity occasionally to mention in conversation that you've changed your mind about something. Develop the confidence of occasionally telling others that you have made a mistake or that new information has enabled you to see a situation or problem more clearly.

If the notion of changing your mind still gives you trouble, try substituting another term for it. Think of it as going through a decision process a second time, with more up-to-date information—I call this re-deciding. You can say to yourself and to others, "I took another look at that problem, and I re-decided on it. Now I think. . . ." Make sure you can re-decide when necessary without feeling guilty or placing your ego in jeopardy. Exercise your occasional right to change your mind, and don't be intimidated by cutting remarks others may make. You can simply say, "Today I'm smarter than I was yesterday. Now I understand it better."

The only man who can change his mind is the man who's got one.

EDWARD NOYES WESTCOTT

being happy: is there life after birth?

The mass of men lead lives of quiet desperation.

HENRY DAVID THOREAU

This year, more than 25,000 people in the United States will commit suicide—the final act of self-defeat for a person who cannot or will not think straight. Most of these people will blast out their malfunctioning brains with firearms of one kind or another, rather than amend their faulty mental models of themselves and their worlds.

Over 12 million Americans are confirmed alcoholics. At least a million of those, according to the American Hospital Association, are teenagers. Possibly another 10 million people have so much difficulty in working out the puzzle of life that they have become borderline alcoholics.

More than 6 million people this year will reside in or temporarily visit mental hospitals. Over 25,000 psychiatrists earn an average of more than $40,000 a year treating unhappy Americans who look for solutions to their problems in a therapeutic setting. Tranquilizer drugs such as Valium, which act to depress the entire central nervous system (and to dim one's awareness of problem thoughts), now outsell all other prescription drugs—including antibiotics—by a wide margin.

Clearly, homo sapiens—thinking man—still has much to learn. The ability to maintain a positive state of mind and to face, solve, and adjust to life's problems as they come along is the functional thinking skill of happying. And it obviously does not come naturally for a great many people.

> Most people are about as happy as they make up their minds to be.
>
> **ABRAHAM LINCOLN**

The chronically unhappy person seems to labor under the cruel delusion that he is unhappy because of unfortunate circumstances, events, and processes happening in his world. He doesn't realize that he is unhappy because of *his evaluation* of these circumstances, events, and processes. The unhappy person fails to grasp the all-important fact that positives and negatives do not exist in "nature;" that "success" and "failure" do not exist as elements of the flow of reality processes outside his head. This person doesn't realize that these are *mental constructs*, which he superimposes on his perceptions of the world. The chronically unhappy person fails to grasp the fact that one *decides* to be happy or unhappy.

> I had no shoes and I complained, until I met a man who had no feet.
>
> **ANONYMOUS**

It's remarkable to me how willing some people are to be unhappy; how they habitually confirm their negative evaluations of their relationship to their world. A person may stay miserably married for years, never making a move to break out of a toxic life pattern. Another person may work for years at a job he hates, at a place he hates, with people whose company he doesn't enjoy, for people who treat him like dirt. Others may continually complain about their lost opportunities and the raw deals life has handed them. All of these people have one thing in common—*inaction.* They drift with their circumstances, settling for much less than they could have, chalking it up to the unfairness of the world, and marching along on the treadmill to oblivion. A person who isn't busy living is busy dying. Each of us *chooses* to be happy or unhappy, and we act out our choices in the ways in which we construct our lives.

> *The three great requirements for a happy life are: something to do, something to love, and something to hope for.*
>
> JOSEPH ADDISON

Alfred Korzybski liked to identify three categories of human functioning in terms of the ability to perceive reality, construct mental models of it, and to modify and match these models successfully against that reality. He believed that probably fifteen percent of people fell into the category of downright crazy—so maladjusted as to warrant the label of *insane.* At the other end of the conceptual scale, according to Korzybski, we find the fifteen percent of truly *sane* people, who have developed their mental modeling and reality testing skills well enough to liberate themselves from a great deal of the everyday frustration in dealing with their worlds.

And making up the great majority at the center of the "bell curve" of human adjustment, we find the merely *unsane* people. They make up the majority of "normally maladjusted" human beings, able to grow up reasonably well, get jobs, have careers, raise families, pay taxes, live pedestrian lives, grow old, and die. Korzybski's unsane person corresponds to Thoreau's "mass of men (and women) who lead lives of quiet desperation," to de la Bruyere's person who simply "forgets to live," and to my definition of the "mechanical thinker."

One of the hallmarks of maturity and personal adjustment, and an important difference between the highly sane person and the unsane person, is simply the conscious *acceptance of responsibility* for one's life. The highly immature person wants to hold anyone and everyone else accountable and responsible for his happiness. This person has learned to blame his troubles and unsolved problems on circumstances, family background, ethnic origins, parents, boss, mate, or just bad luck. By externalizing responsibility, he avoids having to make choices, having to take risks, and having to live with the consequences of his own actions. Many immature or poorly adjusted people seem to spend their lives in a kind of half-hearted "cruise" mode, not going anywhere in particular, not exactly satisfied with where they are, and not sure what to do. They seem to be more or less waiting—as if somehow a lucky accident will suddenly make them happier.

Responsibility, n. A detachable burden easily shifted to the shoulders of God, Fate, Fortune, Luck or one's neighbor. In the days of astrology it was customary to unload it upon a star.

AMBROSE BIERCE

Another important component of personal adjustment involves actualizing your most important personal values on a day-to-day basis. To the extent that you act in accordance with your primary values and needs, you make yourself happy and you grow as a person. To the extent that you give up on your values in order to please others, gain material possessions, earn acceptance or approval, or avoid conflict, you work against yourself and undermine your personal sense of harmony.

A story attributed to Mark Twain illustrates the way in which our values shape our behavior. As a boy, he once had an opportunity to steal a watermelon from an unattended fruit wagon. He carried it off and sat down in a secluded spot, ready to devour it. "As I looked at that watermelon," Twain is said to have remarked, "a funny feeling came over me. I couldn't eat it. I knew then what I had to do. I carried it back to the fruit wagon, put it back, and took a ripe one."

Another key aspect of personal adjustment involves your general social competence. So many books have been written about getting along with other people that one would think the subject must be very complicated. It isn't, in my opinion. Getting along well with others mostly means getting them to like you—to feel attracted to you rather than repelled by you. If people like you and want to be close to you, then you can work many kinds of magic in dealing with them and persuading them. If they don't like you, very little else you can do will make things go smoothly.

In every human heart are a tiger, a pig, an ass and a nightingale. Diversity of character is due to their unequal activity.

AMBROSE BIERCE

My formula for making people like you starts with a very simple policy: the "no-bust" policy. Those who go around "busting" other people—acting abrasively, putting them down, ridiculing them, combating them, refusing to cooperate with them, imposing on them, rejecting them, and refusing to nurture them and support them make themselves undesirable to others. Those who go around affirming and supporting others, helping them, cooperating and compromising with them, and helping them to feel good about themselves make themselves desirable and extremely attractive to others.

We can achieve more of our potential, grow and mature more fully, and live happier and freer lives by consciously following our own values. We can revoke the authority over our feelings which we have vested in others, and release ourselves from excessive obligation to low-level wants and fears such as

1. The fear of failing.
2. The dread of other people's scorn, ridicule, anger, or disapproval.
3. The dread of aloneness.
4. The useless emotion of guilt and the manipulation by others it permits.
5. The slavish need to conform to the standards of others.
6. The squalid ego kick of one-upping other people.
7. The grim compulsion of power seeking.
8. The self-betrayal of status seeking.
9. The treadmill of pursuing money for its own sake.
10. The pathetic dependency on the approval of others.

The ancient Chinese philosopher Lao Tzu had some thought-provoking observations about living skillfully. His legacy, *The Way of Life*, contains the distillation of many centuries of Chinese thinking on human values. Witter Bynner has translated Lao Tzu's work into an inspiring little book, written in English verse. Here is one of my favorite excerpts from *The Way of Life According to Lao Tzu*:

> Not to have edges that catch
> But to remain untangled,
> Unblinded,
> unconfused,
> Is to find balance,
> And he who holds balance beyond sway of love or hate,
> Beyond reach of profit or loss,
> Beyond care of praise or blame,
> Has attained the highest post in the world.

LAO TZU

7

finding facts and facing facts

 Get your facts first, and then you can distort them as much as you please.

MARK TWAIN

The functional skill of *fact finding*, together with the willingness to face facts squarely and to keep an open mind to them, enables you to supply yourself with the necessary material of thought. While the mentally sedentary person usually seeks out information about the world only as a reaction to specific requirements to solve problems or get what he wants, the mentally active person makes a general habit of tuning in to what's going on. A mentally active approach to living places faith in the value of finding out things. Whether you call this habit of the adaptive thinker curiosity, inquisitiveness, or just taking an interest in life, it involves a specific set of skills and specific actions. The skill of fact finding means providing your brain with a steady flow of information, ideas, possibilities, and new points of view so that you can solve problems and get what you want by dealing with situations competently when they arise.

how do you know what you know?

We don't know one millionth of one percent about anything.

THOMAS EDISON

Think about this: How much of what you presently "know" came to you by means other than your direct personal observation? Think about all your so-called academic knowledge, such as historical facts and figures, literature, news information, economics, mathematics, and the like. You probably got much of this information by reading books and by hearing people tell about it. It would, of course, be impossible for you to know from personal observation what really went on at the Battle of Hastings in 1066, or even if there really was a battle or a Hastings, and if there were, which side won, and so on. You quite routinely rely on other sources of information to augment the limited information-gathering potential of your own observation.

History records the names of royal bastards but cannot tell us the origin of wheat.

JEAN HENRI FABRÉ

As discussed in Chapter 5, the four levels of verifiability, or "directness," are personal observations, reports, inferences, and assumptions. How would you assess the approximate proportions of these four levels of uncertainty in supplying your knowledge? My estimate would look something like Figure 7.1. Probably a very small fraction of our practical, everyday operational knowledge comes from our own direct observations. A huge proportion comes from reading, talking to other people, making inferences from available information, and making reasonable assumptions.

WHAT YOU "KNOW"

Figure 7.1   How do you know what you know?

The next question, which we can only answer subjectively as well, is: *how much of what you think is true really isn't true?* How many of the reports you receive could actually be erroneous, deliberately contrived, or colored by the biases of those who give them? How many unexamined inferences and assumptions might you have made and might you be taking as absolute unquestioned truth, which might not stand up to logical scrutiny if you had more facts?

The perceptual malfunction of *inference-observation confusion,* or accepting inferences uncritically as if they had the strength of observed facts, can lead to a great deal of confusion and misunderstanding. A story involving a small boy making a purchase in a drugstore illustrates how uncritical inferences can influence one's behavior. The lad went to the counter and asked to buy a widely-advertised brand of feminine napkins. The lady behind the counter asked him which of several varieties his mother wanted. "They're not for my mother," he replied. "Oh," mused the clerk, "your sister, then?" "Nope." Intrigued, she said, "If you don't mind my asking, who are you buying these for?" "For myself," the boy replied. "The magazine advertisement said with Tampax you can swim, ride horses, and play tennis. That's for me."

As a practical matter, all of us must proceed with the business of living by relying on "maps'" of the world which we have taken on reasonable faith and which we have not tested and often cannot test. You have no choice but to live your life based on a constant stream of reports, descriptions, judgments, inferences, and assumptions coming from a multitude of sources. From this abundance of uncertain information, you piece together a collection of stored mental "models" of the world and its workings, which becomes literally your world view. As shown in Figure 7.2, your brain calls various of these memory models into play as you think, mixing them strategically with the incoming current sensory data. This mixture forms the basic subject matter of your thought at any one moment, and your thought processes about it result directly in your specific behavior. In closed-loop fashion your behavior affects some portion of your world, and you again perceive the world (at least potentially) as changed. In this way you adapt continuously to the ongoing world outside your head.

It's interesting to pause occasionally to reflect on how much of our information about the world we have taken utterly for granted. How many of our common beliefs might not really be true? Is your heart really located on the left side of your chest, or squarely in the center? Do drowning people really come up three times? Did George Washington really throw a dollar

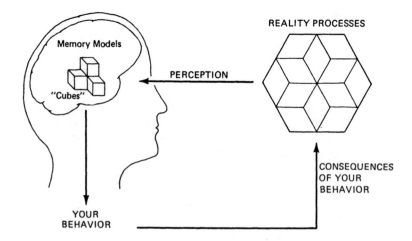

Figure 7.2   Your brain builds memory models from its perceptual experience.

across the Potomac? Is it against the law to deface an American coin? Does lightning never strike twice in the same place? Will hot water freeze faster than cold water? Did Abraham Lincoln write his speech for Gettysburg on the back of an envelope?

In his intriguing book, *The Dictionary of Misinformation*, Tom Burnham gives some alternative reports on a number of matters of widely accepted "common knowledge." For example, with respect to the common notion that Abner Doubleday, an American, invented the game of baseball, Burnham says

That Abner Doubleday invented baseball at Cooperstown, New York in 1839, is so firmly enshrined in the American consciousness as to amount to an article of faith, an attack upon which verges on heresy. Yet this is far from historical fact; it was, rather, simply arbitrarily decided by a commission appointed by the president of a sporting goods company, A.G. Spalding . . . None of them had any qualifications as researchers or historians.

. . . That there certainly was an English game very nearly identical even to baseball as played today is obvious from a description of "Rounders" in The Boy's Own Book, first published in London in 1828.

. . . The founding of the Baseball Hall of Fame at Cooperstown in 1939 has, of course, tended to establish and maintain the Doubleday story as gospel. [1]

Burnham goes on to demolish the notions that Lizzie Borden was an axe murderer (she was acquitted, he says), that Charles Darwin was the first person to advance the ideas of evolution and survival of the fittest, and that the Declaration of Independence was signed on July 4, 1776.

These provocative reports may make you pause and take stock of this business of knowing and not knowing. Of course, we must remind ourselves that Burnham's book is itself a report and could be said to contain a number of inferences drawn from reports available to him. Many of these inferences might seem to fit the reported facts better than the commonly accepted notions. But we must nevertheless remember that Burnham is asking us to substitute one set of verbal maps for another.

So apparently all of us are destined to be continually misinformed about many things. We know many things that are not so, and we still manage to live our lives and function reasonably well in the face of such an uncertain "data bank" about the world. We live in a mental domain, which Adelbert Ames, an early investigator of perceptual psychology, called our *assumptive world*. However, people do vary considerably in the extent of their misinformation and in the degree to which they actively seek out new information, take opportunities to correct or update their mental models, and expose themselves to new sources of information.

[1]Tom Burnam, *The Dictionary of Misinformation* (New York: Thomas Y. Crowell, 1975), p. 20. Used with permission.

Life is the art of drawing sufficient conclusions from insufficient premises.

SAMUEL BUTLER

Semanticist Alfred Korzybski drew a distinction between two alternative mental orientations a person might have with respect to the getting of information about the world. On one hand, a person might employ a strong *intensional orientation* characterized by heavy reliance on his stored memory models when he needs information with which to think about the world. The other, the *extensional orientation*, involves a highly adaptive reliance on one's own senses to acquire new information and to keep his memory models up-to-date.[2]

The intensional orientation, when taken to extremes, leads one to rely on reports, memories, inferences, and assumptions so heavily as to get dangerously out of touch with reality in certain areas. In some cases, what you don't know can kill you. For example, three burglars reportedly tried to open a safe in a small factory in Vang, Norway. They attached an explosive device to the door and hid in the next room until it went off. Unfortunately, the explosion was so powerful it demolished the entire building and buried them under a pile of rubble. The safe contained no money—it contained explosives.

An old story about three men of the cloth who went fishing together also illustrates the potential impact of not knowing what one needs to know. The three friends were a rabbi, a Catholic priest, and a Baptist minister. They were sitting quietly in their boat in the shallow murky water just off the shore. After a while, the rabbi got up, stepped out of the boat, walked across the top of the lake to the shore, picked up some items from their campsite, and returned the same way. The priest didn't look up, but the minister was flabbergasted. Not wanting to appear naive, and certainly not unspiritual, he suppressed his amazement and said nothing.

Presently the priest got up, stepped out of the boat, walked across the water to the shore, and took care of a similar errand. Again the minister was dumbfounded, but made no comment.

Eventually the minister had an errand to take care of himself. Not wishing to appear uninitiated, he stood up, bravely stepped out of the boat onto the surface of the lake, and immediately plummeted out of sight. As he was floundering about in the water trying to get back to the boat, the rabbi leaned over and said to the priest, "I think we'd better tell him where the rocks are."

Assumptions can be especially dangerous mental strategies characteris-

[2]For the original theory, see Alfred Korzybski, *Science and Sanity* (Lakeville, Conn.: International Non-Aristotelian Library Pub. Co., 1933), p. 171. For a much more readable explanation of the concepts of general semantics, see S.I. Hayakawa, *Language in Thought and Action* (New York: Harcourt Brace Jovanovich, Inc., 1939, revised 1972).

tic of the intensional orientation. Although you could not possibly go about the business of livng without making countless assumptions every day, it does pay to keep an eye on the more important assumptions you make and to try whenever possible to subject them to the test of investigation.

One of my favorite illustrations of the extreme intensional orientation concerned a child in art class, busily drawing and coloring a picture. When the teacher asked him what he was drawing, he said, "This is going to be a picture of God." A bit flustered, the teacher said, "But—nobody really knows what God looks like." "Well," said the youngster with some assurance, "they will when I get this picture finished."

Much of what passes for education in our institutions amounts to the transference of various abstract maps of world processes from the book to the teacher's notes to the student's notes without passing through the mind of either. In *Language Habits in Human Affairs*, Irving J. Lee cites the following example:

In a little school just outside Baton Rouge, Louisiana, the teacher had been hearing a class read a lesson on birds in one of the standard textbooks. To drive home a point from the lesson, she asked a boy, "When do the robins come?"

The pupil promptly answered, "In the fall."

"Now, Jimmie," urged the teacher, "read the lesson carefully again."

After he had droned out the text a second time, she said cheerily, "Now, Jimmie, when do the robins come?"

More hesitantly and sullenly, he answered again, "The robins come in the fall."

"James, James!" shouted the teacher, "read that lesson again. Now tell me when do the robins come?"

Almost in tears, the boy finally answered, "The robins come in the spring." And so they do—in Boston where the text was written. But in Louisiana, just in order to avoid the northern winter, they come in the fall, as the boy well knew.[3]

A story concerning General George S. Patton illustrates the alternative orientation to the intensional one, namely the extensional orientation. As the leaders of an Allied armor division were stalled near Coutance, France, studying their rudimentary map and trying to figure out where they could ford the Seine River, Patton came stomping up and demanded to know what was holding them up. When they reported that they hadn't yet discovered a place shallow enough to ford, Patton pointed to his wet trousers and calmly informed them that he had just personally waded across the river at a point a few hundred yards away. They hurriedly investigated the river for themselves and proceeded to get their unit moving again.

[3]Irving J. Lee, *Language Habits in Human Affairs* (New York: Harper & Row Pub., 1941), p. 118. Excerpted with permission from the Greenwood Press edition.

One look is worth a hundred reports.

JAPANESE PROVERB

the art of awareness

I who am blind can give one hint to those who see—one admonition to those who would make full use of the gift of sight: Use your eyes as if tomorrow you would be stricken blind. And the same method can be applied to the other senses. Hear the music of voices, the song of a bird, the mighty strains of an orchestra, as if you would be stricken deaf tomorrow. Touch each object you want to touch as if tomorrow your tactile sense would fail. Smell the perfume of flowers, taste with relish each morsel, as if tomorrow you could never smell and taste again.

HELEN KELLER

In the late 1930s and 1940s, a researcher named Adelbert Ames performed some experiments with human perception, which produced some very interesting results and triggered a much wider interest among researchers in the phenomena of human awareness. The most intriguing experiment involved a specially constructed room, visible only from the restricted angle of a peephole. The view of this room, as a perceptual input, defied all efforts of the viewer's brain to make sense out of it. The design of the room violated a rule deeply imbedded in western visual tradition—it had no rectangular surfaces and no right angles. For example, the wall farthest from the viewer was higher than the closer wall, and the ceiling actually tilted upward as it receded from the viewer. The side walls were shaped to fit the end walls and the ceiling so that the whole arrangement, if seen from a distance, would form a trapezoidal box, similar to the illustration in Figure 7.3.

Ames wanted to experiment with the tendency of the human brain to reinterpret ambiguous features of the environment and to reorganize its images of them to fit known patterns. In particular, Ames theorized, a western thinker lives in a highly rectangular visual world with an enormous number of right angles, perpendicular planes, and square corners. (Think about this as you look around you; how many rectangular shapes do you see?) Ames believed that the western brain learns to use a certain reinterpretive rule starting from early childhood, namely, "When I see a surface which appears to my eye to be shaped like a trapezoid, it is actually a rectangle which is momentarily turned at an angle to my line of sight." The brain "learns" this rule because a person sees so many rectangular objects and sees them moved about within his field of view. When you look at a piece of paper square-on, you see it as a rectangle. But when you tilt the top edge away from you, your retinal image of the top edge gets smaller while that of the near edge stays the same. Your brain now sees a trapezoid,

Figure 7.3   This "distorted," non-rectangular room confuses the brain by eliminating the customary structural cues. (Photo © Norman Snyder)

but your memory enables you to "correct" the image and to assume it is still the same rectangle you saw a few seconds ago. Ames called this effect the phenomenon of *constancy*.

Ames theorized that this mental rule—the long side of a trapezoid is actually the near edge of a rectangle—was so deeply imbedded in the western brain, because it worked almost infallibly in the situations most people experienced, that the brain might be fooled in some circumstances. The brain might apply this rule inflexibly in ambiguous situations and actually "see" rectangles when there were none to see.

This is indeed what happened. When subjects looked into the peephole at the unusual room, they reported seeing a regular room. Then Ames placed a person in the room and had him stand at various points while the subject peered through the peephole. This became a disconcerting experience for many viewers; the person seemed to grow larger and smaller as he walked about the odd-shaped room! Standing close to the front wall, the person seemed normal in height. As he walked toward the back wall, he became shorter in relation to the height of the ceiling, which actually got higher. With one person standing in the near zone of the viewer and another standing near the far wall, the confused viewer would get the impression that the distant person was almost a midget, while the near one was a virtual giant. Apparently their brains were more willing to believe that people could grow and shrink than to abandon the rule that the long side of a trapezoid is really the near edge of a rectangle.[4]

The difference between science and magic rests with the beholder, and his knowledge.

ANONYMOUS

The subject of human awareness—the process by which our brains find out what little they can about the ongoing world—has fascinated investigators for centuries. We have learned that perception, the neural mechanics of awareness, takes place not in the sense organs but in the brain itself. For example, the French scientist and mathematician René Descartes proved that the eyeball actually produces an upside-down image, which the brain learns to interpret. Descartes mounted the eyeball of a recently slaughtered ox in an aperture on his window shutter. Having carefully scraped away the surface tissue on the back of the eyeball, making it nearly transparent, Descartes could peer through it in the direction of the lens and see an inverted image of the scene outside his room.

The brain can be fooled rather easily, since it can only process the sensory data delivered to it. If the input arrives in unfamiliar form, the brain must try to make sense of it. For example, a hard blow on the back of the head may produce the subjective impression of "seeing stars" for a split second, because of the sudden stimulation of the neurons of the visual cortex located in that region. When you become dizzy, your brain may represent the room and the objects in it as seeming to spin or to jump back and forth in fragmentary arcs.

You can do a simple experiment to demonstrate how easily you can fool your brain into misinterpreting what it's receiving. Stand on your right foot with your left foot tucked behind your right leg for good balance. After a few seconds, when you have balanced yourself stably, close your left eye and look with your right eye at some convenient point or object. Now very carefully and gently press with your right index finger on the outside of your right eyeball, making sure you press on the eyelid rather than directly on the eyeball. As you gently displace the eyeball ever so slightly horizontally toward your nose, keep looking at the object. You will probably find that you immediately begin to lose your balance and sway to the right side, as your brain automatically sends out motor commands to correct what it erroneously decides is an out-of-balance condition. Try this with both sides of your body, switching to the left foot and left eye. You may even notice this effect while sitting down, as your upper body automatically sways toward the side of the eyeball you press on.

[4]Rudolf Flesch describes the Ames experiments briefly in Rudolf Flesch, *The Art of Clear Thinking* (New York: Harper & Row Pub., 1951), p. 21. See also Earl C. Kelley, *Education for What Is Real* (New York: Harper & Brothers, 1947).

The magician also depends on the fact that your brain gets confused when it receives ambiguous inputs. He contrives to have you believe a certain thing, and the essence of the trick is the surprise you feel when he demolishes your perceptual set with something you didn't expect to see and considered impossible.

> *Miracle, n. An act or event out of the order of nature and unaccountable, as beating a normal hand of four kings and an ace with four aces and a king.*
>
> **AMBROSE BIERCE**

Have you ever sat in your car waiting for a traffic light to change? Perhaps you got interested in some other sight, such as someone of the opposite sex walking along the street. When you glanced back at the light and found that it had changed within two or three seconds, did you reflect for an instant on the perishable nature of your awareness of your world? Perhaps the light switched at the very instant you looked away. Television personality and writer Hugh Downs told a story during one telecast that illustrates this sampling feature of perception.

I came into the recording studio one morning, ready to tape a show. I had to wait a little while for the crew to get things ready. As I sat down on a bench, I leaned forward and rested my face in my hands. For a few seconds I rubbed my eyes with the palms of my hands. When I lifted my head and opened my eyes I couldn't see anything! Utter blackness! For a few seconds I felt panicky, until I heard the hubbub among the crew. By one of those perversities of nature, we had a power failure at the exact moment I closed my eyes. I'll always remember how I felt at that instant, when I was afraid I'd gone blind.

Not only do your perceptual processes influence your current thinking, but later on they influence your memory of the situation you've perceived. Your brain automatically and inevitably distorts your experiences to some extent at the very instant of perception, and it is these perceptions that you remember rather than the original input. All of your memory is to some extent *interpretive* memory—consisting of "facts," evaluations, and reactions which your brain assembled from the sense impressions delivered to it, filed away for later use, and eventually recalled within the context of some mental task. Your brain's handling of the mental task that creates the need to recall something can distort the memory model again, just as if you were perceiving it for the first time. Many experiments have shown that we don't always recall things exactly as they were, but rather we tend to recall them *as we feel they should have been.*

A group of experiments at Harvard University during World War II focused on this process of *interpretive recall* in connection with the development and spread of rumors. Experimenters showed a series of pictures to various people, and thereafter asked them to describe in as much detail as possible what they had seen. They found that most people tended to reinterpret ambiguous features of the scenes in their individual characteristic ways and to reproduce them in more "recognizable" form. The reports came out more like the pictures *should* have been—in the unconscious judgments of the observers—than they actually were.

Perhaps because most of the test subjects were white, the razor that started in the hand of a white man seen in a picture arguing with a black man ended up in the black man's hand. A movie marquee with a sign announcing a movie with GENE ANTRY got translated into GENE AUTRY. A road sign showing distance in kilometers came out as one showing miles.[5]

British psychologist F.C. Bartlett studied this memory process extensively, showing that the brain's normal mode of operation is to try to make its memory models match up with convenient mental patterns to reduce the amount of attention it must give to the task of filing and retrieving data. According to Bartlett, "Remembering is an imaginative reconstruction or construction . . . it is hardly ever exact."[6]

The same aspects of perception that can lead you to distort your experiences can lead you to distort your memories when you attempt to recall them. For example, if you describe to another person some past incident you found disconcerting and embarrassing, you might be tempted to change the relative emphasis and to describe it in terms less critical of yourself. Have you ever heard two children give their competing descriptions of how a fight started? They may not actually lie, but their imaginative reconstructions of each other's unreasonable behavior may show a great deal of mental flexibility. Each of us has certain personal interests and biases in any situation in which we need to recall something, and these biases are bound to play a part in the way in which we reconstruct our images of the world at some previous time.

In some cases, the words you use to talk about what you perceive can strongly influence the way in which you remember it. In one experiment, people were asked to look at simple line-drawing figures and to reproduce them immediately afterward from memory. Each of the figures was slightly ambiguous and could be described in several ways, for example, a crescent moon or the letter "C," a pair of eyeglasses or a dumbbell, and a trowel or a pine tree. In naming the figures, the experimenters used one set of terms with one group of people and a second set of terms with another group. A large number of people in each group unwittingly distorted their reproductions of the simple figures in ways that emphasized visual features corresponding to the names given by the experimenters.

For most of us the visual channel provides by far the richest source of sensory input. Your brain relies so heavily on information from your eyes

[5]Flesch, *The Art of Clear Thinking*, p. 22.
[6]Ibid., p. 21.

that you tend to consider your visual field identical with the outside world. Like most people, you have relied on your vision ever since you were a small child. You have probably come to think about your images and the real world interchangeably and to believe without even thinking about it that what you see is "reality." But, in fact, what your brain "sees" is merely a pattern of electrical stimulation at the nerve ends.

Biofeedback researchers Elmer and Alyce Green say

. . . no one has ever seen the outside world. All that we can be aware of are our interpretations of the electrical pattern in the brain. Our only view of the world is on our own living internal television screen. The occipital (visual) cortex is essentially the screen, and the eyes are two cameras that give us information about the frequencies and intensities of light. When the eyes are open we say we are looking at the world, but it is the occipital cortex that we actually "look" at. What we "see" are millions of brain cells firing in appropriate ways to display the retinal activity.[7]

For this reason the study of perception focuses primarily on visual processes. We can also extend the findings of visual perception to cover auditory perception, especially of spoken language. These two primary forms, visual perception and hearing other people speak, provide the largest share of our information about the world.

In the following sections, we will study human perception in terms of five interrelated principles:

1. Recognition
2. Interpretation
3. Expectation
4. Intention
5. Context

the principle of recognition

The principle of *recognition* means that most of your perception simply involves trying to match selected cues from the world outside to your stored memory models. Through a typical day, you switch your attention rapidly from one point to another to another, merely checking the elements of the situation. Relatively rarely do you concentrate closely on some unfamiliar sight. Instead you usually recognize the dominant cues or key features of what you see. As you read the words on this page, your brain picks up the shapes of the letters, and in some cases whole word patterns, and finds matching patterns in your memory. This automated recognition frees your cortex for the more complex task of deriving an abstract meaning from the verbal message.

[7]Elmer and Alyce Green, *Beyond Biofeedback* (New York: Dell Pub. Co., 1977), p. 119.

Because your brain is so thoroughly optimized as a pattern-recognizing organ, you have very little trouble in recognizing anything you've seen a number of times before. You can derive meaning from a relatively abstract version of a world process, based on the important cues. A story concerning the famous artist Pablo Picasso illustrates this automatic process of recognition. A young sailor had been introduced to Picasso and was questioning him about the "meaning" of modern art. The sailor did not particularly like abstract visual forms, preferring something more familiar. "All this abstract stuff is junk," he said. "I like something that's real—something that shows the world exactly the way it really is." A few minutes later in the conversation, the sailor had occasion to mention his girl back home. He pulled a photograph out of his pocket and showed it to the famous artist. "She's very pretty," said Picasso. "But tell me—is she really this tiny?"

The more familiar you are with a particular thing, the less time your brain tends to spend in perceiving it. When you come to an unfamiliar feature, you automatically slow down and study it in a more concentrated way, since your brain cannot readily classify it. Abstract art, for example, challenges this process in your brain.

This factor provides an opportunity to teach your brain to concentrate better and possibly to improve your ability to discriminate detail quickly. You can occasionally flick your eyes from one object to another, looking at each for no more than a second. Each time you refocus, your brain goes back to a high-interest mode, tuning in carefully to the features of the new object. After about a second, you recognize the object as familiar, and your level of attention to it drops sharply.

Your brain's pattern-recognition capability also enables you to determine the number of objects in a group at a glance, without having to count them individually. Called *subitizing*, this skill seems to stem from repeatedly seeing things in small groups. Try glancing at various words on this page for a split second each and estimate the number of letters in each without counting or analyzing the word. You will probably find that you can reliably count up to about six or seven letters before your subitizing skill becomes overtaxed. Try this with other groups, such as people at a bus stop, items in a shop window, birds on a rooftop, or coins in your hand.

The perceptual process of recognition enables you to deploy your attention far and wide without becoming bogged down in details that may have little or no value for you. On the other hand, it can also lead you to "recognize" something that doesn't actually match one of your memory patterns, and it can lead you to overlook details that might be significant. If you have a watch with mechanical hands, cover the watch face for a moment and try to recall what it looks like. How many numbers does it have? Are they Arabic or Roman numerals—or does it have any numbers?

Can you recall what the American flag looks like? Having "seen" it so

many times, can you remember the color of the top stripe? The bottom
stripe? How many red and how many white stripes does it have?

The standard telephone dial has ten numbers, one through nine plus
zero. But it doesn't use all twenty-six letters of the alphabet. Which two
letters do not appear on the dial?

Some people become disgruntled when they see a painting or sculpture
they cannot "recognize"—and consequently classify—as something familiar; others find no particular necessity to decide what something "is." One
artist created a series of pictures to play havoc with the common attitude of
demanding that a painting be something. The artist painted a still life of
several items of fruit, with each cut in half to show its interior. But the
inside of the lemon looked like the inside of an apple! The apple seemed to
have the interior of an orange, and the partially peeled banana had the
texture of a watermelon. I was intrigued by the painting in a shop, and I
noticed that many people would stop and show the same characteristic
reaction of surprise, amusement, and heightened interest that I had. Conversely, the other, more conventional paintings went largely unnoticed.
The next time you stroll through a museum, take a moment to note the
reactions of the other browsers to various pieces of art. How many people
just walk from one item to another, simply recognizing the content of the
picture—the "information" it presents—and how many pay attention to
the picture itself?

In perceiving verbal information especially, the brain may tend to leave
out various details because of the high level of "information" contained
in our verbal symbol system. Read the following sentence only once,
counting the number of times you see the letter "f" as you go:

FIVE OF OUR FINEST FACTORY MANAGERS HAVE OFFERED SOME OF THEIR
TIME FOR THE DEVELOPMENT OF THE AFFIRMATIVE ACTION PLAN.

How many did you count? Double-check to make sure you saw all of
them. Might you have overlooked a few, especially those at the ends of
certain two-letter words? Actually, the "f" appears eleven times in the
sentence. If you overlooked some of them, perhaps your brain simply
narrowed its definition of an "f"—taking in only those at the beginning of
words. Because most of us read partially "by sound," that is, we "hear" the
words in our minds as we read along, the "f" occurring at the end of a word
might sound like a "v" and not qualify for recognition.

the principle of interpretation

The perceptual principle of interpretation means that when the brain
has difficulty in recognizing what confronts it, it will nevertheless try to

make sense of it. In making sense of the unfamiliar, the brain automatically tends to begin with the familiar. It searches its library of familiar memory models, trying to find one that fits the ambiguous situation closely enough so that it can assign it a recognition tag and then continue scanning the environment for other new and novel inputs. Sometimes the brain will choose a pattern that does not represent the world feature very well, but will use it anyway. A great deal of misinterpretation, misunderstanding, and perceptual confusion stems from false recognition due to interpretation. When we expect to see a particular thing or when we want to see it, or when we have become so thoroughly accustomed to seeing it, we may see it even if it isn't there.

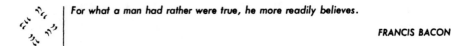

For what a man had rather were true, he more readily believes.

FRANCIS BACON

Some years ago, Hadley Cantril, a researcher and contemporary of Adelbert Ames, experimented with the same trapezoid-rectangle phenomenon mentioned earlier in this chapter to examine the two interwoven perceptual functions of recognition and interpretation. He constructed a replica of a window frame with a trapezoidal distortion. The frame had vertical sides of unequal length, so that the top and bottom sides were no longer parallel, as illustrated in Figure 7.4. Cantril enclosed this curious "window" in a tunnel-shaped compartment with a viewing hole at one end, and he arranged it so that it rotated on a spindle about a vertical axis through its center.

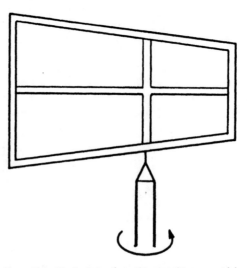

Figure 7.4 The brain tends to interpret this trapezoidal "window" as a rectangular window seen from an angle.

The experimental subjects who viewed Cantril's window were dumbfounded at what they saw, or thought they saw. When they looked at the window straight-on, that is, perpendicular to the plane of its construction, they saw a trapezoid. However, their westernized brains interpreted the trapezoid as it "should" have been, namely a square tilted at an angle to their line of sight. Perhaps your brain did this when you looked at Figure 7.4. This interpretation established a mental set that prevented them from properly interpreting the window's motion. The viewer expected the short side of the trapezoidal window, which he erroneously assumed to be farther away than the long side, to appear progressively smaller until the window had turned edge-on to his line of sight, whereafter it would proceed to grow in appearance until it seemed equal in length to the side that was actually longer. Then, the viewer assumed, it should continue to rotate until the other side (actually the longer side) was the farthest away, when *it* would become the "smaller" side because of its distance.

What really happened was that the long side of the trapezoid was sufficiently longer than the short side so that it *always* seemed longer, no matter what the orientation of the frame. The viewer kept expecting the two sides to exchange characteristics, the short one becoming the apparent longer one and vice versa. The rotating frame seemed to do strange things, like reverse its direction and turn itself inside out. Once the viewer's brain had incorrectly interpreted the trapezoid as a rectangle, he could not make sense out of what he saw. I've seen a replica of Cantril's window in the science museum in San Diego's Balboa Park. Even though I could walk to the other end of the apparatus and see the entire rotating frame through the unobscured plexiglass wall of the tunnel, nevertheless my rectangularly programmed brain had quite a challenge at first to perceive it accurately as a trapezoid.[8]

Optical illusions often make use of rectangular structures, because the westernized brain has learned so well to recognize certain lines and angles as representing rectilinear structures. The entire artistic principle of perspective drawing rests on this usually reliable interpretation process. Another well-known illusion, shown in Figure 7.5, invites the brain to interpret an image as a three-dimensional object, when in fact the object does not completely obey the rules of visual perspective. This "object" doesn't seem to hold still in space. But, in fact, what jumps around is your brain's conclusion about what it sees. First, it tries to interpret it as a three-pronged object of some sort. But as your eye follows the direction of the prongs, at a critical point your brain suddenly changes its interpretation and decides it is seeing a two-pronged object. Since you can't see both at the same time, and since your brain can't resolve the image to only one of the two possible interpretations, you can't arrive at a satisfying interpretation. Notice how your feel in the face of such an ambiguous feature of the

[8]See Hadley Cantril, *The "Why" of Man's Experience* (New York: Macmillan, 1950).

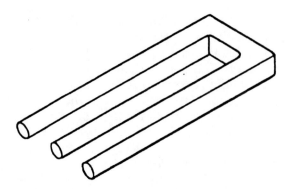

Figure 7.5   What makes this impossible "object" seem real?

world. You lack that comfortable feeling of having classified a perceptual object, and you may feel vaguely dissatisfied and even slightly annoyed.

In addition to matching its stored patterns to the principal cues it finds in the perceived object, your brain sometimes "fills in" missing information to make a complete pattern when none exists. For example, Figure 7.6 provides some suggestive cues without actually presenting a complete figure. As you look at the lines, see whether your brain tries to make a complete star out of it by mentally adding what perceptual psychologists call *subjective contours.* Can you deliberately avoid seeing a completed figure by keeping the image broken down into its original lines?

Conversely, your brain may conveniently "edit out" features that don't readily match up with familiar patterns. Take a moment to glance at the triangle in Figure 7.7 before reading any further in this paragraph. What did you see? Look carefully. Many people completely overlook the repeated word in the phrase. In many cases, your brain converts the incoming data into what it "should" be, sometimes at the expense of fully grasping the meaning.

Figure 7.6   Can you avoid "seeing" a star?

Figure 7.7 What do you see when you read this?

The perceptual effect of interpretation often shows clearly in the language of children. One grade-school child wrote an essay in which he mentioned that a famous writer had been given the "Bullet Surprise."

One Sunday school teacher had the children draw pictures of religious scenes during one Christmas season. When she looked at one child's drawing, she saw an extra, unidentifiable person at the Nativity. It was a fat, nondescript man who seemed to have no particular part in the scene. When she inquired, the child answered, "Him? Oh, that's Round John Virgin."

Still another aspect of the function of interpretation involves *projection*—a process by which some special interest or preoccupation you may have gets "externalized" and mixed in with the incoming perceptual data and interpreted as if it originated in the environment. The metaphorical term *projection* serves as a convenient analogy, suggesting that one's brain occasionally works like a movie projector, casting vague shadow images of one's own making onto one's perceptual field. Especially when the thing being perceived has highly ambiguous features, the brain may resolve the ambiguity by "seeing" patterns, themes, processes, and relationships with which the person is preoccupied, either consciously or preconsciously.

For example, if you feel extremely hungry, you might tend to interpret ambiguous shapes such as those that flash by on a highway billboard as representing items of food. If you feel guilty about exceeding the speed limit you might falsely recognize a car approaching from the rear as a police car. A hairdresser might notice a person's hair at the instant of meeting him, while an orthopedic surgeon might notice the curve of his spine. Projection involves externalized self-interest.

A classic experiment in projection involved a group of schoolchildren in Boston to whom experimenters showed a group of coins. The experimenters later asked each of the children to show how big the coins were by adjusting a simple gadget to the proper size. All of the children overestimated the size of the coins, but when the experimenters tried the experiment with very poor children, they found that the poor ones greatly exaggerated the size of the coins. They overestimated substantially more than did the children from middle-class backgrounds. As an early Persian poet observed, "What a loaf of bread looks like to you depends on how hungry you are."

Some psychiatrists use projective tests like the famous Rorschach ink-blot series to try to identify thought patterns and unrecognized conflicts that trouble their patients. Because many patients in therapy have great difficulty explaining the nature of their unhappiness, the therapist must sometimes help them to express it in other, roundabout ways. A patient may look at a particular inkblot in the series and describe what it looks like to him. In the words he chooses, the themes he describes, and the feelings he gets in looking at the ambiguous image, the patient projects his own preoccupations into his perceptual field.

I gained a much greater respect for the challenge of really seeing things accurately when I began to learn sketching. I found that it requires close and careful concentration to draw an object *just as the eye sees it*, without substituting a known and expected pattern for the real thing. Adults who first learn drawing almost invariably represent things as they think they ought to be, rather than as they actually see them. Especially in trying to represent perspective relationships and trying to show the foreshortening effects of looking at a person's body end-on, they tend to resort to standard patterns such as frontal views rather than to draw the lines their eyes actually see. Children tend to see things much more naively and accurately because they lack the years of repetitive recognizing and reinterpreting that the adult has undergone. In the words of artist Paul Coze, "The child sees and doesn't know. The adult knows and doesn't see."

The study of photography can also teach you a new way to see. If you think of using your camera to *make* a picture, rather than simply "taking" one, you will find yourself visualizing the entire scene as it will appear in the final form. You will learn to pay attention to background features, colors and color relationships, symmetry, and the effects of major lines and features. Try reading a basic book on photography and composition, and then go around for a day or two looking at things with the eye of a photographer. You may be surprised at how much more of the world you begin to see.

the principle of expectation

 Miracles do not happen in contradiction to nature, but only in contradiction to that which is known about nature.

ST. AUGUSTINE

The perceptual phenomenon of *expectation* means a strongly held readiness to perceive some particular thing, which makes the brain much more inclined to perceive it than to perceive alternative possibilities. Sometimes this mental set becomes so strong that one perceives what he expected to perceive even though it didn't really happen.

For example, physician Frederic Loomis cites an incident in his book, *Consultation Room*, in which his expectations in a situation differed greatly from the patient's expectations.

I learned something of the intricacies of plain English at an early stage in my career. A woman of thirty-five came in one day to tell me she wanted a baby but that she had been told that she had a certain type of heart disease which might not interfere with a normal life but would be dangerous if she ever had a baby. From her description I thought at once of mitral stenosis. This condition is characterized by a rather distinctive rumbling murmur near the apex of the heart, and especially by a peculiar vibration felt by the examining finger on the patient's chest. The vibration is known as the "thrill" of mitral stenosis.

When this woman had been undressed and was lying on my table in her white kimono, my stethoscope quickly found the heart-sounds I expected. Dictating to my nurse, I described them carefully. I put my stethoscope aside and felt intently for the typical vibration which may be found in a small but variable area of the left chest.

I closed my eyes for better concentration, and felt long and carefully for the tremor. I did not find it and with my hand still on the woman's bare breast, lifting it upward and out of the way, I finally turned to the nurse and said, "No thrill."

The patient's black eyes snapped open, and with venom in her voice she said, "Well, isn't that just too bad? Perhaps it's just as well you don't get one. That isn't what I came here for."

My nurse almost choked, and my explanation still seems a nightmare of futile words.[9]

You can easily see how your brain can set up an expectation—a mental set that prepares you for a happening you believe will surely come about. Expectations dominate much of our perception, sometimes for better and sometimes for worse. We tend to organize our thoughts in each situation in terms of an expected outcome; many times this is what brings us to the situation in the first place. Only when our expectations do not match the happenings of the situation do we momentarily slip out of touch with reality.

Often the brain will respond to certain cues within the perceptual field and set up a strong expectation based on them. In such a case, the tricky arrangement of the inputs leads to a mental set that induces the brain to interpret the situation in a certain way. For example, if someone tells you

[9]Taken from Irving J. Lee, *Language Habits in Human Affairs* (New York: Harper & Row Pub., 1941), p. 46. Lee attributes it to Frederic Loomis, M.D., *Consultation Room* (New York: Knopf, 1939), p. 47.

Figure 7.8   Do you see an old woman? a young one? or both?

that the movie you are about to see is poorly done and in bad taste, and if you accept that value judgment, you may well expect to see a "bad" movie. If someone applies a familiar verbal label to an ambiguous image or scene, you may tend to expect to see something that corresponds to the verbal label. For example, can you see an old woman as you look at the form in Figure 7.8?[10]

This form usually produces some interesting responses when people try to figure out what it "is." It "isn't" anything, of course, but a collection of marks and dark patterns on a white background. The human brain *gives it* meaning by the way it interprets the ambiguous information. If you can find only one image, either the old woman or the young girl, study the figure from different angles. Try to destroy the mental set that limits you to only one interpretation. Turn it upside down, or tilt it and look at it from the left and from the right. Stare at certain key features and let your preconscious visual processes reorganize the others. To what extent might the caption and the sentence you read just before you looked at the figure lead you to expect to see an old woman?

The old expression "love is blind" probably encodes the principle of expectation as well as any other. Reorganized into a more explicit, although certainly less romantic form, the expression would become "the

[10]Like many other popular concepts and illustrations, the origin of this figure seems to be obscure. Consequently, although I'd like to credit the originator, I can't. So far as I know, it is most commonly used in publications of the International Society for General Semantics, P.O. Box 2469, San Francisco, CA 94126. A typical publication is Sanford I. Berman, Ph.D., *How to Lessen Misunderstandings*, 1962, a pamphlet that uses the illustration (without attributing credit) on the cover.

brain of a person who becomes infatuated with and psychologically dependent on another adopts a powerful mental set, which leads it to pay attention selectively to just those characteristics of the loved one which merit positive evaluation."

A series of experiments by psychological researchers in 1970 demonstrated the powerful effects of expectations on the attitudes of people in the helping professions toward their clients. Dr. David L. Rosenhan, professor of psychology and law at Stanford University, had eight people have themselves admitted to mental hospitals even though they were adequately adjusted. Typically, one of these people would walk into a mental hospital asking for help. He would report hearing strange voices, for example, and would give a contrived story about himself. After being admitted, he would begin to tell the truth to anyone who cared to listen.

Rosenhan found, predictably, that the hospital staff, including the interviewing doctors, diagnosed the person as seriously maladjusted, ranging from "neurotic" to "schizophrenic." In no case did a hospital refuse to admit one of the subjects, and in no case was the subject immediately released after telling the truth. The hospitals kept them for periods ranging from seven to fifty-two days. The average stay lasted nineteen days. Reports indicated that in many cases the other patients could identify the test subjects as impostors, but apparently in no case did the hospital staff identify them.

Rosenhan concluded from these experiments that psychiatrists bring very powerful unconscious expectations to the situation of dealing with a person within the setting of a mental hospital, and this mental set tends to lead them to respond to patients as "crazy people"—which might start a closed-loop, self-fulfilling prophecy effect. Perhaps this is why doctors and nurses usually wear distinctive uniforms in the hospital setting—so they can tell the sane people from the crazy ones.

the principle of intention

The perceptual principle of *intention* deals with your purposes in perceiving anything. From one point of view, you cannot simply "perceive." You perceive *something* in order to take action about it. Stated another way, you virtually always look *for* something as you look *at* many somethings.

Intending to perceive something means searching for it within your perceptual field. And searching means *filtering* out everything that does not match up with what you want to find. The more intensively you search, and the more specific the thing you want to find, the more closely you will concentrate and the more heavily you will filter out the rest. As a simple experiment, look over this page of printing and count the number of periods you see. As you do so, try to make yourself aware of the process of seeking out the periods and aware of leaving out many other features of the page. How many periods did you see? Could you sense other information creeping into your perceptual field as you discovered how easy the task was?

Your brain can search rapidly through a great deal of information, paying only enough attention to each bit of data to decide whether to accept or reject it, according to its apparent relevance to the task at hand, that is, your intention in perceiving. Study the following string of letters carefully and see if you can find a familiar phrase there:

CApiTeaCHMEndiclFecYOUrCeamAN

What did you see? Did you find two familiar phrases with interspersed letters? The capital letters spell out one phrase and the lower case letters spell out another. Notice how your brain selects only one of these threads of meaning at a time, rejecting the other. You'll find it very difficult to pay attention to both at the same time.

Another experiment I have conducted a number of times in seminars on creative thinking demonstrates how well we can pay attention and how accurately our senses can detect subtle cues. With about a dozen people sitting in a circle, I give each of them an orange. First I ask them to take a good look at the orange and to study it as long as possible before they become "bored" with its features. This usually takes no more than about fifteen seconds. Then I propose a test of their perceptual skills. We shall all close our eyes and pass the oranges around the circle to our right, without seeing them. Then, keeping our eyes closed, we are to search for our original oranges, identifying them by whatever cues we can.

The prospect of having to identify their own oranges with their eyes closed usually sparks the participants into renewed interest in the details of their respective oranges. They close their eyes and study them with their fingertips, searching for any features that might help to identify them when they pass through their hands again. Remarkably, almost all of the seminar participants I have worked with in this experiment have had no trouble picking out their original oranges from the rest. Groups of up to fifteen people—the approximate logistical limit for an eyes-closed cooperation exercise—have reached unanimous agreement, despite the inevitable mixing of oranges, dropping them on the floor, and people holding on to two or three at a time. This experiment never fails to generate a new respect in the participants for the effectiveness of their perceptual processes.

Much of what some people call dumbness, stupidity, or craziness in other humans merely amounts to inattention. Not everyone pays attention equally well to all things. Not everyone intends to perceive the same thing in the same situation. A driver may sit in his car behind another driver at a traffic signal. When the signal changes, the first driver may be paying attention to someone else. He may be staring at the sky, looking at a display in a shop window, or tuning out the news on his car radio. After a few seconds the driver behind may become impatient and begin blowing his horn, uttering the time-honored expression, "That stupid #@$%$&! What's the matter with him?" The answer is: There is nothing the matter with him. He probably isn't stupid. And he probably isn't a #@$%& either. He just hasn't paid attention to what the second driver wanted him to. Many people are called stupid or crazy when their real malfunction is merely inattention.

Paying attention becomes much easier if you have a good idea what to pay attention to. You can consider your attention as analogous to a radio or television receiver, which you deliberately tune in to selected stations. Just as the radio is equipped to receive some kinds of transmissions—say, AM or FM, both AM and FM, or shortwave—and not others, so your brain has become better prepared over the years to perceive some things and not others. You have developed many recognition models, which operate like so many perceptual pigeonholes for your thoughts. These pigeonholes allow you to recognize many aspects of your environment easily and to know when you've seen them. But although you may possess many useful recognition models in your brain, you probably also have a number of blind spots, which cause you to overlook aspects of your environment that may be important.

Did you know that you have a visual blind spot—a small area in the field of view of each eye where you can't see anything? Just about fifteen degrees to the outside of each eye's point of focus is the angle where the optic nerves going to the brain merge with the sensory nerve cells inside the eye. That place on your retina has no receptor cells, and the part of the visual image that falls on that point is lost. You usually don't notice these blind spots because your eyes move about quickly, and your short-term visual memory enables your brain to fill in the missing visual data.

Figure 7.9 will enable you to find the blind spot in each of your eyes. Hold the book at a comfortable reading distance, about ten to fifteen inches from your eyes. Close your left eye, and look at the large dot with your right eye. Now slowly shift your focus to the numbers on the left of the dot, looking at each one in a very slow succession. As you do so, stay aware of the dot which will still be in your field of view. As you proceed farther from the dot, you will come to a point where it seems to disappear. It drops out of your peripheral field altogether. This is the angle at which the image of the

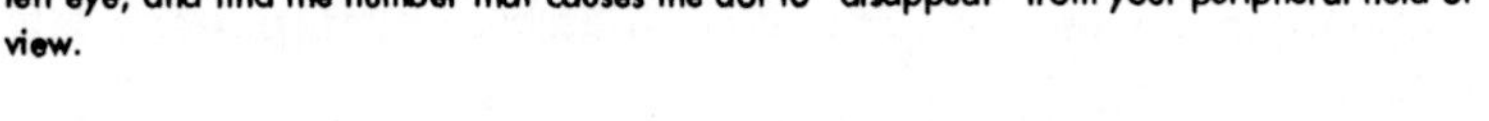

15   14   13   12   11   10   9   8   7   6   5   4   3   2   1   ●

Figure 7.9   Find your visual blind spot. Hold the book at a normal reading distance, close your left eye, and find the number that causes the dot to "disappear" from your peripheral field of view.

dot falls upon your right eye's blind spot. As you proceed still farther along the line of numbers, you will soon become aware of the dot again as it emerges from the blind spot. You can find the blind spot in your left eye the same way, by turning the book upside down and repeating the procedure with your right eye closed and your left eye moving along the line of numbers away from the dot.

A much more striking demonstration of the blind spot involves a lighted candle. Place it on a table or other convenient surface and stand across the room from it. With your left eye closed, first look at the candle flame and then begin to shift your gaze slowly away from it, moving your eye inward toward your nose. When you have placed the blind spot at the angle of the incoming image of the candle, it will disappear altogether. By moving your point of focus around carefully, you can explore the size and shape of the blind spot, noting at what point you can again detect the light from the candle.

Just as we have visual blind spots, so by analogy we can have other perceptual blind spots. We may simply not intend to take in some aspects of situations which could help us to deal with them better. Many people seem to have blind spots about the feelings and reactions of others. If a person in a situation becomes so preoccupied with his own feelings and interests in a situation, he may fail to tune in the signals the other person sends and may engage in behavior that irritates, offends, or intimidates the other person. To the extent that someone is unaware of his impact on other people, he is unable to adapt effectively to their needs and interests. In the long run, this blind spot will probably work to the person's disadvantage in getting what he wants from other people.

the principle of context

The perceptual principle of context means that the way in which your brain interprets certain features or cues in a situation depends to some extent on the overall nature of the situation. Your brain takes in the general arrangement of a given perceptual situation and uses that pattern as a backdrop for figuring out what to make of the specific cues that it finds.

A simple example of the context phenomenon would involve a group of coins on a table, say, beside a plate in a restaurant. If you were in the United States, you would probably assume they were American coins. The context invites you to see them as American, especially because your past experience has often confirmed this kind of an interpretation. If you examine them and discover that they are really coins from another country or that they are just coin-shaped bits of metal, your mental set will then fall apart. You will begin to see them in a different way.

The phenomenon of context has such an all-encompassing effect on your brain's perceptual processes that you seldom notice it. In every perceptual situation, your brain needs a place to start—a point of departure for making sense out of the impressions the senses bring it. Your brain examines the overall situation and derives certain organizing concepts from it. For example, you may look at the conventional objects in a room for a few seconds. Whether you realize it or not, your brain has recognized most of them and assigned each one a given *function* with respect to you and with respect to the others in the perceptual field. It also abstracts *relationships* among the objects, or among the people in the situation. These two aspects—function and relationship—form the basic ingredients of the context your brain establishes for every perceptual situation. It draws on past history and decides what assumptions to make about the present situation.

When your brain makes a mistake in either of these two assumptive factors, you may have difficulty interpreting certain features of a situation, or you may become unnecessarily constrained in the flexibility with which you can view the situation. An awareness of contexts and of how your brain creates them can help to free you from automatic responses to patterned situations.

A number of visual illusions demonstrate the effects of relationships on your brain's attempt to perceive specific features of a situation. Figure 7.10 shows how one element of a situation seems to interact with another element. Does the line with the diverging ends seem longer than the line with the arrowheads? This famous figure, the Müller-Lyer illusion, and others like it, have intrigued perceptual researchers for some time. The eye seems to follow certain lines according to the way they are arranged, and this slight motion may lead the brain to evaluate those lines as covering more territory than others. The arrowheads in the figure seem to lead the eye back toward the center of the line, giving the impression of covering a smaller territory.

Figure 7.11 shows how one feature of a situation may actually seem to change another feature. Do the two long lines seem straight, or do they appear to curve? The interaction of the lines radiating from the center confuses the brain as it tries to examine the straight lines.

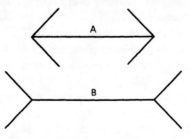

Figure 7.10   Which line is longer, A or B?

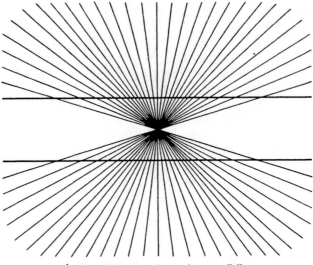

Figure 7.11   Are the two lines parallel?

The contextual cues in a situation also play an important part in understanding another person's behavior. For example, a high school teacher was monitoring an examination consisting of true-false questions on history. He noticed one student in the back of the room flipping a coin and writing down his answers. The teacher thought, "Well, it's his business how he wants to take the test." Later, just before the time limit for the exam had expired, he noticed the same student flipping his coin very rapidly. As the students were leaving the classroom, he pulled the student aside and asked, "I don't care how you take the test, but would you mind telling me why you were flipping the coin again at the end of the exam?" The student replied, "I was just checking my answers."

In the early days of perceptual research, an interesting experiment in problem solving shed a great deal of light on the effects of context in human thinking. The exact form of the experiment varied as different investigators replicated it, but the basic elements were the same. The experimenters would ask a small group of people to try to solve the problem of retrieving a ping pong ball undamaged from the bottom of an old metal pipe that stood on its end, firmly attached to the floor. The pipe was about three feet long and slightly bigger in diameter than the ball. The room also contained a number of other items that the group members were free to use as they saw fit. These might include wire, broomsticks, coat hangers, string, glue, pliers, thumbtacks, and rags.

The experimenters would generally control one particular factor in the arrangement, varying it from one group to another. In one situation, among the many items in the room would be a full table setting, complete with white tablecloth, silverware, crystal glassware, and a pitcher of ice water.

In very few cases would a group seize on the solution of pouring the ice water into the pipe to float the ping pong ball to the top. But when the experimenters placed the water in a dirty old bucket, almost all of the groups found the water solution rather quickly.

The experimenters hypothesized that the test subjects had fallen victim to a phenomenon they labeled *functional fixation*, that is, assigning narrowly limited functions to the elements in the situation and being unable to use some of the items in unconventional ways. Apparently the group members unwittingly saw the ice water as "locked" within the context of the table setting, which seemed to be a perceptual unit all its own. The subjects who saw the water in its more "available" form had no trouble making use of it in formulating a solution. In the one case, the context of the situation lead them to define the water as "something you drink," without realizing that they had done so. In the other case, the context lead them to define the water as "something you pour."

Functional fixation as a perceptual phenomenon often runs deep into one's whole system of "definitions"—his framework for deciding how to deal with the various piece-parts of the world. Probably the strongest influence in defining the function of something is the verbal label one learns to apply to it. In a seminar on thinking, I mentioned the distinction between "things" in their own right and the labels we apply to the things. One participant insisted that everything "is" something or other. I suggested that what something "is"—with the emphasis on the quotation marks—depends solely on how I expect to relate to it. I picked up a chair and asked, "What is this?" She replied, "A chair." I turned it upside down and held it over my head and said, "And if I use it to keep the rain off my head?" She said flatly, "It's still a chair. You're just using it for some other purpose." Then I sat on the edge of a table and asked, "Is this a chair?" She said, "No. *That's* a chair. You're sitting on a *table*." I asked, "What makes that a chair and this a table?" She answered, "Don't play word games. A chair is a chair, and a table is a table. You can use them however you want, but that doesn't change what they are."

Later on in the seminar, I conducted an idea-production exercise using the task of finding as many uses as possible for a common building brick. Although most of the participants could freewheel fairly easily, coming up with outlandish and novel uses, the woman who insisted that a chair was a chair couldn't seem to name any functional application for a brick other than to construct some commonplace structure, such as a wall, a walkway, or a barbecue pit. Her system of verbal categories apparently imprisoned her thinking.

Because our behavior is governed by the assumptions we make in establishing the perceptual context of a situation, we sometimes fall victim to manipulation by others who realize that. A young man posted himself at the door of a popular singles bar on a very busy Friday night. For about fifteen minutes, he collected a two-dollar "cover charge" from each person who came into the bar. Then he departed with a sizable income for a few minutes of "work."

reality testing

Others will tell you to try to prove you are right. I tell you to try to prove you are wrong.

LOUIS PASTEUR

Now that we have abandoned the naive conviction that we see things as they "are," and we have accepted the fact that our brains cannot see beyond the nerve ends that supply them with sense impressions, we can adopt a general policy of paying attention to attention—we can develop an awareness of awareness. As mentioned in a previous chapter, your brain creates memory models from its perceptual data and uses them as building blocks for thought. This process goes on automatically all during your waking hours. The skill of *reality testing* involves evaluating these mental models from time to time against new information. Whereas most of your perceptual processes operate automatically, reality testing requires a conscious and deliberate process. This is the extensional orientation cited by Korzybski.

Some people, however, have learned faulty thinking habits, which interfere with their reality testing processes so much that they become rigid, mechanical thinkers, unable to adapt to the changing world about them. They habitually and unknowingly block their own reality testing processes. By recognizing the mental habits that lead to this blockage, you can eliminate most of them from your thinking patterns and develop a high level of reality testing skill.

These mental habits will probably seem familiar at this point, now that we've studied the perceptual process and the ways in which the brain constructs its mental models. The most common reality blocking habits are

1. The intensional orientation
2. Opinionitis
3. Value judging
4. Ego thinking
5. Wishful thinking

Each of these mental habits tends to distort or constrict the perceptual process by establishing a strong mental set, which keeps one from taking in the information that would enable him to reevaluate a situation, approach a problem differently, revise a viewpoint, or change his mind. Each of them has a reductive influence on perception. They lead to close-mindedness instead of open-mindedness.

A strong mental set, for example, a fixed opinion, leads directly to *selective perception*, the taking in of only that information which aligns with the established bias. The incoming information has the effect of justifying the mental set, making it even stronger. The stronger mental set leads to even more selective perception, and so on. For example, if you've made up your mind firmly about some particular approach to a problem, you'll probably become more alert to notice the advantages of that approach and to screen out findings that don't support it very well. Only if the opposing features become so obviously noticeable that you can no longer reject them will you find it necessary to break out of the mental set and reevaluate the factors involved.

> *Opinion has caused more trouble on this little earth than plagues or earthquakes.*
>
> VOLTAIRE

Another common mental malfunction, which usually originates in ego thinking, is *rationalizing*. Rationalizing means putting the factors of a situation together in a special way, so as to establish a socially acceptable explanation for one's behavior. Whenever people do something they think might elicit the disapproval of other people whom they respect or whose opinions they value, and yet they have strong reasons for having done it, they will tend to develop an explanation of their actions in terms of factors they believe the other people do approve of.

> *Man is the only animal that blushes—or needs to.*
>
> MARK TWAIN

Because all normal human beings value the acceptance and approval of others to some extent, and because many of them value approval so highly that they imprison themselves by seeking it, many people engage in rationalization fairly often. A young boy may feel jealous of his younger sister and may decide to push her down the sandpile. When mother asks what happened, he may offer the story that the little one was falling and that he made a heroic attempt to save her. In its extreme form, a rationalization is simply a lie. However, these kinds of rationalizations are not confined to children. A company president may offer virtually the same explanation, reworded appropriately, for forcing another executive out of the organization—a form of behavior startlingly reminiscent of the childhood sandpile setting.

Mother: Billy, why did you kick your sister in the stomach?
  Billy: I couldn't help it. She turned around too fast.

Another important area often in need of reality testing involves one's own self-image—one's view of oneself as a person and one's relationships with others. If you have certain blind spots concerning the way you treat other people, or if you don't want to face the facts of your motivations in certain situations, your behavior will probably prevent you from fulfilling your needs rather than help you to do so. In some cases, you may create your own problems by dealing with others in overly aggressive or abrasive ways, or conversely by failing to assert your own wants and interests. The kinds of inputs that will help you test your model of yourself against external reality are the facial expressions and other nonverbal cues others give in response to things you say and do; the extent to which they seek you out for companionship and casual conversation; the extent to which they feel comfortable with you; and the extent to which they value your interests in dealing with you. You can also ask low risk questions of other people to find out specific aspects of how they react to you.

> O wad some power the giftie gie us,
> to see oursels as ithers see us:
> It would fra monie a blunder free us,
> and foolish notion.

ROBERT BURNS

Advertising designers have learned, through a great deal of trial-and-error research, to package their products with the proper "rational" arguments for buying them, but to make sure that the real "hidden persuaders" show through clearly enough to reach the actual motivational structures of the consumer. Typically, appeals to the desire for social status, the desire for feelings of power, and fantasies of sexual experience, when connected either loosely or closely to the product, will arouse the buying impulse in most people very reliably. The human brain seems to have the curious faculty of keeping two opposing thought processes separated into logic-proof compartments and preventing them from ever colliding. The same person who will preach to friends in a conversation about thinking for himself and not trying to keep up with the Joneses will respond to a highly manipulative advertisement and obediently buy a luxury car, an item of jewelry, or the latest consumer gadget. Somehow, by selective attention, he can keep these two sets of ideas apart in his brain.

Stanford researcher Leon Festinger studied this phenomenon of building isolated "thought packages," especially in the context of responses to advertising. Festinger coined the term *cognitive dissonance* to describe the subjectively experienced mental "tension" resulting from the potential conflict of two ideas coexisting in one brain. Festinger believed that whenever a person felt this dissonance, it signaled a partial overlap of his logical categories, and that the person would automatically adopt perceptual and cognitive strategies that would isolate the ideas from one another and reduce the dissonance. Rationalizing, Festinger believed, often played an important part in the unconscious reduction of cognitive dissonance.

Festinger's research showed that people can sometimes go to considerable extremes in blocking off their reality testing processes when they try to cling to a belief that has fallen into logical jeopardy. He studied the activities of several fanatical cults, whose members believed the world would soon come to an end and that they had been chosen as survivors. He wanted to see what people would do under the extreme circumstances of having made a complete commitment to their belief, that is, having sold or given away all their belongings and separated their ties from the society, and then finding that their prophecy did not come true. How would people with such strongly held beliefs react when those beliefs were unambiguously disconfirmed?

Surprisingly, Festinger found, none of the groups he studied disbanded immediately on finding their prophecy disconfirmed. All of them tightened their ranks, developed a new prediction, and put forth an explanation about why the world had not ended at the appointed time. One group, previously very secretive and unwilling to talk to outsiders, even began to advertise and recruit new members for the second try. Another group faced no less than three successive disconfirmations of its prophecies before it collapsed and its members went back to try to reconstruct their previous lives. Recent studies of cultist behavior, especially among the more fanatical religious groups, has confirmed Festinger's view that certain people under certain circumstances can place a firm and almost unshakeable belief in preposterous doctrines and can become virtually impervious to information.[11]

> Men stumble over the truth from time to time, but most pick themselves up and hurry off as if nothing happened.
>
> WINSTON CHURCHILL

the lost art of listening

I admire the long-forgotten philosopher who said, "If God had meant for you to talk more than you listen, He'd have given you two mouths and one ear." Much of what passes for social conversation, or for problem-solving dialogues in business settings, really amounts to the exchange of

[11]For a general treatment of Festinger's concept of cognitive dissonance, see Leon Festinger, *A Theory of Cognitive Dissonance* (Stanford, Calif.: Stanford University Press, 1957). Festinger reported his studies of fanatical groups in Leon Festinger, *When Prophecy Fails* (Minneapolis: University of Minnesota Press, 1956).

monologues. Each of the participants in these situations might just as well be talking to his reflection in a mirror, in view of the small amount of real listening and adapting that often goes on.

Many lecturers and writers on the topic of communication and human relations seem to tout listening as a form of social courtesy, an indication to the other person that you accept him as an individual and acknowledge his right to express his ideas. While I consider that a fairly important aspect of listening, it seems to me that a factor of much greater importance is *the opportunity to learn something useful*. Good listening amounts to a perceptual skill, not simply a form of courtesy. And it involves much more than simply keeping your jaws together and your vocal apparatus inert while waiting for the other person to finish talking. It involves an investigative attitude, a readiness to see and hear something new, and a willingness to change your point of view if the message calls for it.

Your intentions play an important part in your level of attention, as you probably recognize when you hear someone talk about a subject that bores you or has strayed from the topic of your immediate interest. Your expectations can also color your perceptions of someone else's statements and can lead you to agree or disagree without really understanding what is being said.

Learning to listen effectively requires a firm belief in the value of fact finding as a general process in dealing with other people, especially in complicated situations. Indeed, the more complicated the situation, the more likely you can find out some of the things you need to know by listening carefully.

In a conference with several executives of a client company, I heard one very high-ranking executive state a strong opinion "disguised" as a question, something along the lines of "Why can't we . . .?" A younger and more junior executive responded with a fact that didn't seem to support the senior's point of view. The senior executive shot back, "Just a minute! Now, you're not listening! Don't go opening your mouth before your brain is in gear!" The junior executive patiently waited until the senior had made his point, then politely repeated his fact, which showed the senior that his opinion was based on a mistaken impression of the entire situation. To his chagrin, the senior man discovered that he was the one who had not listened very effectively. Had he not cut the junior off with his scolding remark, he might have had a chance to change his mind gracefully. As it was, the other participants in the conversation changed the subject and politely "rescued" him.

Having proven to yourself the value of fact finding as an everyday thinking skill, you can learn to explore other people's "data banks" to find out what they know that you don't. Many people enjoy sharing what they know, and if you can tame your ego well enough to help them share their knowledge with you, you can enormously expand your own "data base," as well as enrich your entire outlook on the world.

developing the investigative attitude

> I kept six honest serving men,
> they taught me all I knew;
> their names were What and Why and When
> and How and Where and Who.
>
> RUDYARD KIPLING

If I were asked to choose only one of mankind's symbols as potentially the most important for human thought, it would be this one:? I wonder if all cultures with written language have their counterparts to our Indo-European question mark? I hope so, because in my opinion it symbolizes one of the most important of all possible mental orientations, namely the intention to find out something and thereby to enrich one's mental storehouse of ideas and information. The *investigative attitude* lies at the foundation of all advances in the human condition, from the progression of science to the ordinary business of living a happy life. It involves the willingness to find out something new—something in addition to what you presently know. And it involves a willingness to expend a little effort to find it out. It also involves a willingness to change your mind under the influence of your findings. To the extent that you can ask questions of your world, including yourself, others, and the physical environment around you, you can keep adapting your mental models to match the external reality reasonably well.

> Aristotle could have avoided the mistake of thinking that women have fewer teeth than men by the simple device of asking Mrs. Aristotle to open her mouth.
>
> BERTRAND RUSSELL

Much of the history of scientific discoveries is the history of people noticing curious things and exploring them further. For example, scientist Luigi Galvani noticed a twitching motion in the detached leg of a frog, and his exploration of it led to the principle of the electric battery. In 1895 the German investigator Roentgen noticed that radiation from a cathode tube could penetrate black paper, and his research led to the discovery and use of X rays. Sir Alexander Fleming became curious when a peculiar kind of mold contaminated his bacteria cultures. He began to look into the interactions between the mold and the bacteria, and he discovered penicillin.

Developing the investigative attitude requires adopting the aforementioned policy of fact finding for its own sake, together with the skill of *asking questions*. To the extent that you can train yourself to habitually inquire into things going on about you, you can enrich your personal data base of ideas and information.

For example, a tourist who got lost among the back roads in the middle of Vermont stopped his car to ask directions of one of the natives. "Say, old-timer," he called, leaning out the window of his car. "Am I on the right road to Montpelier?" The elderly gentleman sitting on his porch looked at him for a moment and drawled, "Ee-yup." The tourist drove away, but no sooner had he gone a few hundred yards than he had a strange hunch. Something didn't seem quite right. He put the car in reverse, backed up to the house, and called out to the old man once again. "Say," he asked, "am I going in the right direction?" The old-timer managed just the shade of a grin as he replied, "Nope."

Asking questions effectively requires having a pretty good idea what you want to find out, or at least the ability to recognize when your questions are taking you in a productive direction. Some kinds of questions tend to open up the area of investigation; others tend to narrow it down. Practice using both in your conversations, and you will learn to combine them effectively.

Convergent questions tend to produce *convergent thinking.* They have the effect of narrowing down the topic of thought or discussion and focusing on a smaller range of possibilities. Convergent questions include

1. Concrete questions
2. Binary questions
3. Leading questions
4. Loaded questions

A concrete question asks for a very specific kind of answer and usually helps to surface key facts and exchange useful data between people. Concrete questions tend to clarify a confused situation by bringing the discussion from a highly abstract level down to a more readily understood concrete level. Children tend to ask very concrete questions, and often they want very specific, concrete answers.

For example, a nine-year-old boy approached his father one afternoon and said casually, "Dad, where did I come from?" His father, caught by surprise at the child's simple approach, didn't know exactly how to proceed. After thinking for a few seconds, he sat the boy down on the couch, took a deep breath, and went through a carefully worded explanation of birds, bees, flowers, mothers, fathers, and babies. After listening patiently for a full ten minutes, the boy said, "Yeah, Dad. I know about that stuff. We had that in school. But what I want to know is where I came from." His father was baffled, and his expression showed it. The boy said, "Well, Steve said he came from Baltimore, and Yoko said she came from Japan. I want to know where I came from."

Binary questions, or two-valued questions, encourage the other person to answer in only one of two possible ways. It simply invites him to make a choice between two options, both of which are included in the wording of the question. Although binary questions can quickly narrow down the topic, sometimes they narrow it down too far for convenience. In casual conversation, for example, extensive use of binary questions sometimes takes a conversation into a dead end or prevents it from even getting really started. A typical binary dialogue at a cocktail lounge might sound like this:

"Hi, there."

"Hi."

"Nice place, huh?"

"Yes."

"Do you come here often?"

"No, not really."

"Are you from around here?"

"Yes, I am."

(Awkward silence)

"Do you like the music?"

"Yes."

"Would you like to dance?"

"Okay."

What should have become a friendly exchange of pleasant but inconsequential small talk turned into an exchange of grunts. If one person is rather shy or unsure of the situation, and the other person provides nothing more than binary questions in hopes of getting a conversation started, it probably won't get started.

Leading questions may have some value, but it makes good sense to keep aware of the effect they have on thinking processes. A leading question actually tells the hearer how he or she is supposed to answer. From one point of view, a leading question is really an opinion dressed up to look like a question. As a lecturer, I frequently get questions from members of an audience such as "Dr. Albrecht, don't you think people should try to develop all of their thinking skills and to become as fully rounded as possible?" The words "don't you think" signal me that the questioner holds the opinion expressed in the remainder of the sentence, and he or she would like to see that opinion expressed—or at least endorsed—by the lecturer. I may agree with the opinion, but it is an opinion and not really a question. The effect of the leading question is to cause our thinking to converge to a preselected point, not to offer me an opportunity to share my views. A good rule in asking questions is: Don't ask a question unless you can live with any of the possible answers.

The *loaded question* does the same thing, and I find it a very difficult technique to advocate in most circumstances. Attorneys often use loaded questions, such as those carefully worded to invite a witness to contradict himself so that he will look foolish before the judge or jury. In cases where I've provided expert testimony in legal proceedings, I've found it is a very effective strategy to identify a leading or loaded question and ask to have it reworded properly before answering. This usually disarms an aggressive attorney completely, because the attorney usually hasn't developed any alternatives to this tried and true verbal tactic.

Divergent questions, on the other hand, tend to foster *divergent thinking*. They have the effect of opening up the topic for wider discussion and broader fact finding. Divergent questions include

1. Open-ended questions
2. Abstract questions
3. Speculative questions
4. Reflective questions

Although the exclusive use of divergent questions would probably turn an ordinary conversation into a confused tangle of highly abstract topics, a few carefully selected ones could help to keep the discussion moving in a direction that meets the needs of the people involved. For example, the cocktail lounge discussion mentioned previously might have gone in a different way.

"Hi there."

"Hello."

"How do you like the band?"

"Oh, I like them very much. They're really good."

"Me too. What kinds of songs do you like the best?"

"Oh, I like almost anything except acid rock. Jazz, mellow rock, folk songs—you name it. I just love music of any kind."

"So do I. I've been learning to play the piano lately, so I enjoy watching musicians play even more than I did before."

"Oh, you play the piano? So do I."

"Really, what kinds of music do you play? By the way, would you like to dance?"

"Sure."

The difference is obvious. Divergent questions—in this case, open-ended ones—invite the listener to supply information well beyond the cues contained in the question. This kind of inquiry requires an active mental process on the part of the other party and stirs him or her toward concentration and interest in the topic. After all, the primary function of small talk of this kind is to give the two people something to do, that is, to structure their interaction while they get to know each other and begin to feel comfortable with each other. The skilled conversationalist gives the other person something to talk about and elaborate on.

An abstract question invites the hearer to explore a large topic area and to share fairly complex ideas. This also has the effect of keeping the discussion fairly broad, to enable the participants to explore a wide variety of topics or subtopics. For example, I occasionally like to ask rather abstract questions of the executives in client organizations for whom I serve as a consultant. Questions like "How does your company relate to its competitors?" or "What seems to be the market for your particular service?" or "How would you state your overall corporate strategy in the simplest possible terms?" invite them to think broadly about what they want to do with their organizations.

Similarly, speculative questions invite the hearer to think about more possibilities than those currently known to exist. Questions like "What do you think might happen to the demand for your services if the bottom dropped out of the XYZ market?" or "How would you react if the employees in your organization petitioned to form a union?" invite them to reflect on possibilities that might deserve more careful consideration than they usually get.

A specialized kind of a question, the *reflective question*, really is not a question at all. It merely restates the other person's statement in the form of a question. Reflective questions have certain specialized uses, such as in counseling situations and investigative work. For example, a patient in therapy might say, "Maybe I'll just kill myself." The therapist might respond gently, "You sometimes feel you want to kill yourself?" Or a witness to a disturbance might say, "I think management did some stupid things in handling the workers' grievances." The investigator might reply, "You feel that management could have handled the situation better?" In most cases, when a person makes a strong statement that gets a reflective question in return, he tends to continue along the same line of thinking, rather than stop and move in some other direction, which a more convergent question might suggest. If you want to get to know more of what another person knows, divergent questions often help to keep ideas and information flowing your way.

In addition to using questions effectively for fact finding, you can also help another person to change his mind with questions. As a personal challenge, you might try to rearrange the thinking processes of someone who expresses a particularly dogmatic opinion simply by asking polite divergent questions that lead him to think about alternative points of view You might be surprised at how readily the person might express his views in less dogmatic form and show a willingness to entertain other points of view. A great deal of dogmatism seems to be primarily verbal dogmatism, that is, the tendency to use dogmatic terminology which channels one's thinking into narrow paths. By inviting the other person to discuss the situation or issue in "nonallness" terms, you invite him to think with a nonallness orientation and to accept new possibilities.

Practice asking questions as you go through your normal daily activities. See how many extra questions you can ask in a single day, that is, questions which might bring you a bit more useful information. Test your fact-finding skills at every opportunity. When you hear a confused, complicated explanation from someone, try using concrete questions to clarify the matter. When you hear someone giving strong categorical statements of opinion, try using divergent questions to help him open up his field of view. Try using an occasional reflective question to encourage a person to continue with his line of reasoning. The person may be going somewhere you don't know about, and that direction might be useful or informative for you.

Teach yourself the skill of double-checking information. How often have you asked someone for directions and received a completely erroneous explanation? The person who says "No, Laurel Street doesn't go through the park; you have to go around," may not have visited that part of town since the road department extended the street. In travelling around Europe and Japan, I learned that many people are reluctant to say, "I don't know," and they may very well make a guess. More than once I became the victim of unnecessary politeness. Two reports that matched completely usually gave me much more confidence and made me much more willing to invest shoe leather in trying to find some out-of-the-way place.

You can also take a conscious approach to the process of educating yourself and developing your curiosity by identifying the kinds of things you want to know and giving yourself opportunities to find them out. Think of yourself as placed within an *information stream* of your own choosing, consisting of books, magazines, newsletters, professional or trade journals, lectures, informative television shows and movies, and relationships with interesting people. Each of these sources can enrich you in some way, providing you with new, interesting, and useful information about your world. By consciously arranging your information stream, you can develop a healthy appetite for ideas, and you can make fact finding a permanent habit.

8

using your logic

Man is not rational—merely capable of it.

JONATHAN SWIFT

Two electronic engineers were sitting in an office in New York City. One of them had just finished a telephone conversation with their colleague in Los Angeles. The other had been daydreaming while the first was on the telephone, when a curious fact occurred to him. "You know," he said, "Harry could probably hear your voice in Los Angeles before I could hear it in this room, because the signal travels over the telephone line at nearly the speed of light, while your voice travels over across the room to my ear at only the speed of sound. So Harry knew what you were saying before I did." The other engineer agreed that this was indeed an interesting and very "logical" conclusion.

That evening one of them happened to recall the incident and mentioned it to his wife at dinner. "Did you know," he said, "that if I were talking on the telephone to someone in Los Angeles and you were sitting across from me in the same room, that the person in Los Angeles would hear my voice before you did?" His wife replied casually, "Of course." "Of course?" he said, a bit irritably. "You mean you already knew that?" "Sure," she said. "Everyone knows it's three hours earlier in Los Angeles."

This strikes me as a very interesting little story. Think it over for a moment. Before you succumb to the superior feeling and label the engineer's wife a nitwit, ask yourself what, really, was wrong with her logic. What makes this an illogical conclusion, or indeed is it illogical? In this chapter we will try to strip away the academic and theoretical trappings that often surround the study of logical thinking and show how we can use some very simple and effective logical tools to help us organize our thoughts and deal with the problems that confront us every day.

In his entertaining and useful book, *With Good Reason*, S. Morris Engel writes about the value of studying logic. He says

By acquainting us with the conditions that must always be fulfilled in good reasoning, logic makes it easier for us to know when to withhold our assent and

159

when we may safely offer it. Through learning to identify the soft spots in our own and other people's reasoning, we become more exacting of ourselves and others.[1]

what is logical thinking?

Logic, n. The art of thinking and reasoning in strict accordance with the limitations and incapacities of human misunderstanding.

AMBROSE BIERCE

Logical thinking is simply the use of one bunch of statements to support another bunch of statements. Inasmuch as logic is a conscious verbal process, it is merely a matter of stating ideas in a linear sequence of words, such that the entire construction "seems" right. We can't do any better than that, really.

As discussed in Chapter 2, the cognitive function we call logical reasoning seems to reside primarily in the left hemisphere of the brain, the side that seems to process data by representing it in linear, sequential structures, such as words, phrases, sentences, and sequences of sentences. Logical reasoning amounts to the left-hemisphere function of creating useful linear "word pictures," which interrelate in such a way that they help you to understand your world and to build your more complex memory models of that world.

Sometimes people confuse themselves with illogical descriptions of the situations they want to deal with. One lady, for example, complained to her friend, "My husband cheats so much, I'm not even sure my last child was his." The thinking skill of *accurate description* plays an important part in clear, logical thinking.

Scientists still don't know precisely how logical reasoning works within the cerebral cortex. It seems to involve making "preferred" associations between one idea or set of ideas and another. In our personal experience we recognize that reaching a conclusion involves "going" from one idea—point A, so to speak, to another idea, point B. When you make a logical step, such as you do hundreds or thousands of times a day, you pass from the first idea to the second with a subjective feeling that the step is correct—the conclusion is somehow "right." But your brain makes the transition so quickly and so deftly that you can't slow down the process and examine it. It simply "happens" inside your brain.

For example, you may say, "It's raining outside. Guess I'll take my umbrella." Your brain has gone through a fairly complex logical process, and you've probably paid very little attention to it. If you were to expand the thought process to a larger form (which you probably would not do), you might say, "It's raining outside. If I go out in the rain without an

[1]S. Morris Engel, *With Good Reason* (New York: St. Martin's Press, 1976), p. 13.

umbrella, I get wet. If I use an umbrella when I go out into the rain, I don't get wet. I plan to go out. I don't want to get wet. Therefore, if I take my umbrella I won't get wet. So, I will take my umbrella."

Your brain solves this little logical problem very deftly at the preconscious level, as discussed in Chapter 2, with only a very fragmentary verbalization of the pieces of the problem. Notice how each of the ideas simply seems to follow from the one preceding it; yet you still cannot see the connection itself. In a way, your brain puts the connection there, as a result of having associated the two ideas together many times in the past. The apparent logical "connection" between one idea and the next is merely evidence of your brain's willingness to place them in that order and to derive a subjective sensation of comfort with the arrangement. Logical connections exist only in your brain, not in the world outside your brain.

In this chapter we will take for granted the brain's ability to carry out simple logical processes such as deciding to take the umbrella. We will focus our attention on the more complex verbal reasoning processes by which people solve problems, work together, manipulate and cheat one another, make themselves crazy, and make themselves sane. We will develop a brief vocabulary of terms to study logical thinking, learn how to verbalize logical propositions, and learn how to analyze logical propositions we see and hear. The goal of this exploration is to increase our skill of using logical reasoning more effectively, to solve problems better, and to keep from getting confused by the reasoning processes other people try to use with us and on us.

logical propositions

Let us not dream that reason can ever be popular. Passions, emotions, may be made popular, but reason remains ever the property of the few.

GOETHE

To develop our logical skills, let's borrow a few tools from the logician. We need to understand the following five concepts:

1. Logical propositions.
2. Premises.
3. Arguments.
4. Inferences.
5. Conclusions.

These terms, together with a few others we'll add as we go, are all we need to understand how to think more logically and to avoid being victimized by the illogical thinking of other people. Let's define these ideas and then see how they work.

A *logical proposition* is simply a complete reasoning process, neatly packaged into words so we can take a look at it. Here, we will use the term *logical* in a strictly neutral way, without connotations of positive evaluation. A logical proposition, for our purposes, is simply a reasoning process that someone offers for acceptance. When we label it *logical*, we mean only that it *purports* to arrive at a conclusion by a logical process, not that it is necessarily true or that it represents effective thinking. Although we usually use the term *logical* in everyday conversation as a general term of praise for a thinking process with which we agree, we use it here in a narrower sense, merely to indicate a thought process having a certain structure.

A logical proposition is really just a verbal map consisting of three parts, which indicate the progression of thought. These three parts are

1. The premises, or "facts" we start with.
2. The argument, or the way in which we put the premises together.
3. The conclusion, or the result we arrive at by applying the argument to the premises.

Again we must use our terms carefully. The term *argument*, when used in discussing logic, does not refer to a shouting match, but merely to a structured process of relating the premises to one another. For example, if the premises take the form of numbers or measurements, the argument might be a mathematical relationship, such as "I need three thousand dollars for my vacation trip to Europe. I have two thousand saved so far. That means I have to get another thousand dollars." In this case, the premises are the first two statements. The argument is the implied relationship: Amount needed minus amount presently available equals additional amount to be acquired. The conclusion of the proposition is the last statement in the group.

In defining premises above, I chose to include the term "facts" in quotation marks as a reminder that the structures of our verbal maps always limit our ability to know anything for absolutely certain. Every statement of fact we can make inevitably rests on human descriptive processes, and except for the simplest, most basic incidences of direct observation, they always have a shade of doubtfulness about them, even though we may willingly take them as "true."

Note that when we try to spell out the argument of the proposition, we must try to verbalize the process by which the brain associates the premises with the conclusion. For mathematical arguments, this does not pose much of a problem. But for more complex verbal arguments, we must sometimes settle for a general statement, which more or less "captures" the essence of the relationship. For example, we can examine a proposition such as "I want to buy some new furniture, but I want to spend as little as possible. I heard that XYZ store will have a sale on the kind of furniture I want next month. I think I'll wait till then to buy what I need." The first two sentences constitute the premises. The last sentence expresses the conclusion. We could spell out the argument in a number of ways, but we might find it just as satisfying to take the argument in its "invisible"—that is, un-verbalized—form. The argument in this case "feels right." In some other case, where the argument seems strange to us, we might want to press further and chase it down more explicitly.

We can see that the argument of the proposition serves as the invisible "glue" that binds the premises to the conclusion. We speak of arguing for the conclusion, as a matter of simply connecting the premises in a certain relationship, so that the conclusion seems to follow from them in a satisfying way. Logicians also use the term *inference* with a completely neutral connotation. Although we often hear the term used in a derogatory sense, such as "You're making an inference!", in this context we use it interchangeably with the term *argument*. To argue for a certain conclusion means to infer it from the premises.

So far, so good. We've established that a logical proposition is merely a complete statement of a reasoning process, consisting of some premises, an argument that is often implicit in the statement, and a conclusion. We get the conclusion from the premises by making an inference, that is, by applying the argument to the premises.

Our exploration here centers not on how the brain carries out logical propositions, but rather on the ways in which people use and misuse them. We can simplify our discussion immensely by counting on the fact that the cognitive function of logical reasoning resides in the tissue of your cerebral cortex. You cannot learn to reason logically; your brain already knows how. But you can learn to deploy that powerful computer-logic capability more effectively by learning how to verbalize and analyze some of the logical propositions that play a part in your everyday thinking processes.

To simplify even further, we can note that people tend to use logical propositions with varying degrees of definiteness. That is, many of them are submerged within the flow of conversation, discussion, and sometimes debate, so that they often go unnoticed or unanalyzed. In addition, people tend to use logical propositions for one of two basic purposes, and usually not for both at the same time. These purposes are

1. To analyze available facts and arrive at a conclusion or a decision.
2. To persuade someone else of a conclusion already arrived at.

Because the second purpose involves many more opportunities for confusing one's self and others, and provides the basis by which many people try to trick, swindle, manipulate, intimidate, and confuse one another, it deserves considerably more study than the first. Therefore, most of this discussion will focus on *logical fallacies*, which are propositions or attempts at propositions that don't stand up successfully to careful scrutiny.

These persuasive propositions come in two kinds. *Overt propositions* present themselves in complete form for your scrutiny, while *covert propositions* tend to hide within the verbal quagmire of human discourse. These hidden propositions, which often won't come out and fight in public, can play some of the worst tricks on human thinking processes. So we must learn to identify the logical propositions operating in various situations, dredge them up out of the verbal swamp, clean them off, state them in straightforward terms, and analyze them.

truth, validity, and soundness

A beautiful theory, murdered by a gang of brutal facts.

THOMAS HUXLEY

A biologist performed a series of experiments with a flea, trying to learn more about the perceptual processes of these tiny creatures. First, he trained a flea to jump on command. He would put the flea on a glass plate, lean over it, and say, "Jump!" The flea would reliably hop straight up. Then he removed one of the flea's legs. At the word "Jump!" the flea hopped just about as usual. Then the scientist removed a second leg. Again the flea hopped up in the air in response to the command, but not quite as high as usual. The scientist continued removing the flea's legs one at a time, until the flea had only one leg left. On the command, it only managed to twitch feebly. After removing the flea's last leg, the scientist commanded, "Jump!" The flea did not move. "Jump!" Nothing. After repeated commands and noting that the flea did not jump, the scientist wrote in his research report, "The hearing organs of the flea are located on its legs."

Something about the story just doesn't "click"—but what's wrong? In this case, we have a logical fallacy. The premises seem right, but the argument is not *valid*. It doesn't match with our experience. By some strange variation of nature, the flea's ears *could* be on its legs, but our common sense tells us to question the validity of the inference.

Actually, a logical proposition can be *sound* only if the premises are true and the argument is *valid*. If either of these conditions is not met, the whole thing collapses under careful scrutiny. Returning to the analogy of traveling from point A to point B, we can now see how to test any logical proposition to determine whether it is sound. As Figure 8.1 shows, only one combination of characteristics of the premises and the argument will produce an acceptable proposition, that is, a believable conclusion.

We have just seen an example of a logical proposition that failed the test of soundness because of an invalid argument. How about one that fails because of false premises? Just such an everyday logical fallacy occurred in my local post office. A man was trying to get change from a dollar-bill

PREMISES + ARGUMENT = CONCLUSION

If the Premises Are:	And the Argument Is:	Then the Proposition Is:
True	Valid	Sound
True	Invalid	Unsound
False	Valid	Unsound
False	Invalid	Unsound

Figure 8.1 Only one combination of premises and argument gives a sound logical proposition.

changing machine. He kept trying to insert the bill into the machine's slot, but it wouldn't accept the money. A woman standing beside him, probably unfamiliar with such machines, offered the advice, "Why don't you fold it over, so it will go in?" Since the bill-changing machine must inspect the entire face of the bill to verify it, this was a false premise. The woman misunderstood the machine's operation.

Note that the term *false premise* does not mean that anyone has deliberately told a lie. The situation might include that possibility, but the term, as we'll use it, merely means that the premises used are "false to facts."

When we begin to think carelessly, hastily, or in self-deluding ways, we tend to construct unreliable, unsound propositions. And when other people try to convince us of various conclusions, they may be tempted to resort to unsound propositions and especially to camouflage them in a variety of ways. In the next section, we will make a fairly complete inventory of these logical fallacies and dodges.

Actually, we should consider even sound propositions to vary in their levels of "soundness." In using our logical brain processes, we need not limit ourselves to pure, "hard" facts, which we can express so concretely that no doubt could exist. We certainly can use premises that are somewhat abstractly stated and open to judgment or evaluation. This makes the premises "somewhat true." For example, we can say that "Rapidly growing corporations tend to have more internal confusion and disequilibrium than those which have settled at a stable size." This statement is rather abstract but fairly characteristic of the kinds of statements we frequently make in describing organizations.

We can add some other statements to this one to make a complete logical proposition, such as: "Since this is a rapidly growing corporation, it would be a good idea to pay attention to the effectiveness of our internal communications and to our production efficiency." We have taken a "fairly true" set of premises and combined them with a "fairly valid" argument, and so we have produced a "fairly sound" conclusion. This process proba-bly describes the overwhelming proportion of our day-to-day logical prop-ositions. Many writers oversimplify the idea of a logical proposition by using an example such as: "All men are mortal. Socrates is a man. There-fore, Socrates is mortal." Such a proposition is certainly true, but it is not especially relevant to the kinds of topics we deal with in our daily ac-tivities. If you ever have occasion to prove to someone that Socrates was mortal, you will have the situation well under control. But for the most part, we must make our approach to the use of logic sufficiently practical so that it enables us to attack real problems that need real solutions.

Two other features of logical propositions will complete this brief dis-cussion. These are the processes of *deduction* and *induction*. A *deductive argument* proceeds from a broad set of premises to arrive at a rather specific conclusion. Conversely, an *inductive argument* starts from specific prem-ises to arrive at a rather broad conclusion.

A deductive argument might run as follows: "To practice law in this state, one must have passed the bar examination. This person practices law here, so I assume he has passed the bar exam." The deductive proposition goes from the general to the specific. The Socrates proposition given above, also known as a logical *syllogism*, is an example of a deductive argument. In the strictest sense, the term *deductive* describes those arguments in which the conclusion *necessarily* follows from the premises.

An inductive argument might run as follows: "I've seen many more fat people in America than I have in most other countries I've visited. Ameri-cans must be more overweight, as a group, than people of most other countries." In an inductive argument, the conclusion follows only *with probability* from the premises. The example of the scientist and the flea constitutes an inductive proposition.

Another way to understand the difference between deductive and in-ductive arguments is to recognize that in the inductive argument we venture beyond the information given in the premises. In the deductive argument, all the information necessary to the conclusion exists in the premises themselves. Of course, as noted above, either a deductive propo-sition or an inductive one can give a "fairly sound" conclusion.

You can improve your ability to analyze situations logically by forming the habit of *verbalizing* propositions. In a confused situation, when faced with a complex problem, or when listening to a persuasive but suspicious argument, stop and break it down into its three component parts—premises, argument, and conclusion. By applying the simple tests of truth and validity, you can decide how much faith to place in the proposition. You can also figure out how to make it clearer or more trustworthy by correcting the premises, or by improving the validity of the argument.

Practice explaining your ideas to others in terms of clearly stated logical propositions. Give the facts and assumptions on which you base your conclusions. Then clarify the arguments you used in arriving at them. And share with the other person your overall thinking process to gain the advantage of his or her feedback and ideas. To the extent that you can clearly verbalize a logical proposition, especially one that has been hiding from direct view, you can keep your own thinking straight, and you can base your views and conclusions on clear logical processes.

recognizing logical dodges and fallacies

I realized that, regardless of persons or topics of discussion, the same tricks and dodges recurred again and again and could easily be recognized.

SCHOPENHAUER

Sometimes people succumb to the temptation to try to manipulate or confuse one another by clever use of words. In fact, this seems to have achieved the status of an art in American advertising, in politics, and to some extent in business. In other cases, people may merely put their ideas together in confused, illogical patterns. If you can program your crap detector to recognize the varieties of ways in which people misuse logical arguments, you can make yourself virtually immune to manipulation and confusion. Understanding illogical thought processes can help you enormously in thinking more logically and in spotting the kinds of trickery other people sometimes use and logical traps they can innocently fall into.

In this section we deal mostly with persuasive propositions, both overt and covert, and we focus on those that people may use to advance their own objectives by trying to get others to accept their conclusions. Let us take an inventory of the various types of logical tricks and see how they work.

We can divide logical tricks into two broad categories: *logical dodges* and *logical fallacies.* A logical dodge is any attempt to get a person to accept a conclusion without actually giving logical arguments of any kind to support it. The expert user of the logical dodge wants to distract you from logical thinking altogether, so that you will accept his or her conclusion without examining the basis for it from your own point of view.

A logical fallacy consists of a logical proposition that doesn't stand up successfully to the twin tests of truth and validity. The user of the logical fallacy does offer you a logical proposition, but he or she hopes you won't test it. The user chooses the premises or the argument, or both, in order to impress you so much that you won't apply your logical tests.

Thus, we can actually divide logical tricks into three categories: logical dodges and two kinds of logical fallacies—those of faulty premises and those of faulty argument. We can break these down a bit more, according to how they actually operate in the process of persuasion. The following classification should help in studying them methodically:

1. Logical dodges
2. Faulty premises
   a. factual errors
   b. misleading terms
3. Faulty arguments
   a. fallacies of cause and effect
   b. fallacies of relevance

Figure 8.2 shows these in the form of a "family tree," with the various techniques assigned to their categories. Let's list them here for reference.

1. Logical dodges
   a. begging the question
   b. red herring (irrelevant issue)
   c. personal attack
   d. trick question
   e. false analogy
   f. absurdity
   g. special immunity
2. Faulty premises—factual errors
   a. incorrect facts
   b. weak facts
   c. the big lie
   d. irrelevant data
   e. suggestion
3. Faulty premises—misleading terms
   a. epithet
   b. euphemism
   c. misleading metaphor
   d. word magic
   e. personification
   f. either-or
   g. equivocation
   h. double standard
4. Faulty arguments—cause and effect
   a. post hoc
   b. false cause
   c. false dependence
   d. false correlation
   e. oversimplification
   f. rationalization

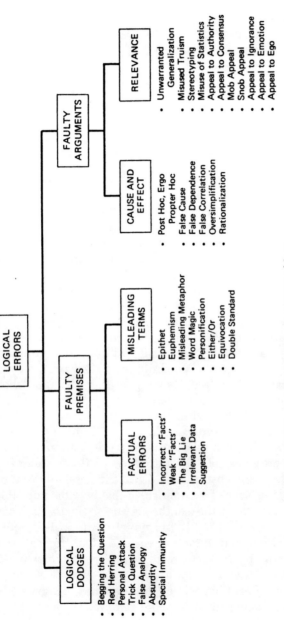

Figure 8.2 Logical errors come in a variety of forms.

169

5. Faulty arguments—relevance
   a. unwarranted generalization
   b. misused truism
   c. stereotyping
   d. misuse of statistics
   e. appeal to authority
   f. appeal to consensus
   g. mob appeal
   h. snob appeal
   i. appeal to ignorance
   j. appeal to emotion
   k. appeal to ego

Now let's examine each one briefly to clarify its definition and the way it operates.

All seven of the logical dodges listed have as their purpose the evasion of logical argument, rather than the construction of one.

The ploy of *begging the question*, sometimes by means of circular reasoning, simply doesn't deal with the question at issue. The conclusion drawn from the premise is itself offered as proof of the premise. Mayor Richard Daley of Chicago offered the classic answer of this type when a news reporter asked why Hubert Humphrey failed to carry Illinois in the presidential election. Said Daley, "He didn't get enough votes."

The *red herring*, or irrelevant issue, involves introducing a thesis that has nothing to do with the conclusion in question and then arguing that thesis. The term comes from a technique used by escaping prisoners. They used to toss a spoiled, or "red," herring on the path behind them to interfere with the bloodhounds' delicate sense of smell. For example, "The government should not interfere with cigarette advertising, nor should it discourage cigarette sales. Cigarette smoking is not as harmful to health as many people say. Besides, the tobacco industry is extremely important to the economy. It provides jobs for hundreds of thousands of people." The speaker has tried to substitute an argument unrelated to the health argument, namely the issue of economics, probably in the hope that by substantiating that thesis, he or she can then return to the original conclusion and get the hearer to accept it without noticing the logical detour.

The ploy of *personal attack*, a very common logical dodge, involves trying to discredit the person who advances a certain thesis, instead of proving that the thesis is not a good one. Name calling, ridicule, and bringing in irrelevant aspects of the opposing person's life all provide ammunition for personal attack. For example: "That guy is a socialist, and everybody knows it. Take what he says about wage and price controls with a grain of salt."

The ploy of the *trick question* attempts to put the respondent in a logical dilemma in which he will discredit himself no matter how he answers. The age-old joke questions like "Do you still beat your wife?" and "Are you still drinking as heavily as you used to?" illustrate the logical trap effect of the trick question, also known to logicians as the *complex question*. On a radio interview show, a news writer asked a political figure, "Mr. X, you were recently quoted as saying you favor the ABC bill. Are you being inconsistent in your position on this matter or have you simply compromised with the White House for your own convenience?" Other forms of the complex question, perhaps of less practical interest, include linguistic riddles or impossible questions like "If God can do anything, can he make a stone big enough that He himself can't lift it?" Another classical example of this kind of *sophism* is the ancient trick statement made by the Cretan that "All Cretans are liars." If you think about the statement and its underlying concept, you have trouble making it "hold still." These logical curiosities form an entire subject of study for some theorists. I've never lost much sleep over them, myself.

The ploy of the *false analogy* also appears frequently in persuasive conversation. The speaker offers a dramatic illustration of his or her point by means of an analogy, which unfortunately does not resemble the situation under scrutiny. One old chauvinist commented, "A good wife is like a good rug. You have to beat them both occasionally to keep them good." Using analogies effectively requires that they resemble the situation of interest in important ways and that differences be confined to unimportant areas.

The ploy of *absurdity* involves turning the entire issue or situation into a joking matter, in hopes that others will forget that the speaker hasn't proved the conclusion. Many people also use this ploy to "disprove", that is, shoot down, another person's proposed course of action. For example, a man in a business conference might offer a new idea, which he has not completely thought through. It might form the nucleus of an important advance for the organization, but someone else might reply, "Where did you get that one, Tom? Out of a fortune cookie?" In the ensuing laughter, the idea might shrivel up and die while the group goes on to more "serious" matters.

Using the creative dodge of *special immunity*, one simply declares the entire matter at issue beyond the reach of logic. A few topics, such as human nature, romantic love, astrology, fortune telling, extrasensory perception, communication with the dead, religious doctrine, and artistic inspiration, seem to enjoy this kind of special immunity to logical discussion. Person A might insist that person B do something that will benefit person A—perhaps agree not to date other people—but which might not be in B's best interests as B sees it. Person A may say, "But I love you. You know that if you date anybody else, I get jealous. Why do you hurt my feelings that way?" This tactic also forms part of the appeal to guilt, classified under logical fallacies of argument. When person B begins to inquire into the nature of the situation, asking for a definition of the terms involved, person A may retreat to the time-honored statement and say, "But why do you have to analyze it? Love is love. You can't define it. You can't analyze it. Just go with it." In my personal opinion, if one wants to grant special immunity from logical review to some topic, then he or she has no right to ask others to accept "logical" conclusions drawn from that topic as if they had the same degree of soundness as other conclusions drawn from nonexempt topics.

> *Faith, n. Belief, without evidence, in what is told by one who speaks without knowledge, of things without parallel.*
>
> AMBROSE BIERCE

Next, in examining the kinds of logical fallacies that stem from faulty premises (whether involving factual errors or misleading terms), we will see that the factual inputs to the reasoning process suffer in various ways, thus preventing one from reaching a trustworthy conclusion. First, we consider those faulty premises that involve factual errors.

The fallacy of *incorrect facts* speaks for itself. A speaker who begins with completely untrue premises will very likely reach an unsound conclusion. For example: "A policeman wears his badge on the left side of his chest, so that if he gets shot the badge will protect his heart." To the best of our medical knowledge, the vast majority of human hearts lie squarely in the center of the chest. A bullet passing into the left side of the chest would probably just graze the heart. Many of our popular fallacies rest on "facts" like the one stated above.

The fallacy of weak facts is more or less a variation on the fallacy of incorrect facts. When the speaker offers as facts certain statements that rest on rather shaky ground, the soundness of the proposition comes into jeopardy. For example: "The students at this college are dissatisfied with the impractical, theoretical orientation of the business administration curriculum. We need to improve the real-world orientation of our programs." The "strength" of the facts presented here, that is, the "degree" to which they are true, will depend on the way in which the speaker gathered the evidence. A few casual conversations would not provide facts with the same strength as a thorough survey supported by extensive individual and group interviews. Another version of the fallacy of weak facts involves carefully selecting only the information that will support the conclusion.

The *Big Lie* fallacy rests on making an extreme statement and promoting it heavily until many people accept it. Once they accept it as a fact, one can build logical propositions on it, which they will also accept. Adolph Hitler observed that the masses of people will more easily fall victim to a great lie than to a small one. Perhaps most of us wouldn't have the nerve to tell an outlandish lie, and so we assume that the person telling an outlandish lie wouldn't either. We may unwittingly reason that "He wouldn't be saying that if there weren't some truth to it."

> The men the American people admire most extravagantly are the most daring liars; the men they detest most violently are those who try to tell them the truth.
>
> H.L. MENCKEN

The fallacy of *irrelevant data* depends on the use of facts and figures that, although perhaps true, have no real bearing on the issue. A television commercial for a certain toothpaste claims that "Three out of five of the dentists we surveyed recommended XYZ toothpaste." It sounds authoritative, but it offers no particular reason why *you* should use the product—that is, it does not provide premises and a valid argument to prove the value of the toothpaste for your own teeth.

> A truth that's told with bad intent
> Beats all the lies you can invent.
>
> WILLIAM BLAKE

The fallacy of *suggestion* operates by hinting that something is or is not so and then letting other people jump to conclusions from there. A newspaper account might say, "Senator A made no mention of whether he had accepted bribes or campaign contributions in the XYZ affair." This innuendo might be entirely the creation of the writer, yet taking it on face value, the reader may conclude that the writer had some facts or possible facts that made the statement relevant. Marc Antony's technique of suggestion, coupled with repetition in his famous "Friends, Romans, Countrymen" speech, accomplished the same thing. After he had repeated the statement ". . . and Brutus is an honorable man" for about the fifth time, the crowd began to doubt the honorable intentions of Brutus in killing Caesar. Antony never said that Brutus was dishonorable; in fact, he said just the opposite. But his skillful use of suggestion got the real message across.

The second kind of fallacy of false premises, *misleading terms*, involves the manipulation of meanings and connotations of words in such a way that the hearer becomes more willing to accept the conclusion than if it came packaged in simpler or less carefully worded terms. The choice of words makes the argument "go down easily" because it capitalizes on the hearer's automatic responses to certain connotations.

The familiar fallacy of the *epithet* places a strongly derogatory label on a person, an idea, an institution, a point of view, or a course of action. The speaker intends to establish a judgmental bias in the mind of the hearer, so that the hearer will tend to accept the conclusion being offered or reject the one being attacked, without taking the trouble to examine the available evidence. A magazine article dealing with the U.S.-Soviet Strategic Arms Limitation Talks (SALT) used the title "Salt II—Blueprint for Disaster." After reading the article, one might have derived enough facts to make his or her own judgment, but the bias of the article showed clearly in the title. You can recognize the fallacy of the epithet quite easily once you start listening for it.

Euphemism works just the opposite from the fallacy of the epithet. By choosing a label with a predominantly positive emotional connotation, the speaker invites the hearers to adopt a judgmental bias in favor of the conclusion advanced. For example, a campaign commercial described a candidate for office as ". . . a taxpayer, a homeowner, and a family man. He's a working lieutenant governor." The individual in question may or may not have made a good whatever-it-is he was running for. This partially hidden proposition simply fails to shed any important factual light on that question.

The fallacy of the misleading metaphor uses a figure of speech to establish a biased point of view and then proceeds to argue for the conclusion by using the various terms that one naturally tends to associate with the metaphor. For example, a person might justify taking advantage of others by saying, "Look—life is a game. There are winners and losers. If you get more chips than the other guy, you win. If he gets the chips, you lose. It's as simple as that. I play to win." Notice how the original metaphor—the idea of a game—brings with it a variety of other ideas that are verbally associated with it. They all reside in the same verbal ballpark, and they tend to reinforce one another as they come to mind. The choice of the metaphor gives the conclusion a kind of artificial "verbal armor," which protects it from logical scrutiny. The only way to overcome this misleading orientation is to set aside the metaphor and make a new description of the situation. The English language abounds with metaphorical structures that can mislead and confuse us if we don't pay attention to them.

The fallacy of word magic involves the use of emotionally "loaded" words, that is, those we tend to respond to with unwitting value judgments. An advertisement for a perfume named "Tigress" might read, "Tonight, become a tigress. He'll love you for it." The partially stated proposition is that if you wear this kind of perfume, you will become an aggressive, highly sensual creature and the man of your dreams will fall in love with you. The choice of words tends to influence the listener's thinking in much the same way that magical phrases and incantations do.

A good catchword can obscure analysis for fifty years.

WENDELL L. WILLKIE

The fallacy of *personification* involves describing an inanimate object or an abstract institution in terms that imply it has human characteristics or that it functions like a living thing. Such phrases as "the stock market rallied today, flexing its muscles on heavy trading" tend to lead the hearer into conceiving of some living, breathing creature actually behaving in some measurable way, rather than to consider that a large number of people took certain kinds of actions. Although the use of personifying terms does not in itself constitute a fallacy, basing conclusions solely on personification may well amount to one. For example, one might say, "I just couldn't leave XYZ company. The company's been good to me. It wouldn't be right to quit, even for more money." In this case, the speaker has based a conclusion on a misleading verbal map—the idea that some imaginary "person" called the company would somehow be hurt or disappointed if he or she quit. News reports sometimes personify government agencies with terms like "the CIA denied any involvement in the matter," or "the White House said that plans are underway for the new project." Many people refer to America as "she" and talk about "her spirit," "her attitude," and "her mood." Personification does not always produce unsound propositions, but the risk is much greater than with concrete descriptive terms.

The *either-or* fallacy operates by expressing an argument in terms of only two mutually exclusive choices and by arguing for one of them as the conclusion. This conveniently eliminates other alternatives which might offer acceptable courses of action. A classic example of the either-or fallacy, also known to logicians as the fallacy of *bifurcation*, is the statement "You're either part of the solution or you're part of the problem." This sounds heroic and challenging, but it excludes other options that someone with a different point of view on "the problem" might want to entertain. Other well-known examples include "Better dead than red," "Fifty-four-forty or fight," and "Give me liberty or give me death!"

The fallacy of *equivocation* involves shifting the meaning or the usage of a key word somewhere between the premises and the conclusion. Returning to the example at the beginning of this chapter concerning the engineer's wife who knew that it was three hours earlier in Los Angeles, we can see that the innocent fallacy derives from shifting the meaning of the word "time," which actually never appeared in the conversation. The man's concept of the other person hearing his voice before his colleague did involved the idea of sequential events. His wife introduced a different unspoken definition of time as a matter of the position of the hands on the clock and the difference between clocks in New York and those in Los Angeles. In a similar vein, I once attended a lecture entitled "Scientific Proof of Reincarnation." When the speaker offered to prove that reincarnation actually took place, using Newton's three laws of physics, I was eager to hear. Having been educated as a physicist, I felt well equipped to understand such an eminently logical approach. However, after the speaker summarized Newton's three laws, which deal with physical forces and the motions of bodies acted upon by those forces, he proceeded to employ the terms *force* and *energy* in a very loose, nonphysical sense. He referred to energy fields and force fields that presumably exist but cannot be measured, and he used the term force in a highly metaphoric sense. While I still find the hypothesis of reincarnation interesting, his technique of equivocation—shifting the meaning of the two crucial words—did not advance the case one inch toward a logical proof of the hypothesis.

The *double standard* fallacy operates by changing the descriptive system used from one case to another in order to invoke two different sets of values or judgments and to get the hearer to respond differently in two similar situations. A typical example concerns the corporate executive who lectures to the Rotary Club luncheon on one day about the evils of government intervention in free enterprise. The next day he vigorously lobbies for government legislation to protect his products from "unfair" competition by foreign manufacturers, conveniently sidestepping the fact that American consumers will pay more for his products than for the foreign-made ones if the government grants his demands. What is sauce for the goose is definitely not sauce for the gander in the fallacy of the double standard, also known to logicians as the fallacy of *special pleading*. A story concerning a small town preacher illustrates how the double standard attitude can backfire. He harangued the congregation with ". . . and I say to you, if any man in this room has committed adultery, his tongue shall cleave to the woof of his mowf!"

Moving next to the third class of fallacies, those involving faulty arguments, let's look at the first subset called fallacies of cause and effect. These include attempts to show that one event follows from another, when in fact it does not, or when we cannot reasonably expect it to as a general matter.

The fallacy known as *post hoc*, after the Latin term *post hoc, ergo propter hoc*, meaning "after this therefore because of this," rests on the simplistic idea that if event B came after event A, then A somehow must have caused B. The brain has a natural tendency to associate events that happen close together in time sequence, so this fallacy can easily arise in complex situations. Mark Twain once commented, "When the (civil) war broke out and commerce on the Mississippi River ceased, my occupation was gone. So I joined the Confederacy. I served for two weeks, and then deserted. The Confederacy fell."

The fallacy of *false cause* works in a similar way to the post hoc fallacy, but it usually involves a more general interpretation of the cause-and-effect relationship between two events or processes. My son was born on the day of George Washington's birthday. When the government decided to promote the policy of long weekends and announced that the holiday would fall on the nearest Monday in February, Steve became somewhat concerned. He thought that perhaps the government had changed his birthday. To a ten-year-old, such things seem a good deal more complex than they seem to adults. The following story about a mathematician also illustrates the false cause fallacy. Because this fellow traveled extensively in connection with his work, he worried about the possibility of a bomb being placed on a plane in which he might ride. His estimates of the probability of having a bomb on board came to about one in a thousand, which he considered unacceptable odds. But one day he had a flash of inspiration. He estimated the chances of there being *two* bombs on board and came up with odds of about one in a million. Finding these odds much more to his liking, thereafter he always carried a bomb in his luggage whenever he traveled.

The *false dependence* fallacy operates similarly to that of false cause, except that it looks backward in time to establish connections. For example: "Roosevelt was a warlike president. He did many things that encouraged the expansion of World War II and America's involvement. If Roosevelt hadn't been president, we would never have been in the war." The fallacy here lies in the contention that American involvement depended on Roosevelt's presidency and that no other state of affairs could have brought about the same result.

False correlation involves connecting two disparate events or situations together and implying that some underlying process causes them both or that one causes the other. Henry Ford is quoted as saying, "If you will study the history of almost any criminal, you will find he is an inveterate cigarette smoker." A study of declining scores on the Scholastic Aptitude Test (SAT) given to high school students concluded ". . . it is perhaps most significant of all that during the past ten years, the curve of the SAT scores has followed very closely the curve of the entire nation's spirits and self-esteem and sense of purpose." In this case, the panel claimed a correlation between a very concrete fact and an extremely abstract concept. Although one might agree with the sense of the statement, it falls apart as a logical proposition because of the unproven and very abstract connection between the two ideas.

The fallacy of *oversimplification* involves too narrow a definition of the premises, usually by claiming that one single factor is the complete cause of some state of affairs. A typical oversimplified proposition might be "We should elect new judges. We have a high crime rate because our judges are too lenient in sentencing convicted criminals." Although we might find the cause cited in the argument to play a part in the situation, it would be very unlikely that one single factor could completely determine such an extremely complex state of affairs. The antidote to the oversimplification fallacy is the *principle of multiple causes,* or as some scientific researchers say, "Everything affects everything else in some way or another." The Sufi scholar Idries Shah likes to tell the teaching story about the Mulla Nasrudin, a kind of folk-wizard who was asked by a scholar, "What is fate?" Nasrudin replied, "Fate is an endless succession of intertwined events, each influencing the other." The scholar replied curtly, "That is hardly an answer. I believe in cause and effect." "Very well," said the Mulla, "look at that." He pointed to a procession passing in the street. "That man is being taken to be hanged. Is that because someone gave him a silver piece and enabled him to buy the knife with which he committed the murder, or because someone saw him do it, or because nobody stopped him?"[2]

> *Everything should be made as simple as possible, but not simpler.*
>
> ALBERT EINSTEIN

The fallacy of *rationalization*, mentioned in previous chapters, involves finding socially acceptable reasons to justify one's actions, when the real reasons would probably draw disapproval if honestly expressed. We can list an endless number of rationalizations, depending on our opinions of the "real" reasons for another's behavior. Probably we can identify our own rationalizations most accurately. To decide that a certain logical proposition constitutes a rationalization involves an inevitable value judgment on our part. For example, I've heard the statement made by staff people of some mental hospitals concerning the continual sedation of the inmates there: "We have to medicate them for their own good. Many of them couldn't function without tranquilizers or sedatives to stabilize their conditions." It seems to me that people who go through their entire waking hours in a stuporous condition stand little chance of learning to deal with their problems effectively, since their more complex thought processes no longer operate clearly. They do, however, become quite docile and easily manageable by the hospital staff, which it seems to me may be the "real" reason for the continual use of drugs. A suspected rationalization should invite further inquiry and closer examination of the premises.

Moving now to the last category of logical fallacies involving faulty arguments, namely fallacies of relevance, we find a number of more or less similar techniques that hinge on very weak relationships between premises and conclusions.

The fallacy of *unwarranted generalization* shows up routinely in casual conversation as well as in political discourse, advertising, and in business settings. Any sweeping statement about a person, group of people, place, idea, course of action, or system of belief probably warrants close examination. A tourist may say, "I'm never going back to Spain. You can't trust those people. I had all my luggage stolen there." The sweeping generaliza-

---

[2] I first discovered this and other intriguing Sufi teaching stories in Robert E. Ornstein, *The Psychology of Consciousness* (San Francisco: W.H. Freeman & Company Publishers, 1972), p. 75.

tion about the Spanish people made from one incident reflects a relatively low order of logical thinking, which we can all fall prey to occasionally. This struck me vividly when I was traveling extensively through a number of countries during 1972. I was in Germany when newspapers around the world carried the story of the shooting of George Wallace. One person, on learning that I came from the United States, asked, "Aren't you afraid to go back to America? It's such a violent country!"

> All generalizations are dangerous, even this one.
>
> ALEXANDER DUMAS

The fallacy of the *misused truism* invokes a broad statement that many people seem to accept as a fact and then applies it to justify a very specific conclusion. Advertisers abandoned the message "Everybody needs milk" after the Food and Drug Administration ruled that not everybody needs milk and that some people find milk harmful to their health because it stimulates allergic reactions and digestive disorders for them. Another example of the misused truism involves the justification given by some cigarette smokers for smoking in the presence of others. "It's a free country. Each person can do what he wants. I have just as much right to smoke as someone else has not to smoke." Bringing the argument down to specific features such as the effect on the health of others in the smoker's vicinity makes this proposition crumble.

The fallacy of *stereotyping* operates in reverse of the fallacy of generalization. In this case, the speaker deduces a characteristic about one member of a class, based on characteristics generally attributed to that class. For example, people may stereotype Chinese as clever and inscrutable, Germans as cold and analytical, French and Italians as romantic and emotional, and other races and nationalities in more damaging terms. Stereotyping very often plays a large part in employment discrimination. A foreman may say, "Look, there's no way in the world a physically handicapped person can do this job." Yet, without specifying the exact nature of the handicap or the exact requirements of the job, this statement presents many applicants with what discrimination specialists call an unrebuttable presumption of incompetence. The fallacy of stereotyping prevents the speaker from taking into account those features of the individual that might differ from the commonly accepted features of the overall group.

> General propositions do not decide concrete cases.
>
> OLIVER WENDELL HOLMES

Misuse of statistics depends on the characteristic tendency of many people to become intimidated and unsure of themselves in the face of numerical data. Some people will give in to almost any conclusion offered in connection with impressive statistics. Two judges were philosophizing as they walked out of the courthouse after a hard day's work. One said, "Well, I figure I've set free just about the same number of guilty men as the number of innocent men I've hanged. So I guess it all averages out." This kind of *fallacy of averages* also befell the proverbial statistician who drowned while wading across a river that had an average depth of two feet. Similarly, a pregnant woman went to see her doctor in a state of extreme anxiety. She had heard that one out of every five babies born in the world is Chinese. Since she had already had four Caucasian babies, she wanted to know whether her fifth would be an Oriental. In a more serious vein, one of the most famous statistical blunders in modern times involved the prediction that Alf Landon would defeat Franklin Roosevelt for the presidency in 1936. The *Literary Digest* conducted a large opinion poll, which showed Landon the likely winner. However, in the election Roosevelt won by a healthy margin. The *Digest's* pollsters had selected a large number of names from the telephone directories of major cities around the country. This produced a highly "skewed" sample, which included only city dwellers with incomes high enough to afford telephones. It eliminated virtually all investigation of the rural population, most of whom apparently favored Roosevelt.

> *There are lies, damned lies, and statistics.*
>
> **BENJAMIN DISRAELI**

The fallacy of *appeal to authority* uses a famous or highly respected individual as a spokesperson for the conclusion, without presenting any facts that might support it. The speaker asks the hearer, in effect, to accept the conclusion merely because the authority figure says he should. Commercials for many consumer products use the famous person ploy in exactly this way. A radio campaign commercial once touted the candidate for a judgeship by saying, "District Attorney A supports Mr. X. District Attorney B has said he trusts him. District Attorney C has pledged his full support. If D.A.'s trust Mr. X, then you can trust him. Vote for Mr. X in the November election."

The fallacy of appeal to *consensus* argues that the hearer should accept the conclusion merely because many other people supposedly accept it. A great deal of advertising uses this approach. One commercial proclaims, "It's the Pepsi generation!" This implies that an entire segment of the American public can be identified as connected with a certain product. With so many people presumably committed to the product, what right do you have to deny that it's the best thing for you?

The fallacy of *mob appeal* calls upon the hearer to align with a large group of people who presumably share a common interest and to accept a certain conclusion without subjecting it to logical evaluation. Antony's famous speech in Shakespeare's *Julius Caesar* began "Friends, Romans, Countrymen! Lend me your ears!" This is probably the best-known example of mob appeal. In this kind of expert manipulation process, the speaker arouses the emotions of the hearers so effectively that they forget to review the facts of the case and compare them against the proposed conclusion. William Jennings Bryan's "Cross of Gold" speech, at a political convention in 1896, had the same effect. As he delivered his famous ending lines "You shall not press down upon the brow of labor this crown of thorns! You shall not crucify mankind upon a cross of gold!" Bryan assumed a dramatic pose reminiscent of the crucifixion of Christ. The crowd burst into thunderous applause, hoisted him to their shoulders, and marched him around the convention hall. That speech played an important part in his nomination for the presidency.

The *snob appeal* fallacy works by inviting the hearer to include himself in a small and select group of special people who stand above the "common herd" in some way. Commercial advertisements for liquor, cars, clothing, hi-fi equipment, and cigarettes often use this fallacy, and it often seems to produce the sales response to the products. As I was writing this particular chapter, I heard an intriguing radio commercial, interspersed with the music I like to have playing while I work. It triggered my crap detector when I realized that the flowery praise given by the announcer to a certain restaurant—"Dine in high style, enjoying the finest cuisine, prepared for your discriminating palate"—purported to describe a restaurant in which I had recently had dinner. One of my friends couldn't finish the plate of food she was served, the other later became sick from eating hers, and I left most of mine on the plate. Discriminating palate indeed!

The fallacy of *appeal to ignorance* simply uses impressive names, facts, figures, or "inside" terms to intimidate the hearer into accepting the conclusion offered, instead of running the risk of seeming foolish by confessing that he doesn't know what the argument means. Most human beings will go to considerable lengths in most circumstances to avoid seeming ignorant or naive. In doing so, they may victimize themselves. A relatively unsophisticated and uneducated patient pointed to the blood pressure kit the doctor had in his hands and asked, "Uh . . . Doc? What's that thing?" The doctor said, "This, Mr. Jones, is a sphygmomanometer." The patient looked rather thoughtful and mumbled, "Oh, I was afraid that's what it was." The commercial that touts "the new miracle ingredient, HO-9" also resorts to the fallacy of appeal to ignorance.

The fallacy of *appeal to emotion* tends to intertwine with some of the others, such as epithet, euphemism, word magic, and mob appeal. It uses terms with highly affective connotations, hoping to substitute an emotional response for critical evaluation of the conclusion offered. Appeals to pity, sentimentality, bigotry, fear, patriotism, race pride, gender pride, school pride, shame, and guilt all work in roughly the same way. A magazine advertisement soliciting funds to help starving children—an idea most of us would presumably support—has a photograph of an emaciated little girl in unbelievably squalid surroundings. The caption reads "You can help Juanita to avoid starvation, by sending your generous contribution. Or you can turn the page." Notwithstanding the question of the worthiness of the cause, this message constitutes a double-barreled appeal to emotions—pity and guilt at the same time.

And the fallacy of *appeal to ego*, probably the most often used in advertising and the easiest to spot once you tune in your crap detector, uses a message that equates feelings of personal significance with doing what-ever it urges, such as buying the product. Similar to the fallacy of snob appeal, it offers the hearer a positive self-evaluation in exchange for certain behavior. Many men buy products such as cigarettes that are promoted with a strong "macho" appeal. Many women buy products promoted with the idea that they will become more attractive to men and more socially acceptable. A classic magazine advertisement asked, "When should you buy your first Cadillac?"

So there we have it. Over three dozen of the most common logical errors stripped naked and held up to scrutiny. Go back over the complete list and make sure you understand how each one works. Can you think of other illustrations or incidences where you have seen various ones come into play? If you can't readily define all of them, read the definitions again and think about the examples carefully. Try to remember the names of as many of them as you can so you can call upon them whenever you need them. As you listen to people talk, especially those who seem intent on persuading you or others to accept certain conclusions, don't expect everything they say to be logically unsound. But do listen carefully for their use of logic. You may be surprised to see how much fuzzy thinking and how many weak arguments or downright fallacies people try to pass off on one another.

You may also find it very satisfying to listen to an argument for or against something, to break it down quickly into its component parts—spoken and unspoken—and to analyze it with relatively little effort. This gives a very comfortable feeling of having your own logical processes in good working order. Also, make sure you handle situations strategically when you dis-cover that someone has put forth a shaky proposition. Avoid the temptation to launch an attack and prove how dumb or illogical the person is. Use your knowledge of logical propositions to enrich your own thinking and to make your interactions with others more effective.

Here are some selected statements on which you can practice your skill of recognizing illogical thinking processes. Try to classify each of them according to the kind of logical error it involves, remembering that some of them might qualify for more than one category, depending on how you view them.

1. Who are *you* to talk? You don't have any credentials in this field.
2. I know it's true. I read it in the Bible.
3. Kids these days have too much money to spend. They don't appreciate the value of a dollar.
4. If your idea was any good, someone would have already thought of it.
5. We don't need another "big brother" law.
6. Old soldiers never die. They just fade away.
7. Camels. They're not for everybody.
8. Sony. Ask anyone.
9. There can be no neutrals in this war, only patriots or traitors.
10. I wouldn't exactly say he's dishonest. But he *is* a Republican, you know.

If you find some of them a bit difficult to classify, don't struggle with them too much. The main purpose in studying logic is just to become more fluent in recognizing premises, arguments, and conclusions. The classification system merely serves as a mental aid for developing that skill.

how to analyze a situation logically

> When you have eliminated the impossible, whatever remains—however improbable—must be the truth.
>
> SHERLOCK HOLMES

The following little problem in logical thinking will test the extent to which you jump to conclusions in dealing with new situations. Visualize five pennies placed on a table so as to form a ring, each one touching its two neighbors. Two players will compete to see who can win by picking up pennies, subject to the following rules:

1. When his turn comes, a player may pick up one penny, or two, provided they are "neighbors," that is, directly touching each other.
2. The player who picks up the last penny wins.

Which player has the best chance of winning, the one who moves first or the one who moves second? *Think this over before reading further.*

This little problem tells me some interesting things when I present it in lectures or seminars on thinking. It shows something of each person's characteristic style in dealing with complexity. Some people immediately jump to a conclusion—*one-shot thinking*—while others begin to examine the parts of the problem to see how it is "put together." The person who works by guess will usually conclude that the first player has the best chance of winning. However, a bit of *if-then thinking* shows that the second player can win every time if he plays properly.

Here is why, in case you haven't already worked it out. On the first move the first player has only two options—take one penny or take two adjacent ones. To work out the remaining logical possibilities, we merely have to spell out the second player's options for each of the first player's possible moves. Assume for a moment that the first player took one penny. This would leave four pennies in an arc. The second player could leave the first player with a losing arrangement merely by taking away two pennies from the inside of the group. This would leave two separated coins. The first player could only pick up one of the coins because they are not touching. This leaves the second player with the remaining coin, which he can pick up to win the game.

Now let's back up to the other possibility: the first player takes two pennies on the first move. This would leave an arc of three pennies remaining. The second player would merely take away the middle penny from the three, leaving two pennies separated from each other. Since the first player could only pick up one of them, the second player would again win by picking up the last one.

This problem and many others of a more practical nature require what psychologist Arthur Whimbey calls *sequential thought*. Whimbey finds that many high school and college students have trouble with word problems, and with mastering subjects like language and history as well, because they have not sharpened the skill of "finding the end of the rope," that is, describing a problem in clear, sequential steps. He says

A significant percentage of the students in an advanced education course at a major university were unable to solve the following problem: What day follows the day before yesterday if two days from now will be Sunday? The ability to proceed through a sequence of analytical steps is the foundation of all higher-order reasoning and comprehension. Low-aptitude thinkers . . . skip unsystematically back and forth through the entire problem, reexamining information that is no longer pertinent and thus confusing themselves. [3]

Whimbey, who teaches thinking courses at Bowling Green State University in Ohio, and Professor Jack Lochhead who does the same at the University of Massachusetts, employ the technique of *loud thinking*—teaching students to vocalize their entire reasoning processes as they deal with a problem, accounting for every single fact and logical step of any importance. They find that students increase their problem-solving competence markedly once they master the loud thinking technique, also referred to as the technique of *accurate description*.

I've used an associated technique to aid in the development of sequential thought, which goes well with loud thinking. This is the technique of using a pen and paper to draw a *thinking diagram*, which helps a person to

[3] Arthur Whimbey, "Teaching Sequential Thought: The Cognitive-Skills Approach" in *Phi Delta Kappan* (December 1977), p. 255–59. See also Arthur Whimbey, *Intelligence Can Be Taught* (New York: Dutton, 1975).

capture the essence of a situation or problem and to represent it in a form that enables him to manipulate the information involved. A thinking model can take the form of a sketch, a cartoon, a list, a time line, a sequence of items, an arrangement of facts or figures in the form of a table, a chart, a graph, or even a physical model.

To gain some practice in using a thinking model and applying the loud thinking approach, try to solve Whimbey's problem given above by writing out the names of the days of the week in their sequence and then vocalizing every step as if explaining the solution to someone else. Point to the various names of the days as you work it out.

We can form a few simple and useful logical habits to help us deal with complicated situations effectively. The more complicated the situation, the more these thinking habits will help.

1. Try to break the problem into parts or a sequence of subproblems; don't try to solve it in one giant leap.
2. Use a pen and paper to make a thinking diagram to help make the problem "hold still" while you work your way through it.
3. Try to get all the known facts together in one place.
4. Look for important relationships between the facts.
5. Try to identify any missing pieces. What fact, relationship, or characteristic do you have to find out to make sense of the situation?
6. Try to conceive of the conclusion to be reached. What might the solution look like when you find it? How will you recognize it?
7. Systematically and patiently investigate the key relationships, keeping the question to be answered clearly in mind. Work out the problem in steps.

These basic habits can serve you well in almost any complex situation, whether it is a puzzle problem, a personal problem, or a business problem. Avoid becoming so preoccupied with jumping at the answer in one step that you neglect to break it into its parts. Develop a certain confidence in the patient, methodical, and persistent approach.

Here is another problem, which provides an opportunity to put these logical thinking techniques into play. Take a pen and paper and make a sketch of the problem. Then try to go through it in "slow motion," applying each of the seven techniques listed above. Even if you see a solution quickly, review the entire problem completely to help clarify the effects of these techniques.

This problem concerns three men who wanted to cross a river. Not having a boat, they approached two boys who had one and offered to pay them for taking them across. The boat could only hold 150 pounds safely. Each of the boys weighed 75 pounds. Each of the men weighed 150 pounds. They agreed to pay the boys one dollar for every time the boat crossed the river. How many crossings did the boat make, and how much money did the men pay the boys for getting them across the river in the cheapest way?

Assume the boys ended up at the same spot where they started when the men came along. (You'll find the answer in the Appendix.)

The problems that face us every day differ from these simple ones only in degrees of complexity. Most personal problems, social problems, and business problems have elements and questions similar to these. By developing the skill of attacking a problem methodically, breaking it down into its individual subproblems, and persistently examining all of them until you find out what you need to solve it, you can put your brain's logical processes to use effectively. Clear, logical thinking pays off, and it quickly becomes a habit for those who take the trouble to develop it.

9

solving problems
and making decisions

The biggest problem in the world
Could have been solved when it was small . . .

LAO TZU

problems, problems, problems

A young man applied for a job that involved operating a small train station along a remote section of the track. The personnel officer of the train company interviewed him carefully to find out his qualifications. Then the personnel officer said, "Well, it looks like you have the basic qualifications for the job. But we need somebody who can think on his feet and solve problems if they come up. Can you do that?" The young man replied, "Well, I think so." The personnel officer said, "Okay, I'll give you a hypothetical problem concerning train operations, and you tell me how you'd solve it. Suppose you find out one day that there's a southbound train headed down the only track that runs by your station. You also find out that there's a northbound train coming up the same track. The engineers of the two trains don't know about each other. What would you do?"

The applicant replied, "I'd get on the telephone and call the stations down the track to notify them of the problem." Said the interviewer, "What would you do if you found out the telephone didn't work?" "Well," said the young man, "I'd use the telegraph." "Suppose the telegraph didn't work either?" "In that case," said the young man, "I'd run outside and throw the switch, so one of the trains would be shunted off onto the spur." The personnel officer said, "And what would you do if the switch was jammed?"

"Well, in that case I'd run home and fetch my brother." This left the interviewer somewhat puzzled. He asked, "Why would you go home and get your brother?" The young man replied, "Because he ain't never seen a train wreck before."

Life presents all of us with problems, large and small, important and unimportant, complicated and simple, just about every single day of our lives. And we manage to solve most of them to some degree of satisfaction.

We usually tend to our personal interests more or less automatically as we go about the business of living. But this skill—the ability to solve problems and make decisions—varies widely from person to person. When a person is very inept at solving the ordinary problems of living, he or she is psychologically maladjusted—unable to adapt to the basic requirements of getting along in the world. One view of maladjustment considers it merely the inability to size up life's ordinary problems as they come along, face them one at a time, and solve them. Conversely, a person who has developed the ability to deal with problems competently as they arise has reached a high level of personal adjustment, and his or her relative state of happiness and enjoyment of life show it.

In this chapter we will deal with the functional thinking skill of *solving problems and making decisions.* We will explore the thinking processes needed to solve various kinds of problems competently, and we will identify the particular mental habits and techniques that will enable us to build these skills.

In the context of this discussion, the term *problem* will mean simply a state of affairs you must change in some way in order to get what you want. That's about the simplest definition I know of the term. My use of the term doesn't involve any particular negative connotation. In saying that we have some problem to solve, we are not necessarily saying that anything has "gone wrong." The term in many cases can be used synonymously with the term *opportunity.* A problem offers an invitation to thought and action.

what's your problem-solving style?

Success comes to those who realize it isn't coming to them, and who go out to get it.

ANONYMOUS

Whether or not you realize it, you probably have a characteristic *problem-solving style,* a distinctive way in which you deal with those situations that present you with the need to make choices. Over years of living, you have probably formed certain habits that shape your response to your perception of a problem that needs solving. By understanding your problem-solving style, you can assess your problem-solving effectiveness and improve it if you want to. Here we shall explore two dimensions of problem-solving style, timing and *analysis.* We will combine them effectively into a strategically sound approach to solving problems.

The timing of your attack on a problem refers to when you decide to deal with it. Sometimes trying to deal with a problem prematurely can be just as ineffective as waiting too long. Probably most people lean much more toward a *reactive* style in dealing with their problems than toward an *anticipatory* style. That is, they simply don't recognize that some problem needs to be solved, or even that it is a problem, until it descends on them. When it does, they may have lost many of their best options for solving it and may find themselves trying to salvage something from the situation rather than trying to get the best of it. They work mostly by *accidental decision making.* For most people, solving problems amounts to an unconscious process of responding to crises and making decisions accidentally. Indeed, many people live their entire lives accidentally. A strictly reactive habit pattern lies at one extreme of ineffectiveness; an overly anticipatory pattern lies at the other extreme. In the center of the scale lies the strategic compromise between too soon and too late. Every problem has its "season"—the time when it ripens and requires action. Knowing how to determine that season is a basic skill in effectively timing your problem-solving attack.

The analysis of a problem refers to the amount of time, energy, and thought you choose to put into solving it. Not all problems deserve the same amount of study. Trying to open a bottle when you've lost the opener doesn't generally merit the same intensity of thought as buying a new car. Deciding which of several attractive places to visit on your vacation probably doesn't need as much analysis as deciding how and when to change your entire career. Probably most people don't take the trouble to analyze deeply enough the major problems that face them, nor do they look broadly enough at the range of available solutions. But one can also spend so much time analyzing a problem that he or she fails to deal with it when it ripens. Psychologists use the terms *reflective* and *impulsive* to describe the two contrasting extremes in the amount of thought given to problems. The overly reflective person wastes time and energy in studying unnecessary details and issues, possibly because of anxiety about committing firmly to a course of action. The overly impulsive person jumps the gun and leaps without looking carefully.

We can combine these two scales—reactive-anticipatory and reflective-impulsive—into a grid-square diagram as in Figure 9.1. This gives the four general extremes of problem-solving styles characterized by "paralysis by analysis" and "extinct by instinct" on the overly reactive side, and "premature panic" and "burning bridges ahead of you" on the overly anticipatory side. The effective combination of the two dimensions of timing and analysis, portrayed as the center portion of the grid, constitutes the policy of *creative procrastination.* This means taking as much time as is available to think about the problem before you will begin to pay a penalty for taking any longer. By first deciding when to decide, that is, when the problem will ripen, you can determine how much time and mental energy should go into it, and you can begin thinking about it ahead of time. By setting a decision deadline, you can consciously suspend judgment on the matter without fear that it will descend on you unexpectedly. Then you can keep your

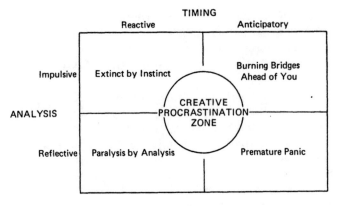

Figure 9.1   What's your own problem-solving style?

options open and indeed stay alert for new options that might develop as circumstances change and as you learn more about the situation. Creative procrastination does not mean just letting the problem or issue lie dormant. It means consciously lifting it out of the network of day-to-day processes and setting it up for special scrutiny, deciding how and when to make the decisions that are central to solving it, and then continually gathering facts and ideas as necessary, so that when it ripens you will be prepared to resolve it effectively and take the proper action. This is *premeditated decision making* rather than *accidental decision making.*

Take a close look at the model shown in Figure 9.1 and assess your own problem-solving style. Where does your general approach to solving problems and making decisions fit in the territory? How do you feel about your effectiveness in this critical area of functional thinking skills? As we examine the techniques and skills of problem solving in this chapter, keep in mind your assessment of your style and look for ways in which you can improve it if you feel it needs improving.

advantages of an organized approach

In the country of the blind, the one-eyed king can still goof up.

LAURENCE J. PETER

It's my general opinion that the world is somewhat underorganized. Most people seem to live their lives more or less by accident, drifting from one reaction process to another. Many people describe their lives in terms of a "logical" sequence of events and processes, completely unaware that they probably just responded automatically to the limited range of options presented to them at the various turning points and merely took the continuous line of least resistance. The typical human life seems to be quite unplanned, undirected, unlived, and unsavored. Only those who consciously think about the adventure of living as a matter of making choices among options, which they have found for themselves, ever establish real self-control and live their lives fully.

> *There are only three important events in a man's life: birth, life, and death. He is not conscious of being born, he dies in pain, and he forgets to live.*
>
> JEAN DE LA BRUYERE

By approaching the interplay of life's processes with a general mental framework for dealing with them, you can bring your mental skills into play strategically. You can make choices and solve problems on your terms, not merely on the terms of others who urge you to do what is best for them. This overall attitude of problem awareness (with the neutral connotation of "problem" as a state of affairs you want to influence in some way) can help you to live your entire life effectively as well as deal effectively with the large and small matters that come along every day.

In this section we will study the entire thinking process of problem solving as a *cycle*, which closes on itself and which involves six distinct steps or stages. We can analyze each stage in terms of the skills and techniques needed for it.

Psychologists recognize two distinctly different kinds of thought processes associated with problem solving. These thought processes differ in the manner in which the brain handles the information that forms the "subject matter" of the problem. One kind, *divergent thinking*, consists of expanding the picture of the problem. It involves stating the problem in various forms, turning it over and looking at it from various points of view, questioning and requestioning basic facts and opinions, identifying values and key factors, gathering more facts and ideas, and generating various options for solving it. Divergent thinking is expansive—it creates a bigger and bigger picture, to make sure we understand the problem well before we proceed to make the choices available to us.

Convergent thinking operates in just the reverse way. It narrows down the problem to a smaller, more manageable size and perspective. It casts out various options in favor of a selected few. It zeroes in on key factors, magnifies them, analyzes them, and evaluates the options to prepare the way to make the choices. Convergent thinking is reductive; it creates a smaller and more detailed picture to prepare us for action.

Both divergent thinking and convergent thinking play equally important parts in effective problem solving. Probably the most important single skill in problem solving is knowing when to diverge and when to converge. Unfortunately, many people habitually lean more toward one kind of thinking than the other. A habitual *diverger* may produce many new ideas and may develop very flexible points of view, but he or she may be unable to "get down to business" and settle the matter. We often use the term "scatterbrained" to describe the habitual diverger who can't converge effectively.

Conversely, the habitual *converger* may jump to conclusions and make snap decisions without adequately exploring the various ramifications of the problem. This person may have such a rigidly developed habit of narrowing every issue down to simple terms and lunging immediately for familiar solutions that he or she cannot easily produce new ideas or adopt new or novel points of view. We describe this person as narrow-minded.

If you can combine the divergent and convergent modes of thinking, and employ them flexibly according to the needs of the situation, you have the skill of the innovator together with the skill of the practical realist. The remainder of this chapter deals with the key techniques and skills characteristic of these two thinking modes, and it shows how to develop and apply them in everyday problem solving.

The model I propose for studying the problem-solving process has a stage of divergent thinking called the *expansion phase,* followed by a stage of convergent thinking called the *closure phase.* The six steps that make up this two-phase process are

1. Problem finding.
2. Problem stating.
3. Option finding.
4. Deciding.
5. Taking action.
6. Evaluating results.

Figure 9.2 shows how these two phases with their six steps relate to each other in the form of a continuous loop. Let's look at each of the steps briefly to see how the entire model works. The following sections will then explain each of them in greater depth.

Problem finding takes place in one of two ways. Either you find the problem or it finds you. If you make a habit of looking to the future and identifying emerging problems or questions or issues that will eventually

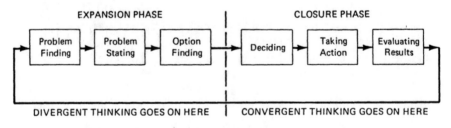

Figure 9.2   The steps of effective problem solving form a closed cycle.

require action on your part, you can prepare for them ahead of time. If you habitually drift along, dealing with various problems only when they present you with the necessity for action, you can only respond to them in terms of the options and information available when they strike.

Problem stating can also involve conscious choice or it can simply be a matter of automatic reaction. Many studies of people who are fluent problem solvers and innovators show that they have developed the skill of stating a problem or situation in a variety of ways, and they don't imprison themselves in the point of view that accompanies their first-reaction statement of the problem.

Option finding can consist of a conscious process of divergent idea production, aimed at assuring that you have a number of effective potential solutions, or it can simply degenerate to snap-reacting with the most familiar solution or the one with the stamp of tradition and the force of habit. Idea production techniques, such as those described in Chapter 10, can form the nucleus of an effective search for solutions.

The step of actually *deciding* forms the beginning of the convergent-thinking, or closure, phase. Making a decision simply amounts to choosing among the known options, with each option expressed in terms of a specific course of action. The better the job you have done in option finding and the better you understand the problem you want to solve, the more effectively you can make the choices. The two-phase model shows clearly the intimate relationship between the quality of the decision and the preceding thinking process that lays the groundwork for it.

Taking action simply means making a commitment to get the results by putting the decision into effect. In the vernacular of the parachutist, "It won't mean a thing if you don't pull that string." A well worked out solution to a problem includes a clear definition of the action you must take and a specific measure of its accomplishment.

The *evaluation* step, probably the most overlooked part of the problem-solving process, calls for studying the situation to see to what extent the action you took actually solved the problem. Many people erroneously equate the step of deciding or the step of taking action with the end of the problem-solving process. Keep in mind that you have not really solved the problem until the state of affairs you wanted to change *has actually changed*. That may take minutes, hours, days, weeks, months, or even years. To evaluate the results of your action properly, you must have determined *what you will take as evidence that the problem has been solved*. These objective conditions will serve as the basis for evaluating your solution.

This last point has a very important bearing on the problem-solving process and emphasizes the cyclic nature of the model. A great deal of everyday problem solving, especially in business organizations, amounts to *open-loop problem solving*, that is, a course of action undertaken on the assumption that it will solve the problem, but without any follow-up investigation. Having your car repaired offers an example of an open-loop, problem-solving process. If you take your car to a shop and the mechanic replaces certain parts, you leave with the assumption that it will work properly thereafter. If you don't return, he assumes that he has solved the problem. But you might find that the car still doesn't work, and other circumstances might prevent you from returning. If the mechanic defines "the problem" as getting you out of the shop minus your money, then for him it has been a *closed-loop problem-solving* process. But if he defined the problem as making sure your car operates properly, he has no feedback about the results, and consequently it becomes an open-loop process.

It usually makes sense to try to approach our problem-solving processes as closed-loop propositions, with feedback and evaluation built into the solutions wherever possible. The more important the problem, that is, the higher the consequences of a successful or unsuccessful solution, the more important it becomes to close the problem-solving loop.

problem finding

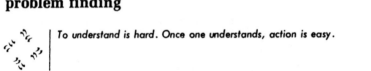

To understand is hard. Once one understands, action is easy.

SUN YAT SEN

You are constantly surrounded by problems waiting to be solved—situations or conditions that warrant your action in order to make things better for you in some way. Unfortunately, only some of these problems will present themselves to you in obvious, recognizable form. Your car may break down, you may need to get a job or change jobs, you may want to improve your health and physical fitness, you may need to stop smoking or to drink less, your mate may want to break up the relationship or get a divorce, you may receive an excellent job offer in some other city, your bank may make a mistake on your account, your friend may do something to damage your friendship, you may lose your wallet. All of these kinds of problems present themselves to you. You can hardly avoid dealing with them, to say nothing of not perceiving them.

In addition to these kinds of problems, you also have around you an indefinite number of "invisible problems," which do not or will not present themselves to you in obvious ways. These fall into the category that Professor Edward deBono calls the problem of "no problem." Because of the relative adequacy of the present situation in some area of your life, you do not experience it as problematic. Therefore, you see no need to change anything about it. Yet if you were to study such an aspect of your life situation carefully, you might decide that indeed you do want to make some changes. You can only deal with these invisible problems by an active searching process, by taking the initiative to evaluate various aspects of the situation and "finding" them.

Problem finding involves several specific mental habits. First, it calls for the willingness to question the status quo from time to time. You can review various aspects of your life, your career, or any other situations you consider important, and decide whether they warrant further attention. In what ways can you add value to those situations?

Second, the habit of problem finding often involves looking at a bigger picture than the one that immediately presents itself. To avoid inadvertent decision making on important issues, you can form the habit of looking for the larger context and determining whether a quick decision would fit the situation or whether you are only seeing the tip of an iceberg. You can find many invisible problems in the course of conversations with other people about problems that seem relatively straightforward and small in consequence.

Third, problem finding often involves looking into the future. This means detecting those conditions or developing trends today that you think may have important implications for your future. If you will find it necessary to face some developing problem some time in the future, it might pay to begin thinking about it early, so you can deal with it most effectively when it ripens.

Anticipatory problem finding has the great advantage of putting time on your side. By spotting a developing problem when it is still small, you can often deal with it more easily and effectively. You can use the time you have to understand the problem well, to find out more about it, and to think it through thoroughly. This sense of timing plays an especially important part in executive decision making, and it can also help a great deal in personal decision making.

John F. Kennedy once commented on this skill of time-sense, as follows:

The great French Marshall Lyautey once asked his gardener to plant a tree. The gardener objected that the tree was slow growing and would not reach maturity for 100 years. The marshall replied, "In that case, there is no time to lose; plant it this afternoon."

Some of the invisible problems surrounding you might be self-caused. That is, you might have certain blind spots concerning your actions toward others or your policies for living that prevent you from seeing their effects. The inability to look at your self and your surroundings dispassionately, and to assess your own effectiveness in dealing with them, can lead you to perpetuate situations that limit your personal effectiveness and your happiness.

For example, an executive with a domineering and abrasive style of dealing with subordinates may unknowingly keep them so defensive that they hide their problems, conceal important but controversial information, and refuse to share new ideas with him for fear of having them criticized. In such a case, he has inflicted certain problems upon himself, even though he may choose to rationalize the situation by saying "You just can't get good people anymore." He may have trouble deciding what to do about low morale, infighting among the staff, and a flourishing rumor mill.

Similarly, a man who insists on maintaining a role-locked relationship with his docile wife may find that their marriage loses all of its spontaneity and affection, not realizing that her needs for autonomy and self-assertion are not being met. He may wonder "What's wrong with her?", not realizing that his behavior contributes substantially to her reaction of withdrawal and avoidance of him, and even possibly looking for respect and affection from someone else. Sometimes we build our own hills without knowing it.

You can improve your skill at problem finding by occasionally listing some of the happenings, situations, and trends you can see around you that may eventually present you with the need to make decisions. This calls for a very thoughtful form of *strategic thinking*. You can keep a problem or decision list tucked into your personal calendar and browse through it from time to time, picking out those developing problems that might warrant some preliminary thinking or even a concerted logical attack. Consider a wide range of areas in your life, such as your career, personal health and well-being, social relationships, family, finances, and so on. By finding as many problems as possible before they find you, you can meet them and solve them more effectively.

problem stating

The uncreative mind can spot wrong answers, but it takes a very creative mind to spot wrong questions.

ANTONY JAY

According to one story, a skilled computer programmer applied his techniques to the problem of investing. He worked for many months writing a program that would analyze stock prices and work out an ideal investment strategy. His program, much like a chess-playing computer program, would search through the stock market data to detect significant patterns from which it would derive an optimal investment rule or policy. After a great deal of effort, he got the program de-bugged and running. He fed in the daily prices on the New York Stock Exchange for a full year's trading. Then he pressed the start button and waited. For a long time the computer sat silently, searching rapidly through the enormous quantity of data. Finally, the printer chattered for a fraction of a second and stopped.

He ran over to look at the result, expecting an answer that would make him rich. The computer had printed "Buy low; sell high."

A common mistake in problem solving, especially in business situations, is to assume that there is such a thing as the "real problem." Many times I've heard several people discussing a problem that someone has stated in some particular form, when one of them will say rather confidently, "The *real* problem here is product quality (or inspection procedures, material handling, cost control, morale, supervision, or whatever)." Rather than search for some ideal definition of the problem, I would much rather work out a number of alternative statements of it and see how each of them can help to illuminate our thinking.

During the first three stages of the six-stage process of problem solving described earlier, we engage primarily in divergent thinking. We try to prepare the way for intelligent choice making by developing as many attractive options, or potential solutions, as we can. And one of the most effective techniques for doing that is versatile problem stating.

The more ways we can look at and describe a problem, the more attractive options we can generate for solving it. By recognizing that there is no one "real" statement of the problem, but rather that there are as many plausible statements as we can think up, we avoid limiting ourselves to a fixed angle of attack. In this section we will examine several problem-stating techniques that can help us to turn a problem around and look at it from many angles and to give ourselves the freedom to approach it in innovative ways.

Even simple changes in the way we frame up a problem can help or hinder our thought processes. To take a simple example, solve this simple arithmetic problem in your mind *before reading further:* How much is two-thirds of one-half?

Did you come up with one-third as the solution? Would you have found the problem easier by restating it: How much is half of two-thirds? The second statement means just about the same as the first, but it seems to make the problem much easier to solve.

As another example: Dick is shorter than Tom. Harry is taller than Tom. How does Dick relate to Harry? Work this one out *before reading further.*

Did you decide that Dick was shorter than Harry? Suppose the problem had said: Harry is taller than Tom. Tom is taller than Dick. How does Harry relate to Dick? This particular way of verbalizing the problem makes it considerably easier to think about, doesn't it?

And versatile problem stating does the same thing for the problem solver. It makes the problem easier to grasp, easier to visualize in many cases, easier to break down into its component parts, and easier to think about in terms of options for solving it.

Sometimes you must go through an uncertain, groping kind of exploration process when the problem seems so confusing that you cannot state it clearly. In this case, asking many kinds of questions may help. For example, a young man who lived on a remote farm decided to go to town to buy a car. He had saved $500, but being unwise in the ways of the city he wasn't sure how to go about it. He took a bus into town and walked up to the first used car lot he saw.

He spotted a nice-looking car with a sign on the windshield announcing that the price was exactly $500. He called the salesman over and offered to buy it. As they were going through the process of the sale, the young man pulled out his cash. The salesman said, "Oh, you're going to pay cash? In that case we take off ten percent." "What do you mean, 'take off ten percent'?" he asked uncertainly. "Oh, yes," said the salesman. "We take ten percent off for cash." The young man said, "I'm not so sure I want to go through with this. I'm going to think it over for awhile, and I'll be back."

As he sat at the counter of a nearby coffee shop puzzling over the matter, the waitress came over to fill his coffee cup. "Can I ask you a question?" he said. "Sure, go ahead." "If I gave you $500, how much would you take off for cash?" She smiled and said, "Well, would it be all right if I kept my earrings on?"

One useful technique for creative problem stating involves simply verbalizing the various aspects of the problem as widely as possible. When I work with groups of managers in problem-solving sessions, I like to see how many different statements of the problem we can put up on a chalkboard or newsprint-covered wall surface. My simple question "What is the problem?" usually generates one flat statement, usually from the most confident or most talkative member of the group. Then I ask, "What else is the problem?" This usually produces another two or three statements, which go up beside the first. Then I ask, "Do you know any other ways in which we can phrase the problem?" At this point the group will usually begin to freewheel, recognizing aspects of the situation they had not previously seen and had not considered part of the problem as first stated.

In some cases the focus of the problem-solving activity will make a dramatic shift, and a previously unrecognized factor might emerge as the most important one the group wants to deal with. In other cases it may increase the number of factors they choose to include in their study of the situation. Only for simple situations does it result in a reduction of the scope of the problem. Occasionally it will become clear that only two or three options really dominate the process.

Following the verbal freewheeling approach, we can also ask a variety of divergent questions, which broaden the view of the problem even further. I like to ask questions like "Why is this a problem?" "How does it manifest itself to the group? To person A? To person B? To others?", and "What undesirable conditions does it cause?" Other useful questions include "How might this problem resemble other problems we have already solved?" or "How is it different?" "Might someone else, somewhere, have already solved this problem or a similar problem?" Or one might ask, "Are we sure *we* have to solve it?" and "What would probably happen if we did nothing about it?"

Some of these questions will have simple and obvious answers; others may provoke considerable thought. The *why challenge* technique, that is, successively asking "Why?" of the person who first stated the problem, will rapidly enlarge the picture of the problem. A "why sequence" might go as follows: "We want to build a new recreation center." "Why?" "To keep kids constructively occupied during the summer." "Why do you want to do that?" "To keep them from getting into trouble." "Why do you want to do that?" "To make a safer and more peaceful community." "Why do you want to do that?" And so on. Notice how quickly the why challenge takes the discussion back to very basic objectives and values. When used sparingly and constructively, it can help to establish a convenient problem-solving perspective.

Sometimes it helps just to review some of the basic variables of the situation, especially the ones you can control. Since problem solving involves changing some situation, you might try looking for a key factor or variable you can change. How might the situation change if you did more of something, less of something, stopped doing something, started doing it, increased the size, used more of them, used less of them, and so on? This kind of general search process quite often can help you strike upon a key factor you might otherwise have overlooked.

At a certain point in our searching process, we will begin to develop a general feeling about the "size" of the problem, that is, the number of factors we want to include, the range of possible solutions we will entertain, the extent to which we might be willing to overturn tradition in developing innovative solutions, and the general scope of the situation we want to change. This can range from a limited scope including only ourselves, to a much broader effort requiring that we enlist the support and cooperation of many other people. Establishing the general scope of the problem we choose to deal with requires that we have carefully thought through the problem-stating stage and have reached a general consensus with the other people involved in the overall problem-solving process.

We will also want to determine the required timing for the solution. That is, we must decide when it will become appropriate for our chosen solution to be put into action. By setting a decision deadline, we lend perspective to the entire problem-solving process, and we can begin to use our time effectively. If we have to decide within minutes or hours, then so be it. But if we have several weeks before the problem fully ripens and requires action, we can think it through carefully, reach a decision at the appropriate time, and put it into play when we choose to, rather than snap-reacting to a surprise issue.

We can conclude the problem-stating stage by establishing a decision objective or the goal of the problem-solving process. A decision objective answers the question "What will we accept as evidence that we have completely solved the problem?" We can specify a definite state of affairs we want to exist as a result of the actions we will eventually take. Once we have a clear idea of our goal in solving the problem, we have a standard against which to compare the various options we will identify in the next stage.

option finding

Don't refuse to go on an occasional wild goose chase. That's what wild geese are for.

ANONYMOUS

Option finding constitutes the last divergent stage of the six-stage problem-solving process before you make a radical change in your thinking mode and enter the convergent closure phase. If you do your work well in this stage, you will have a variety of options to choose from, with the feeling that at least one of them offers the likelihood of solving the problem effectively.

The amount of time and energy you will need to spend in the option-finding stage depends largely on the kind of problem at hand. If the stages of problem finding and problem stating have clarified the situation quite well, you might already have a good inventory of attractive potential solutions. In that case, you might review them briefly to make sure you haven't left out any important ones and then proceed to the deciding stage.

But if the problem is very complex, and if the first two stages have not given you a comfortable feeling that the known options will work very well, then you may feel somewhat blocked. You may want to employ some of the *blockbusting* techniques that have emerged from the study of creative problem solving.

In this section we will deal briefly with both of these aspects of option finding, first cataloging the recognizable options and then blockbusting to produce more options to choose from. Chapter 10 describes a number of these techniques for deliberate *idea production*, the functional thinking skill associated with what is commonly known as "creative thinking."

The first part of the option-finding process, *cataloging the recognizable* options, involves a fairly straightforward procedure. If you are the only person working on the problem, you can write down all the reasonable approaches you can think of. However, if a group is working on the problem, it only takes one compulsively convergent thinker to put a damper on the kind of freewheeling process that can generate a number of effective options. If one or more people in the group do not understand the value of the divergent option-finding process, they may follow their automatic tendencies and zero in on one or two favorite or well-known approaches and begin to advocate them. The first phase of the problem-solving process, the expansion phase, is *no time for advocating*. The purpose of this phase is to prepare well for the second phase, which does involve zeroing in on one or a few preferred solutions. In a group situation, the participants must all understand the nature of the problem-solving process in order to get the most out of it. This makes it very important to have and consciously use a clear-cut problem-solving model such as the one explained in this chapter.

It's difficult to know when to reject a potential solution and when to keep it under consideration. For example, between acts of a play at a small Jewish community theater, the stage manager came out from behind the curtain and announced, "Ladies and gentlemen, I'm afraid we must cancel the rest of the show. We've had a terrible tragedy. The leading man has suffered a fatal heart attack. Please accept my apologies, and I'm sure you'll understand why we can't continue." An old Jewish lady stood up in the balcony and shouted, "Quick! Give him some chicken soup!" The stage manager looked aghast, composed himself and said, "I'm sorry—perhaps I didn't make myself clear. His heart attack was fatal." The old lady shouted, "Never mind! Just give him some chicken soup!" In exasperation, the stage manager shouted, "Madam, the man is *dead!* What good could chicken soup possibly do?" Undaunted, she shouted back, "What harm?"

If the people working on a problem can suspend the judgment process until they have listed all the recognizable options for consideration, they may find themselves with a much more extensive and valuable list than if they had tried to evaluate too soon. Once you have a reasonably complete list of options, you can review it to determine whether you want to spend more time with some energetic blockbusting techniques or whether you can confidently proceed to the closure phase and begin narrowing down the options for a decision.

Blockbusting techniques include

1. Mass idea production
2. Hypothesizing causes
3. Shifting the point of view
4. The "how-to" technique
5. Restructuring the situation

Each of these techniques, explained in the following paragraphs, involves stretching your imagination to find and examine unlikely ideas and options.

Mass idea production, described in greater depth in Chapter 10, involves the use of verbal association, especially in group situations. One form of idea production is the well-known *brainstorming* technique, pioneered in business organizations by Alex Osborn. A brainstorming session simply amounts to a group of people throwing out ideas as they think of them, with each person's idea triggering associations in another person's brain. The participants must obey two important rules for brainstorming to work effectively. First, they must completely suspend judgment until after the session. They must accept all ideas for the time being, without evaluating them in any way. And second, the group must simply strive for quantity—the more ideas the better—on the assumption that a larger harvest of total ideas will have a greater chance of producing more winners when the group later evaluates them.

The technique of *hypothesizing* simply involves thinking up as many potential "causes" of the problem as you can, in order to surface some new possibilities for action. You can freewheel in this process just as you can in idea production, with yourself or a group coming up with as many hypotheses as possible. Sometimes the more absurd hypotheses turn out to contain a grain of truth, or they may trigger verbal associations that bring up more realistic factors, which might not otherwise have surfaced.

Shifting the point of view might also produce some extra options. You can systematically inventory the points of view of various people in the situation and use these elements as starting points for idea production.

The *"how-to"* technique goes down to the operational level of specific effects you want to bring about in solving the problem. You can ask, "How can we stop X from happening?", "How can we get more money for ABC?", and "How can we persuade Mr. A to do such-and-such?" The more how-to's you can state, the more possible actions you can identify. An interesting puzzle exercise in problem solving illustrates this how-to effect very well. The problem concerns a golfer who approached the green to find that his ball had rolled right into a small paper sack that had blown onto the course. His problem at first seems to be "how to get the ball into the hole without losing a stroke." Another how-to statement might be "how to get the ball out of the bag without losing a stroke." By stating as many how-to's as possible, we eventually come to one that seems to suggest a plausible action, such as "how to get rid of the paper bag." Then the mental light bulb flashes with the option of setting the bag on fire, letting it burn to ashes, and going ahead with the putt. Whenever you feel blocked, try to reorganize your concept of the problem with some how-to questions.

A fifth technique for option finding, *restructuring the situation*, involves looking at those features of the problem that we have accepted as immune to scrutiny and that have such a dominating effect on everyone's perception of potential solutions that they warrant reconsideration. This relatively sophisticated and creative problem-solving technique can occasionally bring a dramatic revision of your entire approach to the situation. Chapter 10 deals with this technique in the context of idea production. You can sometimes restructure by asking yourself what obvious and important features more or less "define" the situation. Edward deBono calls this process "identifying the *dominant idea*." Sometimes you can successfully challenge an established tradition or long-accepted way of doing something merely by pointing out that changing it would solve a certain problem effectively.

One novel approach that sometimes works well simply declares the problem to be "no problem." That is, by changing your viewpoint you might decide you can live with the situation quite readily. For example, a man came to his wife one evening and confessed that he had had a mistress for quite some time. She immediately became enraged that he would do such a thing. But after a long discussion in which he promised to break off the extramarital affair, she decided to forgive him—on one condition. She had to know who the woman was. He said, "She's one of the chorus girls at the show-bar downtown." She said, "I want you to take me there tonight. I won't make any kind of a scene. I just want to know who she is." They went to see the show, and as they were having a drink at their table and waiting for the show to start, he said, "By the way, Bill Jones who lives next door to us also has a mistress. She works in the chorus line, too." His wife became quite interested in this. She said, "I want you to point her out to me, too."

As the show started and the line of chorus girls came out, she said, "Which one is yours?" He pointed and said, "The third one from the right." "And which is Jones's mistress?" "The one on the left end." She looked at the two women for a moment and mused, "You know—I think ours is better."

All of these techniques for option finding have one common purpose: to make sure that you arrive at the stage of deciding well-armed with potential solutions for the problem. A thorough job of option finding can free you from the prison of tradition; it can open up many more effective solutions than you might otherwise have; and it can give you the confidence to proceed with action.

deciding

Nothing would be done at all if a man waited until he could do it so well that no one could find fault with it.

CARDINAL NEWMAN

In a sense, deciding becomes the easiest part of the problem-solving process if you have done a good job on the first three stages. If you have not, it will probably become the hardest part. Making a decision sooner or later comes down to choosing one course of action out of a number of plausible options.

You only need two basic ingredients in making a decision. One is the courage to make it. The other is a systematic way of evaluating your options against your objective. Both of these can be easy or difficult, again depending on how well you prepared for the decision and on your own particular decision-making style.

Having the courage to decide means overcoming the residual *decidophobia* that wells up in all of us from time to time when we don't know how to proceed for certain. Each time we commit to some course of action, we recognize the existence of some level of risk—the possibility that we have chosen incorrectly and that we may end up losing ground instead of gaining. But many times a person may suffer from decidophobia unnecessarily. If you find yourself reluctant to make a decision on some issue, pause and ask yourself what you are anticipating. Many of the decisions you have to make every day are not high-value decisions. That is, you don't stand to lose very much or gain very much, regardless of which options you choose. For the most part, deciding where to go for lunch is not a high-value decision. You can adopt a policy in dealing with the many low-value decisions you face of simply making a fairly reasonable decision and getting on with it. A hundred years in the future, how much will it matter where you went to lunch today? Just pick a nice place and go.

You can also reduce your decidophobia substantially by recognizing that, in many instances, two or more of the choices seem to offer roughly equal benefits. If the decision has relatively low consequences—and perhaps even if not—you can probably make any of the better options work out well. So it *doesn't really matter very much which* one you choose. Think this over for a moment. In some cases, you can't really tell the difference between the "best" option and the "second best," because the differences between them are smaller than the uncertainty in your ability to assess the benefits. In those cases, it does pay to agonize over the difference.

Between two evils, I always choose the one I never tried before.

MAE WEST

Actually, your effectiveness in solving a problem depends more on your ability to implement the course of action you choose, to follow through on it, and to adapt it if circumstances change while you are putting it into effect, than it depends on small differences among the options themselves. Once you choose a course of action, you will probably devote your best efforts to making it work. You will be so intent on proving yourself correct that you will probably make it into a self-fulfilling prophecy.

So, one useful guideline for overcoming decidophobia and getting down to action is: If more than one of the options seem very good, and if you cannot find a great deal of difference from one to the other, then go ahead with confidence; you probably have more than one "good" solution, and you only need one. Just choose one of them and proceed with it. As a practical matter, you will never know whether one of the others would have worked better anyway. You can even flip a coin to decide. The important point in such a case is that the difference in potential consequences is beyond your ability to estimate.

Most of the more sophisticated decision-making techniques, which involve more than flipping a coin or just choosing according to our hunches, come into play when we can't easily compare the differences among the options. When the options vary substantially in potential effectiveness in solving the problem and they also vary in their costs and risks, we need to think them over much more carefully than we would in the cases cited above.

The "balance sheet" model probably offers the greatest usefulness in view of its simplicity. If you have a certain number of possible courses of action, for example, five of them, you can simply list them on one side of a sheet of paper, putting the pro's and con's of each in separate columns. If, for example, you wanted to choose one of five different kinds of vacations, you would think about each of the possibilities and spell out the attractive features of each and the relative drawbacks when compared to others. Then you could think about all of them in comparison, and having the pro's and con's in front of you in a single, well-organized picture would help to establish your preferences.

If, after studying the balance sheet model for your problem, you still feel you need more insight into the options and their costs and benefits, you can proceed further with a few approaches that involve a bit more detail. For example, you might find that some of your options include suboptions—choices within choices. You may not know how many choices to consider in all and how to keep the thinking process from getting too complicated. In such a case, you can use the well-known "decision tree" model, a diagram which enables you to see all of the important options in a single picture.

A decision tree model of your vacation problem might look something like the one in Figure 9.3. One possible breakdown of categories, or "branches" of the tree diagram, includes joining a tour group, traveling alone, or going with a small group of friends. For various reasons, you might not want to consider all five places to visit under each of these categories. For example, your friends might only be willing to visit the United States, Canada, and Hawaii with you. You might only want to consider joining a tour group for the Orient or Europe. By organizing the various possibilities in the form of a decision network, you can be sure you have accounted for all of them, and you can begin to compare them as part of an entire collection. You might also decide to eliminate certain options as you look at the choices in this way.

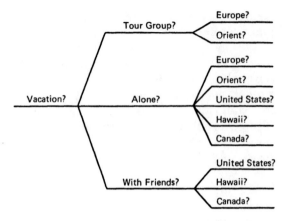

Figure 9.3   A "decision tree" organizes all available options into a single picture.

If you still find it difficult to select an option, and you aren't suffering from simple decidophobia, then you can use a slightly fancier decision model in the form of a point-scoring system. You can assign points to a variety of factors in terms of their relative importance to you. For example, you might consider free time and flexibility more important than logistic convenience. You could give the two factors different numbers of decision points, based on your subjective judgment of the importance.

The typical way to use a point-scoring system is to consider that you have a total of, say, 1,000 points—imaginary points whose abstract value has no significance, but whose relative differences show how you rate the various factors. You can allocate them according to several categories, such as logistic convenience, freedom and flexibility, cost, newness of experience, language difficulty, and degree of relaxation. You would assign a certain number of points as the maximum "value" to you of each of the factors you consider important, with the total of all categories accounting for all 1,000 points.

Then you can evaluate each option against these decision factors, and score it a certain number of points depending on how well it meets your desires in each category. For example, you might have allocated a maximum of 300 points out of the 1,000 to freedom and flexibility, indicating that you consider this factor quite important. In evaluating a three-week tour of Europe, you might only grant that option 100 points out of the maximum 300 it could possibly earn. You might score a trip by yourself to Canada as higher in flexibility, giving it all 300 points. Figure 9.4 shows how the point scoring system might look in the form of a chart.

You would score all of your options in each category, and very probably no option would score the maximum number of points in every category.

DECISION FACTORS	Maximum Points	VACATION OPTIONS									
		# 1	# 2	# 3	# 4	# 5	# 6	# 7	# 8	# 9	# 10
1. Logistic Convenience	150	75									
2. Freedom and Flexibility	300	150									
3. Cost	100	90									
4. New Experiences	100	100		E	T	C	•		•	•
5. Language Problems	50	10									
6. Relaxation	200	100									
7. Miscellaneous Factors	100	50									
TOTALS	1000	575									

Figure 9.4   A point-scoring model helps to clarify your preferences and priorities.

Each would have some strong features and some weak ones. Then, by totaling the points you awarded to a given option for all six categories, you would have a rough numerical indication of your preference for that option. Comparing the scores for all of the options would give you an idea of how strongly you favored them in comparison to one another.

For all of its apparent analytical precision, don't let the point-score technique mislead you into thinking that it will actually make the decision for you. The option that scores the highest number of points is not the "best" option. The system simply expresses your own personal biases in numerical form, and although this helps to organize your thoughts, it does not resolve the decision in and of itself. You still have to assign the points and decide how each of the options stacks up. The point-scoring system can provide a great deal of food for thought, and it can help immensely in clarifying your preferences. But don't mistake it for anything more than a way to organize your subjective judgments.

With these simple tools, together with the courage to make the decision and live with it, you can tackle the vast majority of decision issues that confront you in your personal life, your career, or in business settings. If you use pen and paper as thinking aids, and if you use simple models like these to organize your thinking, your decision-making "track record" will probably be much higher than that of many other people who make their decisions inadvertently and accidentally. Premeditated decision making with an organized approach will give you a high score in the long run.

taking action

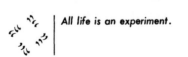

Nothing comes from doing nothing.

SHAKESPEARE

The most important part of the action stage of problem solving is having a very clear idea of your course of action and following through on it. This may seem like a simple matter, yet probably more good ideas have failed to pay off because no one really pushed them through to completion than for any other reason. The stage of spelling out the action to be taken sometimes deserves more attention than it gets, often because the person working on the problem wants to get going and believes that having a general approach in mind will be sufficient.

If you have overcome decidophobia and have picked out the preferred course of action, you need to begin doing everything you reasonably can to make sure the approach will work well. This means accounting for the various details involved, and it means anticipating obstacles that might arise. If the undertaking is rather large or complex, you will probably find it worthwhile to write out a plan, however brief, for all the things you have to do. This might amount to a list of "action items," with a deadline beside each, or it might include a schedule chart or time line that shows how the various actions will relate to one another in time sequence. You can go over each of the action items to define the work involved in getting it done, especially if you will need the cooperation of anyone else. Which of the actions will cost money, and how much? When will you need the money? Do you have it now, or must you get it? Which actions are really critical to the success of the project? Which ones might involve some risk of failure? How can you reduce or minimize those risks?

Sometimes it helps to have a "fall-back" option or plan in case things go wrong or unforeseen obstacles come up. By choosing your options flexibly, you can often work out a plan that offers a higher potential of success. In some cases, it may even help to take action on two or more options, even when one of them has a high potential for achieving the objective. In such a case, you may spend some extra effort or resources to reduce the risk of not reaching the objective or to save time in case obstacles arise.

By anticipating some of the obstacles, you can build safety provisions into your plan to avoid getting thrown off the track easily. Ask yourself, "Suppose X doesn't happen, or suppose it happens much later than I had expected? How can I move ahead in spite of it?"

All life is an experiment.

OLIVER WENDELL HOLMES

Once you have a clear idea of what you want to do, and you have a plan for getting it done, the action stage becomes one of persistent attention to doing the necessary things. Set some specific goals for yourself, work out the timing carefully, and set deadlines you can work to. In this way, you can fit the work to be done in solving the problem into your day-to-day flow of activities, and you can get it done without unusual disruption of your other affairs.

> *The great end of life is not knowledge but action.*
>
> THOMAS HUXLEY

evaluating results

> *Those who will not learn from history are obliged to repeat it.*
>
> ANONYMOUS

You can only "close the loop" on the overall problem-solving process by evaluating results. What disparity do you find between what is and what ought to be? Returning to our definition of a problem as a state of affairs you have to change in order to get what you want, you can see the necessity of knowing clearly what you want. If you worked out a specific statement of your objective—the conditions you would take as evidence that you had solved the problem—then you know how to evaluate the results of your actions.

Whereas open-loop problem solving merely depends on the assumption that the action taken will solve the problem, closed-loop problem solving includes as one of its steps the process of following up to make sure the problem went away. The time scale of the changes you want to bring about may take minutes or months or years. You may find it interesting to review some of the existing conditions in your life right now and see which ones relate directly to specific problem-solving processes you went through some months or even years ago. What decisions did you make five years ago that led to your current sense of satisfaction with life? Did you make any decisions that resulted in a current state of affairs you now want to change? What process or condition or habit or arrangement has turned into a liability after being an asset for a number of years?

Perhaps you've noticed at times that an action you thought would solve a certain problem only made it worse. Presumably you changed your course when you discovered your mistake. In some cases, you may have unwittingly paid a high price before discovering your error. This kind of self-cancelling action, known as the phenomenon of "paradoxical effect" or *paradoxis*, comes into play often in human activity.

A person may persist in an unsuccessful course of action without consciously recognizing or accepting the fact that paradoxis has set in. Examples of paradoxis include a parent trying to badger a teenage son or daughter into giving up smoking; a boss who threatens and intimidates employees and yet wants them to work independently and use their initiative; and a government consumer-protection regulation that prevents competing companies from reducing their prices.

Not only must you look ahead in evaluating the results of your decisions, but you must occasionally look back as well. Just as the consequences of today's decisions will manifest themselves to you at some time in the future, today is the "future" you wanted to change at some time in the past when you made a decision.

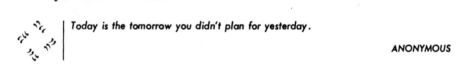 *Today is the tomorrow you didn't plan for yesterday.*

ANONYMOUS

The importance of the closed-loop approach to solving problems becomes evident when you recognize that circumstances change, situations change, people change, and your preferences and values change. You must adapt your solutions to the changing times, and this means occasionally rethinking the solutions entirely. The stage of evaluating the results of your actions feeds right into the problem-finding stage, which begins a new cycle of problem solving. You need to change your approach as the world changes around you.

Change is not always improvement, as the pigeon said when it got out of the net and into the pie.

C.H. SPURDGEON

An open-minded approach to evaluating results occasionally requires the willingness to concede that a certain course of action has not worked as well as you had expected. If you inadvertently get your own ego tangled up with a certain course of action, which can certainly happen if you thought it up, pioneered it, advocated it in the face of opposition and ridicule, and persuaded others to try it, you might have a substantial perceptual blind spot in recognizing that it hasn't panned out. The ability to sacrifice your own brainchild now and then requires a great deal of objective thinking, intellectual courage, and personal self-confidence. If you can carefully distinguish being "right" from being objective, you can stay out of the ego-thinking trap. And as we have seen in Chapter 6, ego thinking is probably the most damaging form of mental rigidity because it blocks adaptation.

If you can say "I've made a mistake" and "I've changed my mind" easily and without feeling unduly defensive or embarrassed, you have the most important mental skill required for successful evaluation of your results and successful problem solving—the skill of open-minded adaptation.

10

producing ideas

 There is one thing stronger than all the armies of the world: and that is an idea whose time has come.

VICTOR HUGO

idea producers and idea killers

One of the most exciting feelings a human being can ever have is the sudden flash of a new and effective idea. This insight experience—the "Aha!" that comes when the parts of a mental puzzle suddenly fall into place—is a physically enjoyable sensation. When you suddenly realize how to do something, or you conceive of a clever solution to a problem that had you stumped, or you simply pop out with a neat idea that is interesting but not especially important, you may feel a surge of pleasure. Your entire nervous system expresses the delight you feel as a result of your new idea. Your heartbeat quickens slightly, your muscles become slightly tense, your body posture shows your increased arousal level, the electrical activity of your brain steps up its tempo, and you feel a surge of well-being and potency sweep across your body. Having a really good idea is a pleasurable experience for anyone—a sort of "cerebral high." Even the least-educated, least intellectually oriented person feels this same enjoyment when he or she gets a good idea.

Yet, if you had a dollar for every good idea that was killed because of someone's clumsy and narrow-minded thinking, you would probably be the richest person who ever lived. A great irony of human thinking is our simultaneous love for new ideas and our reactive fear of them. For me, this paradox makes the functional skill of *idea production* one of the most fascinating and intriguing subjects I've ever studied.

The ironic part of idea production is that, despite the joy people experience when they produce effective ideas, they so often kill new ideas at the instant of their birth, missing the opportunities for enjoying them. It is no exaggeration to say that the typical person unwittingly kills most of his own best ideas out of mental habit and kills a great many ideas that other people have in his presence. It is almost as if human beings feel simultane-

212

ously fearful and charmed by the new and the novel—simultaneously frightened and uplifted by it. We seem to have the idea producers in our world who habitually create and express new ideas, and the idea killers who habitually gun down new ideas before they draw breath. Unfortunately, the killers seem to outnumber the producers by a wide margin.

There is nothing more frightening than ignorance in action.

GOETHE

We also seem to have a curious double standard in our culture about the way we respond to those who challenge the status quo. Many people speak of the need to believe in one's ideas, to face the scorn and disapproval of others, and to proceed courageously even when others consider him wrong. Yet, these same people will turn around and play the role of idea killer against someone else, shooting down fragile ideas, ridiculing an untried approach, and "proving" why the new concept is worthless. We may speak in favor of innovation, but we may not always act in favor of it.

In his thought-provoking book, *Self Renewal*, John Gardner points out our tendency to recognize and appreciate innovators only long after their ideas have been shown to work.

Today Galileo is a popular historical figure, and we feel wise and emancipated as we reflect indignantly on his persecution for supporting Copernicus. But if he were to reappear today and assert something equally at odds with our own deepest beliefs, his popularity would plummet like one of those lead weights dropped from the Tower of Pisa. Our affection is generally reserved for innovators long dead.[1]

Laughter, ridicule, scorn, and open hostility often greet the person who seriously and energetically tries to overturn a closely held belief within his or her culture. "Innovation is fine," the unspoken message seems to say, "so long as you don't try to overturn my boat." It is almost a cliche of our culture to talk about famous innovators who faced ridicule, persecution,

Snap Judgment Killing a Budding Idea. From LANGUAGE IN THOUGHT AND ACTION, Third Edition by S.I. Hayakawa, copyright © 1972 by Harcourt Brace Jovanovich, Inc. Reproduced by permission of the publisher and George Allen & Unwin (Publishers) Ltd.

[1]Excerpted from p. 32 in SELF-RENEWAL by John W. Gardner. Copyright © 1963, 1964 by John W. Gardner. Reprinted by permission of Harper & Row, Publishers, Inc.

and even personal danger at the hands of those whose fear of losing their certainty drove them to try to exterminate the person who tried to make them think.

Toward no crimes have men shown themselves so cold-bloodedly cruel as in punishing differences in belief.

JAMES RUSSELL LOWELL

This paradoxical treatment of new ideas leaves most people with an intense *fear of being wrong.* Most people have faced laughter and ridicule so often in their young lives that they have learned to express their ideas only when they feel sure others will accept them. Gardner believes that this fear of failure blocks most people from developing their innovative skills.

One of the reasons why mature people are apt to learn less than young people is that they are willing to risk less. Learning is a risky business, and they do not like failure. In infancy, when the child is learning at a truly phenomenal rate—a rate he will never again achieve—he is also experiencing a shattering number of failures. Watch him. See the innumerable things he tries and fails. And see how little the failures discourage him. With each year that passes he will be less blithe about failure. By adolescence the willingness of young people to risk failure has diminished greatly. And all too often parents push them further along that road by instilling fear, by punishing failure or by making success seem too precious. By middle age most of us carry in our heads a tremendous catalogue of things we have no intention of trying again because we tried them once and failed. . . .[2]

As Chapter 9 explained, divergent and convergent thinking operate quite differently, and each of them can play an important part in your thinking processes. If you have both of these skills in about equal measure, and if you can bring them into play according to the needs of the situation, you can think innovatively as well as put your ideas to work.

Unfortunately, many people have overlearned one orientation—either the divergent or the convergent—at the expense of the other. The diverger habitually uses divergent thinking, but cannot effectively close in on practical solutions, narrow them down, evaluate them, choose one, and put it to work. He or she comes up with many new ideas, but cannot seem to do anything practical with them.

The converger, on the other hand, makes a religion of "getting down to brass tacks" without ever getting up to steel tacks, plastic tacks, income tax, sailing tacks, racing tachs, syntax, or contacts. He has made such a long-term habit of converging immediately on virtually every matter that comes up that he has lost the use of most of the divergent-thinking skills he had a as a youngster.

[2]Ibid., p. 14.

Actually, since the human brain operates primarily as a convergent organ, seeking to simplify, organize, and arrange into convenient patterns all that it takes in, human beings are automatically inclined to think convergently. The brain habitually seeks and moves toward closure. Consequently, when a group of people talk over a problem together, they tend to think convergently in their collective processes. This means that, for all practical purposes, *we innovators live in a convergent world.*

Some of the most rigid thinkers, who cannot innovate very well and who cannot accept innovation from others, have unconsciously become so because of the demands imposed on them by their careers and life-styles. Among professional people, some of the most rigid, unimaginative, and intolerant thinkers are doctors, lawyers, military officers, and business executives. Except in relatively few cases, their jobs usually demand habitual convergent thinking. They narrow down options and look for workable solutions. If these people don't pay attention to the value of idea production and the innovative skill, they soon lose it. In the general population, convergers probably outnumber divergers by a wide margin. Probably a fairly small minority of people have learned to balance the two orientations.

the myth of
the "naturally" creative thinker

Imagination is more important than knowledge.

ALBERT EINSTEIN

A peculiar labeling process, built into our patterns of social conversation, has probably done more to stifle human thinking skills than any other factor. This process, by the connotations of the terms it uses, conveys the impression that only a few people are "truly creative," and the rest of us poor clods are, therefore, simply "uncreative."

This kind of either-or way of talking forms a subtle verbal trap that tends to imprison the thinking of the person who uses it. If you have been taught to use words in this way, you have concluded in effect that there are only two possible ways to "be." You can be born creative and play in the league with other gifted people, or you can be born uncreative and be part of the common herd. This verbal trap allows for no in-between area. A person subject to this way of thinking faces a forced-choice situation in personal evaluation. And given the enormous tradition of self-disparagement built into our culture, together with the huge number of negative evaluative messages each of us receives as a child, it should come as no surprise that most people accept the label of uncreative without putting up the slightest resistance.

Curiously, most people who describe themselves as uncreative cannot offer a simple, *verifiable* definition of creativity. Few people can say in simple objective terms what they mean by creative thinking, yet, ironically, they "know" they cannot do it. When pressed for a definition, many people will confidently offer a few vague and abstract phrases, try to refine them a bit, and finally resort to defining by example. "Well, take Picasso. Now there's a really creative person." Or, "My Aunt Marge is really creative. She's always coming up with far-out ideas." And they may conclude, "But I've never really been creative myself. I wouldn't even know which end of the paint brush to hold."

We must revise our attitudes—and our talking—about the concept of creativity. From now on, let's get rid of "creativity" in its noun form, which is vague, abstract, and virtually impossible to deal with in action terms. Instead, use *verbs*, which point the way to specific actions, skills, and results we can observe. Rather than refer to someone as "being creative," let's substitute "He (or she) *thinks creatively*," meaning that the person produces very specific results when using his or her brain in a certain way. Let's adopt this working definition: *To think creatively means to produce and express new, novel, and occasionally useful ideas.*

With this definition, we can see that the skill of thinking creatively ranges along a continuum scale from low to high. Just as each person has a level of physical strength he can measure, develop, and put to use, so each person has a level of skill in producing ideas which he can measure, develop, and put to use.

Let's look at the key words—new, novel, occasionally useful—in this definition to see how we can observe the results of thinking creatively.

First, an idea need only be new *to the thinker* or to those to whom he or she expresses it, in order to qualify under this definition. If it is new to you, then you have met the first condition of thinking creatively.

Second, if the idea strikes you as novel—that is, if it elicits that characteristic reaction of pleasant surprise from you or from the person to whom you express it, then you have met the second requirement for thinking creatively. Expressing the idea, by the way, does not require that you express it to someone else. In my definition, you must merely frame up the idea in some way that makes it comprehensible, at least to yourself. For many new and novel ideas, you will probably choose to express them in words. But you could just as well decide that a picture, a sketch, a musical tune, or a physical structure would best capture the essence of the idea and communicate it, if only to yourself.

Third, and even less stringent than the first two, if the idea seems to you or to anyone else somehow relevant to a particular area of interest or to some problem that needs a solution, so much the better. An idea that you consider highly relevant to a practical matter may also become useful. And usefulness, of course, tends to make new ideas become popular.

One final and very crucial point may encourage you to feel much more confident in laying claim to the skill of thinking creatively and in placing yourself somewhere up on the scale. Remember: A new idea is simply a combination of two or more known ideas. I defy you to refute this assertion. Take as long as you want. Search your mind for any "new" idea you have ever heard of that you cannot express as the coming together of two or more other ideas that, taken together, acquire a whole new meaning. Try it with consumer products: hula hoops, pet rocks, frozen apple pies. What about Disneyland? What about the space program? How about art: Michelangelo's Sistine Chapel painting, Dali's *Last Supper*, even Andy Warhol's can of Campbell's soup? The Panama Canal? The giant parabolic arch at the gateway to St. Louis, Missouri? Hybrid corn? Decaffeinated coffee? Movable type? Mass transit? Christianity, Buddhism, or Shinto? Trial by jury? Chopsticks? Credit card? Ball-point pen?

If thinking creatively means producing and expressing new, novel, and occasionally useful ideas, how do you do this? Simply by the *active mental process* of taking available ideas, combining them, and recognizing the novelty and possible usefulness of the new arrangement. According to my definition, you have probably thought creatively many times in your life. Every time you came up with an idea that gave you the "Aha!" reaction, you thought creatively.

You can let your ideas flow more easily by adopting the habit of *connecting*—simply linking ideas together for the fun of it, without requiring that they be immediately useful or important. Respecting and cherishing new combinations for their own sake enables you to mass produce new ideas, which increases the total number of ideas that will strike you as novel and useful. You must teach yourself to respect new and unproven ideas and to defend them against early criticism. According to an old story, a convergent-thinking political figure once scoffed at Thomas Edison's new electric light apparatus and demanded, "But what good is it?" Edison is said to have replied, "One day, Mr. X, perhaps you'll be able to tax it."

A crank is a man with a new idea—*until it catches on*.

MARK TWAIN

Another essential part of the idea production process involves supplying your brain with a steady flow of new ideas and information with which to think. If you don't read books, talk with interesting people, go to interesting lectures and courses, visit interesting museums, or hear interesting points of view, then you will probably have very few ideas in your mental storehouse to begin with. That will limit you in making new and novel connections. But if you use your fact-finding skills to bring in a great deal of information about your world, you will find that associations come rather easily and that you can let your ideas flow much more readily. Curiosity plays a very important part in thinking creatively.

> Chance favors the prepared mind.
>
> LOUIS PASTEUR

Try an interesting and enlightening experiment that will show you how much more you can use your mind and how much you can learn in a short time. Turn off your television set and leave it off—completely—for thirty days. After a full month of not looking at the screen, decide what part you want that device to play in your life. Don't just "cut down"—cut it out. To help you overcome the temptation (or pressure, if you have children living with you), unplug the power cord from the wall, take a scissors, and cut off the plug. Throw it away. A month later, if you still want to use the TV set, you can repair it with little effort. But you might find you enjoy thinking and learning so much, as well as having the extra time, that you have little desire to watch TV except for special programs.

breaking through your "invisible fences"

> Man's mind, stretched to a new idea, never goes back to its original dimension.
>
> OLIVER WENDELL HOLMES

Because your brain operates mostly by means of patterns and routines, you can inadvertently imprison yourself in too narrow a view of some problem, too strict an interpretation of some situation, too limited a perspective, or too small a range of options for proceeding. Every problem has two basic kinds of constraints or limitations on your ability to deal with it. One kind is the situational constraint—the "real" one—such as limited time, limited money, your age, your gender, your racial origin, your height, your educational status, something that has already happened (the spilled milk), a law of nature, or a law of society. You must face these "facts" of life in searching for a solution. They constrain you to some extent in what you can do.

The second kind of constraint is the mental constraint—your self-imposed barriers, many of which you may have unconsciously adopted. In dealing with a situation or problem, you might take for granted one or more constraints that do not really exist in the situation. That is, you might have unconsciously put the constraint there. These mental constraints might include *assumptions* about limited funds, uncooperative attitudes on the part of others, not enough time, the unworkability of some particular approach, the notion that an executive would not approve a certain action, the notion that the other person would not want to make love, the idea that a restaurant could not prepare some unusual kind of dish or late night snack, and so on.

We can detect and deal with situational constraints much easier than mental constraints. Some of your mentally imposed constraints might be conscious and quite reasonable—that is, you have thought about the situation and decided to accept certain constraints and to work around them. But you might impose just as many constraints, and perhaps more, unconsciously and unnecessarily. The essence of a *mental block* is an unnecessary and unconsciously accepted mental constraint that keeps you from reaching a satisfactory solution or resolution to the situation. *Blockbusting* amounts to searching for, locating, and getting rid of various blocking patterns and blocking assumptions. This invariably has the effect of *increasing the number of available options*, which is what adaptive thinking is all about.

Look at the following thinking games to help you get an idea of how blocking patterns and blocking assumptions work. The formulation of each of these little problems invites you to fall prey to *pattern thinking* and to build an *invisible fence* around your thinking. The effect of the invisible fence is to hem you in mentally, keeping you in the "neighborhood" of limited and unworkable solutions. If the effective solution happens to lie outside the invisible fence, obviously you cannot take advantage of it. As you study these problems, try to become more aware of the possibility of invisible fences around your thinking. Ask yourself what mental patterns, relationships, and assumptions about the problem and the solution might be limiting the number of options open to you.

The famous nine-dot problem shown below is a good example of the powerful effects a visual pattern can have on one's thinking processes. Take a few moments to examine it, and try to solve it before reading further.

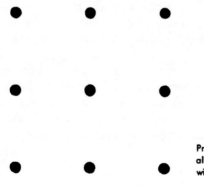

Problem: Draw 4 straight lines that pass through all 9 dots without picking up your pencil and without retracing.

If you had difficulty solving it, probably you organized the problem in your mind in terms of a very familiar—and tyrannical—pattern, namely a square. Probably, you first began looking for solutions that involved squares or other right-angle line structures, and you soon ran out of options. Indeed, your brain probably "saw" a square that was not really there (there were only nine individual dots; the square they supposedly "form" is a perceptual artifact of your westernized, industrialized memory system). If you haven't reached a solution, study the possibilities further from this point of view. If you still can't solve it—and many people can't—check the solution in the Appendix. (Eskimo children, by the way, usually solve it rather quickly, presumably because their world includes relatively few rectangular forms.)

Patterns play a very important part in our thinking, don't they? Here are a couple of easier ones. Rearrange the letters in each of these nonsense words to make it into a meaningful word. (The Appendix gives the answers.)

BIRAB
PILNEC

Here you can observe a very important aspect of pattern thinking. Note how the arrangement of letters in each case looks somewhat like a plausible word. It seems phonetically reasonable and pronounceable. Because it forms an "acceptable" pattern, your brain may tend to cling to it at first. As you begin rearranging the letters, the tyranny of the original pattern begins to break down, and you free your brain to search for other, more acceptable combinations. This example is a miniature representation of exactly the same kind of pattern thinking that can take place on all levels of your thinking. It happens to all human beings from time to time, and to many of them on a routine basis. It causes problems ranging from family feuds to business disasters, from manipulation to racial prejudice, and from personal maladjustment to international warfare.

The next thinking problem will invite you to make certain *blocking assumptions*. See how quickly you can overcome the initial pattern and search for approaches outside the invisible fence. Here is a word picture of the problem.

Six ordinary drinking glasses are standing in a row. The first three are empty, and the next three are full of water. By handling and moving only one glass, you can change the arrangement so that no empty glass is next to another empty glass, and no full glass is next to another full one. How can you do this? Think it over before reading further. (The Appendix gives a solution.)

If you felt blocked for a few moments—and most people do in dealing with this problem—you probably made certain necessary assumptions about the solution. You may have unconsciously assumed that a glass and its contents had to form an inseparable unit, that the water could not leave the glass. If so, your invisible fence put a very simple solution out of your reach. As soon as that option occurred to you, you broke through the fence and it no longer constrained you. Consider also the possibility that the verbal description of this problem may have channeled your thinking in certain directions.

Invisible fences can sometimes imprison our thinking, and, indeed, they frequently do for many people. But the thinker who knows about them and who frequently checks to see whether they might have sprung up around him tends to overcome them more often and to find novel and effective solutions. Sometimes the mere knowledge of a few simple facts can prevent you from fencing yourself in. For example, I once went into a delicatessen with a friend to buy a sandwich and some fruit for lunch. After I had paid for my order, I heard my friend, who was behind me in line, place an order for a half-sandwich. I probably looked at him with a "that's no fair" expression on my face, and I said, "I didn't know you could order a half-sandwich. That would have been plenty for me." He looked at me, smiled benignly, and offered that age-old piece of empty wisdom, "Well, now you know." The truth will set you free, I suppose.

See how many blocking assumptions you can name which you or someone else might make in dealing with various problem situations. Consider the possible blocking assumptions:

1. Somebody has not already solved the problem facing you.
2. You are the one who must solve it.
3. It even *is* a problem.
4. You cannot get any help in solving it.
5. You know everything you need to know about it.
6. You must solve it without spending any money.
7. You must solve it by some deadline.
8. You must solve it completely; a short-term, interim, or partial solution won't do.
9. The presently known candidate solutions are the only acceptable ones.
10. You must deal with it as someone else has stated it; you can't reframe it to make more sense out of it.

Make it a regular thinking habit to scan the situations you find yourself in, and see how often you can spot the effects of patterns and assumptions in other people's actions and in your own approaches. Learn to ask "why?" Why do we do it this way? Why not do it that way? Why should we do this at all? And teach yourself to search for the constraints in a situation. Try to identify any unnecessary "musts," "must nots," and "cannots" that might lurk at the edges of your conscious picture of the problem. Bring them out into the open whenever possible and evaluate them. Keep them if they make sense, and junk them if they don't.

techniques for idea production

Anything one man can imagine, other men can make real.

The late Alex Osborn, once president of the advertising firm of Batten, Barton, Durstine and Osborn and founder of the Creative Education Foundation in Buffalo, New York, said about creative idea production, "I submit that creativity is an art—an applied art—a workable art—a teachable art—a learnable art—an art in which all of us can make ourselves more and more proficient, if we will."

Osborn's pioneering efforts in developing idea production techniques have played an important part in the increasing popularity of creative problem-solving courses in the United States. In his book, *Applied Imagination*, he describes many instances of small groups of people applying techniques for idea production in working together on product designs, community problems, marketing and advertising projects, military problems, and business problems.[3]

The following techniques seem to work especially well in small group situations where the people have consciously chosen to generate mass quantities of ideas on the conviction that *quantity inevitably brings quality.* You can also use them in your individual thinking processes, and even to some extent as a member of a group where not everyone realizes the value of divergent thinking. For convenience we will divide them into three categories:

1. Suspended judgment
2. Practical techniques
3. Skill-building games

The technique of *suspended judgment* enables people to think up and save ideas that might not make much sense at first hearing and to wait until later to see whether they might have some value. You can sometimes get group members to agree to this strategy just by saying, "Suppose we just make a list of all the ideas we can think of—good, bad, or indifferent—and then cut the list down later, after we run out of possibilities?" If the objective becomes to make a list rather than to decide, often group members will abide by the policy of not killing any idea too soon.

To use the technique of suspended judgment, it helps to know the most common habitual ways for killing ideas and head them off when they arise. *Nonverbal put-downs* frequently come up automatically, especially on the part of the habitual converger or the ego-builder who doesn't want anybody

[3]Used by permission of Charles Scribner's Sons from APPLIED IMAGINATION by Alex Osborn. Copyright 1953 © 1957, 1963 Charles Scribner's Sons. For more information on Osborn's methods, contact the Creative Education Foundation, 1300 Elmwood Ave., Buffalo, N.Y. 14222.

222

else to get credit for having good ideas. The snicker, the condescending chuckle, the rolling of the eyes, the scornful look—all of these signal disapproval. And even though an idea might survive this nonverbal blow, it might be so wounded in the unconscious estimation of others that it gets a prejudiced evaluation later.

Verbal put-downs include *killer statements*, things people say that have the effect of disapproving of new ideas or of limiting the extent to which they can get a serious hearing. Some typical killer statements are:

1. We tried that years ago.
2. Oh, Mr. X (or the accountants, or the union, or the parents, or the community, and so on) will never go for that.
3. We don't do it that way here.
4. We're not set up to do that; our bookkeeping system (or student records, or computer, or stock room, and so on) couldn't handle it.
5. We can't justify the costs.
6. If we do that in this case, we'll have to do it in every case.
7. It's against policy.
8. That sounds kind of impractical.
9. I don't think that's very realistic. It's okay in theory, but when you get down to cases, it's another matter.
10. Sounds like too much of a hassle.

You can probably add three times as many killer statements to this list, based on your experiences in group discussions. By keeping on the alert for killer statements and by persuading the other people not to use them at the instant when someone first tosses out an idea, you can help the group come up with a much larger supply of ideas.

But don't underestimate the strength of the negative thinking habit in some people, or the lengths to which they will go to build up their egos at the expense of someone else's ideas. Some people in the group might take more interest in impressing others with how smart they are and how dumb and impractical others are. They may shoot down new ideas with perfectly "practical" ammunition. When confronted on their continually negative comments, they may defend their policies by saying something like, "Look—I'm only trying to tell you what works. I've tried a lot of these things. We've got to be practical. We can't sit here and 'blue-sky' all day. We've got to get down to business." *The negative thinker can find a flaw in any idea, no matter what it is. The positive thinker can find potential in any idea.*

Another good way to protect an idea until it begins to sound familiar and might warrant a closer look is to put it "on probation." When someone mentions a possibility, even a half-baked one, you can head off the tendency to assassinate it immediately by saying, "Do we have to decide yes or no on that right now? Why don't we just write it down with the others and look at it later?"

Edward deBono suggests a technique that I've found excellent for getting people to suspend their judgments of ideas and even to look for positive features of them. This technique requires that anyone who comments on an idea must first offer a positive comment on it before criticizing it. Except for the completely rectangular negative thinker, this will condition most people to look for the best as well as the worst in new approaches. DeBono also suggests commenting on any features of the idea that simply seem "interesting." As I employ the method in problem-solving groups, I call it the "PIN" technique. PIN stands for "positive, interesting, and negative." In offering comment on an idea, one must first say something positive about it, then pick out something interesting about it, and finally—if he or she still wants to—something negative. I have also found the PIN technique a very useful mental aid in many other situations, especially when someone asks me for advice or asks me to evaluate an idea or course of action they've thought up.[4]

Now we come to the principal category of idea production methods—*practical techniques* for use in real situations. My favorite techniques include

1. Group "memory" device
2. Brainstorming
3. Structured associations
4. Hypothesizing
5. Albrecht's leprechaun

By a *group memory* device, I mean using a large surface to draw pictures and record information—images of any sort to help process the problem "data" in additional ways. My favorite technique when working with executives in an organization is to cover an entire wall of a conference room with a four-foot-wide sheet of newsprint paper. I draw a vertical dividing line in the center of the sheet, labeling the left side "Expansion" and the right side "Closure," in accordance with the two-phase problem-solving model in Chapter 9. After briefing the participants on the problem-solving model, I give each of them a felt-tipped marker, crayon, or grease pencil, and we begin putting what we know and think about the problem up on the sheet. As we proceed, we build a comprehensive portrayal of the problem, which everyone can see at a glance. This group memory device stimulates a tremendous amount of diversified discussion and option finding. Each person can draw pictures, diagrams, or cartoons to represent parts of the problem or potential solutions. This overall model of the problem then serves as a useful tool in applying the other techniques of idea production.

[4]This technique is attributed to Edward deBono in David Campbell, Ph.D., *Take the Road to Creativity and Get Off Your Dead End* (Niles, Ill.: Argus Communications, 1977), p. 13.

Brainstorming, the idea production technique pioneered by Alex Osborn, uses a group process in which discipline paradoxically confers freedom. In using the method, group members must abide by two basic rules, which the coordinator must enforce. These rules are

1. Produce the greatest possible *quantity* of ideas.
2. Do *not* evaluate any idea during the session.

A typical brainstorming session follows a recognized plan; it is much more than an undisciplined free-for-all. The group coordinator states the problem for the group in very specific terms. The wording of the problem encourages specific, tangible solutions rather than abstractions or value judgments. The group members make sure they understand what they are to do: Produce as many ideas as possible for solving Problem X. Then the group leader may start a tape recorder, or someone may take down ideas as the members produce them. A chalkboard sometimes becomes a mixed blessing; members may tend to produce ideas only along the lines of the most appealing ones listed on the board. The coordinator's job at this point is merely to keep the association process flowing and occasionally to remind members of the rules. He should discourage approval of ideas just as he discourages disapproval. The coordinator should take care not to "lead" the idea-production process in any particular direction. When the group seems to "run dry," he can toss in a few ideas to get them started again. The coordinator can challenge them to reach some target number of ideas before finishing.

Only after the group decides it has pretty well exhausted its storehouse of ideas does the coordinator wind up the session. A typical session may run from fifteen to forty-five minutes. The coordinator will have the list of ideas typed and organized for use at the next meeting. Breaking the process into two meetings means that members will not feel impatient to converge on "the" solution. They see their mission for the first session as simply to mass produce ideas. At the second session, the coordinator conducts a discussion of the ideas the group generated and invites members to add any new ones. Then, depending on the problem and the exact nature of their problem-solving project, they will probably proceed to narrow the field of ideas down to the most attractive and work out a plan for putting them into action.

Structured associations can help in any idea production situation, and they especially help to extend the range of production in brainstorming. Osborn recommended a number of "idea-spurring" questions, which have the effect of producing more associations. These questions include

1. Put to other uses? New ways to use as is? Other uses if modified?
2. Adapt? What else is like this? What other ideas does this suggest?
3. Modify? Change meaning, color, motion, sound, odor, taste, form, shape? Other changes?

4. Magnify? What to add? Greater frequency? Stronger? Larger? Plus ingredient? Multiply?

5. Minify? What to subtract? Eliminate? Smaller? Lighter? Slower? Split up? Less frequent?

6. Substitute? Who else instead? What else instead? Other place? Other time?

7. Rearrange? Other layout? Other sequence? Change pace?

8. Reverse? Opposites? Turn it backward? Turn it upside down? Turn it inside out?

9. Combine? How about a blend, an assortment? Combine purposes? Combine ideas?[5]

Professor James Adams, director of the Design Division of the Stanford School of Engineering, recommends a number of additional verbal manipulation techniques, using terms such as build up, compare, release, relax, display, check, search, guess, symbolize, manipulate, exaggerate, cycle, and repeat. He also suggests representing the problem at hand in visual form as well as in words and using mathematical or numerical formulations of it to broaden the point of view.[6]

Edward deBono recommends the structured association technique of *reversal*, in which you pick out one or more key words used in describing the problem or in describing known solutions, and reverse their connotations. For example, could you have students teaching their teachers? Clients advising the counselor? The customer delivering the product to the store? The rabbit pulling the magician out of the hat? Using antonyms for the dominant words can also produce extra ideas.

DeBono's technique of *random association* also provides a means for getting the idea production process moving again when it seems to have ground to a halt. Keeping the problem vaguely in mind, the group can use one or more words chosen at random to "force" the association process to begin again. The group leader might toss out any words that come to mind—like "golf tee," "candy bar," or "powder puff." The others then try to find connections between the object suggested and the problem at hand. Strange as this technique sounds, it almost always produces a fresh round of associating. You can even open up a dictionary or any book and put your finger down at any point on any page, read the word you find there, and use it to start more association chains.

DeBono refers to these provocative thinking techniques as forms of *lateral thinking*, as contrasted to conventional *vertical thinking* procedures. Whereas vertical thinking processes consist of well-known and comfortable linear chains of thought, with each link leading predictably to the next, lateral thinking means interrupting these chains of ideas and

---

[5]Osborn, *Applied Imagination*, p. 175.
[6]James L. Adams, *Conceptual Blockbusting*. Used with permission. W.W. Norton & Company, Inc., New York, N.Y. Copyright © 1974, 1976 by James L. Adams, p. 66.

"jumping" to other starting points when you don't seem to be heading in a productive direction.[7]

The technique of *hypothesizing* employs the same kind of association process used in brainstorming. Here the group members propose as many "explanations" as they can for the "cause" of the problem. They can also play the freewheeling game of "what-if?" in exploring possible avenues of attack. For example, a group in an industrial organization might be trying to boost sales of a particular product. By freewheeling about possible sources for the drop in sales, they might strike upon a possible course of action they would not have otherwise found. In this case, the wilder the speculations the better. Creatures from Mars, sunspots, gremlins, spies in the organization, forgetful customers, mail carriers who get lost, diabolical stock clerks, and on and on can all provide food for thought. Most of these wild hypotheses will not, in themselves, provide direct solutions. But they may very well trigger certain other verbal association processes which can lead to solutions.

The game of "what-if?" allows you to play with ideas and courses of action that you know will not work, in order to keep the ideas flowing. You can say, "What if we could manufacture our product at no cost?" This absurd angle might lead to useful associations, like cutting the materials cost, finding ways to transfer some of the assembly process to the customer, having it manufactured by a shelter organization for handicapped people which charges lower rates, or making the product part of a larger and more economically manufactured product. Just as with far-out hypotheses, the what-if ideas do not necessarily represent solutions, but some of them may lead you close enough to useful solutions that the verbal association process can establish the final link.

The fifth technique for producing ideas is one I developed for overcoming mental blocks that limit the number of attractive options. I've modestly named it *Albrecht's leprechaun*. To use this provocative technique, you just visualize the problem as clearly as you can, review it from as many angles as you can, and then imagine that you have called in a leprechaun to help you solve it. To the Irish, a leprechaun is a magical little person who can do many things. According to legend, if you catch a leprechaun, he must reveal to you where his gold—your solution—is hidden. Ask yourself, "How would the leprechaun solve this problem?" Then let your mind spin freely, imagining all the magical things the leprechaun might do, unfettered by the normal laws of nature and humans. Could he snap his fingers and make someone or something disappear or appear? Can he perform miracles? Can he make it rain or prevent it from raining? Can he get inside someone's mind and change their opinion? Can he charm them

---

[7]Edward deBono, *Lateral Thinking* (New York: Harper & Row Pub., Inc., 1970).

into or out of a particular course of action? Can he build an otherwise impossible part, device, or machine? Can he show you an important piece of information you need to know? Can he use pixie dust to solve the problem?

The use of Albrecht's leprechaun is a projective technique. You temporarily set aside your self-imposed constraints and project your unfettered thought processes into the problem, finding additional options by associating with the magical possibilities you can picture in the form of the leprechaun. As with the hypothesizing technique, the leprechaun will usually not present a working solution, but he may very well lead you to think of a possibility that will work, just by bringing you conceptually nearer to it.

The third group of idea production techniques consists of skill-building games to free your association processes and let them flow easily. Learning to make many associations simply and quickly will enable you to think flexibily in almost any problem situation. You can play these games to amuse yourself when alone, when driving with friends in a car, or with children on a trip. It's fun to slip one of them into a casual party conversation for a few seconds. Some of the skill-building games you can play include

1. Memory search.
2. 101 uses.
3. Forced association.
4. Mental hotfoot.
5. What-if?
6. Hypothesizing.
7. Bug list.

The memory search game involves coming up with words or ideas that fit a certain requirement. For example, you can try to name as many items of food as you can that have a certain color. Or name as many kinds of birds as you can (easier than you may think). Try coming up with a boy's name and a girl's name for each letter of the alphabet, or a proverb or folk expression starting with each letter of the alphabet. This kind of activity tends to improve your ability to scan your memory and reach for relevant ideas when you need them.

The game of 101 uses provides an excellent classroom technique as an introduction to divergent thinking. To play, you merely think about some common object of almost any kind—a brick, a coat hanger, a thimble, a burned-out light bulb, old automobile tire, a key—and pretend that it has no name and no known function. Then you proceed to name as many possible uses as you can for the item. Try to come up with at least 101 uses. A group can play this game in the brainstorming style, or the individuals can make separate lists and then combine them. This game also enables an instructor in a thinking course to demonstrate some of the practical techniques for idea production explained previously. For example, the participants can first produce lists of uses for a common object and count the number of uses they found. Then the instructor can demonstrate the Osborn "idea-spurring" questions, for example, and the members produce even more ideas using these methods.

The *forced association* technique offers more of a challenge to your idea production skills, and it enables you to see associations between ideas that others would not see. To play this game, you simply take two randomly selected words, preferably concrete nouns, and put them together. Then you study the association and try to make something useful or interesting out of it. In playing a game, one person can select the two words while the other must name some useful or plausible results. For example, you might take two ideas, such as house plant and typewriter, and try to think up a consumer product based on the combination. This game is easier than it first seems, and it can stretch your imagination quite effectively.

Another very useful exercise for developing your creative thinking skills involves *continuous-flow idea production*. Choose a time and place that allow you to concentrate closely, relax, close your eyes, and think about a common object such as an ordinary paper clip. Now begin thinking up other applications for the paper clip, one after another, *without pausing*. Don't worry about making them "good" ideas; just keep getting them for as long as you possibly can without a break. See if you can come up with twenty or even more. Any application qualifies, no matter how strange, unusual, trivial, or unimportant it may seem. Emphasize continuity of the idea stream, trying to get as many items as you can in a steady flow. Next try some other familiar object and repeat the process. Practice this exercise from time to time and you will find yourself becoming much more fluent at idea production.

The *mental hotfoot* game involves coming up with novel ideas or phrases by combining simple ideas or by modifying well-known phrases. Comedian George Carlin coined the term to suggest the surprise effect such a novel phrase can have on the hearer's mind. "Why," says Carlin, "are there small craft warnings, but no large craft warnings?" I find this game the most enjoyable when I come up with novel statements on the spur of the moment. Sometimes I'll hear someone use the same hackneyed expression for the hundredth time, and a new way to look at it will suddenly occur to me. The novelty of the thought catches my interest. Here are a few mental hotfoots (hotfeet?) to start you thinking:

1. Can you give someone a "coldfoot?"
2. Why isn't there a special name for the tops of your feet?
3. You can have a heart-to-heart talk with somebody; could you have an eye-to-eye talk? A nose-to-nose talk? Knee-to-knee? Back-to-back?

4. Can you fight city hall?
5. Does a sweeping generalization use a broom?
6. If a rooster can crow, can a crow rooster?
7. Have you ever watched a pot boil?
8. Have you ever really seen a brick outhouse?
9. Have you ever seen a man bite a dog?
10. Have you ever seen someone tickled to death? Tickled pink?
11. Have you ever seen a person scared white as a sheet?
12. Have you ever seen an audience rolling in the aisles? Glued to their seats? In the palm of a performer's hand?
13. Boys will be boys; what else will they be?
14. We call something sweet as a nut or brown as a berry, but nuts aren't sweet and berries aren't brown; sometimes nuts are brown and berries are sweet.
15. Why don't they have divorce licenses, divorce ceremonies, divorce gowns, and divorce receptions?
16. Gentle as a lamb—have you ever seen a mean lamb?
17. Thanks, you're all heart. No soul—but all heart.
18. He wouldn't harm a fly. People maybe—flies, no.
19. Think or thwim.
20. How many games in a mental set?

You can have fun and improve the novelty of your own associations by injecting a mental hotfoot into a conversation from time to time. Keep alert for new turns of phrases, new ways of expressing things, and new applications of often used expressions. You may find this game fun to play with a few friends on a spontaneous basis during conversation.

The game of *what-if?* encourages you to examine alternative possibilities in situations where conventional "wisdom" tells you they won't work. The idea is to freewheel with imaginative speculations and see how extensively you can visualize the unusual and the implausible. In some cases you might find that your ideas are not entirely implausible; some of them might become solutions to important problems. To play "what-if" you simply ask a question beginning with "What if . . ." and let your imagination fill in the rest. For example, one person might say, "What if you had eyes in the back of your head?" Others might respond by naming some of the possible effects that this change to human anatomy might have, such as:

1. Hats would have to be redesigned.
2. One pair of eyes could rest while the other pair worked.
3. You wouldn't need rearview mirrors in cars.
4. You could tell if the person sitting behind you was enjoying the movie.
5. Teachers could keep an eye on their students while writing on the board.

Try playing "what-if" with a number of other statements, and you will soon see how effective the game can be in developing your imagination and your ability to associate. Try questions like "What if people didn't sleep?", "What if we could read one another's minds?", and "What if all countries used the same system of money?"

The game of hypothesizing can help to develop your association skills, as well as produce practical solutions in problem-solving situations. To play this game, one person merely asks a question beginning with "Why?", and the others offer as many hypotheses as they can to answer the question. The more outrageous the hypotheses the better, in terms of stretching your association processes. Try hypothesizing about the following questions:

1. A car approaching you on the freeway has its lights on in the middle of the day. Why?
2. One cow is standing alone in the pasture, 100 feet from the rest of the herd. Why?
3. A woman suddenly goes on a huge spending spree, after having been known as poor and thrifty for many years. Why?
4. You don't receive any mail for three days. Why?
5. Someone who has been very unpleasant to you for a long time suddenly begins treating you very pleasantly. Why?

The more freely you can hypothesize, the more flexible you can approach various problem situations. By developing this skill you can supply yourself with many more options than the person who steadfastly clings to the known and the proven. Don't be afraid to freewheel in problem-solving situations as well. Sometimes an outrageous hypothesis might contain an element of truth, or it might trigger another hypothesis, which might turn out to be correct.

The idea production technique of the bug list, suggested by James Adams, involves naming as many unsolved problems as you can, in terms of things that "bug" you. In *Conceptual Blockbusting*, Adams offers the following and many more as idea starters:

1. Bumper stickers that can't be removed
2. Pictures that don't hang straight
3. Glary paper
4. Blunt pencils
5. Dirty aquariums
6. Changing from regular glasses to sunglasses
7. Reading road maps while driving
8. Bras
9. Door-to-door solicitors
10. Vending machines that take your money with no return

A group can use a bug list to develop starter material for mass idea production. Each item could form the basis for a brainstorming session, especially when the group has not worked together and would like to have a preliminary training session in the techniques of brainstorming. The bug list game can also produce some intriguing possibilities for consumer products if used by inventors or product developers in corporations.[8]

All of these idea production techniques—suspended judgment, practical techniques, and skill-building games—have one basic factor in common. They enable you to maximize the *use of association* in putting new ideas together from the raw material of existing ideas, and they invite you to foster and develop new ideas rather than kill them before they draw breath.

becoming an innovator

Anyone, anywhere, in any situation, and in any walk of life can become an innovator by developing the attitude of respecting and protecting ideas, and by using the basic techniques of idea production in everyday situations. Whether you are a nuclear physicist, a student, a manual laborer, a homemaker, an artist, an accountant, or a vagabond, you can innovate in your own way in your own situation. If you are willing to respect your own ideas as your personal intellectual wealth and to let them flow and develop, you can bring fresh and innovative approaches to virtually any situation in which you operate. *No situation is too simple, too ordinary, too unimportant, or too mundane for innovative thinking.*

As you master the techniques and attitudes of idea production, you will probably find that the greatest obstacles to expressing your new ideas come in the form of other peoples' habitual idea-killing responses. The compulsively convergent thinker who wants to show you how smart he or she is and how stupid you are can offer a formidable threat to the freewheeling approach. You must learn to live with criticism, ridicule, laughter, and narrow-minded thinking on the part of some people you meet and to take it in stride.

> *Stupid men, knowing the way of life*
> *And having once laughed at it, laugh again the louder.*
> *If you need to be sure which way is right, you can tell by their laughing at it . . .*
>
> LAO TZU

As mentioned previously, innovation is more talked about in our society than encouraged and rewarded. Much of our cultural programming tells us to criticize and downgrade ourselves, and to leave the artistic, creative, productive, imaginative, innovative ideas to some special chosen few. The innovator must overcome these messages and develop confidence in his or her own innovative skills, not making comparisons to others, but simply

---

[8]James L. Adams,*Conceptual Blockbusting*. Used with permission. W.W. Norton & Company, Inc., New York, N.Y. Copyright © 1974, 1976 by James L. Adams, p. 84.

using his or her own abilities to the fullest. Men in particular seem to receive a great number of programming messages that tell them not to create, not to innovate, not to appreciate or express the artistic and productive sides of their personalities. Psychologist Abraham Maslow comments on the typical way in which men crimp their creative processes:

> One thing I . . . have been interested in recently in my work with creative men (and uncreative men too) is the horrible fear of anything that the person himself would call "femininity," or "femaleness," which we immediately call "homosexual." If he's been brought up in a tough environment, "feminine" means practically everything that's creative. Imagination, fantasy, color, poetry, music, tenderness, languishing and being romantic are walled off as dangerous to one's picture of one's own masculinity. Everything that's called "weak" tends to be repressed in the normal masculine adult adjustment. And many things are called weak which we are learning are not weak at all.[9]

The history of scientific innovation has been the history of people who were willing to fight for their ideas in the face of ridicule, scorn, and even hostility. Guglielmo Marconi, father of radio, tried for years to interest people in the potential of wireless communication over long distances. When Marconi proposed to send a wireless signal across the Atlantic, the "experts" almost unanimously declared it theoretically impossible. They correctly pointed out that the earth's curvature between the two points of land was so great that the straight-line path of the signal would take it off into space; it would never reach its destination. However, Marconi tried it anyway, and in 1901 he succeeded in transmitting the Morse code letter "S" from Cornwall, England, to Newfoundland. Only later did researchers discover the ionosphere, an electrically charged layer of the atmosphere which has the effect of bending low-frequency radio waves and causing them to follow the curvature of the earth. Marconi's belief in the value of experience panned out, but not without a great deal of initial embarrassment and humiliation at the hands of those who "knew" it wouldn't work.

Dr. Robert H. Goddard, generally considered the father of modern rocketry and one of the pioneers of space flight, faced much the same ridicule and opposition when he proposed that rockets could be developed to carry space vehicles beyond the earth's atmosphere. Some people were still claiming in 1926 that a rocket could not operate in space because the escaping exhaust gases would not have anything to "push against." Goddard's dedication and years of work finally proved the point and led to the extensive development work that brought rocketry into its own and paved the way for the exploration of space.

One of the greatest scientific innovators of our time, Dr. Hans Selye, once told me, "To make a great dream come true, you must first have a great

[9]Used by permission of Charles Scribner's Sons from A SOURCE BOOK FOR CREATIVE THINKING by Parnes and Harding, Copyright 1962 Charles Scribner's Sons, p. 97.

dream." Along with the mental techniques of innovation must come a sense of purpose and the *intellectual courage* to stick to your guns when very few other people accept or even understand your idea.

Every great oak was once a nut that stood its ground.

ANONYMOUS

Psychologists who have explored the behavior of people who think creatively have found a marked connection between creative thinking and positive thinking. Those who take a positive "can do" approach to situations that confront them tend to produce more ideas and better solutions than those who tend to throw in the towel immediately.

A sense of humor also plays an important part in the kind of mental flexibility that leads to innovation. The same kind of mental flexibility and appreciation of novelty that underlies a sense of humor also underlies the idea production skill. People who have a well-developed sense of humor—who can laugh easily and who can tell a joke easily—tend to look at things in new ways and produce novel ideas. Humorless people, who go around with grim faces and negative thoughts, seldom come up with new or novel ideas. The same mental rigidity that leads them to see the world as a grim and unpleasant place also prevents them from mobilizing their ideas and producing new ones.

Training in idea production techniques might have the side effect of increasing one's sense of humor, possibly by increasing appreciation for novelty and by enabling generation of new combinations of ideas and clever alternatives such as those involved in jokes. These activities, together with some positive thinking techniques, might form the basis for a greatly improved outlook on life. The ability to laugh—frequently, freely, and heartily—forms a basic part of one's ability to adjust to the world. The world can be a very grim place or a very ridiculous place, depending on how you choose to see it.

John Gardner identifies four specific learnable capabilities of the innovator as

1. Openness to new experience
2. Independence of the opinions and biases of others
3. Flexibility, or tolerance for ambiguity
4. Capacity to find order in experience

He points out that the small child has all of these capabilities in abundance, and by the time the child has grown into young adulthood, he or she has surrendered most of them to the surrounding forces of conformity.[10]

[10]Excerpts from pp. 35, 36, 37, 38 in SELF-RENEWAL by John W. Garnder. Copyright © 1963, 1964 by John W. Gardner. Reprinted by permission of Harper & Row, Publishers, Inc.

You must adjust . . . This is the legend imprinted in every schoolbook, the invisible message on every blackboard. Our schools have become vast factories for the manufacture of robots.

ROBERT M. LINDNER

Here are a few basic policies you may find useful in developing your own innovative skills.

1. Keep taking in new information; read, listen, watch, talk with others.
2. "Listen" carefully for your new ideas; make deliberate associations and verbalize them; keep an "idea list," writing down your ideas as you think of them with others who will respect them.
3. Surround yourself with people who stimulate your thinking and who think positively and innovatively; don't limit your acquaintances to those who have the same ideas and interests you currently have.
4. Meet new ideas with kindness, respect, and protection; practice the PIN technique in reacting to new ideas—positive, interesting, and negative features.
5. Make a habit of questioning the status quo; ask why, why not, and what might happen if?

Although many people seem to consider creative thinking somehow contradictory to logical thinking, I believe we can easily blend them into a very harmonious and effective combination. The ability to think logically does not exclude the ability to think divergently and to produce new ideas. By learning and using both skills—convergent thinking and divergent thinking—you have the best of both. You can become an effective innovator by producing new ideas and by making them work.

11

better thinking
in the business world

ALBRECHT'S LAW: Intelligent people, when assembled into an organization, will tend toward collective stupidity.

KARL ALBRECHT

the prevalence of fuzzy
thinking in organizations

In his provocative book, *De-Managing America*, Richard Cornuelle gives an interesting example of what happens to intelligent people who live within organizational settings.

> . . . I encountered a young woman solemnly attending a giant plastic-molding machine. Every few seconds, the machine would clank and spit out a plastic form that looked like a cover for a large cake plate. The young woman would take the part, spin it skillfully around in her gloved hand and then add it to an enormous pile that surrounded and nearly engulfed her.
>
> She turned off her machine and we talked. She told me matter-of-factly that her job was really very simple. She was to take each new molding off the machine and to look at it carefully. If she saw no flaw, she was to pack it in a cardboard carton. If she saw any imperfection—a bubble or a crack or a bulge—the molding was to be tossed in a rubbish bin. She was puzzled only because the rubbish bin the management had supplied was so small and had overflowed so long ago. The machine had not produced a passable cake plate for ever so long. But she was comfortably and confidently doing exactly what she had been told to do.[1]

This incident didn't surprise me, only because in my work as a management consultant I've seen it again and again in organizations. Of course, the person changes, the machine changes, the product or activity changes, and the organization changes, but the result is common to many situations. Cornuelle has cited an example of what I have come to call "collective stupidity." By this I mean that intelligent people who can think and act

[1]Richard Cornuelle, *De-Managing America* (New York: Random House, 1975), p. 43.

236

very effectively as individuals can, as a group, exhibit the most profoundly stupid and counterproductive responses to the demands of their environment. Almost anyone who has worked for very long in and with organizations can rattle off a dozen or more stories nearly as absurd as Cornuelle's example. Collective stupidity occurs fairly regularly in business organizations.

When a person sees himself as filling a certain specific role within the abstract set of programmed relationships that people call an organization, that person's behavior will almost automatically take on certain patterns that encode his perceptions of that role. An organization person tends to behave in certain very different ways from an individual person. Every organization, as a structured set of roles and relationships, brings a mixed set of blessings. By defining what people are supposed to do and the kinds of interactions they should have, we can focus the efforts of a number of people toward a common goal or expected set of results. At the same time, when they take on these patterned ways of relating to one another, they inevitably experience certain constraints on the ways in which they can approach problems, especially unfamiliar ones. For the most part, the organization chart tells each person *what he can't do*, as well as what he should do.

In some of the organizations I've worked with, it would seem more accurate to replace the term *department* with *compartment*. The abstract organizational structure in many situations becomes a *partitioning system*, which tends to emphasize territorial and jurisdictional subdivisions at the expense of the higher sense of mission. People refer to themselves as members of Marketing, Engineering, Finance, Nursing, Administration, or even Management. These relatively arbitrary subdivisions become as real for the members of these tribes as rivers, mountain ranges, or fences that might separate them from one another. In conflict situations, they tend to fall back to their tribal identifications and to do battle from behind their organizational fences. More often than not, my role as a consultant in working out various improvements in an organization's operation has been to serve as a facilitator of communication and effective interaction across these compartmental boundaries. Very few managers, I've found, can climb above their assigned jurisdictional territories for sufficiently long periods to see how the entire organization operates and to identify ways in which the various groups can cooperate more effectively.

We trained hard—but it seemed that every time we were beginning to form up into teams, we would be reorganized. I was to learn later in life that we tend to meet any new situation by reorganization, and a wonderful method it can be for creating the illusion of progress while producing confusion, inefficiency, and demoralization.

PETRONIUS ARBITER

So many jokes and complaints about management—or the lack of it—fly about in a typical large organization that a visitor might think that these particular people somehow had a monopoly on collective stupidity. But a review of a number of organizations shows clearly that collective stupidity is an inevitable part of all large human endeavors. Therefore, it makes more sense to deal with it matter-of-factly, to stop condemning and complaining about it, and to learn to understand it and modify it to meet our needs. From time to time we must pay attention to the organization structure itself and try to assess the part it plays in the collective effectiveness of the people who have accepted it as their common pattern for relating to one another.

Some of the consequences of rigid organizational structures manifest themselves in such collective malfunctions as

1. Lack of a clearly defined sense of organizational direction; prevalence of the classical "activity trap," where motion substitutes for accomplishment.
2. Postponed thinking; problems insufficiently thought out, plans half made, commitments half made, major issues insufficiently studied.
3. Lack of follow through; frequent use of "somebodyoughta;" infrequent setting of goals, priorities, and specific accountability.
4. Insufficient advocacy; important projects spread across the organizational structure without a single highly involved "quarterback" responsible for getting results.
5. Insufficient attention to human values; slavish preoccupation with the financial bottom line at the expense of the human and social bottom lines, which could benefit the organization as a whole.

The organization's social "climate"—the sum of the perceptions of its people about norms, values, rewards, and punishments—usually has a very strong impact on the people who work there. The extent to which they value creative thinking, innovation, logical problem solving, and advocating new approaches depends strongly on whether their leaders have rewarded or punished them for engaging in them. Unfortunately, the counterproductive behavior about which a manager complains may very well be "incentivized" by built-in organizational processes, or by the manager's own actions. Conversely, there may be definite "disincentives" operating within the organization which discourage certain desirable actions. Too often, the organizational climate rewards obedience, conformity, and convergent problem solving, while it punishes nonconformity, risk taking, and unsuccessful attempts at innovation.

> The first efficiency expert was Simon Legree.
>
> H.L. MENCKEN

In *Self Renewal*, John Gardner observes that as organizations get older and larger they tend to foster innovation less and less, and eventually end up reducing it to a residual minimum. During the early stages of a new organization's growth, according to Gardner, the innovators tend to lead the field, dominating its social processes and making many of the decisions. When the organization becomes much larger, innovators tend to give way to connoisseurs, who specialize in doing things "the right way." Organizational equilibrium, and sometimes stagnation, sets in along with a well-defined set of norms, procedures, and processes, which begin to dominate day-to-day life. Unfortunately, this latter stage almost always increases the risk attached to innovation and challenging the status quo.[2]

From the point of view of the business organization, we can define innovation as *a process by which people find new and better ways to achieve worthwhile goals.* Managers can learn to innovate by applying the specific skills of idea production and mental flexibility; they can teach employees to innovate in the same way, and they can reward innovation on a day-to-day basis rather than punish it. These same processes apply at the executive level. The effective executive can keep an organization in a continuous mode of renewal, can encourage, foster, and reward innovative behavior, and can enable people to make greater use of their thinking abilities. In a self-renewing organization, people work together toward collective intelligence instead of collective stupidity. This chapter deals with the possibilities for making those things happen in an organization.

the phenomenon of groupthink

Where all think alike, no one thinks very much.

WALTER LIPPMAN

A curious psychological phenomenon seems to dominate a great many of the thinking processes that go on in business meetings. This is the phenomenon of *premature closure,* in which the members of a group switch too soon into a convergent thinking mode and jump at a particular conclusion, usually under the influence of a few strong personalities. Psychologist Irving Janis gave this phenomenon the name of groupthink. It results, Janis believes, from insufficient awareness on the part of the group members that they are engaged in the process of making a decision and a lack of inclination to entertain diverse alternatives.

Janis studied the interpersonal dynamics among the members of President John F. Kennedy's cabinet and advisory staff members during the Bay of Pigs disaster, involving American encouragement and support of an invasion of Cuba by a group of exiles. In Janis's opinion, the members of the

[2]Adapted from pp. 75–78 in SELF-RENEWAL by John W. Gardner. Copyright © 1963, 1964 by John W. Gardner. Reprinted by permission of Harper & Row, Publishers, Inc.

inner circle of the group had made up their minds to support the adventure, and when the topic came up for discussion they strongly advocated it. Those who hadn't given it much thought tended to capitulate to the pressure of the others and to go along with the decision even though they didn't feel comfortable with it. According to Janis, several of the members began to have serious doubts about the wisdom of the undertaking, but they never expressed their ideas forcefully because of the strength of the developing consensus and because of the subtle signals they received from the in-group members telling them that they had better join the consensus or risk their status as Kennedy's confidants.

According to the theory of groupthink, most people place such a high premium on convergent thinking and have so little confidence in their own thinking abilities that they tend to accept the points of view, opinions, and courses of action proposed by a minority of people who speak out forcefully—whether they know what they are talking about or not. Psychological experiments with problem-solving groups have shown that many people will readily abandon their viewpoints and sometimes even accept obviously erroneous "facts" when several planted stooges strongly advocate them.[3]

My research into group dynamics has led me to conclude that in every group of people who sit down together to solve some problem or decide what to do about something, several things happen almost universally.

1. They preoccupy themselves almost solely with the *content* of the problem and pay almost no attention to the *process* by which they attack it.
2. Almost anyone with a strong voice and a confident manner can launch the group along a certain course of action or a certain approach to dealing with the problem.
3. There exists a key psychological point along the unconscious time-line of the group's activity, at which they *shift* from predominantly *divergent* thinking processes to primarily *convergent* thinking processes; they begin to establish "the solution."
4. They very probably will not realize that they have made the transition from divergence to convergence, nor will they realize the extreme importance of the transition.
5. The changeover tends to come quite early in the meeting; the remainder of the time usually goes to working out the implementation of the solution, which one or two vocal members have managed to sell to the group.
6. Once a nucleus of people forms, establishes the consensus, and begins working convergently, they become the in-group; the uncommitted others, especially if they are not familiar with the concepts of divergent and convergent thinking, tend to feel a subtle pressure to accept the consensus and to join the in-group members in working it out.

[3]For a brief treatment, see Irving L. Janis, "Groupthink," *Psychology Today* (November 1971), p. 43. For a fuller discussion of Janis's ideas, see Irving L. Janis, *Victims of Groupthink* (Boston: Houghton Mifflin, 1973).

7. In-group members tend to apply pressure, either obviously or indirectly, to the uncommitted members, urging them to capitulate; recalcitrant members may find themselves ostracized, isolated, and held up to scorn or ridicule by in-group members.

This key psychological event—the changeover from divergent thinking to convergent thinking—signals the end of problem stating and option finding, if indeed the group has done any. The essence of the groupthink phenomenon, in my opinion, is this key transition and the enforcement of it by the vocal members of the group.

Most of what passes for logical problem solving in group situations in American business really amounts to a battle of personalities in which one or two people "win" the conference by getting the others to accept the course of action they propose. The amount of creative problem solving or real exploration given to the problem may have been virtually nil. Unfortunately, the "losers" of the conference—those who capitulated against their will—may not wholeheartedly support the solution later, having no personal commitment to it. This distinctly American style of personality interaction contrasts with the Japanese style, for example, in which it is considered crude and inelegant to rush to a conclusion before everyone has had a chance to review the facts and factors involved in the issue. In many Japanese organizations, consensus depends on a careful and deliberate process in which each person in the group has a chance to speak about it. When the members leave the meeting, each has a firm personal commitment to making the solution work, because each had a part to play in making the decision.

A problem-solving group can avoid falling into the groupthink trap by having and consciously using a step-wise problem-solving model like the one described in Chapter 9. In my work with problem-solving groups, I help the members to keep their minds on the process as well as the content and to make sure that everyone works on the same stage at the same time. This produces much more effective solutions, and it gains much greater involvement and commitment on the part of the less vocal members.

questioning motherhood

It takes a very unusual mind to make an analysis of the obvious.

ALFRED NORTH WHITEHEAD

The trouble with thinkers—the innovators, the iconoclasts, the idea producers—is their detestable habit of asking "Why?" In their freewheeling style of fact finding, crap detecting, and idea producing, they continually overturn the applecarts of tradition and dogma. They threaten the comfortable predictability of custom by proposing things we have never tried before. They frighten us; they jar our sense of the "rightness" and stability of things. They can even question something as basic as motherhood. And most people don't like them for it.

In every organization, and especially in the older "mature" ones, there exists a body of custom—ways of doing things that the members of the group have accepted as "the right way." More often than not, a custom or procedure or rule to which they accord the status of "motherhood," that is, "obviously" proper, correct, and desirable, merely represents a mechanically simple and convenient way of doing something. Many of the rules, regulations, and procedures in organizations have survived because of their convenience for the individuals who carry them out rather than because of their effectiveness in getting results. When an organization has sharply defined internal compartments, people in these individual "camps" will tend to interact with one another in increasingly structured, repeatable ways over the long run. As their ways of doing things become solidified and institutionalized, each member of an individual tribe tends to revert to his or her standard procedures rather than to deal with each new problem in terms of its current reality.

It takes a very brave individual to question motherhood in an organization, and a clever one to get away with it. People who profess themselves as open-minded problem solvers can react angrily and viciously when someone starts questioning the effectiveness of their particular customs and ways of dealing with others. Apparently, the liking for order and predictability in work life runs so deep in the typical individual that anything that threatens that routine seems to threaten the person's very well-being. And especially when the innovator offers a new and untried idea, the person who clings to ritual and custom tends to find all the reasons why it won't work and shouldn't be tried. Very few new ideas come along with a completely worked-out written proof that they will work.

> An idea that is not dangerous is unworthy of being called an idea at all.
>
> ELBERT HUBBARD

As an unreformed innovator, I've often found it most effective to sell my ideas to others by helping them to question motherhood themselves and to feel comfortable with new ideas. Once a person in an organization begins to broaden his perspective and think in terms of options and new ideas, he can usually accept the possibility of change and experimentation if it promises to produce positive results. I've concluded that the surest way for the innovator to get assassinated—figuratively or literally—is to barge into peoples' territories with new and threatening ideas. Only by preparing someone to listen to a new idea can you sell it to him. And sometimes you have to help the person discover it personally and take it as his own.

Helping others to take credit for your ideas has a drawback in that it denies you the ego gratification of having other people praise your thinking abilities, but it accomplishes two higher and more rewarding objectives. First, it gets the results you want. Second, you will be teaching other people to do what you do—produce new ideas for themselves. And anything that increases the population of innovators in an organization is a positive contribution.

group problem solving

A camel is a horse designed by a committee.

ANONYMOUS

Many people mistakenly conceive of decision making in organizations as a process confined to executives or other people formally designated as managers, and done in special decision-making meetings. Actually, the vast majority of everyday decision making in organizations goes on in peer groups. In countless daily meetings, business people at various levels discuss various matters and make agreements about how to deal with them. Only occasionally do they "package" a decision issue formally for resolution by a high-level manager. And by the time such an issue arrives at the executive's desk, those who have brought it there have already shaped it extensively by their previous interactions. To the extent that people working together in peer groups pay attention to the process of problem solving and decision making, they can work together more effectively.

The commonly heard jokes and jibes about committees and their lack of effectiveness probably express a desire for more effective methods for group problem solving. From time to time, an executive in a typical large organization will appoint a committee to "work on" some problem. After a few weeks or months of floundering about, the committee members may lose interest in the problem and take any of several avenues to wind up their activities and get it over with. They may or may not have reached a workable solution to the problem assigned to them. They might simply stop meeting, say nothing about it, and hope the executive has forgotten that he appointed them. They may publish a memorandum explaining why the committee approach doesn't suit the problem, and try to hand the matter back to the executive. Or they may simply patch together some semblance of an approach, write it up in a memorandum to the executive, and disband themselves, hoping he won't appoint them to carry it out. In a small number of cases, an appointed committee will work through the problem methodically and effectively, come up with a workable solution, and advocate it confidently.

Why the difference? What makes one group operate effectively and decisively while another flounders about? The difference is team operation. One group works effectively as a *thinking team*; the other simply lurches along without focusing its energies effectively.

We might use the term *committee* to refer to the more typical case of a floundering group and reserve the term *team* for a specific kind of group operation. In problem-solving groups in organizations—both committees and teams—many of the same limiting factors operate again and again. The factors that tend to make a group into a committee instead of a team can include any of the following:

1. The executive who gave them the problem may not have stated it effectively, or may have failed to make clear the specific goal of the group's efforts, or may not have given them any way to tell when they have solved the problem.
2. The group may lack a competent leader—a person formally in charge who has the practical and social skills required to manage their activities.
3. The members may not pay sufficient attention to their own internal processes; they may busy themselves with the content of the problem without using any kind of a conscious problem-solving model or plan to guide their efforts.
4. The group leader may not provide an adequate method or procedure for the group's attack on the problem; he may not plan the project well enough that each member knows what part he should play.
5. The group members may not push their efforts through to a firm conclusion; they may come up with a solution stated in vague, general terms, or they may not follow through to a complete and workable solution with an action plan.

A team attack on a problem requires a well-specified goal, a well-chosen group, a competent and effective leader, a conscious approach such as a problem-solving model and a plan for attacking the entire project, and a thorough follow-through to a complete and workable solution. Many organizations, by this definition have never actually tried team problem solving. Many have only used committee approaches.

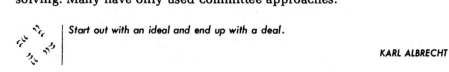

Start out with an ideal and end up with a deal.

KARL ALBRECHT

In working as a management consultant with various organizations, I have frequently used an approach I call the "horizontally organized tiger team" method, which involves forming a special team of action people from various key departments, having one of them appointed team leader, and working closely with them to attack the assigned problem. The team's objective may involve bringing about a major change in the organization itself, solving some problem or difficulty that has arisen unexpectedly, or going after some key opportunity such as a new product or a new program.

Depending on the time and resources available, I try to train the team members in creative problem-solving strategies and help them understand the importance of generating and nurturing ideas rather than killing them. At a minimum, I like to teach them to distinguish between divergent thinking and convergent thinking, and make conscious choices about when to do each. This basic approach helps them to use their ideas effectively.

In helping a group to explore a problem, especially when idea production plays an important part in generating options, I've found it helpful to invoke the concept of "round" ideas and "square" ideas, developed by management consultant Walton Boshear. According to Boshear, most people hold conversations by exchanging square ideas, that is, those that fit neatly with one another and make up a consistent logical pattern of relationships. But many useful ideas first take shape in a person's brain in round form—they come out as half-baked, half-expressed, or only partially understood. By analogy, Boshear says, a round idea tends to "roll away" unless someone catches it and holds on to it in whatever form it might momentarily have. By jotting it down or otherwise keeping it available for later exploration, group members can perhaps make it into a square idea that helps to solve a problem. Using the term *round idea* enables a group member to present an idea in vague form without feeling defensive about it. By saying, "This is a round idea," he or she signals to the group that a fragmentary thought is to be captured and saved for later development. This helps to prevent idea killing and encourages other group members to share their round ideas as well.[4]

Generally, if I can just get the team members to adopt a simple problem-solving model such as the one described in Chapter 9, and help them to move through it one step at a time, they can usually solve the problem very effectively. Using a common conceptual model for their processes tends to keep all of the members doing the same thing at the same time, to conserve and focus their mental energies, and to ensure that they give the problem enough divergent thinking and creative idea production to develop highly effective solutions. The use of such a model also tends to eliminate the groupthink effect because every person can have an opportunity to offer ideas and to ask questions without getting attacked by any consensus-promoting in-group. In simple terms, an effective problem-solving team is a well-organized thinking team.

[4]Walton C. Boshear and Karl G. Albrecht, *Understanding People: Models and Concepts* (La Jolla, Calif.: University Associates, 1977), p. 68.

executive decision making

To the bureaucrat: when in charge, ponder; when in trouble, delegate; when in doubt, mumble.

JAMES H. BOREN

A high school football coach who fancied himself quite a manager faced a very difficult problem in the midst of the big homecoming game, the high point of the team's season. Within a few minutes, both his first- and second-string quarterbacks were taken out of the game with injuries, just before half time. The only available quarterback was an untried third stringer who had never played in a game.

The coach called for a time-out and summoned the green quarterback for a conference. "Now, listen," he said sternly. "I want you to do just exactly what I tell you to do—nothing more, nothing less. We have the ball on our thirty-yard line. Go out there and just hang on to the ball and let the clock run out. Just do three quarterback sneaks and then punt. Then we can get to the half-time break and decide what to do. Don't get clever. Do you understand me?" "Yes, sir," said the lad. "Now, remember," admonished the coach as the boy headed for the field. "Three quarterback sneaks and a punt."

The boy did exactly as he had been told. On the first play he charged through the line and managed to gain fifteen yards. This brought the entire team alive and created justifiable excitement among the hometown fans. On the second play, the green quarterback repeated the performance. The crowd went wild. With the ball on the opposing team's forty-yard line, the boy pulled still another sneak play and managed to advance the ball to the opposition's twenty-yard line before they caught him. His team was bursting with confidence and determination, the opposition was obviously worried, and the alumni in the stands were rabid. On the fourth play, the lad called for a punt. After the half-time gun had sounded, the players were trudging off the field. The coach came running up to the quarterback, beside himself with anger and utter disbelief. In barely controlled rage, he demanded, "Would you mind telling me what you were thinking about when you called for a punt?" "Yeah!" retorted the boy, obviously angry in his own right. "I was just thinking what a dumb coach we have!"

Managerial decision making requires a certain degree of flexibility. While we can apply a certain amount of science to the process of guiding a group of people, we must also respect the necessity to adapt to changing situations. Most executives get to be executives not necessarily because they make better decisions than anyone else, but because they do make decisions. Anyone with a certain amount of confidence and the courage to make decisions can come out moderately well in many executive positions.

By working faithfully eight hours a day, you may eventually get to be a boss and work twelve hours a day.

ROBERT FROST

However, *excellence* in decision making is quite another matter. While some executives chalk up decision-making skill to "instinct," "experience," and "art," others attribute it to the overall process of using organizational thinking resources to equip themselves with the kinds of facts and ideas that will enable them to choose effectively. An executive armed with the courage to make decisions, the lessons learned from experience, and some useful models and techniques for making them can easily pull ahead of other, less well-equipped people in establishing a long-term "track record" of performance.

In this section we will review several of the unconscious thinking habits that can severely limit the decision-making effectiveness of an executive or manager and show how to overcome them. The habits that seem to me to play the most significant part are

1. Making the wrong decisions at the executive level; inundating himself with decisions he should delegate to subordinate managers; conversely, leaving important decision issues unattended so that subordinates make the decisions by virtue of the random interplay of their individual actions.
2. Failing to anticipate key problems and decision issues; failing to recognize developing issues until it becomes too late to handle them effectively.
3. Open-loop problem solving, as described in Chapter 9; failing to maintain surveillance over a particular course of action as a part of a long-term problem-solving process; failing to evaluate results and consciously check the effectiveness of decisions previously reached.
4. Unwillingness to abandon a course of action or a program because of ego involvement or unrealistic expectations; unwillingness to "redecide" an issue when events make it appropriate to do so.
5. Inadequate use of the efforts of staff members to provide the facts, ideas, options, and points of view needed to deal with a problem effectively.[5]

Don't put off until tomorrow what you can get someone else to do today.

ANONYMOUS

Just as the football coach should have delegated the decision about the fourth play to the quarterback, so the executive or manager at any level should delegate as many decisions as possible to subordinates. Many a

[5]For a thorough discussion of effective executive management, see Karl Albrecht, *Successful Management by Objectives* (Englewood Cliffs, N.J.: Prentice-Hall, 1978).

manager falls into the pattern of giving a decision on every issue that subordinates bring to him, when he should first ask, "Does this issue really need my attention or can this person make the decision?"

Lack of anticipation of major decision issues can severely limit the effectiveness of a manager's decision processes as well. A manager and his staff can usually deal with a problem much more effectively when they can see it coming over a period of weeks or months than if it simply pops up one day and demands immediate resolution. The lead time that comes from consciously searching for upcoming problems and going out to meet them enables the problem solvers to gather facts, gain perspective on the problem, generate options, and encourage diversity of viewpoints well before convergent thinking becomes necessary. Anticipatory problem finding and problem solving form a vital part of effective organizational planning.

Open-loop problem solving probably accounts for a great portion of the mistakes and disasters that befall business organizations. Trial and error is probably the most common way of approaching business problems. The tendency of many managers and staff people to live from day to day and week to week often prevents them from detecting the longer term processes and trends in their activity that signal the need for corrective action. Many managers—perhaps most—fail to keep tabs on the results of their decisions and to close the loop on the problem-solving process as described in Chapter 9. They often fail to recognize that today's circumstances are the consequences of decisions they made and actions they took at various times in the past. Because they lack a closed-loop concept of their decisions and actions, such executives and managers may not appreciate the necessity for follow-through on the actions required. I'd like to have a dollar for every staff meeting in which the executive or manager made a decision on some problem and the group disbanded without determining specifically who would do what and how. As the saying goes, "One reason why things don't seem to be going according to plan is that there never was a plan."

A manager's unwillingness to abandon a favorite project, product, or course of action that hasn't worked out relates very closely to open-loop problem solving as a thinking malfunction. Many times what a manager conceives of as a problem once appeared to someone else—perhaps even himself—as a solution. In my work as a management consultant, I often get involved in solving problems that seem to show evidence of a good idea having gone bad. For example, in working with a high technology company in the nuclear power field, I was asked to review a very complex system of written engineering procedures and to recommend a way to make them "work." I asked the client executives, "To what problem in the past did this system seem to offer a solution?" This led us back to the original purposes of the system, which had been taken to extremes and made much too large and complex.

The original problem was to maintain control over the huge quantity of engineering drawings, specifications, and reports required to build a nuclear reactor. By returning to that requirement, which the procedural system had not met, we reopened the original problem-solving issue. I recommended that the company throw out the entire hodgepodge of procedures and prepare a simplified engineering manual oriented to the original objective. What had kept the company from abandoning the approach that had never worked was the existence of a special department appointed to write procedures. These people didn't want to put themselves out of their jobs, so they continued to write procedures long after they should have recognized that the procedures were becoming a problem rather than solving a problem.

There is no right way to do the wrong thing.

ANONYMOUS

More than one organization has floundered and some have gone out of business because the chief executive refused to accept the evidence that his favorite product no longer fit into the marketplace. Sometimes the ability to rationalize, to persist in the face of facts, and to avoid reassessing the originally attractive course of action can delay the necessary adaptation processes so long that the organization does not recover. In the words of an anonymous executive of yesteryear, "There'll always be a market for a good buggy whip!"

Business is what, if you don't have, you go out of.

ANONYMOUS

And, finally, inadequate use of staff resources, time, information, and talent often means that the executive must make important decisions based on guesswork, hearsay, and the opinions of opposing factions within the staff. Some executives even take pride in their ability to make "gut judgments" without bothering to gather facts or explore upcoming problems very extensively. Most of these "hip-shooters," in my experience with organizations, have had uniformly poor long-term track records as decision makers. And many executives who seem to make decisions effectively on the spur of the moment actually study their decision issues over extended periods. Often, what looks like a snap decision by the effective executive actually amounts to putting the final piece into the puzzle and completing the reasoning process. The completion of the decision process came simultaneously with the new piece of information, but the process itself preceded that event by a considerable period.

By using a conscious problem-solving model in discussions with staff, an executive can help them to understand the nature of the decision he must make, and can assign them their various missions in gathering the facts and ideas needed to support the judgment he must sooner or later make. By anticipating major decisions, the executive can use staff resources effectively. He can also get the benefit of their individual ideas and points of view when he must resolve a controversial issue. By encouraging diverse viewpoints instead of squelching them, the executive enriches his point of view on the issue and equips himself to deal with it effectively.

Some executives make the mistake of pitting one strong-willed subordinate against another in battling out opposing points of view on an issue, under the mistaken assumption that the person who can sell his opinion most aggressively must have the "best" opinion. A much more effective approach is simply to encourage staff members to think about the problem from various points of view and to make sure they supply all of the available facts and factors bearing on the decision. In the end, it doesn't matter which of them favored the course of action he ultimately chooses, if he approaches his decision-making responsibility effectively. In fact, it makes more sense to avoid such "win-lose" situations among subordinates by making decisions based on evidence rather than opposing personalities.

It is not who is right, but what is right that is important.

THOMAS HUXLEY

training managers in clear thinking

Take care of the means, and the end will take care of itself.

GANDHI

One of the things we know best and forget most often about organizations is: The effectiveness of the collective efforts of a large group of people generally depends more heavily on the capabilities of their managers than on any other single factor. With this fact so firmly established within business organizations, the syndrome of the misplaced manager still prevails. One of the most common ways for an organization to get an incompetent manager is to promote a person into a management job who has demonstrated excellent performance in some specialty. Because most people tend to consider management an informal kind of skill, which one merely "picks up" as he or she goes along, relatively few executives prepare their subordinates for advancement into management, either by training programs or by special assignments in advance of promotion. Probably no more than one new manager in ten enters his or her new profession with so much as a single introductory course in management.

Although some large organizations invest heavily in managerial training, most seem to drift along with sloppy or nonexistent methods for selecting new managers and with minimal fixed-level budgets for training them. Relatively few executives seem committed to training and developing the future leaders of the organization, or to investing the necessary resources in programs to do so.

If I had to recommend only one training course as most worthy of investment of the funds of any organization, I would choose an intensive course in practical thinking techniques for its managers. Training managers in techniques of clear thinking brings a number of measurable as well as qualitative results. The measurable results usually show up in greater effectiveness of the work groups they manage, especially in professional or "knowledge" work in which the group members depend on effective interaction and joint effort. The qualitative results include greater confidence on the part of managers in handling the managerial job, better recognition of the importance of problem-solving and decision-making processes, and a better perspective on the role of the manager in making things happen in the organization.

Although I favor training managers and professional people in the broad gamut of clear thinking skills, the two functional thinking skills of problem solving and idea production merit the greatest emphasis in a business-oriented training course. A manager who can learn to use an overall problem-solving model in personal thinking as well as in group problem-solving activities can make much more effective decisions than managers typically do, and the consequences can often contribute directly to increased profitablity. In addition, the manager who has a good grasp of idea production becomes an innovator who can adapt his solutions to the changing environment in which he functions. This manager can also teach subordinates to produce new and useful ideas, and can encourage innovation on their part. A long-term policy of respect for ideas as the intellectual wealth of the organization leads to more and more idea production and more and more useful approaches to old problems as well as new problems.

We should ask ourselves from time to time "What is the value of a single new idea? What is the value of a steady flow of new ideas?" Application of creative-thinking techniques such as group brainstorming, product value engineering, and employee suggestion programs have saved many millions of dollars for organizations and have brought in many more unexpected profits.

In his book *Applied Imagination*, Alex Osborn cited case after case of practical benefits and substantial dollar payoffs to organizations whose managers realized the value of training in thinking techniques, especially idea production. Osborn says

The Swiss Society of Life Insurance at Berne brainstormed the problem of "How to find new salesmen." The panel produced 225 ideas in one hour. Evaluation

determined that 25 were worthy of immediate adoption and that 125 were potentially usable.

In an effort to economize, the U.S. Navy's Bureau of Supplies wanted to make "one supply ship do the work of three" in the Pacific Fleet's electronic, ordnance and ship repair work. The solution, arrived at through brainstorming sessions, resulted in . . . a total saving of three million dollars a year in salaries and operating costs.

The Berkeley Heights, N.J., School Board anticipated trouble in getting a bond issue approved for a proposed $850,000 school building. So a group led by Dr. Fred Finsterbach brainstormed this problem: "Ways to cut costs of a new school building without cutting quality of education nor quality of building materials." Resultant ideas cut the estimated costs down to $735,000—a saving of $115,000.

As to the use of brainstorming by business, here are a few cases among the many: Aluminum Company of America, Armstrong Cork, Bristol-Myers, Christmas Clubs of America, Corning Glass Works, Du Pont, Ethyl Corporation, General Electric, IBM, New York Telephone, RCA, Reynolds Metals, Rexall, Scott Paper Company, Taylor Instruments, Union Carbide, U.S. Rubber, United States Steel.[6]

Osborn points out that the man who suggested removing the watch pockets from army uniforms saved the taxpayer an estimated $1,600,000 over a period of two years.

Bringing the techniques of clear thinking and innovation into an organization requires only the willingness to try a training program and some group sessions on an evaluation basis. By having a consultant come into the organization to present a training program and conduct some group sessions in problem solving and innovation, executives can see the process in operation and can assess its value as a general approach. Some organizations establish as a goal of one of the idea production sessions the requirement to cut costs or increase profits enough to pay the consultant's fees for conducting the program.

A training program in practical thinking techniques for managers and other professional people might have an agenda something like the following:

1. Overview of managerial thinking skills
2. Using a problem-solving and decision-making model
3. Idea production techniques
4. Decision techniques
5. Innovation techniques
6. Case studies dealing with the organization's needs

More and more executives of business organizations are investing in training programs for their managers in clear-thinking skills, and most of those

[6]Used by permission of Charles Scribner's Sons from APPLIED IMAGINATION by Alex Osborn. Copyright 1953, © 1957, 1963 Charles Scribner's Sons.

who follow through on these programs find out that they pay for themselves many times over, in terms of dollar benefits as well as increased managerial effectiveness. A manager who can think effectively can manage effectively.

12

building brain skills

 To make headway, improve your head.

B.C. FORBES

the importance of mental exercise

The analogy between the brain and a muscle, in terms of the benefits of exercising both of them, applies surprisingly well. The evidence we have compiled so far indicates that you can improve virtually any aspect of your brain's functioning by using it, using it, and using it some more. Many people limit their thinking forever by assuming that thinking skills are somehow genetically fixed and simply failing to challenge themselves. In precisely the same sense that your heart, lungs, and muscles improve their functioning after a few weeks of jogging and continue to improve with a steadily increasing exercise program, your brain skills improve over time if you make steadily increasing demands on them.

All of the basic brain skills enumerated in Chapter 2—concentration, observation, memory, logical reasoning, forming hypotheses, generating options, making associations, recognizing patterns, making inferences and spatial/kinesthetic perception—will respond to exercise. You simply have to decide which skill you want to develop first, give it your attention, and put it through an exercise program.

If you can approach this process of developing your brain skills from the proper direction, working out ways to do it that you can enjoy and continue over a period of weeks or even months, you will begin to notice results. Of course, if you try to undertake some rigorous, overly disciplined training regimen without making it fun, you probably won't stay with it long enough to see improvements.

You'll probably find it helpful to choose your associates more carefully, spending less time with the uninteresting mechanical thinkers and more time with people who stimulate you and challenge you to think. If you especially crave the companionship of highly intelligent people, look into the possibility of joining Mensa, the international society of high-IQ people.*

This chapter prescribes some ways to overcome a mentally sedentary habit pattern, exercise your brain in a way that makes development an enjoyable process, and systematically put your skills to effective use.

how to change a habit

> *Habit is habit, and not to be thrown out the window by any man; but rather, coaxed down the stairs one step at a time.*
>
> MARK TWAIN

The skill of changing your habits serves as a useful starting point in developing other brain skills, because all skill building involves replacing old habits with newer, more effective ones. If you can train yourself to systematically isolate a habit, study it, define a replacement habit, and take the steps necessary to practice it until it does replace the old habit, you can apply this technique to developing any brain skill you choose. You just make the practice of that skill into a habit, and it will come along automatically.

Most people seem to misunderstand completely the requirements for changing a personal habit, or at least it so appears in view of the number who complain that they can't change themselves. In fact, most people who complain that they can't change their habits have never really made a systematic effort to do it. There is a huge difference between complaining about something and actually taking concerted action to do something about it.

Let's start by having you abandon everything you ever believed or thought you knew about habits, and go back to some basic principles. A habit is basically a behavior pattern you carry out repeatedly because your brain knows and likes the mental pattern that governs it better than any other mental pattern. To change a habit you must *change the brain pattern* that gives rise to it. You will find it much easier to *replace* one habit with another than to try to eliminate a habit without a replacement; your brain cannot fully erase the mental pattern behind the habit. But if you give your brain a much stronger alternative pattern to draw upon, it will completely overshadow the undesired pattern, and your behavior will follow it.

You might want to change some specific habits like:

1. Interrupting others in conversation
2. Failing to count your change when you shop

---

*The address for information about Mensa is: American Mensa Limited, Department A, 1701 West 3rd Street, Brooklyn, New York 11223.

3. Cleaning off your plate every time you eat (causing you to overeat)
4. Watching television
5. Neglecting educational activities like reading and taking courses
6. Losing your temper with your children, parents, friends, or coworkers
7. Smoking
8. Failing to exercise
9. Drinking more than you should
10. Forgetting people's names immediately after you meet them

Take a pen and paper and make a list of some habits you would like to replace or establish, and then pick out the one habit you most want to change right now. Use this habit as a three-week case study in learning how to change your habits.

Instead of trying to "make" yourself change the habit in one giant step, you must simply begin to behave in the alternative pattern whenever you think of it. After you have exercised the new pattern enough times, your brain will begin to prefer it, and it will become your new habit. It will become an unconscious part of you just as its predecessor was, provided it brings you some benefit.

You can "sell" yourself on your chosen new habit in such a way that you will acquire it much more easily than if you lacked the enthusiasm for it. The professional salesperson uses a step-wise process of persuading a customer to buy a product, such as:

1. Attention—the customer realizes the product exists
2. Interest—the customer thinks the product might fill his or her need
3. Desire—the customer decides he or she definitely wants the product
4. Action—the customer commits to action; they close the sale

These four steps, abbreviated as AIDA, provide the basic technique for selling yourself on a new habit pattern. Making the change requires first of all that you get to the point of consciously trying out the new behavior—the "action" stage. After that point, simply repeating it consciously will do the trick.

The following formula will enable you to put this self-supporting process to work:

1. Clearly identify the old habit pattern you want to change—in specific, observable terms (attention stage).
2. Clearly identify the new habit you want to "install" in your brain's system of patterns; don't say "stop procrastinating"—that's too vague to act upon; instead, say "leave for work or school on time," "get my reports in on time," or "set deadlines and meet them" (interest stage).
3. Take a period of several days or even weeks to make yourself so fully aware of the situations in which the old habit comes into play that you can consciously replace the undesired behavior with the desired behavior (desire stage).

4. Systematically act out the new behavior again and again until it starts to become unconscious and fully established (action stage).

To use a physical analogy, you can consider your brain's neural structure to operate somewhat like an airplane's autopilot; you have a *mental autopilot* that controls the functions you perform repeatedly. And just as the human pilot can override the autopilot and take conscious control of the airplane, you can take conscious control of a certain behavior pattern. But to do so, you must bring it up from the submerged level of autopilot functioning, from below your conscious awareness, and deal with it deliberately and repeatedly. Once you have consciously substituted a new pattern for the old one and repeated it often enough, you can let it slip back into the unconscious level of autopilot control.

As a rule of thumb, it takes about three weeks of repetition to make something a habit, if you do it about once a day or more. If you do it less often, it will take longer to build up enough repetitions to make it stick. You can increase the number of repetitions by deliberately rehearsing a new action a number of times, making sure you do it in "real-life" situations. Some researchers also contend that you can develop a habit faster by closing your eyes and imagining yourself carrying it out many times. Repeating this visualization method every day may speed up the process.

How can you make yourself aware of the situation in which you want to adopt the new behavior? How can you head off the automatic reaction governed by the old pattern before it comes up? Probably the best way is to subject yourself to an *advertising campaign* designed to carry out the first three steps of the salesperson's four-step model.

For example, when I decided to make running a permanent exercise habit, I began to supply myself with signals that reminded me about running and its benefits. Instead of immersing myself in the subject all at once, I spread out my self-education process over a number of months. I kept a logbook of my runs, left my running shoes out where I could see them, began to associate with other runners, and began to read an article or two each week on the subject. I took plenty of time to interest myself in the possible benefits and to arouse my desire to have those benefits, all the while running for only short periods every other day. I kept the exercise mild and pleasant instead of making it self-punishing, and I reflected frequently on the importance of aerobic exercise for my health.

As a result, I found it easy to establish a running program sufficient for my needs and to give it the priority it deserved. Instead of reading several books that interested me all at once, I read them one at a time, over intervals of several weeks to a month. As my running became a pleasant and reliable habit, I continued the advertising campaign. I still reinforce the benefits in my mind from time to time, and I compare experiences with friends who run for their health.

improving your concentration

The skill of concentration simply means the ability to focus your attention on something and keep it there for relatively long periods of time. If you find that your mind wanders a great deal when you try to study or work, perhaps you need to develop greater discipline in focusing your attention. Of course, it makes little sense to try to concentrate on some arbitrary object or process when it will have no value for you. You can only concentrate effectively on something when doing so will bring some result that you want.

You can improve your ability to work or study effectively by combining two techniques, both of which take advantage of what we know about the brain's operation. First, you can use simple mental exercises to develop your attentional skills. Second, you can use a simple technique to "lead" your attention into a subject you want to concentrate on and eliminate procrastination.

With respect to mental drill, you first have to decide whether you are too mentally sedentary to undertake a few concentration exercises, or whether you are willing to exercise this function for its own sake. If you spend a few minutes now and then doing some brain exercises, you can increase your concentration skill considerably. However, if you're just content to wish you could concentrate better, you probably won't see much in the way of results.

Here is a basic approach to exercising your concentration function, using mental arithmetic. Alex Osborn proved that adults who practiced simple mental calculations for twenty minutes a day over a period of twenty consecutive days learned to concentrate considerably better, and, of course, they became much more proficient at mental arithmetic.

First, find a spot where you can sit down or lie down quietly for five or ten minutes, relax, and close your eyes. For your first session, simply recite the addition table in your mind, starting with "one plus one equals two," and going methodically through each number up to "one plus nine equals ten." Then continue with "two plus one equals three," and so on until you have recited all the sums up to "nine plus nine equals eighteen." Keep your attention closely focused on the mental task and notice when you start to wander from it. If at a certain point you find it takes you longer and longer to come up with the sum, merely tighten the reins on your concentration and bring it back firmly to the task. If you slip off the task completely, return to the beginning and patiently start again. Notice how your brain seems to work as you keep your attention glued to the task. Learn to sense carefully the level of intensity of your concentration and to tighten it up when necessary. This will give you a greater command over the neurological process of concentration.

After a few sessions of mental addition, spread over several days, change to the multiplication table for variety. Go over each product, taking one number at a time and reciting its product with each other number, just as you learned to do in elementary school. As before, pull your attention back to the task if it begins to wander. Practice until you can complete the task fairly briskly, with very few incidences of wandering off. If you like, you can graduate to adding pairs of three- and four-digit numbers and even to multiplying pairs of two- or three-digit numbers together, taking your time and visualizing the intermediate results.

In all of these practice sessions, pay attention to what close concentration "feels" like. Then you will find yourself transferring the sensation to other, more practical tasks. Learn to "snap" your concentration onto some item in your field of view, such as an article you want to read, or someone's voice, or an idea in your head. You will find that you can block out distractions more easily by activiely focusing more closely on the object of your attention.

The second part of your skill-building program in concentration involves the strategy of gently leading your attention into a subject you want to focus on and allowing the subject to take over your mental field of view. For example, if you tend to put off paying your bills, working out your income tax, studying for a course, or writing a report, you can use the following general procedure for "getting into" the task:

1. Set up the conditions you need to go to work; set aside the time, go to the place, get the materials, arrange the items you need, and sit down at the task.

2. Do not try to force yourself to concentrate; instead, take a few minutes to let your mind wander, daydream, or do whatever else you want to do.

3. After a few minutes, gently bring your attention to the general subject you want to work on; start thinking about the overall topic, reviewing the various parts of it in a moderately interested way; reflect on the end result you want to achieve and the benefits of getting it done.

4. Pick up some item associated with the task and begin to get involved with it; select one of the more interesting features of the task—a picture, a diagram, a new idea, or an intriguing fact; use this item to hook your attention more closely into the task.

5. Now gradually narrow your attention to the subject at hand and move toward the logical beginning of the task you have set for yourself; decide specifically what you want to accomplish; once you have picked a starting point, snap your field of view down sharply and lock onto it; keep your attention focused on the task as you proceed.

6. Sense your level of attention from time to time and focus in more closely if necessary just as you did with the mental arithmetic; take an occasional break to refresh yourself physically and repeat the "entry" process to re-establish your level of concentration.

Some research suggests that, along with a number of other physiological cycles going on in the body, attention itself might swing back and forth between high and low levels. From some very preliminary research data, I've postulated that the brain varies over periods of roughly an hour or so in the extent to which it pays attention to sense inputs. I believe we shift from an *externally directed* mode—which I term the X mode—to an *internally directed* mode—the N mode. In the X mode, the brain seems hungry for sensory input: sights, sounds, body sensations, feelings, tastes, and smells. This mode may offer the best time for taking in new information, studying, enjoying entertainment, appreciating art, music, or nature, making love, and carrying out tasks requiring close attention and motor skills. In the N mode, the brain seems to filter out a great deal of the sensory input and turn its attention inward to process and reprocess its current store of memories. In this mode, reverie seems to dominate; thoughts of the past, plans for the future, reminiscences, daydreams, and philosophical thoughts form the substance of the brain's activity. Perhaps the person we call absent-minded spends a greater than average portion of time in the N mode. Effective mental functioning presumably involves an appropriate balance of N and X modes.

Additional research into this aspect of brain function may confirm this hypothesis. At this stage, it seems worthwhile to learn to sense these cyclic variations and to adapt one's schedule of activities to take advantage of them.

improving your visualization skills

The skill of visualization involves remembering information in the form of physical forms and images rather than just in words. Just as you can recall verbal patterns from your memory, you can also recall spatial patterns. Before we explore some of the techniques for improving your visualization skills, we need to eliminate some misconceptions.

Most people probably "visualize" much better than they believe they do, because they have an unrealistic conception of visual memory. Because they cannot close their eyes and "see" any given scene in vivid detail, they seem to believe that they have poor visualization skills. In fact, very few human beings can do this under ordinary circumstances. Most of us do not "hallucinate" our visual memories, but rather we recall them in a general structural form. You may not be able to "see" an object in absolute detail, but nevertheless you can probably remember its visual features well enough to act upon the information.

An example may clarify this feature of visual memory. Imagine that you have three balls in front of you on a table. In a line from left to right, the balls are red, white, and blue. Now imagine that you take the ball on the right and transfer it to the left end of the row. In your mind's eye, check the sequence of colors. What is the new order of colors, from left to right?

As you solved this problem, you probably used a combination of several forms of memory. You could probably "look" at the row of balls and more or less "sense" their colors, even though you may not have pictured them vividly. You probably used your verbal memory to assign names to the colors in the various positions. And you probably used your kinesthetic memory—your memory of the motions your hands make and the sensations of grasping and moving objects—to help you conceive of moving the balls about. So, rather than rely strictly on mental pictures in the purest sense, that is, direct recall of retinal images, you used a mixture of thought forms in working out the solution. This is the way in which your spatial/ kinesthetic processes help you remember things.

This discussion will use the term *visualization* to include *all* nonverbal thought forms that your brain organizes into a spatial pattern, not just isolated mental pictures. As you perceive some physical situation for the first time, your eyes feed their retinal images to your brain, with their aspects of shape, brightness, color, motion, and so on. Your ears feed in whatever they receive at the moment, your nose provides olfactory inputs, your skin and other tactile sensors send their data, and even the taste information from your mouth goes to the brain. In addition to these well-known sense inputs, your whole-body kinesthetic sensation—your "feelings" if you like to simplify the term—goes to your brain. The current status of your feeling response as well as the details of the sensory data form a complete "package" of data, which your brain receives and puts together into a whole pattern. If the scene you are perceiving has a high level of personal meaning for you, then you will tend to imprint it more intensively and later you will be able to recall many of the features of the situation. Using visualization really amounts to recalling whole patterns like these and extracting the needed information from them by examining whatever mode of sensation seems to have encoded it most accessibly.

Some people seem to rely much more extensively on their visualization skills than others during normal activities. Some researchers feel that these differences reflect variations in brain structure and organization; others tend to explain them in terms of differences in the levels of skill development and opportunities to use the skills. In either case, most researchers seem to agree that one can substantially improve his or her visualization skills by paying conscious attention to them and by using them more and more extensively within the normal flow of thought processes.

Some people do seem to have the skill of vivid visual imagery, and presumably a person could build this skill to a higher level by concentrated practice. Little research seems to have been done in this area. Some children, for example, exhibit a visual faculty which psychologists call *eidetic imagery*—the ability to retain in the memory a precise visual structure in all of its detail. Some interesting experiments with "eidetikers," a few of whom are adults, show that such a person can look at two separate patterns of colored dots, one with each eye and at different moments, and later mentally merge the patterns to detect a figure such as a number or letter like those used in tests for color blindness. This provides some intriguing possibilities for speculating about human perceptual ability. Some researchers estimate that as many as eight percent of children have this eidetic imaging skill, yet almost all of them lose it sometime around the onset of puberty.

Having established a clearer picture of the skill of visualization, let's examine some of the techniques you can use to put your visualization processes to work more extensively and allow them to develop more fully by practice. First, you can visualize more accurately if you teach yourself to observe more accurately. And you can observe more accurately if you have a purpose in observing. Try a little observation experiment with a pencil and paper. Take a commonplace object like a book or a cup or a shoe. Look it over for a few moments, with the intention of making a sketch of it. Try to see it in two dimensions, that is, in terms of your retinal image of its shape and basic features. If you look squarely at a book, you will probably see a rectangle. If you then tilt it away from you slightly, you will see a trapezoid. The outline of the book *as your eye sees it*, not as your brain reinterprets it, will form a figure with two parallel sides, with the far side appearing somewhat shorter than the near side. Take your pencil and draw exactly what you see—a trapezoid. This principle of accurate observation forms the basis of sketching. You might find it enjoyable to take a class in sketching to improve your skills of observation.

You can practice looking carefully at various situations around you and trying to form mental pictures of them. In a small shop, someone's home, a business office, or on a street corner, ask yourself what features you would have to remember in order to describe the scene later to someone else in such a way that they could recognize it. Pick out those features, make a note of them, close your eyes, and reconstruct them. Don't worry about vivid detail; just recall the primary features. Then see how many extra details you can fill in from memory. Note the dominant colors, the key dimensions and distances, the most noticeable objects, their spatial relationships to one another, and the general "feel" of the situation. Where are the people? How do they move? What patterns tend to dominate the situation?

From time to time you can close your eyes and recall scenes you have visited. When you feel like reminiscing about a vacation you enjoyed very much, close your eyes and let your attention drift back to that time. Recall the feelings you had at the time and re-experience them as you let the images flow into your mind. Linking the feelings with the images will make both of them easier to recall. Say the names of some of the places in your mind, allowing the words to bring back more images and more feelings. Zero in on some situation you especially liked and explore it closely. Recall what happened, where you were, what you wore, and what you did. Recall some of the things people said and see how those words bring up more images.

You can also improve your visualization skills by using them more extensively in ordinary conversations. If you have occasion to describe an idea to another person, say, over lunch, draw a sketch to help represent it. Paper napkins and placemats probably serve this purpose better than their intended functions. Ask the other person to illustrate his or her idea for you as well.

As you listen to someone else talk, try to form a mental image of the situation he or she describes. Let your mental pictures, sensations, and feelings respond automatically, and just keep following the words. Try to visualize as many of the things or processes he or she mentions as you can. When you talk to other people, choose terms that help to create word pictures. Use metaphors, analogies, and other colorful expressions that help to convey ideas in pictorial form. Coin your own descriptive terms for variety and emphasis.

You can also use games and toys which involve spatial and kinesthetic perception in solving them. Jigsaw puzzles work well for this. You can play mental tic-tac-toe with another person while waiting in a line. The ancient Chinese puzzle called the "tan-gram" offers an intriguing way to work with visual forms. It consists of a square divided up in an elegantly simple way into seven pieces in the form of triangles, a small square, and a parallelogram. You can make an enormous number of interesting shapes with these simple pieces, usually trying to match a given silhouette of the form. You can buy a version of this puzzle in many game stores. Other games of spatial skill, such as three-dimensional tic-tac-toe, can also help in developing your visual observation abilities, as well as the ability to concentrate and reason logically.

You can also use the concentration exercises described in the preceding section to develop your visualization skills. In concentrating on mental arithmetic, try to see the numbers vividly in your mind's eye, and try to sense their size and shape as if you were tracing them with your fingers. You may find that some of them seem to take shape vividly for a second or so and then fade out, leaving only the sensation of their shapes. If you happen to visualize more clearly than most people, you may be able to retain a fairly clear image in your mental field of view, almost as if you are looking at physical number. I've practiced this to some extent by imagining that I'm watching a large digital display, similar to an automobile odometer, and that the digits are ticking away from 100 down to 0. I try to see each of them as a black number on a white background, pausing for a few seconds before giving way to the next lowest digit. This exercise, especially if done in connection with self-hypnosis, can help a great deal to improve concentration skills as well as visualization skills.

improving your memory

Sometimes within the brain's old ghostly house,
I hear, far off, at some forgotten door,
A music and an eerie faint carouse,
And stir of echoes down the creaking floor.

ARCHIBALD MACLEISH

The skill of memory requires that you store things properly so you can later retrieve them properly. Probably very few people have taken the conscious effort to exercise their memory in order to improve it. Most people seem to regard memory as some kind of fixed skill that works as if by magic. A person may say, "I wish I had a better memory," without thinking about the fact that he or she has never done a single thing to develop a better memory. The prevailing notion that one remembers well or poorly depending on a lucky or unlucky arrangement of neurons is not only absurd but extremely self-limiting.

As a first step in improving your memory, start to use it more and rely on it more. As with other brain skills, just as muscle becomes stronger with repeated use, your memory becomes more effective with repeated use. In this section we will study some ways to exercise your memory more strenuously, and we will explore a few simple memory tricks to help you file things effectively.

Take a pen and paper and make a list of situations in which you could use your memory more extensively than you have in the past and in which remembering things better would help you in some way. This might include your work or school activities, taking care of errands, using shopping lists or lists of things to do, remembering key bits of information, learning a foreign language, memorizing a few key facts about a topic, recalling other people's names, or recalling telephone numbers, addresses, or zip codes. Pick out one of these applications to use in your first approach to changing your memory habits. Use the four-step approach to building habits described in a preceding section of this chapter to make yourself fully aware of the thing you want to remember, and teach yourself to recognize opportunities to use your memory when they come up.

If, for example, you would like to learn to memorize a number of items on a shopping list, use the list and your memory side by side for a while. Make a list of the items you want to buy as you usually do and take the list to the market with you, but *don't use it*. Review the list just before you begin shopping. Keep it in your pocket until you have picked up all of the items you can remember, and then check to see whether you remembered them all. The more times you do this, the better you will get at recalling as many as fifteen or twenty items. Apply the same technique to other situations in which you want to remember better. First, write down the things you want to remember, such as errands to do, and don't look at the list until you have made every possible effort to recall them from memory. Writing it down first helps you to form the conscious intention to remember, which is one of the key elements in filing it away to begin with. If you apply this technique repeatedly over a period of about three weeks, whenever an opportunity arises, you will improve your memory to a very noticeable degree. You will find yourself remembering other things more easily and becoming more optimistic and enthusiastic about building your memory.

Over the years, various people who have studied memory have developed mental tricks and gimmicks for filing things away in the brain in such a way as to maximize the probability of recall. Let's explore the aspects of brain function that make these techniques work and then examine a few of the more useful techniques themselves.

Psychologists generally subdivide memory phenomena according to the two categories of *short-term memory* and *long-term memory*. Although the two processes really blend together to some extent, the brain does seem to handle the two kinds somewhat differently. Some research suggests that the two functions may involve distinctly different forms of brain chemistry. A prevailing theory of physical memory processes suggests that whatever you perceive at some instant "reverberates" within certain neural structures for periods of a few seconds up to minutes, and in some cases a few hours. This reverberation effect presumably takes the form of repeating "echo" signals carried by certain neurons. According to the theory, these short-term memory echoes soon die out and are overlaid by the others that come along behind them, unless the brain finds them sufficiently interesting or important so that they become more permanent and form long-term memory traces. Presumably, all memories start out as short-term memories, and very few short-term memories get "promoted" by your brain into long-term memories, which you can retrieve much later. How long an item survives in long-term memory depends on how often you retrieve it. The more often you retrieve it, the more firmly it becomes imprinted. If you seldom or never retrieve it, it will eventually fade.

This physical basis of memory provides a very important clue to the mystery of memory development: To remember something at a much later time, you must consciously increase the probability that it will get transferred from your short-term memory to your long-term memory. The prevailing physiological theory of memory seems to indicate that the transfer of a short-term image into long-term storage depends heavily on the *overall arousal level* of your brain during the few seconds after you perceive the image.

Some theorists believe that a small lump of brain tissue, a portion of the *limbic system* known as the *hippocampus*, plays the part of a "record" button, much like the button you press on a tape recorder to make it record what you say into the microphone. The hippocampus, which also has a variety of other functions, seems to respond to the general emotional level you experience at any one instant. This theory holds that if your brain is not particularly aroused, either because you are not paying very close attention or because you are not very interested in what you are perceiving, or both, the hippocampus tends to have less influence over the transfer of the images from short-term processing to long-term storage. But if you find the scene, object, or idea somewhat engrossing, or if you become more aroused as a result of your recognition of its meaning, the hippocampus presumably sends more and stronger "record" signals to whatever neural structures carry out the long-term imprinting process. This theory has the virtue of explaining several long-known facts about memory, and it points directly to the use of simple brain-arousal techniques for consciously imprinting images in long-term memory.

For example, you can probably recall certain experiences that had a very high emotional content for you, such as the circumstances surrounding the death of a loved one, a personal triumph, or a particularly enjoyable and meaningful experience. You can probably recall movie scenes that you found especially upsetting, touching, or amusing more easily than you can recall many of the in-between scenes that make up the story. Indeed, you may find that you can recall specific scenes years after you have forgotten the story line of the movie.

You can capitalize on this brain-arousal phenomenon to help you imprint the things you want to recall. To do so, you must pause to become fully conscious of the thing you want to imprint and let it echo in your short-term memory for a few seconds. Concentrate your attention on it and then use any of a number of mental techniques, such as those described below, to make it "important" to your brain. This technique, together with the conscious intention of recalling the item at some later time, will cause your brain to imprint it more firmly in long-term storage.

Techniques for using this imprinting phenomenon include

1. Combining verbal, visual, tactile and kinesthetic inputs to form a diversified total "image," which brings more brain activities into play
2. Adding emotional content to the image, such as humor, feelings connected with the item, or a strong sense of its importance
3. Associating the idea with other important ideas you already remember, so that recalling one of those ideas may elicit the new idea

Let's examine each of these more fully. You can use your visualization skills to help you remember a list of items by forming a vivid mental image of each item on the list as well as saying its name. In this way, you combine visual thinking with verbal thinking. You can also add kinesthetic features to the memory image by thinking about how it feels to hold the item, use it, or taste it.

For example, if you want to remember to buy some frozen orange juice, rather than just say "frozen orange juice" over and over in your mind, you can form a detailed mental image of a can of frozen orange juice and imagine holding it in your hand and feeling the intense cold sensation. Imagine tossing it up in the air and catching it, to bring in the motor aspects of your kinesthetic imagination. While you do this in your imagination, say "frozen orange juice" to yourself several times. You can also intensify the memory imprint by saying the words aloud, so that the motor regions of your brain that activate your vocal apparatus come into play. In addition, you can imagine the taste the orange juice will have after you mix it, and you can picture yourself mixing it up and drinking it at some future time. As you do these things, form the strong intention to recall this item later when you shop. With a bit of practice, you can learn to imprint an image like this in two or three seconds.

By using your concentration skills, you can soon develop the ability to go down a list of ten or fifteen items, focus on each one for a few seconds, and file them firmly in your memory. After you buy them, they will just fade out of your memory because you only filed them for a consciously determined time. If you want to remember a list of items for a very long time, you have to form the intention of holding them in memory for that long. Reviewing them from time to time also helps considerably.

A popular technique for imprinting a group of items in your memory involves connecting all of them together into a visual relationship, by exaggerating their features and constructing an outlandish or comical story situation. Apparently this increases the arousal level in your brain enough to transfer the images into long-term memory. For example, I wanted to buy a loose-leaf notebook, some typewriter ribbons, some three-by-five cards, and some envelopes at an office supply store. I created a mental picture of the notebook spread open and flying like an airplane, with the side panels working like wings. I visualized the notebook dropping typewriter ribbons like bombs and also dropping three-by-five cards, which sailed down to fall neatly into the envelopes that were opened to receive them. In this visualization, I emphasized motion and interaction. When I got to the store, I could instantly remember the items I wanted just by recalling the whole ridiculous scene.

These techniques have had the effect of improving my memory overall, so that I can often recall a list of a dozen items by simply intending to recall it, without even spending much time in forming images. From this I conclude that the general function of imprinting, which goes on in my brain when I want to remember, has improved substantially and has become more available to my conscious will. It may be that I have trained my hippocampus, so to speak, and that I don't have to play tricks on it as much. I still play tricks on it when I want to be sure of remembering something, and I find that my use of visualization techniques combines with my intention to remember more and more effectively.

A technique similar to the "outlandish story" technique involves visualizing the items you want to remember as resting upon a sequence of physical locations that are very familiar to you. The ancient Greek orators could memorize long speeches simply by visualizing the topics they wanted to cover in the form of representative objects placed on various steps, walls, porches, and patios of a familiar public building or at various specific points around a familiar courtyard. To keep the speech flowing in sequence, an orator merely "walked" in his imagination along the familiar path while he delivered his speech, and as he saw in his mind's eye the next location, he checked the object he had put there, and he knew what topic to cover next. This technique is a surprisingly easy one. Take a moment right now to try it out in recalling a list of items. First, select a familiar location such as your home, and in your imagination go around the walls and identify the places where you can put things. Choose locations that will not change over a short period, and which you can remember unambiguously. Once you have ten locations selected in a definite sequence, mentally place each of the following items on its respective resting spot:

1. A tennis ball (bouncing up and down, for example)
2. A pitcher of water (overflowing)
3. A sandwich (which you intend to eat)
4. An automobile hubcap (spinning, as if still on the car)
5. A light bulb (blinking on and off)
6. A telephone call (in the form of a phone jumping off the hook)
7. A bicycle chain (moving as if on an imaginary bicycle)
8. A book (with its pages open and turning by themselves)
9. An appointment (as an alarm clock going off at a specific time)
10. Shoes (shining themselves or each other)

The moving forms of the images given in parentheses merely serve as suggestions, of course. Any way in which you can increase the intensity of the image will work to help you imprint it. Now review the list again, making sure that you have imprinted each of them vividly and in some interesting way. Then close your eyes and go through the locations one at a time and recall the items in their turn. If you concentrate on each of them effectively, you will probably recall them with little difficulty.

Before you read about this technique, would you have believed that you could win a bet from another person by memorizing a list of ten items—in order—with about two minutes of study? If you used this technique properly, you can now remember the fifth item, the ninth, or any other you choose. You can recite them forward or backward. This technique demonstrates both the simplicity of the memory function and the powerful effect of using visualization in imprinting information in your brain.

You can apply the visualization technique very effectively in learning a foreign language. To remember that "hon" is Japanese for "book," rather than recite the two words over and over in combination you can form a mental image of a book, or better yet pick up a book and sense it while you say the Japanese word aloud. File the word in your memory along with the mental image, the feeling of holding a book, the motor sensation of turning the pages, and a mental image of the word in printed form. By using this technique carefully and methodically, you can significantly reduce the time required to learn a foreign vocabulary by the conventional method of verbalization.

I've developed several other techniques for using visualization to aid my memory. I use a "mental pegboard" to remember lists of things, as well as other visually novel techniques that occur to me from time to time. To use the mental pegboard technique, visualize as clearly as you can a pegboard—one of those fiberboard panels with holes all over it at regular intervals. Make it about as wide as you can conveniently reach with your outstretched hands, and mentally place it just above your field of view and out in front of you. Imagine that you can see it from the normal perspective of standing in front of it. See the holes at regular intervals as well as the shiny metal hooks on which you can hang the things you want to remember. Put five or six hooks on the board at convenient distances across its length. When you want to keep a short list of items in your memory, just form a mental picture of each one, shrink it down to the dimensions of the pegboard, and hang it up firmly. Check each of the positions from left to right and make sure you can visualize each one clearly and simply enough to recall it later. I often use this technique when I want to remember to buy some item, especially if it occurs to me while I'm busy with something else. I just review the pegboard, check the items there, find a vacant space, and hang up the new object. Later, when I go into a shop or market, I just "look" at the mental pegboard, see which of the items I can buy at the moment, and get them. Then I remove them and make the space available for other items.

This technique probably sounds a bit strange at first, but if you try it you will see how easy it really is and how reliably it works. As an exercise, take five items from the list you just memorized by using the sequence of locations and place them on a mental pegboard. For example, take the second, fourth, sixth, eighth, and tenth items. Put them there with the intention of recalling them tomorrow. Tomorrow you can check to see how well you applied this technique.

Another of my favorite techniques uses an imaginary "cookie jar," although you can use almost any physical image that helps you add interest or visual impact to the thing you want to remember. I may have an interesting idea pop into my head as I'm jogging, and since I don't carry a paper and pen with me (one of the few occasions you could find me without them), I like to capture it with a mental trick. So I just visualize a large and colorful ceramic cookie jar with a lid. In my imagination, I remove the lid from the cookie jar and a jack-in-the-box pops up on a spring. I mentally put a placard in his hands with a key word printed on it in bold letters, which captures the essence of the idea. I say the word and the idea out loud while I think about the idea, and I form the intention to recall it later. Then I mentally push the jack-in-the-box back down into the cookie jar and replace the lid. Before dropping the subject, I make one practice try at recalling the idea. I picture taking the lid off the cookie jar and seeing the ridiculous funny-faced figure pop up with the placard, and I imagine hearing him say the key word in a comical kind of voice. It may seem crazy, but it certainly works!

You can use your visualization skills to remember the names of people you meet as well. When you meet a person, take about five seconds and focus your attention on getting his or her name. Make this a deliberate effort—say the name aloud or ask the person to repeat it, and make sure you have heard it and are conscious of it. You might say something like "I'm teaching myself to remember names, so I hope you don't mind if I take a second or so to get your name clearly." The other person will probably find this flattering, which will serve an additional purpose in starting off positively. As you say the name *aloud* for the second time, visualize the name written in bold letters across the person's chest. Use letters whose shape seems to match with his or her personality or appearance. For example, use a thin and graceful script for a tall person or heavy and rounded capital letters for a plump person. Later, when you want to recall the name, you can assist your regular memory process by looking at the letters and "looking up" the person's name in your visual memory. Give special attention to a positive attitude in recalling peoples' names. Don't tell yourself "I can never remember names," or you won't remember them. Practice imprinting them carefully, and you will notice an improvement in your skill.

You can even remember numbers by carefully using visualization techniques. There are some number memory systems based on forming key words from the numbers, but most people find these uninteresting and rather mechanical. You might prefer using novel mental images for imprinting telephone numbers and the like.

For example, you can remember the telephone number of your favorite theater by visualizing it on the theater marquee in large and colorful letters while you say it aloud. Do this as you dial the number, and you will add kinesthetic thought forms to the verbal and visual information. You can imprint the telephone number of a person you know by forming a picture of that person in your mind, possibly holding a placard with the number printed on it. You will probably have to vary the way in which you represent the number to maintain a sufficiently novel version so as to associate each number distinctly with its owner.

All of these techniques have the same purpose: to enrich the associations, increase the emotional content, and diversify the form of the mental image you want to imprint in your brain. You can invent techniques of your own to serve these purposes. By taking the time to stop and concentrate on the thing you want to imprint, enriching your image of it as explained above, and by imagining yourself recalling it in the future, you maximize the strength of the brain pattern that encodes the item. This will maximize the probability that you can bring it to mind later when you need it.

developing your intuition

I believe we routinely perceive intuitively, at a level beyond our immediate verbalization processes, and we routinely reason intuitively. In this regard, I don't consider it entirely accurate to speak of "intuition" and "logic" as two opposite forms of thought, as is the popular custom. I prefer to consider what we call "logical thought" as merely a *verbal translation* of the intuitive processes by which we do the major part of our thinking. In my definition, intuitive processes are every bit as "logical" as verbal processes, that is, they hold together, obey the rules of proper association between ideas, and they produce reliable results.

I believe that listening to a hunch amounts to giving voice to a preconscious thought process. In fact, we continually draw on intuitive processes and convert them into verbal form. Sometimes we do so without consciously choosing to, because a preconscious thought may create such an arousal in the brain that the verbal centers are affected, and we find ourselves putting it into words.

If this concept of intuitive thinking makes sense, then developing intuitive skills amounts to *listening* to preconscious thoughts and *sometimes* verbalizing them. This approach, fortunately or unfortunately, takes much of the mystery out of intuitive thinking and brings it from the realm of occasional magic to the realm of a commonplace adjunct to verbal thought.

The skill of perceiving intuitively, according to this thesis, involves learning to perceive without verbalizing—something you may at first find surprisingly difficult to do. As an experiment, pick up a commonplace object such as a pen, shoe, or ring, and simply try to look it over without mentally verbalizing about it. As soon as you "hear" labels begin to rise in your mind, stop the process and try again. From time to time in various situations, repeat this process of unverbalized perception of whatever you see and hear. You will find it easier and easier to do as you abandon the tendency to label things. You can teach yourself to stop and dwell on something, and to just pay attention to your subjective impressions of it. In doing this, you are tuning in to your intuitive thoughts, prior to verbalization.

While standing at the edge of the ocean, in the woods, in a park, or while looking at some flowers, try to put your brain in a kind of reverie state, and let yourself be affected by the sights, sounds, and smells in whatever way seems natural. Don't try to "manage" your reaction to it. Just tune in to your own reactions below the verbal level. As soon as you hear your internal voice reciting the names, colors, and other label features of things, interrupt the process and look at the scene as if for the first time. Try to find some aspect of what you see that defies verbalization—that has no known labels. Dwell on a shape, a texture, or some spatial form. This will increase your skill at sensing the intuitive level of perception.

In dealing with people, you can apply the same approach. As you listen to someone talk, you can use your brain's excess data-processing capacity to tune in to other aspects of the situation besides the words. Let your attention scan around in a leisurely way, picking up little features of the situation that seem interesting. Rather than look for anything in particular, just allow your brain to make connections preconsciously without trying to verbalize them. Later, you might want to review the situation and see how much of what you picked up intuitively you can express in words.

Practice making some of your low-risk decisions intuitively. When faced with a simple choice, just pause for a moment and "sniff the air." Listen for an imaginary "voice"—your preconscious decision process—to tell you which choice to take. In deciding whether to go somewhere or do something, pause and see which choice "feels right." Make a deliberate attempt to *avoid verbalizing* about the pro's and con's of the choices. Allow your brain to process this data at the preconscious level. As you do this more and more, keep a "track record" on your hunches to find out how often the consequences came out favorably. I've often found that when I don't follow a hunch that says I shouldn't do something, I usually wish I had followed it. When I follow a hunch that tells me to do something, I often find that it was a good idea. This process of listening to and following hunches simply amounts to capitalizing on the preconscious thought processes that constitute your intuitive level of thinking.

It makes sense to *combine* intuitive thinking with conscious verbal thinking, and to get the best of both. Rather than consider yourself as "basically intuitive" or "basically logical," consider yourself capable of drawing on both forms of thought and combining the results in such a way as to get more of what you want in the situations in which you find yourself.

using puzzles and games to develop your thinking skills

> Come, Watson, come! The game is afoot!
>
> SHERLOCK HOLMES

Those who frequently play mental games and work puzzle problems know the value of these amusing pastimes in developing a variety of thinking skills. Many people who do not probably shy away from them because they anticipate not being able to solve them and because they dread the feeling of frustration they think they will inevitably get. But experienced players know that mental games come in graded levels of difficulty, and they choose games that match their level of skill and the amounts of time and energy they want to devote to them. There are rabid fans of mental games just as there are rabid fans of all other pursuits.

You can find a wide variety of puzzle books, thinking games, and physical puzzles in novelty stores these days. Apparently the public interest in these brain-building games has increased substantially over the past few years. The advent of the microprocessor and the video games it has made possible have also had a part to play in making Americans more interested in developing their mental skills. You might like to buy one book or game every few weeks or months and use it to develop your skills. When you get fairly proficient with it, try another one.

You can also have fun and develop your logical thinking skills with the old party game of "twenty questions," which requires no materials at all. In twenty questions, one person thinks of an object and the others try to identify it by using no more than twenty yes-or-no questions. The most important skill in this game is asking questions carefully and not wasting them on wild stabs. You can get closest to the object by asking a question that has about a fifty-fifty chance of a "yes" answer. In this way, you can progressively subdivide all of the possibilities and eliminate as many of them as possible on each question. This game can help you to develop your skills of questioning, investigation, and fact finding to a very high level.

By choosing pastimes and forms of recreation that develop brain skills in preference to passive processes like watching television, you can increase your mental effectiveness and have fun at the same time. By using them at parties and gatherings with your friends, you can make the time you spend together more interesting, stimulating, and enjoyable.

This section offers twenty simple thinking puzzles and games, which should fall within the range of abilities of a typical reader with average intelligence and a bit of persistence. They represent three levels of challenge. Level 1 includes those you can probably solve just by reading them and giving them a few moments of thought. Level 2 includes those that require some further exploration and perhaps a bit of cleverness in attacking them. Level 3 includes those that require some extra effort with a pen and paper, and possibly quite a bit of methodical work, but no particular mathematical skills or special flair for puzzles. One puzzle at level 3, the "Who owns the zebra" problem, will probably take you about an hour of methodically arranging the facts, either with a sketch or some physical models. It is essentially a problem in logic and persistence rather than puzzle skill.

Set a goal for yourself of getting the answer to each of them and double-checking it to make sure it is right, before looking at the answers in Appendix B. Use each of them to stretch your thinking processes and to practice the kinds of thinking skills it uniquely brings forth. Approach it confidently and persistently, with a flexible attitude of willingness to try various angles to get the solution. If you find these puzzles interesting and enjoyable, try some of the books of mental games and puzzles listed in the bibliography. You can find others in almost any general bookstore.

Level 1 Puzzles:

1. What is the minimum number of coins you need to be able to pay the exact price of any item costing anywhere from one cent up to a dollar?
   (logical reasoning, short-term memory, visualizing)

2. One archaeologist reported finding a Roman coin with Julius Caesar's image on it, dated 21 b.c. Another archaeologist correctly asserted that the find was a fraud. Why?
   (forming hypotheses, logical reasoning, critical perception)

3. Is it legal for a man to marry his widow's sister?
   (analyzing verbal maps, logical reasoning, accurate description)

4. What was Lewis Carroll talking about in this poem?[1]
   John gave his brother James a box:
   About it there were many locks.
   James woke and said it gave him pain;
   So he gave it back to John again.
   The box was not with lid supplied,
   Yet caused two lids to open wide.
   And all these locks had never a key—
   What kind of box, then, could it be?
   (analyzing verbal maps, divergent thinking, forming associations, making inferences, verbalizing assumptions)

5. Rearrange the following patterns to make familiar words:
   a. runghy
   b. flymia
   c. mulcica
   d. dornev
   e. lendraca
   (recognizing patterns, memory search)

6. Move only one of the four matches shown below to form a square.
   (divergent thinking, recognizing patterns, spatial perception, verbalizing assumptions)

[1]Included in Martin Gardner, *More Perplexing Puzzles and Tantalizing Teasers* (New York: Simon & Schuster Pocket Books, 1977), p. 63. Copyright © 1977 by Martin Gardner. Reprinted by permission of Pocket Books, A Simon & Schuster division of Gulf & Western Corporation.

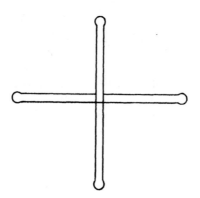

7. Why does the barber in Oatmeal, Nebraska, say, "I'd sooner shave ten skinny men than one fat man?"
   (divergent thinking, forming hypotheses, analyzing verbal maps)

8. The legendary runner Flash Fleetfoot was so fast that his friends said he could turn off the light switch and jump into bed before the room got dark. On one occasion Flash proved he could do it. How?
   (forming hypotheses, analyzing verbal maps, verbalizing assumptions)

Level 2 Puzzles:

9. How can you arrange 6 identical pencils in such a way as to form 4 identical triangles whose sides are all equal, without modifying the pencils in any way?
   (divergent thinking, spatial perception, visualizing, verbalizing assumptions)

10. There are ten bags, each containing ten weights, all of which look identical. In nine of the bags each weight is 16 ounces, but in one of the bags the weights are actually 17 ounces each. How is it possible, in a single weighing on an accurate weighing scale, to determine which bag contains the 17-ounce weights?[2]
    (visualizing, forming hypotheses, logical reasoning, making inferences, strategic attack versus trial and error)

11. Each of these people lives in a state that can be spelled by rearranging the letters of that person's name. For example, Roy Kewn lives in New York. Where do the others live?[3]
    a. Roy Kewn
    b. Nora I. Charlton
    c. Colin A. Fair
    d. Dora K. Hatton
    e. Earl Wade
    f. A.K. Barnes

[2]L.H. Longley-Cook, *Fun with Brain Puzzles.* © 1965 by Fawcett Publications, Inc. Reprinted with permission of the Fawcett Books Group, the Consumer Publishing Division of CBS Inc.
[3]Gardner, *More Perplexing Puzzles and Tantalizing Teasers*, p. 71. Used by permission.

h. J.R. Sweeney
(memory search, pattern recognition)

12. Identify the next term in this series:

88 . . . 64 . . . 24 . . .

(recognizing patterns, forming hypotheses, logical reasoning)

13. In the figure below, can you join each point with its counterpart, that is, "A" with "A," "B" with "B," and so on, by drawing lines which follow the grid and which do not intersect, cross, or touch? [4]

(visualization, short-term memory, logical reasoning)

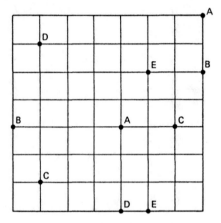

14. Each of these cartoon figures represents a figure of speech which involves a spatial relationship. For example, the first one means "long underwear." Can you translate the others?

(pattern recognition, accurate description, verbalizing assumptions, divergent thinking)

1	2	3
WEAR ―――― LONG	R O ROADS D S	MAN ▭
4	**5**	**6**
ECNALG	MIND ―――― MATTER	R E A D I N G
7	**8**	**9**
YOU _U⟨J C S T⟩ ME	O ―――― M.D. B.S. Ph.D.	AGE BEAUTY

[4]Longley-Cook, Fun with Brain Puzzlers, p. 17. Used by permission.

15. Try to work this one out in your mind. We know the following facts about the four cards shown:
    a. The King is not the top card, but it is closer to the top than either the Ace or Jack.
    b. The Heart is above the Club.
    c. The King is not a Heart, nor is it a Club.
    d. The Ace is neither a Spade nor a Diamond.
    e. The Diamond is below the Club.

    What are the respective faces and suits of the cards, from top to bottom?
    (concentration, spatial perception, visualizing, logical reasoning, short-term memory, sequential thought)

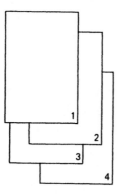

Level 3 Puzzles:

16. Five men of different nationalities live in five separate houses of different colors— red, yellow, blue, green, and ivory. Each has a particular pet, a favorite drink, and a favorite brand of cigarettes. We have the following information about them:
    a. The Englishman lives in the red house.
    b. The Ukrainian drinks tea.
    c. Coffee is drunk in the green house.
    d. The Spaniard owns the dog.
    e. The Norwegian lives in the first house on the left.
    f. Kools are smoked in the yellow house.
    g. The green house is to the left of the ivory house.
    h. Chesterfields are smoked next to the house where the fox is kept.
    i. The Old Gold smoker owns snails.
    j. The Lucky Strike smoker drinks orange juice.
    k. The Japanese smokes Parliament.
    l. Milk is drunk in the middle house.
    m. The Norwegian lives next door to the blue house.
    n. Kools are smoked next to where the horse is kept.

From these facts figure out who owns the zebra and who drinks water?[5]
(persistence, logical reasoning, making inferences, using models, sequential thought)

17. Three cards lie face down on a table, arranged in a row from left to right. We have the following information about them.
    a. The Jack is to the left of the Queen.
    b. The Diamond is to the left of the Spade.
    c. The King is to the right of the Heart.
    d. The Spade is to the right of the King.
    Which card—by face and suit—occupies each position?
    (logical reasoning, making inferences, using models, sequential thought)

18. Four friends are having lunch and discussing their favorite athletic pastimes. We know the following things about the seating arrangement:
    a. Bob is sitting across from the Tennis Player.
    b. The Golfer is sitting across from Ted.
    c. Alice is sitting on Carol's left.
    d. The Jogger is sitting on the Swimmer's right.
    e. There is a man sitting on Bob's right.
    What is the favorite sport of each person?
    (logical reasoning, making inferences, using models, sequential thought)

19. Eight numbered cards lie face down on a table in the relative positions shown by this diagram:

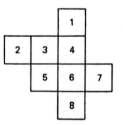

Of the eight cards:
a. Every Ace borders on a King.
b. Every King borders on a Queen.
c. Every Queen borders on a Jack.
d. No Queen borders on an Ace.
e. No two cards of the same kind border on each other.
f. There are two Aces, two Kings, two Queens, and two Jacks.

[5]The zebra puzzle came to my attention by a roundabout route, so I don't know whom to credit for it. Like many of these curiosities, the item became disconnected from the name of its creator, and it circulates among people interested in puzzles without bringing the originator proper credit. Here is my thanks to the unknown (to me) creator of the zebra problem—a novel and intriguing one.

Which kind of card—Ace, King, Queen, or Jack—is card number six?
(spatial perception, sequential thought, testing hypotheses, making inferences,
persistence, short-term memory)[6]

20. In this problem, each letter uniquely represents one number. By analyzing the
relationships among the digits, can you identify the original subtraction problem?

$$
\begin{array}{r}
A\ B\ A \\
-\ C\ A \\
\hline
A\ B
\end{array}
$$

[6]George J. Summers, *Test Your Logic: 50 Puzzles in Deductive Reasoning* (New York: Dover Publications, Inc., 1972), p. 46. Used by permission.

13

what is the potential of the human brain?

 Human history becomes more and more a race between education and catastrophe.

H.G. WELLS

Custom dictates that, in a book like this one, the author offer some speculation about future possibilities. Where are we going? What can we look forward to in the next five, ten, or twenty years, in terms of the ability of human beings to make more effective use of the awesome biocomputers inside their own skulls? Since I enjoy speculating about the future, I welcome the responsibility.

Ten or twenty years from now, history will probably show that I've been naively conservative in my guesses and that I've failed to foresee one or more revolutionizing developments that have given humans the ability to expand their mentality beyond my wildest speculations. Perhaps an advance recognition of that possibility will secure for me a gentler evaluation by those who look back on us from the vantage point of the turn of the century. Things are happening very fast with homo sapiens these days.

My general opinion is that by the turn of the century we will either have eliminated ourselves as a so-called advanced culture, or we will have learned to grow up as a species and to transform ourselves from grasping, greedy, combative, self-centered mental myopes into truly godlike human beings. I don't see that we can continue more than fifteen to twenty years further with our present ungraceful behavior toward the earth and its ecosystem. Indeed, we may need to make a quantum step in our composite racial intelligence, in order to pull off the survival maneuver that we have made necessary.

It is exciting to think that just around the corner, or around a series of corners, may lie advances in human mental function that could put to shame the fantasies of our best science fiction writers. Medical evidence makes this possibility quite plausible. For one thing, we have already seen some few cases of phenomenal mental abilities among unusual human beings. We can only speculate now whether the enormous intellect of a

Mozart, a daVinci, or an Einstein comes from a genetic accident or whether it somehow resides within any human brain.

Psychologists have studied a number of human prodigies—people possessed of extremely highly developed mental powers in one or more categories. The mathematician Carl Friedrich Gauss could perform mental calculations by the age of three. In his adult life he knew the square roots, squares, and logarithms of the first thousand numbers from memory. Another calculating prodigy, G.P. Bidder, could solve complex algebraic equations in his mind as a child.

Chess prodigies like Capablanca, Reshevsky, Evans, and Fischer can memorize dozens of chess games in their entirety and recall them at will. They can visualize variations on the arrangement of the board for many moves ahead, and can maintain intense concentration while evaluating various strategies. George Koltanowsky managed to take on fifty-six players at one time, playing each game *blindfolded* and simply inquiring as to his opponents' moves.

Memory prodigies have also fascinated psychologists for many years. Daniel Webster supposedly memorized the entire Bible, as well as all of Shakespeare's plays. As a stage performer at an early age, James Crichton could answer questions from an audience in any of twelve languages. Professor A.R. Luria of the Soviet Union studied one stage performer over a period of many years, and could never present him with a memory task that "filled up" his storage capacity. The man could commit to memory a matrix of random numbers 100 by 100, that is, 10,000 numbers in all, and could recall any selected entry by its row number and column number. He could memorize long lists of objects, names, pictures, and words with little apparent effort. Luria found that the man's willingness to persevere in the long, boring experiments constituted the limiting factor on the research, not his memory capacity.[1]

Curiously, this person and a number of other mental prodigies whom psychologists have tested had a curious handicap: They could not carry out the normal business of living. Their mental prowess was confined to their highly developed specialties, and they were markedly inept in other areas. In some cases these unusual people confined themselves to protective environments such as family settings because they lacked the ordinary mental skills required to live independently in society. Psychologists refer to these selectively brilliant people as *idiot savants*, a term derived from French, which means roughly "wise idiots." Their mental development is usually well above the level formally designated as the idiot level, yet considerably retarded. How a person can perform phenomenally well in

---

[1]A.R. Luria, *The Mind of a Mnemonist: A Little Book About a Vast Memory* (Chicago: Contemporary Books, 1976).

one aspect of intelligence and so poorly in all the others continues to baffle investigators. The most common hypothesis holds that early in life these people take an absorbing interest in some particular process, like memorizing things, performing calendar calculations, or performing mental mathematics, and focus their attention on it to the virtual exclusion of all else.

Musical prodigies have also provided researchers with some intriguing glimpses into the potential of the human brain. A long line of famous musicians and composers—Mozart, Mendelssohn, Chopin, Dvorak, and more recently Heifetz, Menuhin, and Rubinstein—showed highly developed musical ability by the age range of three to five, and continued to develop thereafter.[2]

We commonly consider these people somehow out of the ordinary, and they certainly were. But to assume that the capabilities they displayed lie beyond the reach of most human brains may foreclose an important possibility for future research and development. If we believe that the "average person" cannot make a substantial increase in his mental skills, then we will never invest much effort in exploring that possibility. I believe our society needs more naive researchers who are willing to pursue possibilities that everybody "knows" to be impossible, much as Marconi pursued the possibility of sending a radio signal across the Atlantic when scientists of his day "knew" that it was theoretically impossible.

Some exciting things are happening in the wide area of investigation that I refer to as human mentality. In this chapter I'd like to trace five specific areas of investigation which seem to me to offer enormous potential for helping us discover, probably within this generation, how to approach the incredible potential of the human brain. I consider these five areas most significant:

1. Brain physiology
2. Infotronics
3. Altered states of consciousness
4. Parapsychology
5. Cognitive skill training

The following sections define each of these areas and offer some possible trends.

brain physiology

A woman sat in her attorney's office as he opened and read her departed husband's will. He scanned through the brief paper for a few moments and

---

[2]For a brief discussion of mental prodigies, see Robert M. Goldenson, *The Encyclopedia of Human Behavior* (Garden City, N.Y.: Doubleday, 1970), 2, 1009–13.

looked up quizzically. "Well," he said, "this is a bit unusual." She looked at him anxiously and asked, "Why do you say that?" "It seems," he said, "that Johns Hopkins Medical School gets his money, and you get his brain."

The architecture of the human body protects the brain so well from external forces that physiologists have found it an exceedingly difficult organ to study. To remove the top of someone's skull and poke around in his brain constitutes such a boldly intrusive procedure that researchers must find other alternatives. Most of what scientists know from direct observation of the human brain comes from autopsies and incidental examinations during radical surgical procedures undertaken for the survival of the patient. A few bold researchers such as Wilder Penfield and Roger Sperry have explored the brain's responses to electrical stimulation during surgery with the patient fully conscious. Sperry's work with patients who had had their cerebral hemispheres surgically separated as a last-resort treatment of severe epilepsy contributed a great deal of what we now know about brain lateralization.[3]

But except for these relatively few instances of limited physical exploration of the living human brain, researchers have had to settle for indirect and inferential data about how it works. They have generally proceeded along two parallel avenues in making inferences about brain structure and function. On one avenue, they experiment with the brains of live laboratory animals, especially cats and monkeys, and try to extrapolate their findings to the human brain. On the other avenue, they study the human brain in its natural setting by experimenting with its "input-output" characteristics, that is, perceptual processes, cognitive and motor activities controlled by the brain, and reports by the subject of his inner experiences. Following these two lines of exploration and trying to merge the findings, researchers have managed to piece together a fragmentary description of the brain's structure and functions.

So far, researchers have faced a frustrating gap between the findings of neurochemical research and the practical questions of how the brain forms a thought, where and how it stores memories, and how it dreams. They have identified and given names to most of the significant structural features of the brain, yet many of them defy simple explanations of their functions. Almost every substructure in the brain seems interlocked with one or more other substructures, and a number of them may share various cognitive and "administrative" processes. Redundancy, function sharing, and diversity of function seem to characterize most of the known brain structures.

From time to time, however, various findings from brain physiology do

[3]For a very readable collection of articles on various aspects of the brain and the correspondence between physiology and thinking processes, see M.C. Wittrock, ed., *The Human Brain* (Englewood Cliffs, N.J.: Prentice-Hall, 1977).

fill in certain gaps in our knowledge and offer useful guidelines for brain development. The relatively recent discovery of brain lateralization offers probably the most dramatic example of this. Many educators have now begun to speculate that our system of public education has too heavily emphasized the left-hemisphere functions of language, mathematics, and linear thought at the expense of the right-hemisphere functions of spatial/kinesthetic perception, music, whole-body skills, and artistic expression. Probably athletics offers the only significant exception to this, and yet even athletics in most high schools and colleges emphasizes strategic, goal-directed, programmed physical activity rather than free and creative expression of physical processes.

The discovery of the cortical arousal phenomenon and its possible connections to memory imprinting, as described in Chapter 12, offers another example of the usefulness of the findings of brain physiology. The hypothesis that the hippocampus operates somewhat like a "record" button clarifies a long-known technique of visualization used by Greek orators, and it also points to other possibilities for the deliberate development of memory skills.

A number of investigators have become extremely interested in the effects of the brain's functional chemicals, the *neurotransmitters*, which convey information pulses across the synaptic gaps between neurons. We have known for a long time that various chemicals in the bloodstream, such as alcohol and other mind-altering drugs, seem to operate by disrupting the brain's chemical processes. The exact nature of the neuron-to-neuron communication processes is now becoming clearer. It appears, for example, that the psychedelic drug LSD has a chemical structure similar to the neurotransmitter called *serotonin*, and may cause the same effects in the brain as overproduction of this substance.

Other researchers have taken an interest in the effects of nutrition and diet on the chemistry and function of the brain. Experiments seem to indicate that eating certain foods can increase the levels of concentration of certain neurotransmitters, and that this presumably would have consequences for the speed and efficiency of neural message transfer. One of the more common neurotransmitters, *acetylcholine*, plays an important part in memory, sleep processes, and motor coordination, and seems to increase in concentration in response to higher dietary intake of foods rich in *lecithin*. Increased intake of the nutrient *tryptophan* seems to result in higher levels of serotonin. Some sketchy evidence suggests that the intake of relatively large quantities of the nutrient *choline*, which contributes to the formation of acetylcholine, can improve short-term memory in test subjects.[4]

Where all of this research may take us is, of course, open to conjecture.

[4]For a brief discussion of the effects of diet on cortical functions, see Richard Wurtman, "Brain Muffins," *Psychology Today* (October 1978), p. 140.

The continued exploration of the structure, chemical processes, and operational functions of the brain may very well enable us to optimize our individual intake of nutrients and achieve a higher level of mental capability simply by feeding our brain better. We may also gain much better insight into practical functions such as memory, visualization, and concentration, and learn to improve them by a combination of better nutrition and more enlightened skill development based on a greater understanding of how they work.

infotronics

The term *infotronics* applies to the rapidly exploding technology of low-cost digital electronics as it is used to support and augment human mental functions. The advent of the integrated-circuit microprocessor has, in my view, opened wide a door into a realm that is bigger, more promising, and greater in potential impact for human beings than any of us can possibly comprehend.

We may soon find it necessary to drop the use of the obsolete term *computer*, in view of the fact that the applications we have made of miniaturized digital circuits have reached far beyond the original concept of the investigators of the 1940s and 1950s, who believed the primary application of their devices would be in making mathematical computations that were too cumbersome to be carried out economically by hand. They called their machines "computers," reflecting the horizon of technology they could see at that time. Now we use microprocessors as decision-making devices and programmers for consumer products, in controlling sophisticated manufacturing processes and machines, in teaching machines, in electronic games and video displays, as generators of artistic and graphic images, and as processors of vast quantities of verbal information in business organizations, as well as in the more conventional applications of office and personal computing. We now need a much broader term to refer to these functions. Perhaps the general term *processor* will become more commonly used, or perhaps we will coin a special word that means "an electronic device that manipulates information in a variety of forms and that interacts with a human being in such a way as to extend and amplify his mental capabilities."

I find it appropriate to include the emerging technology of *biofeedback* under this broad umbrella of infotronics. Researchers such as Joe Kamiya, Barbara Brown, and Elmer and Alyce Green have shown clearly that a human being can learn to control virtually any of the internal body functions that physiologists had always considered automatic, that is, beyond the influence of conscious mental processes, just by observing a signal which an electronic apparatus feeds back to him as a measure of the instantaneous status of that particular internal variable. These people and other researchers have used infotronic systems as *teaching machines* in clinical, experimental, and practical settings.

The Greens report reliable results with a large fraction of patients in eliminating or reducing excruciating migraine headache by using feedback signals that help them learn to control the level of dilation or constriction of cranial blood vessels. Other researchers report encouraging results in teaching hypertensive patients to reduce their blood pressure by biofeedback techniques.[5] Researcher Barbara Brown seems to feel that a person can learn to impose some measure of conscious control over virtually any bodily process—voluntary or "involuntary"—if he can sense its momentary status by means of some feedback signal provided by the appropriate device for measuring it, amplifying it, and displaying it.[6]

We may eventually discover or invent important applications for biofeedback unlike any we can currently imagine. The concept and technique have such far-reaching implications for understanding and developing human mentality that we hardly know which lines of application to pursue first.

I believe the microprocessor will finally make the dream come true of a sophisticated teaching machine for a low price. During the 1950s and 1960s, many educators had great hopes for the teaching machine. Having discovered the enormous potential of self-paced instruction with immediate feedback for teaching basic skills and for building unprecedented levels of student motivation, they wanted very much to see these devices brought into the educational setting. However, the inability of simple mechanical teaching machines to carry out "branching" programs, which led the learner along different possible paths depending on what he knew and didn't know, and the extremely high cost of general-purpose digital computers at that time, kept the idea of their widespread use in the dream stage for many years. The microprocessor solves both of those problems at a stroke. Probably the only resistance to the rapid application of infotronics to basic education will be the threat it poses to traditional organizational structures of the institutions themselves, and to the habit patterns of traditional teachers who prefer to babysit rather than to facilitate learning.

I have a hunch about another possible application of infotronics— merely a hunch. My experiments so far with microprocessor systems, commonly called "personal computers," have pointed to their possible use as teaching machines for developing *basic cognitive skills*, rather than for simply imparting subject matter. My hunch, which I've recently promoted to the status of a hypothesis after some pilot studies, is: A person might be able to interact with a "minicomputer" in such a time-efficient way that he

[5]Elmer and Alyce Green, *Beyond Biofeedback* (New York: Dell Pub. Co., 1977).
[6]Barbara B. Brown, Ph.D., *New Mind, New Body* (New York: Bantam, 1974). See also Barbara B. Brown, Ph.D., *Stress and the Art of Biofeedback* (New York: Bantam, 1978).

could condense a large number of skill-building repetitions of a particular cognitive function—say, memory—into a relatively short period of time, and thereby develop that function to a very high level.

For example, a person who has only one or two opportunities each week to meet new people and remember their names, probably will not exercise this memory function often enough to make it very strong. But if the person could sit with a processor-controlled video tape recorder and "meet" a number of people in a short time, he might very quickly develop the skill of remembering faces and names. Presumably, this concept would apply to a variety of other useful everyday skills.

We have only begun to get an inkling of the enormous potential of infotronics in developing human mentality, and we may see some amazing results in this area. In the short run, the dramatic development of interest in consumer electronic systems, such as video games and home "computers," may very well signal the beginning of an unprecedented interest on the part of Americans in using their brains.

altered states of consciousness

Although human beings have found fascination for centuries in the varieties of their subjective mental experience, scientific investigation of these altered states of consciousness as phenomena in their own right has for the most part begun well within this century, and mostly within the period following World War II. Only recently have we found out some of the things we need to know about bodily processes, brain waves, and other electrochemical signals that accompany various states of consciousness. We have learned that human beings can experience a wide variety of subjective mental states, including full "waking" consciousness, reverie, dreamless sleep, dreaming sleep, the half-way stages between waking and sleeping, intoxication, hallucinations, hypnosis, hysteria, various kinds of emotional arousal, meditation, and, of course, the dramatic experiences of psychedelic disorientation elicited by drugs. Each of these seems to have its own special features, and each seems to have its own relative significance for the growth and development processes of human beings.

The discovery of the "rapid eye movement" (REM) syndrome, which reliably signals the onset of dreams in a sleeping person, and the realization that *every normal human brain dreams every single night*, took place as recently as 1953. Eugene Aserinsky, then a graduate student working in the sleep laboratory at the University of Chicago, discovered the connection between REM and dreaming in his studies with test subjects. Since then we have learned a great deal more about sleep and dreaming, aided, of course, by the recent improvements in electronic technology that have made the electroencephalograph—the brain wave machine—a sophisticated and reliable laboratory instrument.

Some researchers have explored the use of biofeedback techniques for inducing selected states of consciousness, which might play a part in various mental skills. Elmer and Alyce Green at the Menninger Foundation have trained subjects to produce at will the characteristic "theta" brain signals—electrical voltages fluctuating about four to eight cycles per second. These characteristic patterns seem to correspond closely to reverie states that sometimes produce spontaneous and creative images and ideas. Early research seems to indicate that people who can learn to vary their brain states at will can employ their preconscious processes for a variety of constructive purposes.[7]

Hypnosis and self-hypnosis have, of course, played a part for many years in training people to concentrate, to increase their recall of specific incidents, and to control pain. A number of "mind control" training programs and centers have developed, and have met with an enthusiastic group of students. Many of the instructors in these methods carefully avoid labeling them "hypnosis," but most of them apparently use the classical techniques of hypnotic induction and self-hypnotic programming.

Meditation has received most of the attention among those interested in altered states of consciousness since the late 1960s when Maharishi Mahesh Yogi, an Indian priest, introduced the slickly packaged and skillfully marketed "transcendental meditation" technique into Europe and America. Investigators have detected definite physiological correlates of the meditative state and have shown it to have useful calming effects on the human nervous system. I have used various forms of relaxation training, reminiscent of meditation techniques, in stress-reduction training programs for managers and other professional people in organizations.

Interest in the dream state has increased dramatically among psychologists in recent years, and a variety of new techniques offer the possibility of using the study of dreams for self-insight and reprogramming attitudes. Since 1951, when anthropologist Dr. Kilton Stewart reported on an obscure tribe in Malaysia known as the Senoi, who based much of their culture on their dream experiences, researchers have become greatly interested in the notion that a person can not only analyze his dreams as an aspect of his own thought processes, but that he can actually "reprogram" them. According to Stewart, the Senoi share their dream experiences with one another, and especially teach their children to recall and discuss their dreams.

In the Senoi system, a person first learns to recall dreams on awakening, then learns to sort out the various images and processes and relate them to waking thought processes, and eventually learns to channel the dream processes to make them positive and growthful. A characteristic technique

[7]Green, Beyond Biofeedback, p. 118.

of Senoi dream control has the dreamer confront and conquer any hostile, dangerous, or threatening dream image and to reorganize the dream so the dreamer comes out the winner. This may seem like a tall order in view of our western conception of dreaming as a helpless involuntary state, but a great deal of practical application of the Senoi technique by investigators in this country seems to indicate that one can actually learn to do this, and in a relatively short period of self-study and training. In this regard, I've recently began exploring the hypothesis that positive-thinking techniques—positive attention and positive verbalization—as described in Chapter 5 tend to correlate with fewer negative or unpleasant dreams.[8]

Interest in altered states of consciousness has increased dramatically since the mid-1960s, in terms of physiological correlates of various states, subjective experiences of the states, and potential applications of altered states in developing various nonconventional aspects of mentality, such as creative imagery, attitude programming, and various phenomena generally included under the category of parapsychology. We may learn a great deal about mental skills by studying altered states of consciousness, and especially by combining these studies with biofeedback techniques.

Recently educators in Europe and America have become very interested in an unusual technique for teaching languages, based on the use of focused awareness techniques. The Lozanov Method, named after its creator, Dr. Georgi Lozanov of Bulgaria, isolates various components of the so-called "suggestive environment," such as the lighting and mood of the room, the sounds, the nonverbal behavior of the teacher, the attitudes and expectations of the students, and the setting of the school itself. By creating a highly affirmative and rewarding learning environment, and by using special techniques for perceptual imprinting such as chorus readings, instructor readings accompanied by background music, and frequent activation of the student's new vocabulary, Lozanov-trained teachers claim their students can achieve four or five times the learning rate typical of conventional classroom methods. This and other accelerated learning techniques now under development may soon present us with some very useful advances in learning how to learn.*

parapsychology

The field of *parapsychology* has probably caused more storms within the orthodox scientific community in America than any other area of investigation, including unidentified flying objects (UFOs). Ever since Dr. J.B. Rhine conducted his famous statistical tests for extrasensory percep-

[8]For a highly readable account of the Senoi "dream-engineering" techniques, see Patricia L. Garfield, *Creative Dreaming* (New York: Simon & Schuster, 1974).

*For more information about this newly developing area, contact: Society for Accelerated Learning and Teaching, P.O. Box 1216, Welch Station, Ames, Iowa 50010.

tion (ESP) at Duke University in the 1930s, researchers have been sharply divided on the basic question of the existence of human faculties such as direct mind-to-mind communication and a variety of other hypothesized faculties. Rhine contended that human beings do possess a characteristic skill, which he referred to as the "psi" faculty, named with the Greek letter that forms the first syllable of the word *psyche*. He developed a vast statistical foundation for the hypothesis that people can occasionally tell which of five standard symbol cards a "transmitter" person is looking at, presumably by "reading his mind." Rhine also believed many people could predict, at statistical levels far greater than chance, which cards would come up before the experimenter dealt them. Most of the conventional psychologists who agreed with Rhine's theories said little publicly in support of them, presumably because of apprehension about their reputations and their tenure at conservative and prestigious institutions.[9]

During the time since Rhine terminated his experiments, without acceptance by the psychological community and without having been refuted or discredited, a steadily increasing number of serious investigators have entered the field. Unfortunately, most of them have met with some huge obstacles to objective research because the phenomena they sought to investigate have been almost uniformly, frustratingly, and suspiciously fleeting and unpredictable. Researchers have had to wade through a horde of impressionable believers, stage performers, magicians, charlatans, and simple folk who believe themselves possessed of various mystical and magical capabilities. Typical of the researcher's challenge is to investigate the reports of phenomena surrounding the colorful Uri Geller, a charming and outrageously confident Israeli who claims to make forks and spoons bend and broken watches and clocks run again merely by concentrating on them. Some investigators have described Geller as a psychic genius, and others have called him a gifted stage magician. His best results seem to come when tight experimental controls do not exist, as in "spontaneous" situations. Some advocates explain this very simply in terms of a psychic's emotional sensitivity to the presence of people who lack faith in his or her honesty and psychic ability, as well as the notion that these abilities come on a more or less hit-or-miss basis and one cannot predict or control them. These kinds of disputes, although logically legitimate, do make the search for parapsychological phenomena very difficult and frustrating for serious investigators.

Most serious parapsychologists recognize several better known hypotheses concerning so-called psychic abilities, and many of them prefer to explore the evidence concerning one or more of them in preference to others. Some of the major hypotheses within the field of parapsychology are

[9]J.B. Rhine, *New Frontiers of the Mind: The Story of the Duke Experiments* (Westport, Conn.: Greenwood Press, 1972).

1. Telepathy—direct mind-to-mind communication without benefit of sensory processes
2. Clairvoyance—direct extrasensory knowledge of events at a distance, without the agency of another person
3. Precognition—knowledge of the future
4. Psychokinesis—influence over physical objects and processes by mental volition, without the use of conventional physical contact or forces
5. Psychic healing—direct reduction or elimination of health disorders in one person by another who interacts with him or her in some "psychic" way
6. Out-of-body experiences—leaving one's physical body during altered states of awareness and "traveling" with one's consciousness to distant places
7. Communication with people after death, holding conversations, usually by means of an intermediate person—a "medium"—with spirit entities that represent people whose personalities have continued to exist after they have died

Investigators in each of these areas have piled up impressive case histories, anecdotes, reports of experiences, and a limited body of controlled laboratory experimentation that tend to give support to the hypotheses. Yet, skeptical conventional observers consider none of them wholly proven, or even worthy of the weight of accepted theory. Unfortunately, because of the close connections between many of the people interested in these phenomena and various other fields generally identified as "the occult" subjects, preconceived attitudes tend to dominate the evaluation of research results. For those who utterly accept all possible hypotheses as proven fact, research evidence is unimportant and serves only to confirm what they already "know." For those who have made up their minds that parapsychology is quackery, no amount of indirect evidence will decide the issue. And because so many of the battles between these two camps tend to confuse the issues, people of a middle persuasion—like myself—find it very difficult to accept the arguments, pro or con, as presented. Many other scientific hypotheses have achieved the status of accepted theories on much less evidence than that which exists for parapsychology, but because of the magical overtones of the topic, people involved find the evidence very difficult to evaluate "objectively."

In my view, all of the hypotheses mentioned above deserve recognition as logically plausible, and they deserve continued investigation. People such as Elmer and Alyce Green, Gardner Murphy, Thelma Moss, and a number of others in Europe and the Soviet Union, seem to offer realistic approaches to the slowly developing body of evidence in the area. We may learn more important and useful things in these areas than many people presently expect.[10]

A number of topics which scientists once classified under the categories

[10]For a current review of research activities in the field of parapsychology, see Thelma Moss, *The Probability of the Impossible: Scientific Discoveries and Explorations in the Psychic World* (New York: NAL, 1975).

of "pseudoscience," "occult," or "witchcraft" have eventually emerged as respectable after all. Characteristically, once these theories have attained the status of serious acceptance, many scientists turn out to have "known all along" that they deserved serious investigation. Apparently most of us can say "I told you so" much more readily than we can say "You told me so."

For example, American psychologists had heard for many years the reports that yogis and other practitioners of self-control had developed the ability to modify and control various bodily processes at will. Since we "knew" (remember Marconi?) that functions like heartbeat, blood pressure, blood vessel dilation, and others could only be controlled by the autonomic nervous system, and that this part of the nervous system was, by definition, independent of anything a person could do with his thought processes, then obviously these yogis and other "quacks" could not do what people said they could. It took many years before serious investigators examined yogi adepts in laboratory settings and confirmed virtually all of the reported skills. Experiments in India as early as 1961 had been virtually ignored in the United States.

In 1970, in a replication of an earlier experiment, Ramanand Yogi was sealed into an airtight experimental box in front of BBC cameras. The box had a fixed, measured quantity of air inside, and the 46-year-old yogi undertook to survive inside for a period of four hours. Physiological measurements and air samples at half-hour intervals showed that he had succeeded in dramatically reducing his heart rate, slowing his breathing, and reducing his oxygen consumption (metabolic rate) so drastically that the experimenters first suspected an instrumentation error. Ramanand had, for one period of about a half-hour, operated his body at a rate of oxygen consumption that was about *one-fourth* the level which scientists had always believed necessary to sustain life in the most inactive state possible. The wide publicity associated with this experiment lead to the serious examination of other reported data and to similar experiments with meditators in America. These findings, along with the newly developed phenomena of biofeedback, lead physiologists in America to junk a substantial portion of prevailing theory dealing with the "involuntary" nervous system, which now seemed potentially more voluntary than they had ever supposed. The fact of conscious and deliberate control over autonomic functions has now become so well accepted that many people have forgotten that as late as the 1960s, reputable scientists had put it in the same category as the Indian rope trick.[11]

Another incidence of a "weird" phenomenon gaining respectability seems to be the work done by Dr. Carl Simonton in teaching visualization skills to patients with terminal cancer. At his laboratory in Fort Worth,

[11]For an absorbing description of this and other brain research, see Nigel Calder, *The Mind of Man* (New York: Viking, 1970), pp. 81–88.

Texas, Simonton has worked with terminal patients on the notion that, by active visualization, they can block the spread of the disease and even progressively eliminate tumor cells. Simonton hypothesized that the cancer-stricken patient typically had certain attitudes which his or her unconscious thought processes converted into self-destructive physiological processes. This attitudinal syndrome, he believed, included intense feelings of self-pity and diminished self-esteem. Simonton witnessed an encouraging number of cases of what other physicians chose to call "spontaneous remission" in people who learned to visualize their internal processes attacking and destroying their tumors. Simonton's work, although still controversial at the time of this writing, seems to have convinced a number of people that the age-old concept of "mind over matter" may hold true in the literal sense after all. I consider Simonton's work another example of an investigation that scientists have "promoted" out of the category of parapsychology and into the respectable category of "psychiatric adjuncts to medical treatment."[12]

As investigations in the area of parapsychology proceed, I think we can expect to see continued controversy, a continued exasperation with the interplay of true believers and serious investigators, and possibly some dramatic confirmations of one or more of the major hypotheses of the field.

cognitive skill training

I believe the time has come to devote a substantial fraction of classroom hours in American schools and colleges to teaching students how to think more effectively. This can bring some enormous payoffs for our entire society. We have the techniques to do this, and we are developing more and more of them as we go along. From Alex Osborn's work in teaching business people to produce ideas and solve problems creatively to the present day, we have accumulated a wide variety of useful mental concepts and techniques. This book represents my attempt to organize a great deal of what we know into what I believe is the first comprehensive textbook on the entire subject of thinking.

More and more American colleges and universities have begun to include courses in various aspects of thinking in their programs. Professor James Adams teaches engineering students at Stanford University the principles and techniques of creative design and mass idea production, with very successful results. Some high schools have also experimented with thinking courses, generally also with excellent results. Several teachers in San Diego have pioneered a comprehensive program in cognitive skills training for elementary grades, using J. P. Guilford's "structure of

[12]O. Carl Simonton and others, *Getting Well Again* (New York: J.P. Tarcher, 1978).

intellect" model, and have captured the interest of a number of other educators. We have the necessary technology, and we're seeing the increasing interest among members of the educational establishment.

Part of the long delay in bringing the subject of thinking into the classroom stems from a general lack of recognition among educators that thinking can be taught as effectively as it can. Perhaps the lack of an organized methodology such as this book offers has played a part in that delay. I also believe that many of our educators and their institutions have become so "factory oriented" over the years, satisfied to divide the students into standard-sized groups and spoon out the "content" to them, that they have developed a large blind spot to the possibilities for expanding human mentality itself. We have very few people who can just teach; everybody has to be a teacher of *something*. A person interested in art can become an art teacher. A person interested in mathematics can become a mathematics teacher. Each of them teaches a *subject*. Apparently, we will have to make thinking into a subject in order for conventional educators and institutions to recognize it as something they can and should teach. By developing a supply of *thinking teachers*, we can give the development of human mentality the emphasis it needs. Maybe soon a course in thinking will be a required part of every student's curriculum, just like history or English.

The development of educational technology in the area of *cognitive skill training* has recently benefited by increased grant support from organizations like the Department of Health, Education, and Welfare. Professor Jack Lochhead of the University of Massachusetts, for example, has created a Cognitive Development Project within the physics department, aimed at designing specific instructional modes and techniques. Lochhead and his colleagues use the term *cognitive-process-instruction* to describe the subject area. According to Lochhead

We should be teaching students how to think; instead we are primarily teaching them what to think. This misdirection of our educational effort is the inevitable consequence of an overemphasis on objectively measurable overt behavioral outcomes. In brief, we are more concerned with the answers students give than with how they produce them . . . Cognitive-process-instruction is more than a shift in emphasis towards basic skills; it implies a radical change in our current conception of learning. (It) is based on a simple premise: cognitive processes can be studied and students can benefit from the knowledge gained through such studies.[13]

Lochhead cites developing programs in cognitive skills at a number of other institutions, such as the University of Oklahoma, University of Washington, University of Nebraska, M.I.T., Bowling Green State University in Ohio, Carnegie Mellon University in Pennsylvania, the University of California at Berkeley, and McMaster University in Canada.

[13]Jack Lochhead, "An Introduction to Cognitive-Process-Instruction" (monograph, Physics Department, University of Massachusetts, Amherst, Mass. 01003).

During a landmark event in educational technology, a National Conference on Cognitive Process Instruction at the University of Massachusetts in 1978, a number of educators and researchers shared ideas for teaching basic cognitive skills. Much of the development in this area seems to center on teaching people to apply useful mental strategies, referred to as *protocols, heuristics,* and *thinking models.* A protocol amounts to a standard sequence of steps that help a person to arrange his or her knowledge in a useful way, for example, stating a problem as a series of if-then steps and inspecting alternative branching possibilities. A heuristic amounts to an exploratory approach that maximizes the possibility of discovering a useful or relevant fact or relationship leading to a solution, for example, examining the relationship between two parts of a problem. Thinking models, as I use them in thinking courses for adults, consist of simple visual forms that help to organize information so we can manipulate it. Examples include sketches of a physical situation, cartoons, graphs, matrix arrangements of information, decision trees, lists of key factors, time lines, and diagrams that clarify relationships between elements of a problem.

More and more business organizations have taken an interest in thinking skills. A number of management consultants have developed practical training programs for business managers and professional people in creative problem solving, idea production, and various mental skills associated with personal effectiveness. Some training companies offer packaged training programs for business organizations. We will probably see a rapid expansion of materials and techniques for thinking programs in this area.

My belief that cognitive skill training offers a very important avenue to the expansion of human mentality derives directly from my personal experiences with it. Every one of the thinking concepts and techniques described in this book is one I've learned from someone else, discovered for myself, or invented; and I have applied every one of them successfully in practical situations. They work. My personal interest in the human brain and its activity stems from a selfish interest in living my own life successfully and happily. To the extent that the techniques I have learned have helped me to do this, I consider them worth sharing with others. In my view, we have proven that human thinking still is highly elastic and that it can be developed by interest and practice. I think we will see a dramatic increase in interest in this area.

The whole field of human mentality now lies open to thorough investigation and practical development. If we can expand the current research into human thinking processes and cognitive skill training, wake up more of our educators and get them interested in learning and teaching the skills of thinking, and help more people develop enough confidence in their brains to use them more effectively, we can take a giant step forward in human ability. Perhaps within every normal human brain resides the potential for genius, waiting only for its owner to discover and use it.

bibliography

The literature on the "subject" of thinking suffers from an extreme lack of organization and balance, largely because heretofore researchers, educators, and writers have not generally conceived of thinking as a subject in itself. Some areas, like idea production, have received extensive treatment, while areas like fact finding, crap detecting, and thinking on your feet have gone nearly untouched. As the field develops, we may expect to see a well-organized body of literature come together, and probably we will see a number of neglected topics receive their fair share of attention.

In compiling the following list of recommended books I simply chose a variety of representative titles from those I've read and found useful. I've deliberately limited the list to a few recommendations under each of the headings, which correspond roughly to the major topics of this book. Please don't consider these choices the "last word" on the subject. Although I've read a wide variety of works on thinking, I may well have missed some useful books that deserve mention. If you want to explore the subject in even greater depth, the bibliographies contained in these various works should enable you to do so.

general study of thinking

BRUNER, JEROME, and others, *A Study of Thinking*. New York: John Wiley, 1957. An early work on thinking, but still an authoritative coverage of cognitive processes.

FLESCH, RUDOLF, *The Art of Clear Thinking*. New York: Harper & Row Pub., 1951. One of the most widely read and most entertaining of the very few popular books devoted to thinking; however, it concentrates more on what to think about than on techniques for thinking.

KEYES, KENNETH S., JR., *How to Develop Your Thinking Ability*. New York: McGraw-Hill, 1950. A very readable and practical book, based on the principles of general semantics; deals with mental flexibility, accurate perception and description of one's experiences, and ways to lessen misunderstandings among people.

fact finding

BURNHAM, TOM, *The Dictionary of Misinformation*. New York: Ballantine, 1975. An alphabetical listing and explanation of commonly accepted "truths," which the author claims are not true; entertaining and thought provoking, although the author splits a few hairs occasionally.

WALLECHINSKY, DAVID, and others, *The Book of Lists*. New York: Bantam, 1977. Like eating peanuts, reading this vast compendium of topics can capture your appetite—for ideas; like the 7 wonders of the ancient world, Will Durant's list of the 10 greatest thinkers, 20 people on Richard Nixon's list of political enemies, 25 all-time biggest box-office movies, 11 corporations that paid no taxes in 1975, the 10 best-selling books of all time, 7 famous men who were virgins, the 15 safest airlines, the 10 . . . (oops!).

WATTENBERG, BEN J., *The U.S. Fact Book*. New York: Grosset & Dunlap, 1978, and, hopefully, subsequent years. If you don't own a recently published almanac or other fact book, get one and browse through it. Keep it handy, and you will be delighted to see how much useful information you can find by delving into it occasionally.

crap detecting

HAYAKAWA, S.I., *The Use and Misuse of Language*. Greenwich, Conn.: Fawcett Books, 1962. A collection of entertaining articles taken from *ETC: A Review of General Semantics*, dealing with the ways in which human beings manipulate, swindle, intimidate, and fool each other and themselves with words.

JOHNSON, NICHOLAS, *Test Pattern for Living*. New York: Bantam Books, 1972. A pointed analysis of the television-packaged and television-promoted American ethic and the mass consumption life-style, with some creative alternatives, by an ex-FCC commissioner.

POSTMAN, NEIL, and CHARLES WEINGARTNER, *Teaching as a Subversive Activity*. New York: Dell Pub. Co., Inc., 1969. The authors make a convincing case for teaching young people the essential skill of crap detecting and warn that in doing so we must accept the inevitable consequences to some of our fossilized institutions, traditions, and practices. Most educators will find this book highly provocative.

thinking on your feet

Sмiтн, Manuel J., *When I Say No, I Feel Guilty*. New York: Dial Press, 1975. A practical book on assertive communication, which explains the bullying and manipulative tricks we often fall for at the hands of others and presents a variety of verbal tactics to use in countering them.

problem solving and decision making

Gordon, J.J., *Synectics*. New York: Harper & Row Pub., 1961. A thorough description of synectics as a problem-solving methodology and its uses in various situations; emphasizes metaphorical thinking techniques applied to product design, as well as mass idea production.

Kepner, C.H., and B.B. Tregoe, *The Rational Manager*. New York: McGraw-Hill, 1965. A step-by-step problem-solving technique, developed by two consultants and taught in management seminars for business organizations.

Whimbey, Arthur, and Jack Lockhead, *Problem Solving and Comprehension: A Short Course in Analytic Reasoning*. Philadelphia: Franklin Institute Press, 1979. A book by two innovative educators, written for educators. Examines the processes of logical reasoning and gives some techniques for teaching it.

idea production

deBono, Edward, *Lateral Thinking*. New York: Harper & Row Pub., 1970. A thorough treatment of deBono's novel concept of an alternative style of attacking problems, that is, lateral thinking vs. conventional vertical thinking.

Koestler, Arthur, *The Act of Creation*. New York: Dell Pub. Co., Inc., 1967. Probably the most widely accepted theoretical treatment of "creativity." Not for the casual reader; it contains a wealth of research information and a conceptual framework for studying creative thinking.

Osborn, Alex F., *Applied Imagination*. New York: Scribner's, 1953. Well-known and a bit overrated, but an excellent treatment of Osborn's technique of brainstorming. This book has probably had more influence than any other in stimulating interest in idea production among professional people in business organizations.

happying

Dyer, Wayne W., *Your Erroneous Zones*. New York: Funk & Wagnalls, 1976. A highly readable treatment of the mistaken assumptions and thought processes human beings often use to make themselves miserable, and ways to revise them.

JOHNSON, WENDELL, *People in Quandaries*. New York: Harper & Brothers, 1946. A timeless book about human adjustment explained in terms of the thought structures we build inside our heads and the ways in which we use them to make ourselves happy or unhappy.

MEININGER, JUT, *Success Through Transactional Analysis*. New York: Grosset & Dunlap, 1973. A highly readable example of a variety of books dealing with transactional analysis as a framework for analyzing one's self-image and one's relationships with others.

logical thinking

ENGEL, S. MORRIS, *With Good Reason: An Introduction to Informal Fallacies*. New York: St. Martin's Press, 1976. An easy-to-understand book dealing with the various logical dodges and fallacies human beings use to confuse and manipulate one another; how to recognize them and how to deal with them.

language and thinking

FARB, PETER, *Word Play: What Happens When People Talk*. New York: Knopf, 1973. An entertaining and highly informative excursion into the use of words and their effects on the thoughts of people in various speech communities around the world.

HAYAKAWA, S.I., *Language in Thought and Action*. New York: Harcourt Brace Jovanovich, Inc., 1939, 1972. A classic in the field of general semantics dealing with the ways human beings use and respond to symbols, especially language.

POSTMAN, NEIL, *Crazy Talk, Stupid Talk*. New York: Dell Pub. Co., Inc., 1976. A well-organized and thought-provoking book about contemporary language habits that interfere with, rather than contribute to, human understanding and communication.

perception and knowing

GREGORY, R.L., *The Intelligent Eye*. New York: McGraw-Hill, 1970. Well-illustrated treatment of perception, imagery, and illusions.

McKIM, ROBERT, *Experiences in Visual Thinking*. Monterey, Calif.: Brooks/Cole, 1972. Well-illustrated practical treatment of the role of imagery in the thinking process; contains many illustrations, puzzles, experiments, and problems.

ORNSTEIN, ROBERT E., *The Psychology of Consciousness*. San Francisco: W.H. Freeman, & Company Publishers, 1972. An interesting and readable attempt to merge the findings of the Eastern "esoteric psychologies" with the traditional framework of Western psychology.

brain physiology and function

BLAKEMORE, COLIN, *Mechanics of the Mind*. London: Cambridge University Press, 1977, available in U.S. A well-illustrated and readable account of the history of research into the brain's operation, with a useful roundup of our current knowledge about brain lateralization.

FERGUSON, MARILYN, *The Brain Revolution*. New York: Bantam Books, 1973. A tossed salad of reporting on many different areas of brain research, with some speculations about future possibilities.

WITTROCK, M.C., and others, *The Human Brain*. Englewood Cliffs, N.J.: Prentice-Hall, 1977. A collection of interesting and readable articles dealing with recent findings in brain physiology and function; deals extensively with brain lateralization and split-brain experiments.

biofeedback, parapsychology, and other unorthodox fields of research

BROWN, BARBARA B., *New Mind, New Body*. New York: Harper & Row Pub., 1974. A pioneering study of the brain's ability to control aspects of the body's functions that scientists have heretofore considered "autonomic," that is, beyond conscious control; slow reading, but informative, well referenced, and inspiring.

GREEN, ELMER, and ALYCE GREEN, *Beyond Biofeedback*. New York: Dell Pub. Co., Inc., 1977. A very readable account of some unusual and important findings resulting from the use of biofeedback and other instrumentation in the study of human brain processes; contains a serious discussion of the merger between biofeedback research and parapsychological research.

MOSS, THELMA, *The Probability of the Impossible*. New York: NAL, 1975. A report by one of the most respected researchers and reporters on parapsychological research.

thinking games and puzzles

GARDNER, MARTIN, *More Perplexing Puzzles and Tantalizing Teasers*. New York: Pocket Books, 1977. One of Gardner's many enjoyable books of thinking games and puzzles, similar to those he writes for *Scientific American;* most of them lie within the grasp of a typical persistent thinker.

RAUDSEPP, EUGENE, with GEORGE P. HOUGH, JR., *Creative Growth Games.* New York: Harcourt Brace Jovanovich, Inc., 1977. Seventy-five thinking games and mental exercises of various kinds; offers more variety than most books of this type; also offers commentary on creative thinking and problem solving.

SUMMERS, GEORGE J., *Test Your Logic: 50 Puzzles in Deductive Reasoning.* New York: Dover, 1972. A representative sample of the many similar books available; contains some excellent puzzles, challenging but not overly difficult, along with explanatory solutions.

thought-provoking quotations

PETER, LAURENCE, *Peter's Quotations: Ideas for Our Times.* New York: Morrow, 1977. Over 500 pages of the most thought-provoking one-liners, witticisms, and observations ever compiled; a welcome replacement to the dull and dusty drivel of Bartlett's famous doorstop. Peter quotes George Bernard Shaw on the subject of quotations: "I often quote myself. It adds spice to my conversations."

appendix
solutions to puzzle problems

chapter 8

To solve the problem of the men and boys crossing the river, merely recognize that the boat can only cross the river in one of three possible ways: rowed by both boys, rowed by one boy, or rowed by one man. Both boys row the boat to the opposite shore, one stays there while the other rows it back, and then one man rows across. The first boy then brings it back to the starting point. This completes a cycle consisting of four crossings— two each way. Three of these cycles will get the three men across, leaving the boys and the boat at the starting point. Three cycles of four crossings each add up to twelve crossings, so the boys earned twelve dollars.

chapter 10

The solution to the famous nine-dot problem looks like this:

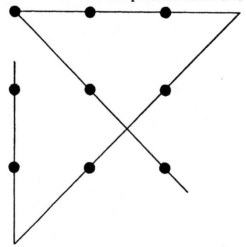

You can rearrange the letters in BIRAB and PILNEC to spell RABBI and PENCIL.

To solve the problem of the six glasses of water, simply pick up the middle full glass, pour the water from it into the middle empty glass, and put it back in its original position. Then you will have produced an alternating pattern of "empty, full, empty, full, empty, full."

chapter 13

1. You need ten coins: 5 pennies, two nickels, 1 dime, 1 quarter, and 1 half-dollar.
2. The dating system using "B.C."—Before Christ—originated after Christ's lifetime. Therefore, a coin maker of that period could not have known about the designation and could not have stamped it on a coin.
3. Could a man marry his widow's sister? It's a moot question, because he would have to die in order for his wife to become a widow. Once dead, he couldn't very well get married.
4. It was a "box" on the ears, that is, a blow with the cupped hand.
5. When rearranged, the words become:
   a. runghy—hungry
   b. flymia—family
   c. mulcica—calcium
   d. dornev—vendor
   e. lendraca—calendar
6. Slide the match at the top of the diagram just slightly in the direction of its length, creating a small square opening formed by the ends of the matches as shown here:

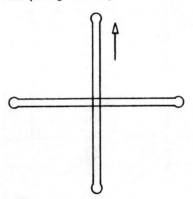

7. The barber makes ten times as much money by shaving the ten men as he would make by shaving the one man.
8. Flash went to bed during the daylight hours.
9. Arrange the pencils to form a three-dimensional figure—a pyramid. The three pencils on the table form one triangle; the three that come to a point in space

above them form three more triangles. Did you *assume* you had to place all six pencils flat on the table?

10. Take one weight from bag number one, two weights from bag number two, three from bag number three, and so on up to ten weights from bag number ten. Put them all on the scale together and see how much they weigh. If they each weighed 16 ounces, then the 55 weights you put on the scale (1+2+3+. . . +10 =55) would total up to 880 ounces. Instead, they will be heavier than that. The number of ounces over that amount is the same as the number of the bag that has the 17-ounce weights.

11. By rearranging the letters of the names, you get:
    a. Roy Kewn—New York
    b. Nora I. Charlton—North Carolina
    c. Colin A. Fair—California
    d. Dora K. Hatton—North Dakota
    e. Earl Wade—Delaware
    f. A.K. Barnes—Nebraska
    g. J.R. Sweeney—New Jersey

12. Each term following 88 comes from multiplying together the two digits of the term that precedes it. So, 88 leads to $8 \times 8 = 64$; 64 leads to $6 \times 4 = 24$; 24 leads to $2 \times 4 = 8$. The missing term is 8, the end of the series. Incidentally, you might try a few other two-digit numbers and see how many steps it takes to reduce the number to one digit.

13. You can connect each point to its mate of the same letter in the following way:

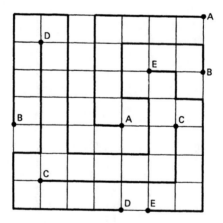

14. The cartoons mean:
    1. Long under-   2. Crossroads   3. Man over-
       wear   board
    4. Backward   5. Mind over   6. Reading be-
       glance   matter   tween the lines
    7. Just between   8. 3 degrees   9. Age before
       you and me   below zero   beauty

15. An arrangement of four cards that satisfies the conditions given consists of:
Queen of Hearts
King of Spades
Ace of Clubs
Jack of Diamonds

16. Surprisingly, this puzzle has two solutions, depending on whether you place the green house immediately to the left of the ivory house, or to the far left. Either the Japanese owns the zebra and the Norwegian drinks water, or the Englishman owns the zebra and the Japanese drinks water.

17. From left to right, the cards are:
Jack of Hearts   King of Diamonds   Queen of Spades

18. Bob swims, Carol plays golf, Ted likes to jog, and Alice plays tennis.

19. Card number six is a King.

20. The original subtraction problem goes:

$$\begin{array}{r} 101 \\ -91 \\ \hline 10 \end{array}$$

$A = 1, B = 0, C = 9.$

index